PAYING FOR EDUCATION

Which type of education should we pay for?

How much education should we pay for?

Can we buy knowledge about how to improve education?

Uniquely presenting a general overview of economic principles applicable to all sectors of education, *Paying for Education* makes key economic ideas accessible to non-economists, whilst drawing on insights from other social science disciplines. It examines the implications of its analysis, especially for two important areas of policy – paying for teachers and paying for teaching in higher education – in order to highlight some underlying issues and consider alternative policy options, as well as reflect on possible futures.

The chapters examine:

- The value of education for the individual
- The value of education for society
- Private and public demands for education
- Choosing a system to supply education
- The cost, efficiency and equity of providing education

Analysing evidence and case studies on a global scale, *Paying for Education* is an essential read for academics, educational administrators, policy makers, leaders in educational organisations and all of those interested in the future of how we pay for education.

Peter Davies is Professor of Education Policy Research, University of Birmingham, UK and Affiliated Professor, Stockholm University, Sweden.

Foundations and Futures of Education

Peter Aggleton
University of New South Wales, Australia
Sally Power
Cardiff University, UK
Michael Reiss
UCL Institute of Education, UK

Foundations and Futures of Education focuses on key emerging issues in education as well as continuing debates within the field. The series is inter-disciplinary, and includes historical, philosophical, sociological, psychological and comparative perspectives on three major themes: the purposes and nature of education; increasing interdisciplinarity within the subject; and the theory–practice divide.

Teacher Education and the Political
The Power of Negative Thinking
Matthew Clarke and Anne Phelan

A Social History of Educational Studies and Research
Gary McCulloch and Steven Cowan

The Creative Self
Psychoanalysis, Teaching and Learning in the Classroom
Tamara Bibby

Materialities and Mobilities in Education
Rachel Brooks and Johanna Waters

The Datafication of Primary and Early Years Education
Playing with Numbers
Alice Bradbury and Guy Roberts-Holmes

Paying for Education
Debating the Price of Progress
Peter Davies

For more information about this series, please visit:
www.routledge.com/Foundations-and-Futures-of-Education/book-series/FFE

PAYING FOR EDUCATION

Debating the Price of Progress

Peter Davies

Routledge
Taylor & Francis Group

LONDON AND NEW YORK

First published 2018
by Routledge
2 Park Square, Milton Park, Abingdon, Oxon OX14 4RN

and by Routledge
711 Third Avenue, New York, NY 10017

Routledge is an imprint of the Taylor & Francis Group, an informa business

British Library Cataloguing-in-Publication Data
A catalogue record for this book is available from the British Library

Library of Congress Cataloging-in-Publication Data
Names: Davies, Peter, 1954– author.
Title: Paying for education / Peter Davies.
Description: Abingdon, Oxon; New York, NY: Routledge, 2018. |
Series: Foundations and futures of education | Includes bibliographical references.
Identifiers: LCCN 2017060475 | ISBN 9781138998353 (hbk) |
ISBN 9781138998360 (pbk) | ISBN 9781315658728 (ebk)
Subjects: LCSH: Education–Economic aspects. | Education and state. |
Capitalism and education. | Education and globalization.
Classification: LCC LC65.D35 2018 | DDC 379–dc23
LC record available at https://lccn.loc.gov/2017060475

ISBN: 978-1-138-99835-3 (hbk)
ISBN: 978-1-138-99836-0 (pbk)
ISBN: 978-1-315-65872-8 (ebk)

Typeset in Bembo
by Wearset Ltd, Boldon, Tyne and Wear

CONTENTS

FIGURES

TABLES

ACKNOWLEDGEMENTS

I owe a legion of debts to colleagues, authors and students who have shaped the thinking and ways of working that have led to this book. The teachings of Julian Lailey and Stan Metcalfe stand out as powerful role models for how to combine passion for a subject with dispassionate analysis. I am also grateful to those with whom I have had the pleasure to work, those who have given their time to discussion and students who have had to put up with my teaching. There is no space to refer to all the influences of which I am aware, and these would only tell some of the story. However, I must acknowledge the impact of Richard Dunnill, Noel Entwistle, Steve Hodkinson, Cecilia Lundholm, Ference Marton, Mick Mayers, Eric Meyer and Ming Fai Pang on my understanding of what it means 'to teach'. I am also very conscious of how my analysis of policy has improved through collaborations and discussions with, among others, Nick Adnett, Robert Coe, Neil Davies, Marco Ercolani, Stephen Gorard, Jean Mangan and Geoff Whitty. Collaborating with Becky Morris and Tom Perry in teaching and research has helped create an environment which made this book possible: colleagues who are worth their weight in gold.

I am grateful to Peter Blatchford, Simon Burgess, Karen Davies, Neil Davies, Marco Ercolani, John Goldthorpe, John Jerrim, Tony Kelly, Rita Kirshstein, Kristian Kristianson, Hugh Lauder, Hank Levin, Geoff Lindsay, Lynn Meek, Tom Perry, Ed St John, Anna Vignoles and Alison Wolf for immensely helpful comments on, and corrections to, earlier drafts of sections of this book. Special thanks to Sally Power for her guidance during the development of the structure and content of the book. The views expressed in the book and its shortcomings remain exclusively the responsibility of the author.

Many thanks to: The Future of Children for permission to reproduce, as Table 3.2, a table from Beller, E. & Hout, M. (2006). Intergenerational social mobility: The United States in comparative perspective. *The Future of Children, 16*(2), 19–36, and to reproduce, as Table 5.2, a table from Barnett, W.S. (1993). Economic evaluation of home visiting programs. *The Future of Children, 3*(3), 93–112; Miles Corak and the American Economic Association for permission to reproduce, as Figure 3.5, the Great Gatsby Curve from Corak, M. (2013). Income inequality, equality of opportunity, and intergenerational mobility. *The Journal of Economic Perspectives, 27*(3), 79–102; Cambridge University Press for permission to reproduce, as Table 3.3, a table taken from Goldthorpe, J.H. (2013). Understanding – and misunderstanding – social mobility in Britain: The entry of the economists, the confusion of politicians and the limits of educational policy. *Journal of Social Policy, 42*(3), 431–450; Taylor and Francis for permission to reproduce, as Table 5.17, a table from Davies, P., Qiu, T. & Davies, N. (2014). Cultural and human capital, information and higher education choices. *Journal of Education Policy, 29*(6), 804–825; the American Economic Association for permission to reproduce, as Table 6.1, a table from Ostrom, E. (2010). Beyond markets and states: Polycentric governance of complex economic systems. *The American Economic Review, 100*(3), 641–672; and the Institute for Fiscal Studies for permission to reproduce, as Figure 7.7, a diagram from Chowdry, H. & Sibieta, L. (2011). *Trends in education and schools spending.* IFS Briefing Note BN121. London, Institute for Fiscal Studies.

1

INTRODUCTION

The focus and scope of this book

I can pay for my education, someone else could pay for me, or I could pay through tax. But someone has to pay, because educating people takes a lot of resources. This book considers who should pay and how much they should pay. Much of the time is taken up with whether these questions should be answered by market forces or governments.

So much is expected of education. Governments talk as if their ailing nation states can be revived through stronger doses of education: to increase economic competitiveness and to foster national cohesion. The New Labour government in the United Kingdom declared that its priorities in the first decade of this century were 'Education, Education, Education' (Adonis, 2012). A White House briefing in 2015 declared: 'President Obama knows we must comprehensively strengthen and reform our education system in order to be successful in a 21st century economy.'[1] The European Council (2015) declared targets for increasing participation in early years education by 2020 as part of its strategy for long-term economic growth based on increasing the quantity and quality of education.

But other voices (e.g. Grubb, 2009; Brown et al., 2011) tell a different story. Some tell us that education is a side-show. Life prospects are forged by global economic power games between nations and corporations. Others tell us that social structures use education as a way of keeping people in their place. Spending more on education only moves the deckchairs.

The stories people tell about education are rooted in powerful ideas not just about 'the way the world works', but about why people do what they do, what they know and what they want. This book takes the view that it is neither desirable nor reasonable to follow one of these stories as a shining path while ignoring or denigrating all others. This stance is *not* based on a view that all these stories are fictions seeking to recruit us to one gang or another. Each story gives us one, valuable, perspective on a very complex phenomenon about which we know some things, but not yet enough. The intention of the book is to juxtapose rather than integrate these stories. Efforts to integrate the stories (e.g. Akerlof & Kranton, 2002) are hugely important, but that task is well beyond the scope of this book which is only able to offer a very incomplete picture of the vast amount that has been written on this subject.

This book focuses on OECD countries and refers chiefly to evidence from Australia, the USA and the UK. Policy and practice in England receives much more attention than policy and practice elsewhere, simply because there is not enough space for more extensive description of other education systems. New analysis of data (largely in Chapter 5) is restricted to England. While there are substantive differences among education policies pursued in OECD countries (including within the UK), this group of nations faces certain similar contextual challenges which affect the consequences of pursuing one policy rather than another. The problems for OECD countries in the twenty-first century are hardly less than those faced in the previous two centuries. Relationships between work, welfare and citizenship are being transformed through information technology, globalisation and demography. International relations are strained by shifts in power, ideology and migration. Global warming casts a shadow over the sustainability of taken-for-granted modes of production and lifestyle. Populism has re-emerged as liberal democracies have struggled to meet voters' expectations.

This chapter sets out some broad positions adopted by this book: on the context for education policy in the first half of the twenty-first century, on the distinctiveness of education and a perspective on social science. The chapter also introduces some major themes in the book and concludes with brief summaries of each of the chapters.

A context for education policy (1): globalisation and national identities

The roles of markets and governments cannot be properly understood in abstract, divorced from time and space. Growth in trade and communications has made many markets more globally integrated over time. The roles that governments take in education in the twenty-first century are very different from the roles they took in the nineteenth century (MacDonagh, 1958). The form of globalisation in the second half of the twentieth century and the morphing of nation states into market states (Bobbitt, 2002) have changed relationships between societies and their governments. By the early twenty-first century only eight countries ranked among the top 25 economic entities in the world.[2] All bar one of the 17 companies in the top 25 operated in the financial sector.

Following the financial crash of 2008, globalisation has met with increasing resistance in the form of populist movements in many Western countries. This form of resistance sees problems in the movement of peoples, the supply of labour and threats to perceived hallmarks of national identity. It has also been accompanied by a rhetoric which imagines that the growth in incomes previously delivered by globalisation can be re-established by resisting globalisation. Many are anxiously waiting to see whether twenty-first-century populism turns out to be less of a tide than a vain attempt to stand against one.

This book treats the financial crash as a stimulus for reconsidering what nations are paying for when they devote resources to education. The form of globalisation and its accompanying rhetoric has positioned the purpose of education as securing the conditions for productive employment: developing skills and aptitudes for an internationalised labour market and creating stable contexts for low-risk production. It has encouraged a shift to viewing education as a phenomenon provided primarily by organisations for individuals (rather than by society for society). It has also changed the constraints upon governments to intervene in the process of education (Kettl, 2000). Education has not always been viewed in this way.

In 1819 only one in 15 children in England received a formal education (Akenson, 2011). However, steadily through the following century the church and then the state set about the task of using education to spread social and moral order in the new industrial age (Soysal & Strang, 1989) or, as in the case of Ireland (Akenson, 2011), the colonial age. In either case, the prime role of education in OECD countries was to build the nation state through socialising the mass of citizens for the industrial age (Green, 1990; Wiborg, 2004). Socialisation was embedded in the vision and interests of the middle classes as described by narratives provided by Apple (1982) for the USA, Power et al. (2003) for England, and the contributions in Blackbourn and Evans (2014) for Germany. The middle-class prescription for an orderly society mapped an education that would prepare sections of society for different types of employment and secure acceptance of norms of behaviour and the distribution of power. These accounts portray education as a national rather than as an individual process.

Over the past 100 years, economic structures and incomes in OECD countries have changed enormously. As blue-collar jobs have disappeared and white-collar jobs have appeared, there has been an increasing expectation for individuals to spend longer in education to improve their productivity. The story of human capital has taken centre stage as politicians have come to view more education as critical for the international competitiveness of their countries. The salvation of the country in the face of the global economy lies in sum of individuals' human capital which make a nation's workforce attractive to international capital (see e.g. OECD, 2007). This message offers an attractive prospect of dealing with the vexed interactions between average income and inequality. If education makes the individual economically productive then providing opportunities for education is a sufficient policy for a fair society: they had the chance. This message has survived the financial crash in 2008 with barely a scratch. Speaking in 2016,[3] the German Chancellor, Angela Merkel, declared: "This means we must empower every young person, through education, to contribute his or her skills to the community." In the same year the UN Special Envoy for Education, Gordon Brown, declared that annual education spending in low- and middle-income countries needed to rise from $1.2 trillion in 2016 to $3 trillion in 2030[4] in order to achieve social reform and to increase average welfare.

But 2008 cannot be so easily swept aside. Several commentators (e.g. Stiglitz, 2013; Wisman, 2013; van Treeck, 2014) have noted the relationship between rising inequality and increasing household debt in the USA before the financial crash. Increasing participation in education had been associated in these years with rising average incomes and rising benefits from higher education, but also with a widening gap in individual prosperity. Education reforms in the nineteenth century took it for granted that education would affect what was considered normal and acceptable in society: not that everyone would think the same but that education would affect the median position around which variation was centred.

Globalisation is changing social as well as economic structures. Some communities have thrived and some have become neglected as patterns of employment and prosperity have shifted. As traditional working-class jobs disappeared, one policy response was to change the curriculum to prepare young people who did not come from managerial and professional backgrounds for 'the new jobs'. Under the influence of human capital theory, policy then switched to increasing the quantity of education in an effort to 'upskill' the entire workforce. More education has to be paid for. But who should pay?

A context for education policy (2): education, economic growth and the structure of employment

Changes in employment structure over the past 100 years have increased the proportion of non-manual jobs that require higher levels of education (Feinstein, 1999). The school-leaving age has steadily risen.[5] Those who were forced to stay on in the first year after the school-leaving age rose earned more than those who left school a year earlier when this was still permitted (Harmon & Walker, 1995; Oreopoulos, 2006). Participation in higher education spread from the few to the masses, fuelled by commissions (e.g. Robbins, 1963; Dearing, 1997) and policies that portrayed growth in higher education as a prerequisite for a growing economy in the information age. Despite fears about over-education, the graduate premium – the difference between what an average individual with given school grades earns if they are a graduate or not – has increased rather than declined (Goldin & Katz, 2007). There has been a positive association over time between increasing average incomes and the length of time individuals have spent in formal education: changing employment structure and increasing average incomes have increased the capacity of societies to pay for education and increased the number of people who face financial incentives to spend a long time being educated.

Increased participation in education requires more teachers, unless the ratio of students to teachers is allowed to increase. But parents and students prefer lower student–teacher ratios. Parents who send their children to private schools in England are willing to pay more when children are taught in smaller classes (Davies &

Davies, 2014). Moreover, increases in average income in England have been associ-ated with reductions over time in the pupil–teacher ratio in private schools (Davies, 2011). However, this adds to the pressure to recruit more teachers to meet rising levels of participation and preference for smaller classes. Since it takes a long time to develop capacity to be a good professional educator and professional educators have capabilities that are in demand in other parts of the economy,[6] teachers have to be paid well. To maintain the number of graduates who choose to become teachers requires teachers' salaries to keep pace with salaries offered elsewhere. When a society requires an increase in the number of teachers there is pressure for teachers' salaries to rise relative to the salaries of others.

Elsewhere in the economy, high labour costs have prompted a switch to different forms of production which require lower inputs of labour relative to capital. Applications of information and communications technology (ICT) have been at the heart of this change, driving substantial increases in productivity in some indus-tries. Unsurprisingly, therefore, there have been many visions of transforming the process of education through ICT (e.g. Allen & Seaman, 2007). Although ICT is starting to change the way in which higher education is provided, universities and schools rely chiefly on face-to-face contact between teachers and students. To some extent this may reflect shortcomings in currently available ICT which limit capacity to replicate or move beyond the quality of interactions between teachers and learn-ers which are widely held to be critical for good education (see e.g. Hattie & Tim-perley, 2007). It may also reflect some advantages of human contact for the emotional and social context that promotes learning. Unless (or until) advances in the design and use of ICT can overcome these problems we are left in a situation in which the conditions of production in education and elsewhere mean that there is an inexorable tendency for the relative cost of providing education to rise over time. This phenomenon (known as 'Baumol's Cost Disease') is not restricted to education (Baumol, 2012), but it plays a substantial role in steadily raising the amount society pays for education. In societies where education is largely paid for through taxation, this creates a problem for governments. People want more educa-tion but they don't want to pay more tax.

Governments which have based their appeal to voters on reducing tax[7] and restricting the scope of government face a major problem. This problem would be exacerbated if low taxation on capital and low government spending were required to attract international capital in the arena of global competition. However, com-parisons between countries do not give clear answers to whether this is actually the case (Garrett & Mitchell, 2001; Dreher, 2006). Greater trade does not seem to be associated with lower welfare spending. Higher corporate taxes are, in fact, posi-tively associated with inflows of capital. One interpretation is that international capital is more interested in highly skilled labour than in low tax rates. But this still leaves a major problem for governments that have managed to convince voters that low taxation is necessarily a good thing.

The problem evokes a range of responses. The Internet is awash with diatribes against governments 'throwing money at education'. Flat or falling productivity in education is read as prima facie evidence of waste (see e.g. Craig, 2008, p. 78). Governments are charged with wanting more education than people want or need. A second reaction is to assert that 'money doesn't matter' in education. What matters is to reorganise schools, teachers and teaching so that more is achieved without spending any more money. While it is perfectly reasonable and necessary to urge (e.g. Grubb, 2009) educators to choose the best available option in teaching and organisation, this is a quite separate matter from the question of whether the total amount of money spent on education makes any difference. Voices bemoaning increases in state spending on education rarely berate parents for spending more on private education. A third reaction is to look for alternatives to spending more money on more teachers. One option has been to hire 'teaching assistants' to take on some jobs that would otherwise have been carried out by lecturers or teachers (see Stevenson, 2007; Muzaka, 2009; Butt & Lowe, 2012). Consequences of changing the combination of inputs to education are examined in Chapter 5.

A social science perspective

Education is a battlefield and there are many casualties. There is a battle for control between the public and private sectors. There is a battle for control of the arguments between exponents of different disciplines: notably between economics and sociology, but also involving political scientists, philosophers and psychologists. There is a battle between the interests of different parts of society. Identities as well as interests are on the line. Because the stakes are high, there is a tendency for combatants to overstate the coherence and certainty of their beliefs. Moreover, everyone has so much experience of education. 'Everyday' beliefs have been reinforced through years of familiarity with what it is like to be taught. People just *know* what is right.

These beliefs foster conservatism in attitudes towards education. Across the political spectrum people hark back to imagined golden days. In England, some long for the return of selective grammar schools,[8] while others regret the erosion of 'common', comprehensive schooling and the days when teachers and schools had immense professional freedoms. Like all memories of golden days these are suffused with confirmation bias,[9] but there is a bigger problem. Education is supposed to prepare people for the future, not the past, and the world changes.

This book attempts to make sense of the arguments by adopting a social science perspective with the following characteristics:

- Drawing upon research by economists, sociologists and, to a lesser extent, political scientists and psychologists.
- Referring to evidence which bears upon the way in which problems are defined as well as the consequences of education policies.
- Aiming to recognise theoretical standpoints which make contrasting assumptions about the basis on which individuals, households, professionals and governments make decisions about education.

This is a broad canvas which entails referring to a large and wide-ranging body of theory and evidence. Nonetheless, it can only be offered as a partial, very incomplete view of the field. The rationale for attempting the task is that since each discipline within social science competes for funding and prestige there has been a tendency for interaction between disciplines to be characterised by more heat than light. The view taken here is that no discipline and no perspective within a discipline has a monopoly on valuable insights on the question of paying for education.

Thus there is a big question about how to organise the material in a way that begins to live up to these ambitions. The approach taken is to use demand and supply as a first layer of organisation. Chapters 2 to 4 build a picture of demand and Chapters 5 and 6 examine supply. Of course, this draws upon introductory economics, but it also offers plenty of space to explore perspectives and evidence that rarely feature in accounts of the economics of education. Demand becomes a social phenomenon as soon as we allow for demand to be influenced by relative outcomes: how education places me relative to others. While looking separately at demand and then supply helps to provide a distinct focus for each chapter, it does make it more difficult to convey consequences of parents and students as suppliers as well as demanders of education. I hope the reader will be patient with attempts to highlight these relationships and the ways in which arguments in different chapters are related to each other.

A second layer of organisation distinguishes between perspectives on choosers in education. Choice may be framed along three dimensions of variation, as presented in Figure 1.1. This creates eight possible combinations and for simplicity of organisation the narrative in subsequent chapters is conflated to just three: (1) consistent

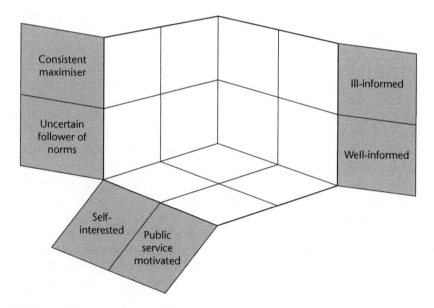

FIGURE 1.1 Three dimensions of choice.

maximisers who are self-interested and well-informed (the standard assumptions of mainstream or neoclassical economic theory); (2) self-interested but ill-informed choosers who may be consistent maximisers or uncertain followers of norms; (3) uncertain followers of norms who are ill-informed and may be self-interested or public service motivated.

The purpose in the exposition is not to try to demonstrate that one characterisation of choices in education is universally superior to others. Each characterisation has advantages and disadvantages, and the stance taken in this book is that individual and collective human behaviour in education is too complex to be completely captured by one characterisation.

The distinctiveness of education

Others (e.g. Dixit, 2002; Adnett & Davies, 2003) have suggested that education has a bundle of characteristics which create a distinctive challenge for markets. This book also takes the view that education cannot be treated *simply* as the same as any other good or service provided by an economy. Some of the characteristics identified by others (difficulty in measuring outcomes and existence of public service motivation) follow when the assumptions of well-informed, consistent and self-interested agents are relaxed. Another (positive externalities) reflects a belief about the role of education in society (McMahon, 2009). Two more characteristics (multiple principals and a tendency towards oligopolistic markets) reflect the conditions under which education is frequently provided.

To these we may add three more characteristics of education. First, the separation of sellers and buyers lies at the heart of the economic analysis of markets. Some people demand something and others supply it, with prices providing the information to efficiently coordinate choices. But students and parents both demand and supply education. A parent who wants their child to be more educated will devote time to providing some of that education. A student who wants to become more educated will devote more effort to their learning. Second, the process of education depends on how learners as well as teachers understand its purposes, their own roles, and the effects of teaching and learning on achieving their goals. Third, formal education is a long process. Compulsory education in the UK begins at age 5 and ends at aged 16, but many experience 18 years or more of formal education.[10] This creates boundless opportunities for the experience of education to feed back into engagement with education, with consequences for subsequent outcomes. Each of these characteristics carries implications for the way in which prices and incentives are likely to work in education. Failing to take account of these characteristics will compromise decisions on when to rely on markets for education.

Education is not unique in possessing any one of these characteristics. It is the combined effect of all four that creates the degree of difference. Regarding education as something done by and for society helps to foreground these characteristics.

Chapter summaries

Chapter 2 examines four types of benefit of education for individuals and households: (1) higher income; (2) greater relative income and social mobility; (3) empowerment and citizenship, and (4) consumption. The chapter proposes that the value of education to the individual or household is the sum of benefits from these four sources. Each type of benefit affects what an individual may be ready to pay for education and, therefore, what a government should acknowledge if it chooses to intervene in providing education or demanding education on behalf of individuals and households.

Chapter 3 looks at the benefits of education from the point of view of the society. Each of the main sections in the chapter examines one source of benefit: (1) increasing productivity and income; (2) reducing inequality and increasing social mobility; and (3) empowering citizens. Shifting from a private to a social perspective means more than recognising social benefits which are likely to be ignored by individuals. It also encourages a view of education as a whole in which demand and supply of education interact. When individuals compete for position it does not mean that the only outcome is relative position. The total amount of education may be affected in the process.

Chapter 4 examines the private and public demand for education. Chapters 2 and 3 identify different sources of value for individuals and society, but the amount of education that is (or would be) actually demanded depends on the constraints which limit actual choices. The chapter considers the implications of information and uncertainty for private and public demand.

Chapter 5 shifts attention to the cost of supplying education through schools. It concentrates on the size of educational institution and the mix of inputs. The whole chapter sticks with the assumption that providers are well-informed and self-interested, since this is the perspective that has underpinned most of the research evidence relevant to this chapter.

Chapter 6 changes the point of perspective on supply from individual providers to systems. The way in which providers operate depends on the system within which they are embedded, The chapter considers three supply systems: markets, hierarchies and networks. How each of these systems is perceived depends on whether we assume that providers are well-informed and self-interested. So the chapter considers the implications of lack of information, uncertainty and suppliers' motivations. The chapter also considers the implication of looking at education as jointly supplied by institutions, parents and children. The consequences of shifting the balance between public and private supply in education depend on the interplay between governance through markets, hierarchies and networks. Each system is always in play. It is never a choice between total reliance on one system of governance or another.

Chapter 7 concludes by examining some implications of the analysis in the previous chapters for two important areas of policy: paying for teachers and paying for teaching in higher education. The section on paying for higher education uses a comparison of systems in Australia, England and the USA to highlight certain underlying issues and to consider policy options. The chapter ends with some reflections on possible futures. These reflections return to themes in this Introduction: if education is valued for the difference it makes to society as well as the difference it makes to individuals *and* if education is provided through societies, not just through educational institutions and if individuals *and* societies will want more education in the future, how will this work out in an age in which ICT is increasingly dominant in communication, economic and social life?

Notes

1 White House (2015). *Knowledge and Skills for the Jobs of the Future*. White House Briefing. Washington, DC, The White House. Available online at www.whitehouse.gov/issues/education/reform.

2 As judged by the 2015 Hale Index. See www.stockinvestor.com/19646/the-2015-hale-index/.

3 Speech to the Royal Society on 1 April 2010. Available online at https://royalsociety.org/news/2010/german-chancellor/.

4 Speech accessed from http://en.unesco.org/news/gordon-brown-building-learning-generation on 13 March 2017.

5 The school-leaving age in England was raised in 1947 and 1973. Like other Australian states, Victoria raised its school-leaving age to 17 in 2009 (see www.education.vic.gov.au/about/department/legislation/Pages/act2006age.aspx) and New South Wales followed suit in 2010, raising its school-leaving age from 15 to 17 (Audit Officer of New South Wales, 2012).

6 The old insult 'Those who can, do; those who can't, teach' derived from George Bernard Shaw's *Man and Superman*, is undermined by teacher turnover figures. In the USA the rate of school teachers leaving the profession each year rose from 6 per cent in 2008/2009 to 8 per cent in 2012/2013 (www.shankerinstitute.org/blog/update-teacher-turnover-us). For detailed analysis see Ingersoll (2001), Boyd *et al.* (2008) and Ingersoll & May (2012).

7 As expressed by UK Prime Minister Theresa May in her speech to her party conference on 5 October, 2016: "We all believe in a low-tax economy." Available at www.independent.co.uk/news/uk/politics/theresa-may-speech-tory-conference-2016-in-full-transcript-a7346171.html.

8 In England the Chancellor of the Exchequer announced on 8 March 2017 that there would be a £320 million boost to education funding for grammar schools. Available at www.gov.uk/government/speeches/spring-budget-2017-philip-hammonds-speech (accessed 13 March 2017).

9 Confirmation bias refers to a problem that besets arguments which ignore all the drawbacks of a position (see Klayman, 1995).

10 If they attend a nursery from age 3 and complete a Bachelor's degree.

2

THE VALUE OF EDUCATION FOR THE INDIVIDUAL

Introduction

Chapters 2 and 3 examine why education is worth paying for. This chapter looks at the question from the point of view of the individual, and Chapter 3 looks at the question from the point of view of the nation. When looking at the value of education from the individual's point of view this chapter also takes account of the household to which they belong. Households routinely make sacrifices so that one member of the household can receive more education, but an individual's education is sometimes sacrificed in the wider interests of the household. This chapter considers four types of benefit for individuals and households: (1) levels of income; (2) social mobility and inequality; (3) empowerment and citizenship, and (4) consumption. The first three are lifetime benefits: education is treated as an investment for the future. The fourth approach concentrates on the here and now: what benefits do learners get *while* they are studying?

Within each section it will be important to recall a difference between the value placed on education, the amount and type of education an individual or household would demand if reliant on their own resources and the value that they *actually* get from education. We return to the demand for education in Chapter 4. Individual expectations of the value of education should motivate participation and engagement. However, there are good reasons to believe that many of these expectations will be inaccurate. Preferences change with maturity and education is generally expected to play a role in developing these preferences. At age 30 a person may value their education very differently from how they valued education at age 15. Moreover, the whole point of schooling is to develop an understanding of the world and the roles a person could play in developing the future. If someone understands enough to accurately predict the future *in general terms*, why do they need to be educated? Finally, even if an individual could accurately predict what the future will typically bring for 'someone like me', they will be uncertain about how typical they will be. This uncertainty will matter if some individuals face more uncertainty than others, or if some individuals are more troubled by uncertainty ('risk averse').

Personal income

According to Human Capital Theory (Schultz, 1961; Becker, 1994), individuals invest in education to increase their future productivity and earnings. The choice they face is usually portrayed as whether or not to participate in an education pro-gramme. Therefore, the cost–benefit decision involves weighing the costs of studying against the benefits of higher earnings later in life. This can be represented in a simple formula used to analyse *any* investment decision:

$$NPV = \sum_{i=0}^{n} \frac{R_i - C_i}{(1+r)^i}$$

Equation [1]

In this formula, the Net Present Value (NPV or value to the person at this moment) of a decision to participate in an education programme is the sum of the difference between *additional* future earnings (R_i) and costs (C_i) arising in each year (i). The NPV is the figure commonly quoted in public references to the 'value of a degree'. In 2010 the Browne Report estimated that an undergraduate degree was worth just over \$200,000 to the average UK graduate, somewhat higher than the OECD average, but less than the \$420,000 graduate premium estimated by Avery and Turner (2012) for US graduates. The costs include forgone earnings while studying as well as any costs (such as tuition fees) directly related to participation. Therefore, the problem for the individual is how to weigh immediate costs against future (income) benefits. The value to the individual of money in one year's time com-pared to money now is shown by the discount rate (r). The subscript r is used because the interest rate on loans is the normal reference point for this discounting. However, an individual who places a relatively high weight on money today rather than money in the future will have a higher discount rate. The examples in Table 2.1 illustrate some implications of tuition fees and earnings for the benefits to an individual of studying for a three-year Bachelor's degree.

   A comparison of rows (6) and (8) in Table 2.1 shows that an increase in the discount rate from 0 to 5 per cent roughly doubles the number of years it takes before the individual feels they have broken even on their original investment (NPV = 0). Anyone who borrows to finance studying for a degree has good reason to pay very careful attention to the rate of interest they will be charged. Comparing students (A) and (C) shows the effect on the overall calculation of tuition fees and part-time earnings while studying. Human Capital Theory requires that all benefits and costs be measured in terms of money. Therefore, if we were to include the value of leisure time in the calculation we would have to place a monetary value on each hour of leisure either gained or lost. The contestability of this kind of

TABLE 2.1   Example calculations on net present value of a three-year degree

	Student			
	(A)	*(B)*	*(C)*	*(D)*
(1) Earnings forgone while studying (over three years)	£36,000	£30,000	£36,000	£30,000
(2) Total tuition fees for three-year degree	0	0	£27,000	£15,000
(3) Earnings from part-time employment during degree	0	0	£15,000	£15,000
(4) Difference in leisure time compared to not studying (hours per week)	0	+10	0	−10
(5) Average additional annual earnings post-degree	+£3,000	+£4,000	+£3,000	+£4,000
(6) Number of years of work following graduation to achieve NPV of 0 with discount rate of 0%	12	7.5	16	7.5
(7) Number of years of work following graduation to achieve NPV of 0 with discount rate of 2%	16.2	10.4	21.9	10.4
(8) Number of years of work following graduation to achieve NPV of 0 with discount rate of 5%	22.7	12.25	39.7	12.25

valuation means that any benefit or cost which is not already measured in terms of money is excluded from the calculation.

Estimates of the income benefits of education are frequently presented in terms of a 'rate of return'. These calculations show the discount rate (r in equation [1]) that will result in an NPV of 0. A review of international evidence (Psacharopoulos & Patrinos, 2004) judged that the average rate of return to an extra year of schooling was 10 per cent, with the average for OECD countries being slightly higher. Rates of return are highest for early years and primary schooling, since early child education is associated with better educational progress later in schooling (Currie, 2001; Dickson, 2007). This underpins the case for additional provision of early years education (Heckman, 2006).

The analytical framework provided by Human Capital Theory has also been applied (e.g. Connelly, 1992) to estimates of the benefits of increasing participation in the labour market by parents of young children. In this case, the additions to income (R in equation [1]) arise from the future employment of the parent as well as the child. Childcare provided for the child increases the productivity of parents through enabling participation in the labour market rather than through raising parents' marketable knowledge and skills. Reducing the cost of childcare increases the likelihood that a mother will participate in the labour market since the pay-off (NPV) is increased. This section concludes by noting four factors which complicate the simple Human Capital story.

First, when people decide whether or not to participate in education they cannot be sure how much difference it will make to their future earnings. Decisions have to be made on the basis of expectations as shown in Equation [2],

$$NPV^e = \sum_{i=0}^{n} \frac{R_i^e - C_i^e}{(1+r)^i}$$
Equation [2]

(where the superscript ^{e} denotes expectations).

This equation retains the assumption that individuals aim to maximise future benefits (they are 'rational actors'), but their capacity to accurately predict future benefits is limited by the gaps in their knowledge and their ability to process that knowledge. Simon (1955) defined this characterisation of individual decision making as 'bounded rationality'. If participation is compulsory and paid for by the government the question becomes whether the government's expectations of future benefits and costs are accurate.

The importance of 'bounded rationality' depends in part on the extent to which it is associated with social class and students' academic achievements (Boudon, 1974; Breen & Goldthorpe, 1997). Students' capacity to form accurate expectations of the benefits of education (in terms of income or other outcomes) may be affected by their level of 'cultural capital' (Tramonte & Willms, 2010). Cultural capital refers to an individual's stocks of knowledge and skills which enable them to 'read' situations and to present themselves in ways that are considered appropriate by others in different situations (Bourdieu, 1973). This idea was originally restricted to 'highbrow' cultural capital esteemed by the ruling classes who were presumed to act as gatekeepers to professional employment and power in society (DiMaggio, 1982). More recently it has been extended to include scientific and technical knowledge, reflecting the importance of these fields in lucrative employment (Prieur & Savage, 2011) and parents' knowledge of how to interact with schools (Dumais & Ward, 2010). Davies and colleagues (2014) found that levels of cultural capital were positively associated with graduate premium expectations of secondary school students in England.

From the perspective of Rational Action Theory (Boudon, 1974; Breen & Goldthorpe, 1997; Breen & Jonsson, 2005), cultural capital is a mechanism which maintains social class divisions because the capacity to interpret and engage with the education system is passed on from parent to child.[1] Lower levels of cultural capital are associated with lower levels of academic achievement (De Graaf et al., 2000; Sullivan, 2001), and students with lower levels of achievement derive less benefit from more education – either in terms of increased achievement or subsequent earnings. Lower levels of cultural capital are also associated (while controlling for academic attainment) with greater reluctance to continue in education (Noble & Davies, 2009; Davies *et al.*, 2014). Children from disadvantaged socio-economic backgrounds have two reasons to place a lower value on post-compulsory education: (1) more education will make less difference to their future earnings than the future earnings of more advantaged, higher achieving students, and (2) the benefits of post-compulsory education will be more difficult for disadvantaged students to judge. Rational Action Theory regards decisions of students from disadvantaged socio-economic backgrounds not to continue in education as rational, class-bound responses to the opportunities and uncertainties they face.

Second, the effect of education on future income depends not only on participation but also on where and what one studies. In secondary education, future income seems to depend more on where one studies. Comparisons of private and state schools and comparisons between state schools have been widely interpreted as showing that some schools are more effective in helping students to achieve higher grades. Mathematics seems to be the only secondary school subject that makes a difference to future earnings (Levine & Zimmerman, 1995; Dolton & Vignoles, 2002; Arcidiacono, 2004; Rose & Betts, 2004). In contrast, degree subject seems to make a much greater difference to future earnings than the university from which one graduates (McKnight *et al.*, 2002; Hussain *et al.*, 2009; Chevalier, 2011).

Third, the length of time spent studying may be less important than the extent to which studying has increased general intellectual capacity (Hanushek & Woessman, 2008). This may be reflected in the degree classification or grade point average (GPA) that a student achieves, given their prior attainment.

Fourth, by concentrating on decisions to participate in educational programmes, applications of Human Capital Theory typically ignore students' and parents' agency (Hill & Tyson, 2009) as characterised by Expectancy-value Theory (Wigfield & Eccles, 2000) and the Theory of Planned Behaviour (Ajzen, 1991). This looks like a serious omission, given the strong evidence that (1) students' efforts affect their achievements; (2) students' beliefs about the efficacy of their efforts affect their achievement (Wigfield & Eccles, 2000); (3) students with the same prior achievement have different expectations about future achievement (Svanum & Bigatti, 2006; Kim *et al.*, 2010; Bong *et al.*, 2012), and (4) students' expectations are positively associated with their subsequent achievement (Perry *et al.*, 2017). Greater effort increases the cost of education to the student, since it entails giving up time for other pleasures. Students' aspirations and expectations of the pay-off to their own efforts are routinely accepted as a critical target for interventions in school, but much less so in higher education (Gorard *et al.*, 2012).

The implication is that the effect of education on future income arises from a combination of participation (the effect of instruction) and the individual's inputs in terms of effort and self-regulation. Looked at the other way, education can add value through the direct effect of instruction, through motivating the learner to devote more effort to learning or through developing the learner's capacity to direct their efforts more effectively.

Relative valuations and inequality

This section considers arguments that individuals are interested in how education positions them in relation to others. Although each of these arguments emphasises relative rather than absolute value, they differ in their treatment of three dimensions: (1) the extent to which value is a calculated (explicit) or taken-for-granted (implicit) motivator; (2) whether relative value is judged in relation to all others or to a specific group, and (3) whether relative value is judged in relation to risk.

The most straightforward version of this proposition suggests that individuals are explicitly motivated by the effect of their choices on their position relative to *all* other individuals in their society. They will value more education if it enables them to earn more *than others*. Frank (1997) found support for this proposition in evidence that self-reported happiness is positively associated with income at each point in time, while increases in absolute income over time seem to make little difference to the self-reported happiness of the person with median income. This evidence gains in credibility through the association between self-reported happiness and 'objective' measures of well-being in the USA (Oswald & Wu, 2010).

The belief that individuals are more interested in relative than in absolute income may be combined with an assumption that education affects future labour productivity. Maximising relative income will motivate an individual to demand more education so long as there is net gain in their *absolute* income. However, students who are motivated by relative income will be influenced by the educational choices of others. As long as others choose not to participate, a student can stay ahead by participating a little. As rates of participation in education rise, there is increasing pressure on students motivated by relative income to increase their own participation. There is a 'bandwagon' effect (Leibenstein, 1950).

The belief that individuals are interested in relative rather than in absolute income may also be combined with an assumption that education does not affect the productivity of labour. But in this case, how can we explain the association between education and individual income? Sorting theories regard education as a mechanism for identifying and labelling individuals according to their *innate* potential for productivity (Stiglitz, 1975; Weiss, 1995). There are two dimensions to this sorting process. Employers are believed to use education credentials as indicators of innate characteristics (including disposition towards hard work and intelligence) through which they *screen* applicants. The value of education to employers is that (if the screening is effective) it reduces recruitment costs by enabling them to quickly rule out unsuitable applicants. The value of education to individuals is that credentials enable them to *signal* their capacities to potential employers (Spence, 1974). Altonji (1995) studied the effect of taking additional academic courses on the subsequent earnings for high school students in 1971/1972 in the USA. Even before controlling for student characteristics he found a negligible relationship between extra courses and subsequent earnings. According to Weiss (1995, p. 139), "These [Altonji's] results are a strong refutation of the huge literature that interprets the correlation between wages and secondary schooling as due to learning in secondary school." However, there are some difficulties in interpreting this evidence. First, it is possible that students who took more courses worked no harder than other students; they simply spread their efforts among more courses. Second, we do not know whether there were differences between the students who took more courses and others which may have counterbalanced an effect of additional study. Students may have taken more courses simply to broaden their general education rather than with a view to future employment. Moreover, students may have taken additional courses because they regretted their initial courses.

Credentialism (Collins, 1979; Fevre *et al.*, 1999; Brown, 2001; Bills, 2003) places sorting in the context of the preservation of social power and privilege. According to this theory, the objective of the education system is to make sure that only individuals with the 'proper' backgrounds are employed in the leading positions in a society. This view of education treats 'choice' as a social rather than an individual phenomenon (people choose what their class background drives them towards) and sorting is a method of excluding certain groups rather than a process of meritocratic competition. Whereas economic models assume sorting on the basis of innate personal characteristics, credentialism assumes sorting on the basis of class background. In economic models of sorting, individuals may try to 'beat the system' by obtaining qualifications which overstate their true productive potential, but the system itself is intended to provide a meritocratic ranking.

Two theories offer accounts of how individuals from disadvantaged social backgrounds may 'select themselves out of education'. The idea of habitus (Bourdieu, 1973; Reay, 1998, 2004) suggests that individuals will tend towards dispositions which reflect the values and life expectations of their parents.[2] These dispositions are not immutable. They may be altered by subsequent experience, notably within educational settings. Nonetheless, children of middle-class parents are likely to assume that it is normal to go to university, while children from working-class backgrounds are likely to assume that it is not. This perspective treats valuations of education as implicit: particular educational trajectories are associated with norms that become embedded through upbringing. Engagement with education is not planned *in order to achieve* desired employment or position (as assumed by each of the perspectives summarised in the previous section). Habitus treats parents as the reference points for implicit valuations. However, parents and parenting are regarded as partial embodiments of norms and aspirations which are dictated by membership of a particular social class. A 'habitus interpretation' of the expansion of middle-class participation in higher education (Blanden & Machin, 2004) requires that young people also reference social class peers in developing their sense of what is normal for themselves. A habitus interpretation of working-class participation in higher education (e.g. Reay, 1998) focuses on the uncertainty of these students about whether they were doing the right thing in 'going against type'.

Prospect Theory (Kahneman & Tversky, 1979) suggests that relative valuation is related to estimates of the risk attached to different outcomes. Lab experiments (e.g. Page *et al.*, 2007) have found that most people prefer a certain small gain to an uncertain large gain. However, the same individuals also prefer an uncertain large loss to a certain small loss. Status Attainment Theory places this difference in the context of social class. This perspective suggests that young people will view the value of education in relation to its prospects for enabling them to achieve employment and social position equivalent to their parents. Therefore, children of graduate parents will regard not going to a university as a certain loss (relative to their parents) which they will have strong motivation to avoid. Children of non-graduate parents are more likely to regard going to university as enabling them to achieve higher status employment than their parents, and their motivation to achieve this gain will be less than the motivation of children from middle-class families (Vossensteyn, 2005; Becker & Hecken, 2009; Malloy, 2015).

Empowerment

Individuals may also value education because it will enable them to become a *certain kind* of person, regardless of how much money they may earn. Education for individual empowerment may focus on an individual's capacity to (1) appreciate, enjoy and contribute to human achievements and cultures; (2) direct their own life; (3) participate in the society to which they belong, or (4) play a role in the development of the worlds they share with others. This was once taken for granted as the dominant aim for education (Noddings, 2003).

Education aims explicitly to develop tastes and, therefore, to change the subjective value which an individual places on their own education. Documents which set out the aims of a school curriculum typically start with a statement to this effect:

> Every state-funded school must offer a curriculum which is balanced and broadly based and which promotes the spiritual, moral, cultural, mental and physical development of pupils at the school and of society.
>
> *(Department for Education, 2013a, para 2.1)*

Parents who pay to send their children to private schools frequently state that their choice is strongly influenced by their aspirations for the children's spiritual and moral development (Beavis, 2004). Gamoran and Boxer's (2005) study of Jewish schools in Chicago found that schools influenced the development of children's cultural capital in this social and ethnic context. We also have grounds to believe that understanding art and culture fosters appreciation of artistic and cultural artefacts (Leder *et al.*, 2004). Schools can, and do, influence capacities to appreciate art and cultures and individuals' readiness to participate in particular cultural activities. Moreover, these outcomes are valued by parents.

Empowerment in terms of capacity for self-determination also features prominently in the mission statements of educational institutions:

> We hope that students will begin to fashion their lives by gaining a sense of what they want to do with their gifts and talents, assessing their values and interests, and learning how they can best serve the world.
>
> *(Harvard College, 2016)*

(Students will develop) a passion for learning that will remain with them beyond their formal education, alongside values that will enable them to become responsible, positive members and leaders of society through a deep-rooted belief that they can achieve excellence in everything they do.

(A small secondary school in an English City with a high proportion of disadvantaged children, judged by the school inspectorate as failing to meet 'floor standards')

Self-determination theory (Ryan & Deci, 2000) makes the case for believing that the capacity to direct one's life is a fundamental human need, implying that education which develops this capacity will be highly valued. This assertion is supported by evidence that students with a stronger sense of self-determination report more positive 'subjective well-being' (Lyubomirsky *et al.*, 2012). According to self-determination theory, human beings have a natural motivation to satisfy three needs: competence, relatedness and autonomy. Education can benefit the individual by increasing abilities to do things, by fostering a sense of belonging and by developing confidence in the capacity for independent action. Confidence in the capacity for independent action is frequently referred to in terms of 'locus of control': does the individual believe that their chance of success in a situation depends on their external circumstances or on the capacities and energy they bring to the situation? But what basis is there for believing that educational institutions *can* live up to their aims and really make a difference? First, locus of control is affected by students' educational experiences and has long-term benefits (Skinner *et al.*, 1990). Second, students' self-reports of their 'subjective well-being' are positively related to their belief in their ability to determine their own success (Lyubomirsky *et al.*, 2012). Third, we have some evidence from students in higher education. Swain and Hammond (2011, 603) provide an example of a self-report of the effect of part-time study for a degree on one mature student:

Um – well at the beginning I was, I started with massively low self-esteem, I hardly knew anybody, I didn't think of myself – I thought of myself as someone who had potential but possibly wasn't ever going to do anything. [...] By the end I'd overcome to a very large extent my illness and increased my self-respect enormously [...] when I left I – I basically thought, you know, that I thought I was someone who might be able to do things, to make something of my life.

Jamieson and colleagues (2009) describe this kind of experience as the development of 'identity capital'. They surveyed part-time, mature students enrolled on courses at two universities in England. Approximately two-thirds of the students were entirely self-funded and the dominant motivation declared by 60 per cent of these students was personal development. This was measured by seven items ('got recognised qualification', 'developed as a person', 'increased overall happiness', 'enjoy learning more', 'improved self-confidence', 'attitude towards learning' and 'moved to a further course'). Using data from the World Inventory of Values survey, del Mar Salinas-Jiménez *et al.* (2011) reported a strong positive correlation between years in education and self-reported life satisfaction. Analysis of the General Social Surveys in the USA (Oreopoulos & Salvanes, 2011) has found a strong positive correlation between number of years spent in education and each of self-reported (1) happiness; (2) job satisfaction, and (3) job prestige. These positive correlations were only slightly reduced by controlling for personal income. A comparison of the later life satisfaction of students in England before and after an increase in the compulsory school-leaving age (also reported by Oreopoulos & Salvanes, 2011) supported belief in a causal effect of length of schooling on subsequent satisfaction with life.

The value of education for participation in society is often referred to in terms of 'literacy'. The idea of 'functional literacy' was frequently used in the post-World War II era to refer to some basic level of communication necessary for participation in employment and social interaction. As noted by Kirsch and Guthrie (1977) and Levine (1982), the literacy required to participate in a society depends on the economic, social and political structure of that society. Yet despite academic worries about the definition of 'illiteracy' it has maintained its currency in public anxieties about schools (e.g. Orr, 2011; Huffington Post, 2014). In the final decades of the twentieth century it became commonplace to refer to 'information literacy' as a prerequisite for participation in the digital age. As with 'functional literacy', education was expected to play a critical role in making sure that all citizens were capable of participating at a basic level (OECD/CERI, 2001). More recently, governments (e.g. US Department of Education, 2001; US Department of the Treasury, 2006) have turned their attention to 'financial literacy' in an effort to instil wise financial personal behaviour. Each of these literacies targets performance in a life role. While 'functional literacy' was primarily focused on the ability to perform as a worker, financial literacy shifts attention to performance as a consumer or as an owner (of financial capital) (Davies, 2015). While each literacy has been presented as benefiting individuals by enabling them to participate more effectively in a life role, the nature of 'effective performance' has been defined by others.

Existing economic, social and political structures have frequently expected different 'functions' of people from different backgrounds. Learning to 'fit in' means something very different for one person than it does for another. Children's trajectories towards adult life have been framed by differentiated schooling (Cookson Jr. & Persell, 2008). However, even a 'common' education may have very different benefits for one person than it does for another and this effect extends beyond the curriculum and the organisation of education. Relationships formed at higher education may have financial consequences through increasing the likelihood of embarking upon a long-term relationship with another graduate (Lewis & Oppenheimer, 2000). For example, Kaufmann and colleagues (2013) reported that women attending elite universities in Chile were more likely to form marriage partnerships with higher earning males than women who attended other universities. Eika and colleagues (2014) reported that the likelihood that a US or Norwegian graduate will have a graduate partner is high but has been declining over recent decades. They also found that graduates in particular disciplines have a very high likelihood of having a partner who graduated in the same discipline. In summary, there is evidence that, for some parents and students, judgements about social well-being are sufficiently important to direct decisions about participation in education, and there is also some evidence suggesting long-term effects of social interactions in educational contexts on future achievement and earnings.

The importance of education in the development of the individual's capacity to influence their world is widely advocated. The United Nations Convention on the Rights of the Child expects universal commitment to allowing children's voices to be heard. This declaration has provided the springboard for proposals for education to foster individual capacity to form and express views about the world and the role those individuals may play in the world. The value of education to the individual may be observed in developing capacities to contribute to decision making within existing institutional structures and distributions of power. There is a strong positive correlation between the number of years spent in full-time education and citizens' support for democracy and engagement with democratic processes (Putnam, 2001). However, this may simply mean that individuals who are more likely to participate in democratic processes are more likely to participate in higher education. Dee (2004) used an instrumental variable approach to judge whether attendance (after compulsory schooling) at a two-year community college in the USA increases the likelihood of voting in elections. He used the distance between a student's home and the nearest community college as an instrument and reported a large positive effect of college attendance on voting. Milligan and colleagues (2004) used changes in laws governing the minimum school-leaving age in the USA and the UK to identify school effects on engagement with election debates. They reported a strong positive effect in both countries. These studies encourage us to believe that more engagement with formal education increases strength of participation in democratic processes. We cannot tell from these studies how *much* this sense of empowerment is worth to these individuals, but that does not mean it should be ignored.

Freire (2006) and others have offered a more radical view of the value of education for empowerment. Education may also develop the capacity to challenge existing conventions and power structures. Individuals with the ability to form persuasive arguments, envisage new possibilities and mobilise widespread support have often been highly educated. Moreover, writers in radical traditions have consistently espoused the importance of education in raising awareness of disadvantage and realisation of other possibilities. We may expect substantial benefits to an individual's subjective well-being from a sense of having stimulated a change in society. However, this may come at great personal cost and the benefits of radical change are more usually measured in terms of value to society as a whole.

Consumption benefits: education and well-being

Education is more than an investment. People spend many years in formal education so it is important to consider the intrinsic value of this experience. In the words of the Head Master of Eton College (Henderson, 2016):

> School should be fun and happy children are more likely to be successful.
> *(welcome to visitors to the school's website)*[3]

Some students express much greater satisfaction than others with their experience at school (Huebner *et al.*, 2000). Moreover, studies of children's satisfaction with school consistently point to the same sources of satisfaction: feelings of academic competence, relationships with peers and relationships with teachers (Verkuyten & Thijs, 2002; Jin & Moon, 2006; Vecchio *et al.*, 2007). 'Self-determination' (Ryan & Deci, 2000) has a current as well as a future pay-off. Psychological studies of well-being stress the importance of social acceptance and interaction for self-reported happiness (Frank, 1997; Myers, 2003). It is, therefore, not surprising that making friends and social acceptance at school are strongly associated with self-reported happiness, attendance and subsequent achievement (Ladd, 1990; Samdal *et al.*, 1999; Osterman, 2000). Conversely, bullying at school is negatively associated with children's sense of well-being (ONS, 2014). Gutman and Feinstein (2008) found that 3 per cent of variation in children's mental health was attributable to school-level effects. Some students regard the major benefit of attending school to be meeting up with friends (e.g. Banks *et al.*, 1992) and, for some students, friendship formation is critical to decisions about whether or not to drop out of higher education (Wilcox *et al.*, 2005). Moreover, satisfaction with school plays a significant role in adolescents' overall life satisfaction (Elmore & Huebner, 2010; Long *et al.*, 2012). From the perspective of the 'value of education' the question is whether spending more on education makes children any happier at school. Private schools have much smaller class sizes than public schools and school fees in England are inversely related to class size (Davies & Davies, 2014). Canadian parents, responding to a survey by Bosetti (2004), cited this as their most important reason for being willing to pay for their child's education. It is also possible that parents are willing to pay for their child to be educated in a more ordered environment in which they will receive more individual attention from the teacher. Since there are also plenty of qualitative studies reporting that some parents have chosen schools on the basis of whether they thought their children would be happy (e.g. Coldron & Bolton, 1991; Bagley *et al.*, 2001; Verger *et al.*, 2016), it is reasonable to assume that parents place a substantial, though difficult to measure, value on children's happiness at school.

Conclusion

This chapter has considered four ways of judging the value of education for individuals. These approaches draw upon different social science traditions and disciplines. Each approach tells us something about the value for individuals of becoming educated. Any account of the value of education which ignores one or more of these approaches is impoverished as a result. The value of a degree is not the same as the net difference in discounted future income. Analyses of the value of education which rigorously employ a single approach are critical to understanding the problem but they are not sufficient for generating policy responses. Young people considering applying to university in England express a wide range of motivations (Davies *et al.*, 2013). Some individuals give more weight to future income, others to status and others to developing technical skill or serving society. But the educational choices of most individuals have multiple motivations. Treating the value of education *only* in terms of one of income, self-realisation or position in society is useful for developing theory. It is not so good at capturing the complex nature of the problem. This creates a challenge for policy and practice, since we do not yet have a sufficiently firm basis for judging how important each motivation is to different individuals at different times.

For example, 'production function' or 'consumer satisfaction' approaches to judging the value of education may be useful in posing the question 'Are these resources for education being used efficiently?' This is a good question to ask, because it discourages waste. But education is not like other forms of production or consumption. The individual is the key resource in their own education. What the student does is more important than what the teacher does. Moreover, the process of education is critical to appreciating the value of education. It is an act of becoming as well as an act of consuming and an act of being fashioned. A singular focus on schools as 'producers of added value' can encourage practices in which teachers work very hard to secure high short-term performance from students *at the expense of* the development of students' capacity to be agents of their own progress. A singular focus on undergraduate satisfaction with what they receive from universities can undermine students' responsibility for their own efforts. There are also tensions between different sources of value in education. Education which improves an individual's future productivity may be at the expense of education which develops their capacity to participate in, and add to, the cultures of the societies in which they live.

Finally, analysis which focuses on the value of education to the individual encourages policy which expects the individual to bear the cost. Why should others pay for what benefits me? This line of reasoning becomes particularly strong when the benefits arrive in the form of future personal income. If someone is going to get paid more in the future, they should borrow now and pay back later. This view reduces financial problems to 'the access which low income families have to borrowing' and 'the risk that individuals will be myopic and not make decisions in their best interest'. However, education benefits which arrive later in the form of empowerment and personal fulfilment and benefits which are enjoyed now through a happy school experience are not (directly) associated with future income. Surely every child has an equal right to these benefits. But turning such principles into policy is very hard. We have to pay more to make school a happy place. And creating schools that provide secure and fulfilling environments costs more for some children than for others. But how much extra should we pay? If we prevent parents from paying schools to provide rich experiences for their children then they will pay others to provide these experiences out of school.

Notes

1 Rational Action Theory is typically combined with Status Attainment Theory in the work of theorists such as Breen and Goldthorpe (1997). In a similar fashion Cultural Capital is associated with Habitus in the work of Bourdieu (1973). However, Rational Action Theory and Cultural Capital are consistent with an 'absolute value' approach to the benefits of education. Status Attainment Theory and Habitus emphasise Relative Value and for that reason they are considered in the next section.
2 Akerlof and Kranton (2002) have encouraged economists to reconfigure their theorising to include this perspective on education.
3 This statement was included in the Headmaster's welcome. Available at www.eton college.com/Introduction.aspx (accessed 31 March 2017).

3

THE VALUE OF EDUCATION FOR A SOCIETY

Introduction

This chapter begins with a brief overview of spending on education in the context of national income in OECD countries. The main body of the chapter examines three broad justifications for national spending on education: (1) Increasing productivity and income; (2) Reducing inequality and increasing social mobility, and (3) Empowering citizens. The following section gathers together objectives to maintain a healthy democracy and a harmonious society with objectives to develop culture and individual cultural appreciation. The main three sections mirror the organisation of the previous chapter. However, there is no simple symmetry between the value of education to the individual and the value of education to society.

The value of education to a country entails more than a simple addition of the value of education to each person in that country. First, education for one person has consequences for others which need to be taken into account. Second, the interaction of supply and demand for education in a country results in a pattern of provision that can run counter to individuals' motivations for wanting more education. Individual demands for more education 'to get ahead of others' do not *necessarily* increase inequality in a society. Conversely, a desire to become more educated for its own sake can have unintended consequences for inequality. Third, causation between education and each of income, inequality, citizens' fulfilment, social integration and well-being runs in both directions. A country with more educated people tends to be more productive and to have a higher income per head. But a country with a higher income per head can afford to provide more education. Partly because governments play such a major role in providing education in OECD countries, these interactions of cause and effect operate substantially as systemic rather than individual relationships. Inequality, democratic stability and social cohesion are, by definition, characteristics of societies rather than of individuals.

Education spending and national income

Countries with a higher national income per person spend much more on educating each student than do countries with a lower national income per person. Higher spending may reflect the length of time a person spends in formal education or the value of resources used at each stage of education. Levels of participation may be increased by raising the proportion of young children in nursery education or by raising the proportion of the population enrolled in tertiary education. Each of these strategies has been argued (Vandenbussche et al., 2006; Heckman & Masterov, 2007) to be beneficial for the future of a country.

The relationship between rates of participation of 3- and 4-year-old children and average income per person is only evident in OECD countries with per capita incomes of less than $30,000 (Figure 3.1).[1] Participation for 20- to 29-year-olds is only slightly associated with average income (Figure 3.2).

The scale of the variation around these weak patterns indicates the extent to which national policies affect rates of participation. The three countries with the highest GDP per capita had relatively low proportions of 3- to 4-year-olds and 20- to 29-year-olds in education. The UK was ranked 7/40 in proportion of 3- and 4-year-olds in education (95 per cent enrolled in education), and was ranked only 36/40 in terms of the proportion of 20- to 29-year-olds in education (19 per cent enrolled). In contrast (and notwithstanding the analysis suggesting that increasing resources per student has little effect on academic outcomes: Hanushek, 2003), spending per student is strongly related to average income (Figure 3.3).[2]

The relationships at national level between spending on education and average income per head may be interpreted in three different ways. First, education may be regarded as an investment which increases productive capacity and

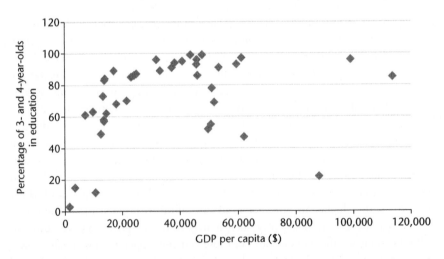

FIGURE 3.1 The percentage of 3- and 4-year-olds in education in OECD and partner countries (2012).

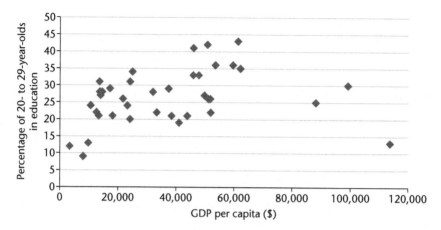

FIGURE 3.2   The percentage of 20- to 29-year-olds in education in OECD and partner countries (2012).

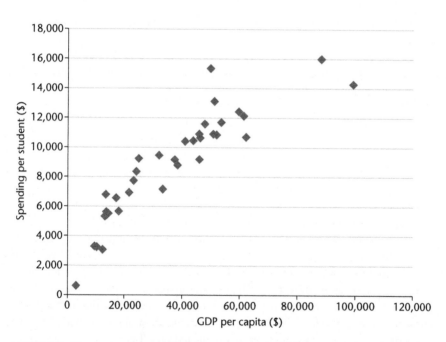

FIGURE 3.3   Total annual expenditure per student and GDP per head in OECD and partner countries (2011).

future income. Countries which spend more on education will experience faster economic growth. Second, as national income grows, so does the government's capacity to spend taxpayers' money. More spending on public education may be seen as a consequence of government bureaucracy and union power in schools such that money is spent inefficiently to the benefit of people working in the public sector. Third, as national income grows, governments are able to spend more on education to combat inequality and to enable individual and collective development of citizens (e.g. in empowerment, cultural awareness or self-realisation).

Productivity and income

The value of education to a society may be judged – just like the value of education to the individual – in terms of the monetary value of what has to be given up relative to the monetary value of what is gained. In order to provide education, a society has to use resources that could have been devoted to providing other goods and services. This trade-off may be analysed in terms of productivity: How productive are the resources devoted to education compared with other ways in which those resources could have been used?

Productivity in an industry (i) is measured in terms of the ratio of inputs to outputs. This ratio may be defined in several different ways:

1 O_i^i/L^i: The contribution to output (O^i) of workers in that industry (L^i) [where output is measured in terms of quantity rather than the value of whatever is produced].
2 O_i^i/w^iL^i: The contribution to output of workers in that industry relative to the cost of employing them [where cost is the total wage bill – average wage (w) X number of workers (L)].
3 $p^iO_i^i/w^iL^i$: The value of workers' contribution to output (O^i) X the price at which this output is sold (p^i) relative to the wage bill.

Rising living standards over time have been associated with increases in physical productivity across all industries $(\sum_{i=1}^{n}O_i^i/L^i)$ resulting from increases in the physical capital intensity of production (such as the introduction of robots in production lines). In recent decades, productivity growth has been strongly associated with the production and use of information technology (Grossman & Helpman, 1994; Black & Lynch, 2001; Inklaar et al., 2005). Oliner and Sichel (2000) estimated that two-thirds of economic growth in the USA in the 1990s was due to investment in information technology. Jorgenson (2001) traced the relationship between falling semi-conductor prices and economic growth fuelled by new labour-saving production methods and cheaper consumer products. The scope for increasing physical productivity in service industries has been demonstrated by the banking industry (Berger, 2003). The expansion of supermarket chains in the retail industry was based on achieving higher physical labour productivity through mechanisation of the retail business and exploitation of information economies (Reardon et al., 1997). The growth of Internet shopping is pushing this process a step further. Taken-for-granted modes of providing banking and retailing have changed dramatically under the pressure of achieving higher labour productivity which increases average living standards.

So what of education? Should we expect to see rising output per worker in schools and universities and should we expect to see falling costs of educating each person? If we were to assume that productivity should increase at the same rate in every industry, then the answer would, of course, be yes. However, Inklaar and colleagues (2005) compared the contributions to national productivity growth of different industries in the USA and Europe over the period 1979 to 2000. They showed that national productivity growth, particularly in the USA, was largely associated with industries producing and using information and communications technology (ICT) (see also Black & Lynch, 2001). The contribution of 'social and personal services' to productivity growth declined over the same period in the USA and Europe. If the pivotal element in 'production' involves face-to-face contact between provider and customer this is hardly surprising. This 'productivity problem' is compounded when 'customers' value a service more highly if the number of workers per 'customer' is increased. Parents in England pay higher fees to send their children to private schools that have smaller classes and more non-teaching staff per child (Davies & Davies, 2014) and the demand for supplementary private tutoring is also positively related to family income (Bray & Kwok, 2003). If parents' 'revealed preference' is for smaller classes, then market forces will encourage physical productivity in schools to fall as average incomes increase.

In principle, there is scope for using ICT to increase productivity in education. This could arise by improving outcomes for students through adding ICT facilities to supplement existing staff–student ratios. However, hopes for substantial improvements in students' achievement through increasing use of ICT in schools have largely failed to materialise (Reynolds *et al.*, 2003; Hurd *et al.*, 2005). Even more positive interventions (e.g. Chandra & Lloyd, 2008) have tended to find that while some groups (e.g. lower achieving boys) have benefited, other groups (e.g. higher achieving girls) have lost out. The lack of overall effect of additional school spending on ICT may have arisen because increasing access to ICT does not necessarily cause teachers to make more use of ICT in their teaching (Cuban *et al.*, 2001).

Alternatively, ICT facilities could be used to replace staff. Given that classroom teachers comprise the majority of the school workforce, this means increasing student–teacher ratios. Evidence from school class size research (e.g. Blatchford *et al.*, 2003) suggests that modest increases in class size would have little impact upon children's achievement. However, as noted earlier, parents tend to prefer smaller classes. The organisation of teaching in HE seems to offer more scope for substantial substitution of IT for staff time. However, several studies have reported that students attending larger classes achieve lower grades (see e.g. Kokkelenberg *et al.*, 2008; De Paola & Scoppa, 2011). Therefore, we do not yet know whether greater use of currently available ICT would increase physical productivity in education.

Relatively static physical productivity (O_t^i/L^i) has clear implications for output relative to the cost of employing each worker ($O_t^i/w^i L^i$). Increases in national productivity raise average wages. If wages of workers in education keep pace, there must be a fall in $O_t^i/w^i L^i$ if O_t^i/L^i is constant. This problem has been dubbed 'Baumol's Cost Disease' (Baumol, 2012). If teachers' wages fail to keep pace with average national growth it will become steadily more difficult to attract people to work in education. So the prospects for the service will depend on how customers value the service as their incomes rise. If customers are prepared to pay the same proportion of their income as they did before, then providers of the service will be able to increase wages in a service with static productivity.

The implications for education ($O_t^e / w^e L^e$) may be illustrated using data from the UK. Between 1984 and 2014 average real wages rose by an average of 1.3 per cent a year with the cumulative effect that the real value of average income in 2014 was just under 50 per cent higher than 30 years earlier.[3] Productivity in UK manufacturing rose over this 30-year period by an average of 1.5 per cent per year. Over this period the pupil–teacher ratio (PTR) fell slightly in state-funded English schools (in primary schools from 22.1 to 20.9 and in secondary schools from 16.2 to 15.5). Thus if we measure physical productivity of teachers in terms of the number of pupils,[4] there was a small *fall* in physical productivity in schools. Moreover, between 1984 and 2007 average salaries for teachers employed in the state sector rose at a rate above the national average rate for all jobs.[5] After taking account of inflation there was an increase of 60 per cent in the cost of providing a teacher for each child (somewhat higher than the average growth in real incomes over the period). This picture of declining productivity and increasing costs has been evident throughout OECD countries (Gundlach *et al.*, 2001). A rise in teachers' wages relative to average wages may be interpreted in different ways. One possible interpretation is that as average incomes rise, people wish to spend a relatively higher proportion of their income on education. When education is provided by the state, governments may be encouraged to prioritise spending on education if this is popular with voters.

Alternatively, a decrease in $O_t^e / w^e L^e$ for teachers relative to other workers ($\sum_{i=1}^n O_t^i / w^i L^i$) could reflect public sector inefficiency and the success of teacher unions in gaining pay rises above the 'market rate' (Gundlach *et al.*, 2001; Hoxby, 1996, 2004). The argument is that increases in teachers' unions' bargaining power (e.g. through favourable legislation and market monopoly) enable teachers to raise their wages well above what would be offered in competitive markets (through 'rent-seeking behaviour'). Hoxby (1996) found that teachers' earnings relative to average earnings were higher in US states which offered a bigger role to unions in pay bargaining. She infers that declining productivity *over time* is attributable to increase in union power over time. In 2004, Hoxby supplemented this union power argument with an argument that productivity declined in US schools because school districts became larger over time, reducing their exposure to market pressure from parents choosing to live in districts where teacher productivity is higher.

If it were the case that US teachers' unions had caused a decline in teacher productivity we might expect to find a similar effect of unionisation in other sectors of the US economy. However, Black and Lynch (2001) found that levels of unionisation were not related to productivity throughout the private sector in the USA (though they may have found different results if they had looked at the public sector). Trade union recognition is routine in the state school sector in the UK but is still relatively unusual in the private sector. The teachers' union most active in UK private schools claimed in 2016 that it negotiated on behalf of its members in only 100 of the 2,600 private schools in the country.[6] Nonetheless, most UK private schools[7] have traditionally linked their pay scales to the rates negotiated in the public sector: aiming to pay similar or slightly higher salaries to attract high-quality teachers. Between 1984 and 2005 the Independent Schools Council (ISC) Census reported annual average pay increases for teachers in ISC schools using the figure that had been negotiated in the public sector. If unions were securing 'above-market wage rates' in the state sector this would have had knock-on effects for the private sector. Other aspects of the state/private comparison present more difficulties for the unionisation/bureaucracy thesis. While pupil–teacher ratios declined between 1984 and 2014 by approximately 5 per cent in the state sector, they declined by approximately 25 per cent in the private sector.[8] Between 1987 and 2005 the Independent Schools Council (UK) provided data on annual wage settlements and tuition fees charged by member schools. Over this period teachers' pay rose by 120 per cent and headline tuition fees rose by 240 per cent. It therefore looks very unlikely that teacher productivity would have declined more sharply in the state than in the private sector over this period.

The third approach to productivity ($p^i O_l^i / w^i L^i$) makes a judgement on the basis of the value of workers' contribution to output rather than on the physical quantity. One way in which education contributes to the value of total output is through childcare provision which enables carers to participate in the labour market. This effect is independent of any long-term effects of childcare on children's capacity for work. The focus here is on the value of production ($\sum_{i=1}^{n} p^i O_l^i$) and productivity ($\sum_{i=1}^{n} p^i O_l^i / w^i L^i$) in the whole economy.

The proportion of mothers of young children who were participating in the labour market rose dramatically in the later decades of the twentieth century. Between 1960 and 1995 the proportion of mothers of young children in the USA who were in some form of employment rose from 20 per cent to 62 per cent (Committee on Ways and Means, 1998). Between 1981 and 2011 the proportion of mothers with children under the age of five in employment in Australia rose from 30 per cent to 56 per cent (Baxter, 2013). These increases were partially achieved through state subsidisation of childcare.

Education may also increase income through effects on productive capacity. It is impossible to be certain about the effect of compulsory education on a country's income, since there is no 'counter-factual' to use to estimate a country's income in the absence of compulsory education. But, from a human capital perspective, we can use the additional earnings of those who have participated in post-compulsory education to judge the difference that further and higher education make to a country's income through increasing workers' productivity. A review of public sector productivity in the UK (Atkinson, 2005, para 9.34) calculated that taking account of effects on future income would add between 1 and 1.5 per cent to estimates of educational productivity. This interpretation implies that the economic growth achieved in OECD countries through the development and application of ICT would not have happened without an increasing supply of more highly educated workers. In line with Galor and Moay (2000), UKCES (2014) envisioned increasing polarisation in the labour market, as highly skilled, hi-tech workers command high salaries, and low-tech service workers (e.g. in catering and retailing) see little growth in earnings. Consequently, the graduate premium has not declined despite huge increases in the proportion of young people attending university (Walker & Zhu, 2008), although there has been an increase in the dispersion of graduate earnings (Green & Zhu, 2010).

National income may also grow through unrewarded effects of highly educated workers on the productivity of others (Chapman & Lounkaew, 2015). Markets should reward workers for 'spill-over' effects in the workplace such as the identification of more effective work practices and management processes. However, it has been widely argued (Nelson & Phelps, 1966; Dowrick & Gemmell, 1991; Walshok, 1995; Machin & Van Reenen, 1998; Psacharopoulos & Patrinos, 2004; McMahon, 2009) that spill-overs in the generation of new knowledge (such as invention and innovation which creates new production possibilities) should be treated as externalities. This idea has become increasingly influential following the development of Endogenous Growth Theory (Romer, 1986). Romer and others suggested that human capital would become increasingly important for future economic growth. Moreover, he suggested that investments in human capital might be less likely than investments in physical capital to suffer from diminishing returns. Successive increases in investment (e.g. through expanding participation in education) would continue to yield similar individual returns, offering the promise of continuous and perhaps increasing levels of growth.

Beliefs about the existence of social (labour market) benefits from education[9] have also been influential in forming governments' policies on the promotion of STEM (Science, Technology and Mathematics) subjects (e.g. Browne, 2010). A case for relatively high externalities to STEM degrees was presented by McMahon (2009). However, there are reasons to be cautious about this argument. First, there are substantial differences between countries in estimates of externalities by subject studied. For example, Bourne and Dass (2003) estimated that externalities for physical science degrees in one Caribbean country were lower than externalities for social sciences, while Winters (2014) estimated substantially higher social benefits for STEM graduates in the USA. Second, the relationship between average and marginal social benefits is unclear. Additional STEM graduates might make smaller contributions than current graduates to social welfare. Third, measures should take account of teaching cost differences between STEM and non-STEM degrees – ignored, for example, by Winters (2014). Fourth, valuation of social benefits from graduates of different degree subjects is contingent on the values ascribed to political, social and cultural benefits which are not fully reflected in market prices. If there are large social benefits from STEM graduates, a more logical policy implication is to increase government spending on STEM research to boost the demand for STEM graduates (Noailly et al., 2011). Encouraging the supply of STEM graduates without boosting demand for STEM-specific human capital appears likely to increase the proportion of STEM graduates employed in jobs which do not require STEM training.

One approach to measuring these effects is to compare changes in the proportion of more educated workers among geographical localities. For example, a US study by Moretti (2004) estimated that a 1 percentage point increase in graduates in a city raised the earnings of non-graduates by more than 1 per cent. The difficulty with these calculations is that they require strict assumptions to exclude other factors which may lead to changes in the wages of graduates and non-graduates alike. Different assumptions (e.g. that increasing the supply of graduates in a locality does not affect the demand for those graduates) lead to more pessimistic estimates of social benefits (Ciccone & Peri, 2006; Lange & Topel, 2006). Therefore, current evidence makes it very difficult to judge claims about the existence and size of these benefits. The case for believing that increasing human capital causes economic growth (either through increasing the proportion of 'highly educated workers' or through enabling innovation) is yet to be proven. Economic growth and rates of innovation have not been demonstrably higher over times as participation in education has increased (Jones, 1995; Temple, 1999), and it has proven difficult to match the elegance of formal expositions of the theory with robust empirical design (Fine, 2000).

Nonetheless, in 2014, the UK Office for National Statistics (Fender & Carver, 2014) estimated that total human capital in the country could be valued at £17.61 trillion on the basis of predictions of future earnings of individuals who had stayed in education beyond the compulsory limit. This enormous figure was approximately 200 times larger than annual public spending on education (Bolton, 2014). It was also more than ten times greater than the UK's total national debt (ONS, 2015). Deloitte (2015, p. 21) estimated that Australian Gross Domestic Product 'was 8.5% higher because of the impact that a university education has on the productivity of the 28% of the workforce with a university qualification'. They also asserted (DeLoitte, 2015, p. 49) that:

> [A] permanent 10% increase in the tertiary education attainment rate in Australia would increase labour productivity in Australia by 1.5–2.0 percentage points, representing around half of the required rate of productivity growth required to maintain our growth in living standards over the coming decade.

These estimates ignore the effects of screening and sorting on the earnings of individuals who have spent longer in education. The value of additional education to an individual is unaffected by whether more education leads to higher wages through greater productivity or through screening. But it matters a great deal to a country. For example, imagine an individual whose lifetime earnings are £200,000 higher because they graduated with a Bachelor's degree. If their degree acted simply as a signal of their innate productivity, the additional education has not added £200,000 to national product. From a signalling/screening perspective, education only adds to national product by helping to achieve a more efficient match between workers and jobs. Chapman and Lounkaew (2015) review several studies which have tried to estimate the proportion of the earnings of the more educated which are attributable to higher productivity and the proportion attributable to screening and sorting. While there are some variations between and within studies, they suggest that the 40 to 60 per cent of additional earnings in Australia are attributable to higher productivity resulting from more education. This provides a rough guide to estimating national productivity effects in OECD countries.

Education, inequality and intergenerational mobility

Education has long been valued as a means of addressing inequality and social mobility in society. Education commissions which prompted the extension of elementary education in England in the late nineteenth century (e.g. the Newcastle Commission in 1861) and the 'Head Start' programme in the USA in the twentieth century (Currie, 2001) expressed firm beliefs in the power of education to overcome disadvantage. Yet education has also been cast as a cause of inequality: preparing school students for different stations in life (Bowles & Gintis, 1976) and subsidising the university education of children from middle- and high-income families (Blanden & Machin, 2004; Bratti *et al.*, 2008). Others have argued (e.g. Goldthorpe, 2016) that education has left social mobility (in Britain at least) unchanged. It is immediately apparent that the impact of education upon inequality and social mobility depends on how education is provided and how the benefits are distributed (Schütz *et al.*, 2008). An increase in total spending on education may leave inequality increased, reduced or unchanged.

Education could affect future *inequality* through effects on the supply of labour or through effects on the attitudes of citizens towards inequality. For example, if there is an increase in demand for more educated workers and the increase in the supply of these workers does not match demand, then the relative earnings of these workers will increase and this will probably increase income inequality. If voters become more tolerant of inequality then governments have less incentive to reduce inequality through tax and welfare policies. A change in education could also affect *intergenerational mobility* by making it easier or harder for a particular group of people to acquire the capabilities or achieve the certification that enable participation in more rewarding sectors of the economy or more prestigious roles in society.

The first part of this section examines two approaches to describing inequality and social mobility: (1) comparing individuals according to their personal income, and (2) comparing groups according to their employment or education. The second part reviews mechanisms by which education may be associated with inequality or mobility. The final part of this section considers how we can place a value on any difference that education may make.

Describing income inequality and intergenerational mobility

Income inequality refers to the distribution of incomes across individuals at a particular point in time. Intergenerational income mobility refers to the association between the incomes of parents and children. Inequality in incomes at a single point in time can be measured through a Lorenz Curve (Figure 3.4). Each 1 per cent of the tax-paying public is placed along the horizontal axis in order, from the people with the lowest income to the people with the highest income. The vertical axis shows the percentage of total income earned by each cumulative percentage of the population. If everyone earned exactly the same, then the income distribution would be shown by the solid line. The distribution of income before tax in the UK in 2013/2014 is shown by the dotted line and the income after tax is shown by the dashed line. Since income after tax is closer to the line of perfect equality we can see that taxation did redistribute income to reduce inequality. However, it is difficult to judge the difference simply by looking at the diagram. The Gini coefficient measures the area marked A (between the line of perfect equality and the line of actual income) divided by the triangle beneath the line of perfect inequality. In 2013/2014 in the UK the pre-tax Gini coefficient was 0.35 and the post-tax Gini coefficient was 0.31. Income inequality was reduced by the tax system.

Table 3.1 illustrates the measurement of inequality and intergenerational mobility. Column [0] presents incomes for ten parents. Columns [1] to [4] imagine different incomes for the children of these parents. Columns [1] and [3] imagine that the average incomes of children are the same as the average incomes of parents, whereas columns [2] and [4] imagine that the average income of children is much higher. Rows 12 and 13 present two measures of inequality at a point in time. Unlike the standard deviation, the Gini coefficient is not affected by a change in average income (cf. Children [3] and Children [4]). The Gini coefficient shows that

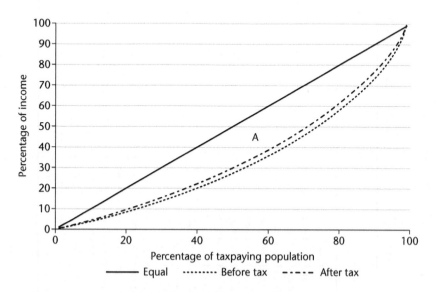

FIGURE 3.4 Income inequality before and after tax in the UK (2013–2014).

Source: Office for National Statistics (2016). Percentile points from 1 to 99 for total income before and after tax. London, Office for National Statistics.

TABLE 3.1 Correlations between the incomes of parents and children

	Parents' income	Child's income [1]	Child's income [2]	Child's income [3]	Child's income [4]
1 Parent and child pair 1	15	21	5	16	34
2 Parent and child pair 2	16	24	22	20	42
3 Parent and child pair 3	20	26	23	15	47
4 Parent and child pair 4	24	27	34	29	50
5 Parent and child pair 5	28	28	35	24	55
6 Parent and child pair 6	29	30	44	28	66
7 Parent and child pair 7	30	32	48	36	74
8 Parent and child pair 8	31	36	125	30	74
9 Parent and child pair 9	35	37	135	35	80
10 Parent and child pair 10	36	38	136	31	84
11 Average income	26.4	26.9	60.7	26.4	60.7
12 Standard deviation	7.41	5.76	50.73	7.41	17.34
13 Gini coefficient	0.15	0.10	0.42	0.15	0.15
14 Spearman rank correlation with parents		1	1	0.84	1
15 Pearson product correlation with parents		0.95	0.85	0.85	0.97
16 'Intergenerational elasticity': Coefficient of logged regression of children's income on parents' income†		0.60	2.97	0.54	0.95
17 Standard deviation in log of income	0.31	0.20	1.02	0.20	0.31
18 Intergenerational elasticity adjusted for change in inequality of income [multiplied by $(SDlnY^{parents}/SDlnY^{child})$][11]		0.95	0.91	0.85	0.95

the incomes for Children [1] are more equally distributed than they were for their parents, while Children [2] experience a very much greater inequality in their incomes. The Spearman Rank Correlation in row 14 only tells us about the mobility of children compared with their parents. Children [1], [2] and [4] occupy exactly the same ranks as their parents, so there is zero absolute mobility. Children [3] have experienced no change in inequality (shown by the Gini coefficient) but there is a small amount of mobility (shown by the Spearman Rank correlation). The next two measures are affected by changes in inequality *and* mobility. The Pearson Product Correlation shows the relationship between parent and child income, constrained to lie between −1 and +1. The correlation for Children [2] is the same as the correlation for Children [4]. However, Children [2] occupy the same ranks as their parents. The difference between the parents and Children [2] is due to a change in inequality. Children [4] have experienced no change in inequality compared with their parents, but they have experienced some mobility.

The intergenerational elasticity shows the relationship between *differences* in parents' incomes and the *differences* in children's incomes (this is achieved by using logarithmic transformations of the incomes).[10] If (as in the case of Children [2]) there is a huge increase in inequality then the intergenerational elasticity may be greater than 1. Whereas 60 per cent of the difference between the incomes of Children [1] and their parents reflects differences between the incomes of their parents, the inequality between the incomes of Children [4] magnifies the inequality between their parents' incomes by a scale of 3. The intergenerational elasticity is much more illuminating than the Pearson Product Correlation and because it shows the ratio between differences in income it is not affected by changes in average incomes between generations. However, it does not distinguish between ranking and inequality effects. Blanden and colleagues (2004) adjust the intergenerational elasticity measure by multiplying it by the ratio of the standard deviation of log parents' incomes divided by the standard deviation of log children's incomes. Using the log of incomes avoids reintroducing a bias due to any change in average incomes.

The extent of intergenerational mobility will be over-estimated by income measures for a single year, since they will include transitory changes (such as brief periods of unemployment) affecting either the parent or the child (Francesconi & Nicoletti, 2006). Ideally, comparisons should use lifetime income, and studies have tried to approximate this, using averages for a period of years. These studies have suggested that studies of social mobility comparing parents and children in a single year produce estimates about twice as high as those which use average parent and child incomes over several years (Solon, 1999).

Intergenerational mobility may also be measured (e.g. Dearden *et al.*, 1997) through a matrix showing the likelihood that children have an income which places them in a particular part of the income distribution. The data in Table 3.2 show a sample of young adult US males from the mid-1960s. Sons whose fathers were in the top 25 per cent of earners had a 70 per cent probability of being in the top half of earners in their generation at their age. As with a Spearman Rank correlation,

TABLE 3.2 Intergenerational income mobility: probability of son's quartile given parents' quartile (a US sample from 1966)

Parents' income quartile	Destination: son's income quartile			
	First	Second	Third	Fourth
First	42	28	19	12
Second	26	29	27	19
Third	18	24	29	29
Fourth	15	18	25	40

Source: Beller & Hout (2006, p. 26) from *The future of children*, a collaboration of the Woodrow Wilson School of Public and International Affairs at Princeton University and the Brookings Institution.

this measure tells us something about mobility but does not reveal anything about changes in inequality (the difference in income between quartiles).

Estimates of intergenerational elasticity (e.g. Behrman & Taubman, 1990; Dearden et al., 1997; Corak & Heisz, 1999; Beller & Hout, 2006) have found substantial differences between countries and within countries over time. For example, intergenerational elasticity is much greater in Nordic countries than in the USA or the UK. Blanden and Gregg (2004) reported that intergenerational mobility by income had declined in the UK between 1958 and 1970. Autor and colleagues (2008) showed that inequality in the lower half of wage distribution increased rapidly in the USA during the 1980s but was relatively stable before and after this period. Wage inequality in the upper half of the income range rose steadily over the period and was strongly associated with the graduate premium and a reduction in income inequality for women. Linear correlations do not capture intergenerational elasticity differences between mobility at different points in the income distribution. Bratsberg and colleagues (2007) found that the greater intergenerational elasticity in Nordic countries was due to considerably greater mobility at the bottom of the distribution rather than greater mobility at all points in the distribution. Differences among countries and differences over time are necessary, but not sufficient to encourage the belief that education affects either inequality or mobility, or both.

The relationship between income inequality and intergenerational mobility has been termed 'the Great Gatsby Curve' (Krueger, 2012). Figure 3.5 shows that a comparison among countries suggests a positive association between inequality and mobility. However, since intergenerational elasticity incorporates any increase in inequality there is an inbuilt bias towards a positive association (Jäntti & Jenkins, 2013).

Sociological expositions of inequality use 'the group' rather than the individual as the unit of analysis. Social groups may be defined by social class, race, gender or disability. This form of analysis may be justified on the basis that preferences are formed through group identities (demand), and access to a good or service is framed by power relations among groups (supply).[12] Two examples illustrate these points

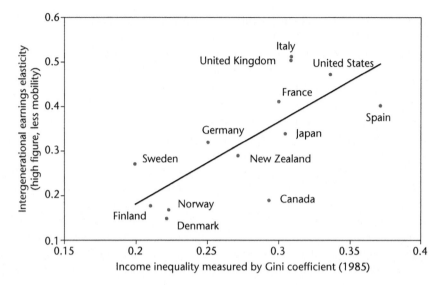

FIGURE 3.5 The Great Gatsby Curve: more inequality is associated with less mobility across the generations.

Source: Corak (2013, p. 87).

in relation to education. The demand side is illustrated by a quotation (from Ball *et al.*, 2002, p. 68), in which a UK-born Chinese student who attended a state school expresses a sense of 'not fitting in' during a visit to an Oxbridge college while applying to university:

> It was a complete shock, it was different from anywhere else I have ever been […] I just didn't like the atmosphere. […] All typical private school, posh people […] posh and white.

The supply side is illustrated by gender inequality in access to university. Universities were established as all-male institutions to which women had to fight for access (Jacobs. 1996), with the first Oxbridge colleges for women opening in 1869, more than 600 years after the establishment of the first Oxbridge college.

These group identity processes in demand and supply interact in the experiences of the individual, as explained by Reay (2004, p. 434):

> Therefore, although the habitus is a product of early childhood experience, and in particular socialization within the family, it is continually re-structured by individuals' encounters with the outside world.

While economists focus on price as a mechanism for harmonising demand and supply, sociologists focus on harmonisation through adjustment in identities and institutions which embody power relations among groups. The default position in economic analysis is continual, small-scale price adjustment keeping demand and supply in equilibrium. The default position in sociological analysis is resistance of institutions and group identities to adjustment such that reproduction of the status quo is the normal reference point for society. Individuals may shift their positions within a society that is stable in its social structure. Changes in the structure itself are likely to be more dramatic if and when they do occur.

Many accounts of inequality and mobility from a sociological perspective have focused on social class. Definitions of social class assume fairly rigid relationships between access to capital, occupational status, and autonomy and income. Occupations lie at the heart of this perspective, defining an individual's role in a materialist society. Bukodi and colleagues (2014) distinguish between the occupation of parents as an indicator of social class and the occupations of an adult's partner and close friends as an indicator of social status. Occupation is structurally connected with family capital through ways in which inherited endowments, access to financial markets and social networks affect trajectories towards the labour market, leading to what Breen and Jonnson (2005) refer to as *'inequality of opportunity'*. From this perspective, therefore, there is a prima facie case for regarding occupation as the best indicator of deep-rooted social inequalities (see e.g. Goldthorpe 2013). Breen & Jonnson (2005) refer to income comparisons as describing 'inequality of condition' that is affected by government policies on taxation and welfare and (voluntary and forced) movements in and out of employment.[13]

On this reading, changes in occupational structure can lead to a change in inequality if there is a change in the proportion of high- and low-status jobs. Goldthorpe (2013) refers to this kind of change as 'absolute mobility'. The number of manual and semi-skilled jobs in the USA and the UK has declined and the proportion of professional and managerial jobs has increased (Autor *et al.*, 2008; Li & Devine, 2011). As noted in the previous section, increases in productivity have enabled societies to devote more resources to health, education and media. Some of these changes are long term but some have been relatively quick. Goldthorpe (2013) uses the term 'relative mobility' to refer to the probability that a child from a low social class background will achieve a high social class occupation rather than a low social class occupation relative to the probability that a child from a high social class background will achieve a high social class occupation rather than a low social class occupation.

Relationships between education, inequality and social mobility

This section turns to the question of whether money spent on education, either by design or by accident, may affect inequality or social mobility through each of four possible conduits: length of time spent in education; stratification; 'resource richness' of education and teachers' expectations and the cultural mediation of teaching. The organisation of the section follows the simplified representation of relationships shown in Figure 3.6. One of the simplifications in the diagram is that it does not portray the dynamic links between children's experience of the education system at

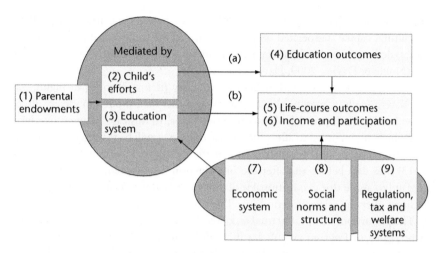

FIGURE 3.6 A model of the mediating effect of education on inequality and mobility.

different ages (as portrayed, for example, by Ermisch *et al.*, 2012, p. 9). This aspect of education experiences is assumed, and it is not highlighted in Figure 3.6 simply to leave space for the interactions between the nature of an education system, the socio-economic context within which that education system is embedded and the outcomes of education for different young people (as argued, for example, by Lupton and Thomson (2015) and Connelly *et al.*, 2014).

Before examining the four possible ways in which education could act as a mediator, we consider the possible causal effects of inheritance and the social and economic structure of society. These two forces set the context for inequality or social mobility. Earlier research tried to match particular genes with educational attainment (Bowles & Gintis, 2002; Björklund *et al.*, 2006; Jerrim *et al.*, 2015; Nielsen & Roos, 2015) and reported modest genetic effects on educational achievements and incomes. In contrast, Branigan and colleagues (2013), from a large meta-analysis of studies estimating the heritability of educational attainment, suggested that genetic variation can explain around 40 per cent of the variation. Rietveld and colleagues (2013) and Okbay and colleagues (2016) reported up to 72 individual genetic variants which were associated with greater educational attainment using large genome-wide association studies. There is increasing evidence that educational attainment is highly polygenic; that is, inheritance of educability appears to be a function of a large number of genetic variants, each of which have a very small effect, but which in aggregate have a large combined effect. However, it is not clear *how* these genetic variants influence children's outcomes in school. For example, we do not know how the children's genetic make-up interacts with their parents' characteristics. For example, children whose parents have endowed them with a particular genetic combination and who have nurtured them in a particular way may gain some of their advantages because either (or both) the education system, the tax and welfare system and the labour market currently operate to the advantage of individuals with these endowments. Children whose parents pass on high levels of 'cultural capital' (associated with the culture of the professional and managerial classes) do better at school (Sullivan, 2001) and they are more likely to go to university (Noble & Davies, 2009; Davies *et al.*, 2014).

Conversely, the 'inherited' structure of society (items [7] to [9] in Figure 3.6) may determine how membership of one group rather than another in society directs individuals towards particular life-course outcomes. In this case, changes in education which are intended to affect life-course outcomes will be thwarted by counterbalancing adjustments in society to maintain the status quo. For example, Goldthorpe (2013) uses data before and after the introduction of comprehensive schooling in England to argue that occupational mobility was not affected and earnings mobility declined over the relevant period (see Table 3.3).

The cohort born in 1958 started secondary school in 1969. A change in government policy in England and Wales in 1965 led to a switch from a selective to a comprehensive secondary school system, but by 1969 fewer than a quarter of secondary school students were attending comprehensive schools. By the time that the 1970 cohort started secondary school in 1981, the vast majority of secondary pupils were attending comprehensive schools (Bolton, 2012). The earliest date for the 1958 cohort entering higher education was 1976, while the 1970 cohort would have been starting to enter university in 1988. Compared to earlier and later decades

TABLE 3.3 Relative social mobility: intergenerational income and occupational inequality in the UK (for two cohorts of children born in 1958 and 1970)

	Earnings quintile (father)						Class† (father)				
	1	2	3	4	5		I	II	IIIA + V	VI	IIIB + VII
Son						1958					
Top	31	22	22	15	11	I	36	28	18	9	9
2	22	22	21	18	17	II	28	27	19	16	10
3	17	17	22	21	22	IIIA + V	16	20	23	19	22
4	15	19	21	22	22	VI	13	17	20	26	24
Bottom	14	19	14	24	28	IIIB + VII	7	9	19	30	34
						1970					
Top	37	19	22	15	8	I	39	23	19	9	10
2	24	25	20	17	14	II	26	28	19	15	12
3	15	22	22	22	18	IIIA + V	16	19	22	24	19[14]
4	14	18	19	24	26	VI	11	15	21	28	25
Bottom	10	16	17	22	35	IIIB + VII	8	15	20	24	34

Source: Goldthorpe (2013, p. 439).

Notes

† Definition of class by occupation: I – Professional and managerial, higher; II – Professional and managerial, lower; IIIA + V – Routine non-manual, higher and lower supervisory and technical; VI – Skilled manual; IIIB + VII – Routine non-manual, lower and non-skilled manual.

this was a period of relatively modest change in rates of participation in higher education (the number of students studying for a first degree rose by only 13 per cent in the whole of the 1980s: Bolton, 2012). Table 3.3 suggests that a period of substantial restructuring of secondary education and modest change in participation in higher education was associated with decreasing relative mobility by income and static relative mobility by occupation. This association challenges the belief that "education policies such as comprehensive school systems and extensive early-childhood education can increase the equality of educational opportunity for children from different family backgrounds" (Schütz et al., 2008, p. 282).

We turn now to ways in which education could influence inequality and social mobility. Social mobility is likely to be reduced by the scope for individuals to choose *how long* to spend in education. This will be the case if parental endowments in terms of financial, cultural and social capital affect these decisions. US children with graduate mothers are much more likely than other children to be enrolled in pre-school education (Barnett & Yarosz, 2007), and young people in the UK are more likely to go to university in the UK if they have graduate parents and above-average cultural capital (Davies et al., 2009a; Noble & Davies, 2009). The role of parents' ability to pay (for nursery education or for higher education tuition fees) depends in part on the existence of 'credit constraints'. Insofar as more education is an investment which will yield higher income in the future, there is good reason for parents to borrow in order to invest in their children's future. The question 'Why do parents with low income and capital not simply borrow to finance education?' is sometimes answered with the suggestion that these parents will find it difficult to secure loans and are therefore constrained by their low current income and assets (Becker & Tomes, 1986).

In contrast to the 'constrained by limited endowments' thesis, families from lower socio-economic backgrounds may discourage their children from participating in early or late education because the economic benefits of doing so are insufficient for these children. This thesis, following the stance of 'rational action theory', predicts that expanded opportunities to participate in education (e.g. through state subsidies) will be largely taken up by the middle classes (Arum et al., 2007). This kind of increase in state spending on education would therefore leave the inequality gap between rich and poor unchanged and was termed 'maximally maintained inequality' by Raftery and Hout (1993). Boliver (2011) and Lindley and Machin (2012) illustrate this pattern using data from the UK.

Spending on education may also affect inequality and social mobility through 'stratification'. The option of private schooling creates a concentration of children from higher incomes in private schools (Epple et al., 2004). State provision of education vouchers to lower income families may ameliorate this tendency (Goldring & Phillips, 2008). Alternatively, the state may pay for all children to attend neighbourhood schools following the meritocratic ambition embodied in the 'common school' in the USA (Cremin, 1961) and comprehensive school systems introduced in Western Europe since the 1950s (Leschinsky & Mayer, 1999). State provision of common schooling intends to redistribute 'peer effects' so that all pupils have similar educational opportunities (Thrupp, 1995; Sacerdote, 2011). However, freedom to choose where to live means that high-income parents can concentrate in particular districts, thwarting ambitions for 'comprehensive schools' unless the state allocates children to 'out-of-neighbourhood' schools and pays the cost of transporting them to schools beyond their locality.

Stratification is also affected by 'tracking systems' between and within schools. In a 'tracking system' pupils are grouped either between or within schools according to their perceived aptitude and judgements about the kind of curriculum that best suits their life prospects. Tracking systems usually divide pupils into 'academic' or 'vocational routes', although the relative prestige associated with each route varies between countries. When children and young people are organised by ability in separate institutions or classes their progress is shaped by four factors: their own expectations, teachers' expectations, the design of the curriculum and opportunities to learn from peers (Vandenberghe, 2006; Schmidt, 2009; Willms, 2010; Schmidt & McKnight, 2012). According to Breen and Jonnson (2005), this tracking effect is most influential in the early stages of education when whole trajectories may be shaped. An international comparison (Hanushek & Woessman, 2006) showed that educational inequalities were greater in countries which began tracking at an earlier age. Using a careful review of evidence from PISA, Schmidt and colleagues (2015) concentrate on the association between experience of the curriculum and the attainment gap between students from low and high socio-economic status (SES) backgrounds. They use the term 'opportunity to learn' to refer to the time allocated to particular subject areas (such as mathematics) and the level of study within each subject area (such as algebra). They (Schmidt *et al.*, 2015, p. 376) found that PISA data show that 'countries with larger average differences in opportunity to learn between high and low-income SES students within the same school tend to have larger differences in performance'. They also reported (p. 381) that the USA, the UK, Australia and New Zealand had some of the highest levels of within-school inequality in 'opportunity to learn' and the strongest relationships between opportunities to learn and achievement gaps. This message is consistent with Gamoran's (1987) earlier US study of data from 'High School and Beyond' and Boliver and Swift's (2011) comparison of between-school differences in the UK before and after the introduction of comprehensive education. Bratsburg and colleagues (2007) attribute the greater social mobility by income at the lower end of the distribution in Nordic countries to the common education system as well as welfare provision in these countries: enabling families with very low incomes to gain access to a similar quantity and quality of education as families with middle incomes.

The organisation of higher education can also affect social inequality through criteria for entry to higher education, rates of participation and stratification between higher education institutions (HEIs). Boliver (2011) reported that stratification has remained stable between types of HEI in the UK. As working-class participation in HE has increased, it has been concentrated in less prestigious HEIs (see also Iannelli *et al.*, 2011). However, there is substantial variation between countries in these patterns, with fee regimes and the distribution of population relative to types of HEI exerting detectable influences (see e.g. Shavit *et al.*, 2007; Mangan *et al.*, 2010a). In HE systems where tuition fees vary substantially between institutions there is greater scope for credit constraints to affect the type of HEI attended (Turner, 2004).

The provision of education may also affect inequality through additional 'compensatory' funding being provided so that more resources are available for the education of disadvantaged children. Additional funding has been dedicated to the schooling of children in state schools defined as having 'special educational needs' (SEN). In the USA in the 1990s (Chambers *et al.*, 1998) and more recently in England (Parish & Bryant, 2015), spending per SEN child was approximately two and a half times spending on other children. In 2011, schools in England were also given additional funding (known as the pupil premium) according to the proportion of pupils on roll who were eligible for free school meals (FSM) on the grounds of coming from low-income families. However, this additional funding was relatively modest, starting at £485 in 2011/2012 and rising to just over £1,000 in 2015/2016. Carpenter and colleagues (2013) estimated that in 2012/2013 the pupil premium accounted for less than 5 per cent of the annual income of most state schools.

Central government allocation of additional funds using simple thresholds (such as eligibility for FSM) has the merit of clarity and equity between localities. However, it does create problems for schools with high numbers of children falling just below the threshold (Marsh, 1995; Parish & Bryant, 2015). It also provides a strong incentive to schools to maximise the number of children defined as meeting the funding threshold (Banks *et al.*, 2015). More complex sliding scales of funding and scope for regional variation in funding (as in the USA: see Chambers *et al.*, 1998) overcomes some of the problems created by simple binary thresholds administered by central government. However, children with similar needs receive very different levels of funding in different states.

Additional funding may be provided through highly resourced schools (e.g. 'special schools' which separate SEN children from their peers). Adaptations to buildings and provision of specialist staff may be more cost-effective if children with similar special needs are educated in the same school (yielding economies of scale). However, this separation of disadvantaged children is deeply problematic from the perspective of social integration and normalisation. Moreover, it creates a tension with policy on parental choice if parents want their children educated with peers in manstream schools (Lindsay, 2003). In addition, a UNESCO declaration in 1994 (The 'Salamanca Statement'), stated that inclusive education is more cost-effective than separate schooling. International evidence suggests that inclusive education has proven a little more expensive than separate 'special' schools, but has yielded better cost-effectiveness due to improved outcomes for children (Beecham & Knapp, 1999; Peters, 2003).

Additional resources may be provided within mainstream schools through more generous staffing (smaller class sizes and teaching assistants) or by changes in teaching practices. The Education Endowment Fund in England has aimed to disseminate research evidence on the cost-effectiveness of alternative strategies through a 'Teaching & Learning Toolkit'.[15]

Finally, education may affect inequality through teachers' expectations and the cultural mediation of learning (Ferguson, 1998). However, proposals (e.g. Flores *et al.*, 1991; Diamond *et al.*, 2004) for addressing this problem typically do not refer to funding. Since this analysis locates problems in the thinking, attitudes and practices of teachers and school leaders the prescription is for schools to adopt different modes of thought. Of course, changing the way in which teachers and school leaders think can be an expensive business and there is little available evidence on which to judge the cost-effectiveness of interventions which would yield the kind of change that has been advocated.

This section concludes by noting some of the differences among countries in terms of inequality, attitudes towards inequality and education spending. Bénabou and Tirole (2006) reported results from an international survey of attitudes towards inequality. They found a positive correlation between social spending in a country and a belief held by survey respondents from that country that luck determines income. Their model helps make sense of the relationship between national education spending and income inequality (shown in Figure 3.7).

This figure presents the relationships between Gini coefficients and spending on education in OECD countries in 2012. The USA is clearly an outlier compared to other (mainly European) OECD countries. It is one of the countries with greatest inequality yet it is also has the highest spending per student. This makes sense if voters in the USA believe (despite the evidence: see Bénabou & Tirole, 2006), that social mobility in their country is high (that inequality is the reward for individual agency) and whether they believe that education promotes 'getting on in life'. Four former communist countries in Eastern Europe also have different patterns from the main group of OECD countries. In these four countries inequality is low but spending per student on education is also low, reflecting the relative low average incomes in these countries. In the remaining countries high education spending is

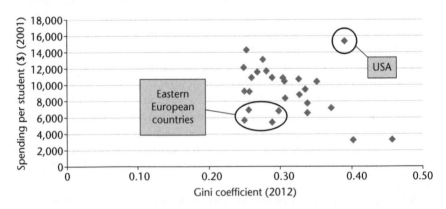

FIGURE 3.7 The relationship between education spending and income inequality in OECD countries.

Sources: Data collated from OECD data on income inequality[16] and Education at a Glance (2014).

associated with lower inequality. This poses a question: Does more education spending reduce inequality (as suggested by Bratsburg et al.'s (2007) interpretation of social mobility in Nordic countries), or does lower inequality increase support for education spending? The answer must depend on how the money is spent, and we will return to this in later chapters.

Putting a value on changes in inequality and mobility

A decrease in inequality or an increase in social mobility may not necessarily be considered a good thing. This section begins with a brief review of several principles which may be invoked to judge the value of changes in inequality or social mobility: (1) meeting fundamental human needs (need); (2) providing just rewards for choices (equity); (3) creating incentives for using resources which benefit society (efficiency), and (4) respecting a parent's freedom to influence their child's development (parental rights). Judgements about whether a particular educational change can be justified by an appeal to benefits for inequality or mobility depends on the way in which each of these principles is defined, the priority given to each principle, beliefs about how an educational change will affect inequality and mobility, and beliefs about how much the educational change will cost. Given this parade of contingencies it is not surprising that commentators often resort to simple heuristics to cut through to clear-cut judgements.

The principle that education meets a fundamental human need encourages a view that any change in education which increases equality of opportunity (Coleman, 1968; Schütz et al., 2008) is necessarily a good thing. Rawls (2009) argued that rational individuals would always prefer equality of opportunity if they were ignorant (under 'a veil of ignorance') of the capital endowment their children would receive. This reasoning gave rise to his 'Difference principle' (p. 303) which has frequently been invoked to justify a judgement that more equal educational opportunity is necessarily a good thing: "All social primary goods – liberty and opportunity, income and wealth and the bases of self-respect – are to be distributed equally unless an unequal distribution of any or all of these goods is to the advantage of the least favoured." This principle provides a justification for 'compensatory education' and 'affirmative action' strategies to provide additional resources and favourable admission for disadvantaged groups (Arcidiacono, 2005). An alternative justification of the 'human needs' argument was offered by Bowles and Gintis (2011). They justify this position by arguing that human beings are genetically disposed in favour of cooperation. Therefore, people will internalise benefits to others and will become happier when society becomes more equal because this strengthens altruistic motivation.

However, a series of studies have indicated that a majority of individuals believe that benefits should be distributed on the basis of effort as well as need (Konow, 2003). On the basis of experiments with 145 US undergraduates, Frohlich and colleagues (1987) argued that people prefer a principle of maximising average income subject to a minimum floor. This study introduced a tension between two principles:

a desire for a 'floor' income reflecting a principle of addressing need, and interest in average salary reflecting a desire for efficiency (and an implication of the acceptability of incentives). The presence of the 'equity' principle in decisions has been illustrated through 'production and distribution experiments' (Cappelen *et al.*, 2013). The first round of these experiments is a production activity. Participants start the second round with different levels of income according to their success in the production round. In the second round they have to make decisions about how the benefits from the production will be shared between the participants. Arguing on the basis of principle rather than on evidence of actual preferences, both Dworkin (1981) and Roemer (2009) agreed that the 'human need' principle is insufficient. Dworkin argued that individuals should take responsibility for their own risk preferences. Roemer argued that while 'capacity to fulfil a life plan' should be covered by Rawls' Difference principle, individuals should take responsibility for their own preferences in their life plan. From the point of view of society, these arguments may be extended to include a principle of efficiency: it is for the good of all if individuals are rewarded for effort.

The principles are illustrated in relation to inequality and intergenerational mobility in Table 3.4. In each alternative we imagine (under a 'veil of ignorance') that parents do not know which of the four income rows their children will occupy. We start by treating alternative (a) as an initial position. Alternative (b) would be preferred to (a) by someone who valued intergenerational mobility, although someone only interested in inequality would be indifferent between the two. However, the comparison between (a) and (b) will also depend on whether mobility is attributed to luck or effort (the equity principle). Alternative (c) would be preferred to (a) by the participants in Frohlich *et al.*'s (1987) experiment since it yields a higher average income (52.25 compared with 51.25) with no change in the floor income. Preference between (c) and (d) will depend on what individuals regard as the appropriate floor income. Alternative (c) yields a higher average income but alternative (d) offers a higher floor which will definitely attract all the 'Rawlsian' individuals focused on the 'need principle'. This comparison also highlights the way in which alternative distributions make assumptions about relationships between equity and efficiency. Comparing (c) and (d) offers a trade-off between higher average income and greater income inequality which contrasts with recent experience in OECD countries (Aghion *et al.*, 1999; Ravallion, 2005). Alternative (e) leaves no scope for parents' income (or parental attributes that affect their income) to be passed on to their children. Jencks and colleagues (1972, p. 8) came close to imagining this option when they asserted that "economic success seems to depend on varieties of luck and on-the-job competence that are only moderately related to family background, schooling or scores on standardized tests". This maximises intergenerational mobility at the expense of the 'parental endowment' principle.

What are the implications of lifting the 'veil of ignorance' for valuations of effects of education on inequality and social mobility? Even if individuals are purely self-interested there are reasons for the majority of a population to prefer lower

TABLE 3.4 Alternative probabilities for intergenerational mobility of income

Parents' income (£'000)	Child's income			
	100	*60*	*30*	*15*
Alternative (a): replication of an unequal society				
100	80	10	7	3
60	10	50	33	7
30	7	33	50	10
15	3	7	10	80
	100	*60*	*30*	*15*
Alternative (b): increased intergenerational mobility but no change in income bands or average income				
100	50	25	15	10
60	25	30	30	15
30	15	30	30	25
15	10	15	25	50
	120	*80*	*30*	*15*
Alternative (c): Replication of an unequal society with increasing average income				
100	80	10	7	3
60	10	50	33	7
30	7	33	50	10
15	3	7	10	80
	90	*60*	*30*	*25*
Alternative (d): Greater income equality but no change in intergenerational mobility				
100	80	10	7	3
60	10	50	33	7
30	7	33	50	10
15	3	7	10	80
	100	*60*	*30*	*15*
Alternative (e): Complete intergenerational mobility but no change in inequality				
100	25	25	25	25
60	25	25	25	25
30	25	25	25	25
15	25	25	25	25

inequality. Parents who expect their child to earn less than average have reason to welcome a decrease in income inequality, whereas a parent who expects their child to earn above the average has reason to prefer income inequality to increase. Nonetheless, since the median in income distribution is typically less than the mean (Borck, 2007), a majority of parents should expect their child to earn less than the average. Therefore, more parents would prefer a more equal income distribution. Moreover, if wealth and income inequality hinder economic growth (Aghion *et al.*, 1999; Voitchovsky, 2009), there is an incentive for everyone to want the level and type of education to reduce inequality. These factors may explain why democratic governments use taxation to reduce income inequality (see Figure 3.4), but they do not explain why these adjustments tend to be relatively modest. Harms and Zink (2003) suggest that the limited scale of taxation on inequality can be explained in terms of (middle)-class interests rather than individual, majority preferences. This theme is taken up in the following section.

The alternatives in Table 3.4 may also be viewed in terms of 'equality of outcome' and 'equality of opportunity'. While none of the alternatives offers anything like equality of outcome, alternative (d) is clearly preferred on this criterion. Alternative (e) offers equality of opportunity in terms of income, but it denies scope for parental influence and it is also perfectly consistent with inequality being distributed at random (denying the equity principle). 'Equality of opportunity' which is defined in terms of providing all children with the same education ignores the effects of parental endowments and ignores the likelihood that any particular form of education will benefit one child more than another. 'Equality of opportunity' is a fine-sounding idea, but as Coleman (1968) pointed out, it all depends on how institutions and social contexts have shaped the world in which education is provided.

Education and the development of well-informed, active and fulfilled citizens

If education is primarily an act of determining the future of a society then it looks more like a collective than an individual choice. But how should that choice be exercised? In traditional societies with stable norms and hierarchies, local leaders oversaw taken-for-granted induction into adulthood which would facilitate a society's replication (Gardner, 2011). One of the features of Western nations since the nineteenth century has been the way in which education has played a dynamic role in relation to change in society. Conway (1974) charts the interaction between debate in society and the provision of increased educational opportunities for women (including training to become teachers) in the decrease in gender inequality in education in the USA in the nineteenth century. Becker and Woessman (2008) show how the spread of Protestantism across Prussia in the early nineteenth century was associated with falling gender inequality in school participation.

The emergence of democracy in OECD countries has been accompanied by governments assuming responsibility for these processes: sometimes to encourage change and sometimes to resist it. The development of schooling in the nineteenth and twentieth century was framed by beliefs about who *should* be educated and this concept reflected those of the 'normal' structure of society. While schooling in nineteenth-century Europe emphasised the development of elites, the 'common school' movement in the USA regarded education as a site for generating equality of opportunity among the white population while entrenching racial disadvantage through no schooling or inferior schooling for blacks (Goldin, 1999). The development of the modern university system in Australia was framed by an expectation that universities would safeguard democracy by spreading enlightenment (Forsyth, 2014). More recently, the European Union has regarded education as a key vehicle for fostering a shared European identity (Naval, Print & Veldhuis, 2002), while the British Prime Minister, David Cameron, spoke in 2014 about his "uncompromising stance on requiring schools to teach *British* values".

So public policy has frequently treated education as a means by which governments can achieve national objectives for the structure of society or national economic competitiveness. However, globalisation has substantially eroded the extent to which higher education has been regarded as a site for the formation of national capacities and perspectives (Altbach *et al.*, 2009). Some commentators (e.g. Robertson, 2005) foresee a similar pattern emerging in compulsory education as national governments are urged to remove barriers to international private providers.

The possible value of education for national coherence and stability may be judged by the consequences of breakdown in social cohesion. The Los Angeles riot of 1992 caused $446 million of property damage and, more importantly, 52 people died (DiPasquale & Glaeser, 1998). The annual cost of programmes to address mental health problems in children and youth was estimated by Perou *et al.* (2013) at $247 billion (an average of $2,000 for each US household). The US government (GAO, 2013) has estimated that the financial crash of 2007/2008 cost $6 trillion in lost gross domestic product alone and the net worth of the average US family fell by almost 40 per cent. If education can improve self-, social and national regulation the benefits could be considerable. It may be that simply participating in more education yields citizenship benefits for society. Alternatively, it may be necessary to change the curriculum for education to yield these benefits. The cost of longer participation is fairly straightforward to measure, but estimating the cost-effectiveness of curriculum change is more difficult. It requires measuring the cost of implementing change, estimating its longevity and taking account of any losses arising from not teaching whatever has now been replaced. This section looks at four dimensions of 'citizenship benefits': democracy, rule of law, religious and ethnic integration, and mental health.

Democratic forms of government require acceptance of the will of the median voter and readiness to engage with electoral processes (see Friedman, 1955, 1962; Lauder, 1991; Wells *et al.*, 2002). The argument is that democracy provides political and legal stability, enabling conflict resolution without civil unrest and violence. This creates good conditions for prosperity and welfare as organisations and individuals can plan more confidently for the future. However, the redistribution of economic power with globalisation has placed a question mark over the role of democracies in economic prosperity (Ohmae, 1995) and this has prompted calls to rework preparation for citizenship to global humanitarian concerns (Torres, 2002).

Nonetheless, the health of national democracies and alliances between democratic nations (such as the European Union) depends on the beliefs and attitudes of the population (Naval *et al.*, 2002, Davies, 2006). Therefore, education is expected to prepare citizens so that they (1) remain committed to resolving national issues through the ballot box, and (2) are persuaded by reasoned argument rather than prejudice or image. In this kind of society, individual fulfilment is judged partly in terms of engagement with, and contribution towards, the social project. The contribution of education to the formation of individual identity and personal fulfilment is framed by objectives for society (see Naval *et al.* (2002) for a summary of European Union initiatives).

Evidence is accumulating to suggest a positive correlation between engagement with democracy and length of participation in education. Figure 3.8 shows that there is a strong relationship between level of education and individuals' belief that they have a say in the government of their country. There is also a positive association[17] between spending per student in these countries and the likelihood that individuals believe they have a say in the government of their country. Unsurprisingly, therefore, there is a strong positive correlation between number of years spent in full-time education and citizens' support for democracy and engagement with democratic processes (Putnam, 2001). Dee (2004) used an instrumental variable approach to judge whether attendance (after compulsory schooling) at a two-year community college in the USA increased the likelihood of voting in elections. He used the distance between a student's home and the nearest community college as an instrument and reported a major positive effect of college attendance on

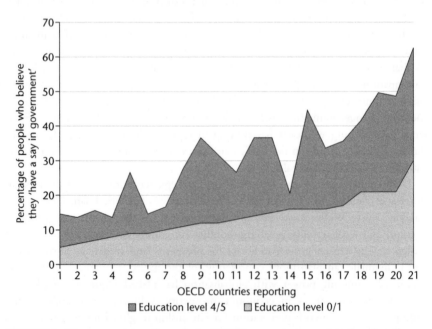

FIGURE 3.8   The percentage of people in OECD countries reporting that they 'have a say in government'.

Source: Data from OECD (2014b, p. 187).

voting. Milligan and colleagues (2004) used changes in laws governing the minimum school-leaving age in the USA and the UK to identify school effects on engagement with election debates. They reported a strong positive effect in both countries. However, evaluation of 'citizenship education' as an element in the curriculum (e.g. Kerr *et al.*, 2004) has tended to focus on schools' engagement and approaches to teaching rather than on measuring outcomes for students. The development of a framework for evaluating citizenship education and international comparisons using this framework (Schültz *et al.*, 2009) are certainly helpful, but firm judgements about this role of education await more substantive evidence of the long-term impact of programmes.

A second theme in 'citizenship benefits' is the role of education in preparing citizens to exhibit reciprocity: not only abiding by the law of the land, but also displaying tolerance and generosity on the basis that this is good for everyone. According to Gardner (2011) and Curren (2013), education plays a critical role in maintaining the fabric of societies. It inducts individuals into conventional behaviours and attitudes, and prepares them for roles which the structure of society requires. This aim is referred to as 'character education'. While moral sentiments and social orientation may develop naturally (as asserted, for example, by Bowles and Gintis (2011)), schooling plays a role in nurturing and strengthening these inclinations towards honesty, altruism and empathy, etc. (Berkowitz & Grych, 2000). The benefits for all have been termed 'civil externalities' (Usher, 1997) and have long been a focus of education systems in OECD countries (McClellan, 1999; DfES, 2007b).

The focus of teaching and the way in which schools manage pupils can affect the development of socially beneficial character traits and behaviours. Belfield and colleagues (2006) reported the finding that an early education programme in Michigan targeted at 'at-risk' children yielded large cost–benefit gains as a consequence of lower crime rates by adults who had participated in the programme as young children. Waddell (2012) reported beneficial effects of in-school deterrents to drug misuse.

Schools also prepare young people for participation in society by seeking to inculcate appreciation of the cultural and artistic achievements of their own society and, usually to a lesser extent, the achievements of other societies. This objective of an education system has sometimes (e.g. Grace, 1989) been expressed as though it entails educating individuals to the point of fulfilment. For Koopman (2005) and Jackson (2007), it is the act of engagement in art and drama that enables fulfilment by developing capacities, and providing a context, for self-expression. Understandably, the voices of pupils captured by a study of arts education in England (Harland *et al.*, 2000) emphasised this personal benefit rather than any broader benefits for society from their continuation of an artistic and cultural heritage. This contrasts with the emphasis in the pronouncements of some of the country's politicians. Education Secretary Michael Gove justified changes to the English and history curricula with a declaration that curriculum reforms which included more emphasis on Shakespeare and British history would "give our young people the broad, deep and balanced education which will equip them to win in the global race" (Gove, 2013). However, since modern democracies typically have rather heterogeneous cultures the espousal of one particular body of cultural tradition appears like an attempt to use education to reinforce the power of a dominant class interest. This reading is strongly associated with Bourdieu's (1973) account of the role of education in privileging 'high-brow cultural capital'. Education which enables the accumulation of 'cultural capital' facilitates progress in education (Noble & Davies, 2009; Davies *et al.*, 2014) and access to influential positions in society as well as personal development.

There is clearly a tension between the promotion of a dominant cultural capital and a role for education in promoting harmony among different religious and ethnic groups. This tension has been exposed through debate in the UK about the role of schools in promoting 'Britishness' (Andrews & Mycock, 2008). There may also be an association here with the positioning of different racial groups with an education system. According to Gillborn (2005), policy discourse on education in England has legitimised Black disadvantage partly by eulogising the achievements of other minority ethnic groups (particularly Indian and Chinese) that have been accepted into the dominant culture. Gillborn's account treats education as a place where the inequality experienced by Blacks is amplified rather than redressed. The unequal school experience of Black Caribbean students in English schools is illustrated by their low value-added between the ages of 7 and 11 (Strand, 2010). They are the only ethnic group to make less progress than white students, with the difference in value-added being similar to that of children eligible for free school meals. However, there are also numerous accounts of how schools and teaching can be changed to encourage religious and racial harmony and a greater measure of equal treatment for different groups (e.g. Banks, 1993; Donnelly, 2004; Tan, 2008). Moreover, a report following racial tension in Bradford, England claimed (Ouseley, 2001, p. 2) that young people in the locality expressed a firm belief that education would overcome the "negativity that they feel is blighting their lives and leaves them ignorant of other cultures and lifestyles". This report argued that citizenship education in schools would be an effective way to reduce interracial tension in the area. Nonetheless, we still do not know a great deal about the extent to which these expectations can be fulfilled, the extent to which effective school interventions to promote racial equality and civil harmony are specific to one locality with its particular challenges, or how much these interventions will cost.

The final citizenship benefit considered in this section is 'mental health'. Mental health problems are widespread among children and adults, and higher income countries spend a great deal on trying to address problems once they have occurred. Torio and colleagues (2015) reported that up to one in five US children experience a mental health problem in any given year and that the prevalence of problems has been increasing. Perou and colleagues (2013) estimated that the annual cost of programmes to address mental health problems in children and youth in the USA was $247 billion. In some countries, though not in the UK, levels of education seem to be more strongly associated than income with mental health (Araya *et al.*, 2003;

Davey Smith *et al.*, 1998). There is now good evidence to suggest that particular types of school interventions (see Payton *et al.*, 2000) do lead to substantive improvements in mental health (Wells *et al.*, 2003), diet and greater physical activity (Wechsler *et al.*, 2000).

So what can we conclude about the citizenship benefits of education? First, the cost to societies of the problems which education might address is enormous. Therefore, there appears to be scope for education to make a financially worthwhile difference even if it does not make that great a dent in the scale of the problems. Second, while there may be benefits of *more* education, the majority of the gains seem to be associated with the *type and organisation* of education. The benefits of more education are concentrated in engagement with electoral processes and this may well be due to graduates believing they have a stronger stake in the existing processes by which a country is governed. Third, while there is increasing evidence of the effectiveness of particular kinds of programme (e.g. in relation to mental health) there is a real shortage of evidence about how much it would cost to change our education systems so that these programmes were more universally applied. Aside from the uncertainty about the cost of implementing these programmes there is the cost of what would be lost from the curriculum if education for citizenship benefits were taken more seriously. Traditional academic curricula are routinely described by governments (e.g. Gove, 2013) as essential for economic progress. However, the only school subject which may be firmly linked with higher earnings is mathematics (Dolton & Vignoles, 2002; Arcidiacono, 2004; Rose & Betts, 2004). The gap between politicians' assumptions and the evidence upon which they are able to draw undermines confidence in state control of the curriculum.

Conclusion

Democratic governments have responsibilities for national economic growth, cultural heritage and development, social cohesion, political participation and equality of opportunity. This chapter has examined the case for believing that education has a strong formative role in relation to each of these objectives. Since education is but one of many influences in each case and because there is no 'counter-factual' for compulsory education, there is room for judgement about how much influence education really has. Nonetheless, the evidence currently available suggests we can go beyond simply saying 'it is a matter of opinion'. First, in a globalised knowledge economy there are spill-over effects from education for economic growth. Second, education nurtures cultural knowledge, interest and participation. Third, education can foster social cohesion and more educated people tend to participate more strongly in political processes. Fourth, education can improve equality of opportunity.

We also know that the contribution of education to social cohesion, political participation and equality of opportunity is greatly affected by how education is organised: how children are allocated among schools and how they are educated separately within schools.

Even when we have a good idea about the direction of influence it is very hard to gauge the scale. But the stakes for governments and their countries are very high. Changing industrial structure in the context of globalisation redistributes income and opportunity within as well as among countries. This is far from a 'zero-sum' game, but rising inequality in some countries and feelings of alienation on the part of large sections of societies pose threats to economic well-being and stability as well as justice (Acemoglu & Robinson, 2012). This has been visible in flat or falling disposable income between 2005 and 2014 for two-thirds of the populations of 25 advanced countries (Dobbs *et al.*, 2016). The threats to stability have also been visible in movements as disparate as the 'occupy' protests (Byrne, 2012) and nationalist protests in Western Europe (Eatwell, 2000). Governments which position themselves as promoting social justice are therefore drawn to spending more on education to meet the twin challenges of resisting inequality and maintaining national identity and stability in the face of globalisation.[18] Conversely, governments that are anxious to please voters and corporations through low taxation find themselves struggling to increase funding for education and attracted by options which claim to offer improvement through reorganisation rather than resourcing. Chapter 4 turns from the value of education to what determines the quantity and type of education that will be actually demanded

Notes

1 In fact, there is a small negative association between average income and the participation in education of 3- to 4-year-olds in countries with average per capita incomes over $30,000.

2 A simple regression of average income per head and average income per head on average spending per student yields an R^2 of 0.88.

3 Figures from the Office of National Statistics United Kingdom Accounts after taking account of inflation available at www.ons.gov.uk/ons/datasets-and-tables/data selector. html?cdid=IHXW&dataset=ukea&table-id=X11.

4 This is the position adopted by Gundlach *et al.* (2001) and Hoxby (1996, 2004) who interpret attainment data as indicating that there has been no change in OECD countries in what the average child knows and understands.

5 Using data from Bolton (2008) and National Economic indicator data for average wages in the whole economy.

6 Data provided on the ATL (Association for Teachers and Lecturers) website available at www.atl.org.uk/why-join-atl/independent-members.asp (accessed 16 March 2016).

7 The 80 per cent of schools which belong to Independent School organisations that participate in the 'Independent Schools Council (ISC)'. See also the guidance given by one private school group affiliated to the ISC available at www.google.co.uk/?gws_rd=ssl# q=teacher+salaries+independent+schools.

8 In schools affiliated to the ISC as reported in the ISC Annual Census.

9 It appears that the general public take a similar view. A survey of public perceptions of the benefits of higher education in England (Ipsos/MORI, 2010) found that three-quarters of respondents agreed that universities were good for the economy (through developing skills and helping businesses) and just under three-quarters agreed that higher education helped develop the arts.

10 Jerrim and colleagues (2014) demonstrated the challenges facing measurements of intergenerational earnings elasticity due to procedures which usually have to be adopted to infer parents' earnings from available variables.

11 Multiplying the coefficient by the ratio of standard deviations is equal to the correlation coefficient. In this case all the expressions are logged, so this correlation coefficient may be different from the correlation coefficient of the unlogged expressions.

$$y = a + bx + e$$

The parameter b may be estimated using the transformation:

$$b = cov\ (xy) \star sd(y)\ /\ sd(x)$$
$$cov\ (xy) = b \star sd(x)\ /\ sd(y)$$

12 Economists have also developed theories of 'group decisions' based on analyses of the evolution of conventions (Young, 1996) and relative consumption (Bagwell & Bernheim, 1996).

13 Nonetheless, economists routinely stress that they aim to compare the 'permanent income' of parents and children by using income data over a spread of years. This addresses the concerns raised by Breen and Jonnson (2005). The idea of permanent income, from Friedman (1957), is that consumption decisions are based on expectations of lifetime income rather than current income.

14 This 19 was marked as significant difference in the original publication, but confirmed with the author that this is a publication typo and should be shown as not statistically significant.

15 Provided on the Education Endowment Fund website available at https://education endowmentfoundation.org.uk/evidence/teaching-learning-toolkit.

16 Available at https://data.oecd.org/inequality/income-inequality.htm.

17 Using a simple bivariate regression, $p < 0.01$ for both levels of education.

18 See, for example, the accounts of New Labour in Britain offered by Whitty (1998) and Adonis (2012).

4

PRIVATE AND PUBLIC DEMAND FOR EDUCATION

Introduction

The previous two chapters have examined how much education is worth to individuals and society. However, the amount and type of education that anyone actually demands depends on the system within which demand for education is formed and expressed. This chapter distinguishes between three systems: market, hierarchy and network (Powell, 2003; Thompson, 2003). Each of these systems creates distinctive norms, constraints and incentives that frame the demand for education. Patterns of demand for education within each of these systems will also be affected by who is choosing. For simplicity, the chapter will follow typical practice in assuming that market demand comes from households and hierarchical demand comes from government. However, demand formed through a network depends on the composition of the network. Within each system demand may be expressed by exit, voice and/or loyalty (Hirschman, 1970). Exit is the dominant form in markets, while voice is the dominant form in hierarchies. All three (exit, voice and loyalty) feature strongly in accounts of networks (e.g. Thompson, 2003), though loyalty receives more emphasis than in accounts of markets and hierarchies. The pattern of demand within each system also depends on how choosers are motivated. Critically, what account is taken of the interests of others? Chapters 2 and 3 have shown how the benefits of education to society may be quite different from the aggregated self-interest of individuals. The extent to which this is reflected in demand for education matters a great deal. Finally, the demand for education depends on what choosers know. The demand for education from choosers with perfect foreknowledge may be quite different from the demand for education from choosers with relatively limited or indeed uncertain knowledge of future outcomes from that education.

Keeping to a format used throughout this book, the major sections in this chapter are: demand for education when demand is rational and well informed; demand for education when demand is rational but based on limited information, and demand for education when choosers are relatively uncertain about the implications of their choice. Each of these main sections is subdivided into 'private demand' and 'public demand'. Demand for education through networks is largely restricted to the final section, since relaxing the 'rationality assumption' opens up more scope for collective decisions. To prepare the ground for the main sections in the chapter, a short, preliminary section provides a brief overview of systems, choosers and motivations.

Systems, choosers and motivations in the demand for education

Demand for education, like any other good or service, can only be exercised within a system which has been established to regulate that demand. There are three main types of system: markets, hierarchies and networks. Markets provide price signals to tell consumers about the value of a service while also constraining demand by making it contingent upon ability to pay. If prices can be trusted to reflect the value of education, then they provide free and reliable information to choosers. Attempts to introduce market forces within state education have sought alternative ways of informing households about the performance of different educational institutions.[1] Markets also constrain demand according to households' ability to pay. Consequences for equity have prompted governments to remove this constraint by demanding education on behalf of households. As a consequence, choice of school has been constrained by where one lives and choice of university has been constrained by grades achieved at school. Since both of these constraints are strongly related to socio-economic background, education is not prevented from reinforcing advantage.

Hierarchies rely on the choices of the few rather than of the many. Those at the top of a hierarchy decide on behalf of everyone else. Ideally, this means that benefits of education to society as a whole will be taken into account. However, fulfilment of this hope rests on the degree to which governments are able to gather information to judge the benefits of education and also whether they are motivated to use what they know in the public interest. Government decisions about the quantity of education (though not usually the type of education) are constrained by the willingness of taxpayers to pay for education.

Networks gather information through formal and informal channels of communication. Considerable attention in education has been paid to the role of social capital within networks defined by socio-economic status, ethnicity and religious affiliation (Coleman, 1988; Perez & McDonough, 2008). As networks increase in size, the difficulty and cost of identifying and synthesising preferences of network members increases enormously (Thompson, 2003). However, this challenge is overcome by strong norms which bind the network together around stable beliefs about the kind of education that is desirable. These norms also constrain demand for education, leading to a bias towards conserving received values. The more tight-knit the network, the less open it will be to new ways of thinking that may change the network's demand for education (Bauman, 2001).

Much of the recent literature on the demand for education has focused on individual (private) choice. Within this literature there is debate about whether it is better to think of individual or household choice. Educational choices for younger children are generally made by parents. As students begin to take more responsibility for their lives they adopt an increasing role in educational choices. However, the resources and attitudes of other household members remain important to the educational choices as students move towards adulthood. Parents fund or underwrite the costs of higher education for some students (Christie & Munro, 2003; Avery & Turner, 2012) and students claim that information from parents influences their higher education choices (Mangan *et al.*, 2010b).

There are also difficulties in the definition of public choice exercised by and through government. The locus of decisions made by the state depends on the degree to which power is concentrated at the top of government, or delegated to public officials or professionals employed by the state. Even when we restrict the locus of control to central government, decisions arise from struggles for control between different political and civil service interests. These struggles sometimes lead to policy fractures such that it is difficult to reconcile strands of policy emerging from different arms of government (Davies & Hughes, 2009). For economy of words, 'private demand' will refer in this chapter to demand for education from either individuals or households, and 'public demand' will refer to choices made by politicians or public officials.

Judgements about systemic effects on demand[2] are contingent upon beliefs about how choosers are motivated. An attraction of the core argument for market systems is that an assumption that everyone is purely self-interested does not prevent prices from guiding buyers and sellers towards the best possible outcome for society. It is understandable, therefore, that exponents of market analysis are happy to judge between alternative systems on the basis that, in any system, everyone will be self-interested.[3] The assumption of universal, complete self-interest, independent of the system for regulating demand (and supply), is very strong. Different systems place individuals in different relations with each other and, given individuals' interest in their position relative to each other (Sen, 2017; Deci *et al.*, 2001; Rawls, 2009), there are prima facie grounds for anticipating motivation to be somewhat different in one system than in another. Moreover, studies of motivation (e.g. Watt & Richardson, 2008; Davies *et al.*, 2013; Firestone, 2014) consistently find variation in motivation among individuals and this seriously challenges any assumption that all individuals are motivated in the same way.

Therefore, judgements about the best way to frame demand for education hang on beliefs about what decision makers know, how they are constrained and how they are motivated. Table 4.1 presents two stylised possibilities. Answer (1) idealises private demand, and answer (2) idealises public demand. Since one of the recurring themes in this book is that idealisations of private or public sector behaviour undermine good policy it will be no surprise to find that this chapter examines the implications of more equivocal answers to the questions.

TABLE 4.1 Public or private? Two stylised answers

	Answer (1)	*Answer (2)*
What do they know?	Individuals and households are well-informed and know their own needs better than any government could.	Governments are much better informed than individuals and households because they have far greater resources for collecting and analysing information.
How are they constrained?	Demand for education is not constrained by income.	Governments face minimal constraints on their demand since they can increase taxation to fund additional educational spending.
How are they motivated?	To be consistent we must assume that governments and public officials are as self-interested as private individuals and households.	Governments and public officials will act in the public interest, taking no notice of their own interests.
Private or public?	Private demand should be preferred.	Public demand should be preferred.

Demand for education when actors are self-interested, well informed and rational

In this section we assume that decision makers make rational, self-interested choices that are well informed. They are only prevented from achieving perfect outcomes by external constraints which limit their options. Table 4.2[4] summarises what this means for private demand. Chapter 2 identified four sources of value or utility which are listed in the left-hand column. A self-interested, rational and well-informed individual will try to maximise the overall value they get from education and this involves attaching some weight to each of the four sources of value in Table 4.2. Maximisation is subject to the constraints of income and the price of education relative to other goods and services wanted by the individual or household. Table 4.3 looks at this maximisation problem from the perspective of politicians, public

TABLE 4.2 Characterising maximisation of educational benefits to the individual or household subject to constraints

Utility or value of the education to the individual or household		*Constraints on capacity to buy education*
[1] Future income [2] Relative well-being [3] Empowerment [4] Consumption	Subject to	(Y) Income (individual or household, current or lifetime) (P) What has to be given up (opportunity cost or price)

TABLE 4.3 Characterising maximisation of educational benefits to a government subject to constraints

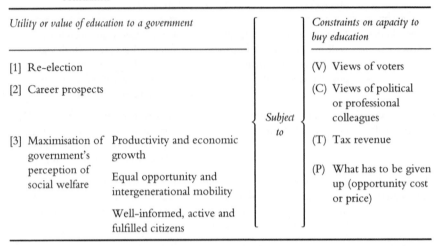

Utility or value of education to a government		Constraints on capacity to buy education
[1] Re-election		(V) Views of voters
[2] Career prospects		(C) Views of political or professional colleagues
[3] Maximisation of government's perception of social welfare	Productivity and economic growth	(T) Tax revenue
	Equal opportunity and intergenerational mobility	(P) What has to be given up (opportunity cost or price)
	Well-informed, active and fulfilled citizens	

Subject to

officials and professionals who play a role in the enactment of government. Self-interested politicians will want to get re-elected. Therefore, they will want to please the median voter. This entails responding to the willingness of the median voter to pay taxes that can be spent on education. Government spending on education is also constrained by the price of education relative to other goods and services the government could buy. However, politicians, public officials and professionals will also be interested in the views and esteem of their colleagues, since this will affect their career prospects. Table 4.3 also allows for public motivation to maximise the welfare of society as perceived by a politician, public official or professional. Motivation may stem from a desire to realise an idealisation of society. Political power creates an opportunity to impose one's views upon others and, regardless of how this may be judged by others, it is a source of satisfaction for those in power.

Well-informed, rational demand for education from individuals and households

Mainstream economics treats lifetime income rather than current income as the relevant constraint upon educational choice. The permanent income hypothesis (Friedman, 1957) proposes that consumption decisions be based on individuals' expectations of lifetime income and this applies with particular force to major financial commitments such as buying a house or a car. When transposed into the human capital view of investment in education, lifetime income becomes a choice, contingent upon the individual's choice of how much education to demand. Since the theory assumes that everyone is well informed, banks and individuals will share the same accurate assessments of future income. As long as demand for more education is based solely on the expectation of higher income, well-informed banks will be happy to lend to students. Therefore, there will be no short-term barrier to accessing finance (credit constraint) to restrict participation in education (Runkle, 1991; Strawczynski & Zeira, 2003). Individual and household demand will, however, be constrained by any innate characteristics which limit students' capacity to improve their productivity through education and by their time preference. Individuals who are myopic (placing high value on current consumption relative to future consumption) will be less likely to forgo current income in order to participate in education. However, studies (e.g. Eckel *et al.*, 2007; Callender & Jackson, 2008) which have included measures of 'debt aversion' in analyses of demand for higher education have yielded mixed results.

Does extending sources of the value of education to the individual beyond income (as in Table 4.1) make any difference to the conclusion? The critical point here is that benefits of education in the form of empowerment or consumption provide no financial security to encourage banks to lend to cover the cost of education. Education for these purposes does not pay for itself through higher lifetime income. Therefore, we may expect variation in access to credit to affect individual and household demand for education which is motivated by empowerment or consumption. Assuming that individuals are well informed, rational and self-interested predicts that demand for education will be constrained by capacity to benefit from education, individual and household preferences for current or future consumption and by credit constraints bearing on some motivations for education. That is, inequality in participation in education will appear to be a largely 'natural' reflection of free choice.

The extent of predicted inequality in participation will depend on the degree of inequality in household incomes. Even in more equal societies (such as in Scandinavia) there are large differences between individual earnings. The OECD 'Better Life Index' reported in 2015 that the top 20 per cent in Norway earn approximately four times as much as the bottom 20 per cent. Income inequality is much greater in other countries. Moreover, in the USA, the proportion of national income going to the top 1 per cent of earners virtually doubled between 1985 and 2007 (OECD, 2014b). The implications of these income inequalities may be inferred from data on non-compulsory participation in education.

We now turn to associations between income and private demand for education in different contexts. We start with parents' demand for their child's education. This demand is constrained by *parents'* lifetime income, since it is normal to assume that parents do not expect their children to repay parents for costs they have incurred for their child's education. The story starts with parents' decisions about where to live. When state school places are allocated either totally or partially by proximity to the school, there is an incentive for parents to buy a house near a 'good' school. School quality becomes one factor in choice of neighbourhood as outlined by 'Tiebout Choice' (Tiebout, 1956). We can estimate how much parents are prepared to pay to live near a good school by analysing house prices. A standard approach is to measure the effect of school quality on house prices through multiple regression analysis which controls for other factors expected to influence house prices (this approach is referred to as 'hedonic pricing' and is presented in Equation 4.1).

$$\ln(P_i) = \beta_{0i} + \beta_1 H_{it} + \beta_2 N_{it} + \beta_3 S_{it} + u_{it} \qquad \text{[Equation 4.1]}$$

Where at time t:
$\ln(P_i)$ is the log of the price of house i
H_i is a selection (vector) of characteristics of house i which affect its price
N_i is a selection (vector) of characteristics of the neighbourhood in which house i is located that affect its price
S_i is an indicator of the quality of the nearest school to house i

Various approaches to estimating relationships in Equation 4.1 have found substantive positive associations between measures of school quality and house prices in US districts. Black (1999) reported that parents were willing to pay 2.5 per cent more for a 5 per cent higher average test score in schools in the suburbs of Boston, USA. Downes and Zabel (2002) found a similar pattern using a difference analysis of house prices in Chicago. Reback (2005) found a similar pattern in Minnesota, using a discontinuity caused by a change in school choice policy, while Gibbons and Machin (2008) reported similar findings for house prices in London. Since similar types of houses tend to be grouped together, localities become strongly differentiated by residents' income and socio-economic background (Watson, 2009). Ethnic groups are also unevenly distributed by locality (van Kempen & Özüekren, 1998). When students attend their local school, residential segregation is translated into educational segregation (Taylor & Gorard, 2001) or 'school choice by mortgage' (Wolf, 2010). However, this process seems to operate largely through parents taking account of peer groups and absolute school performance rather than school quality as judged by value-added measures (Urquiola, 2005; Rothstein, 2006).

Studies have found that private demand for childcare is, unsurprisingly, positively associated with parental income (Bainbridge et al., 2005) and negatively associated with price (Blau & Hagy, 1998). However, there appears to be little relationship between indicators of the quality of pre-school provision and either the amount that parents pay for childcare (Waite et al., 1991; Blau & Hagy, 1998) or parents' satisfaction with their provider (Barraclough & Smith, 1996). In contrast, a study of state provision of pre-school education in Brussels (Vandenbroeck et al., 2008) reported that higher income families made more use than lower income families of higher quality provision.

Children from households with higher income are also more likely to attend a fee-paying private school (Dearden et al., 2011). Beavis (2004) reported that the proportion of Australian children whose parents earned more than $100,000 was 40 per cent in private schools and 11 per cent in state schools. Parental income is also a factor in choice between private schools. Tuition fees vary considerably between private schools (Davies & Davies, 2014), although we do not know the extent of the relationship between parental income and choice of private school by 'sticker price' tuition fee. However, we do know that parents choosing to send their child to a private school report that they are motivated by their child's happiness, security and broad cultural opportunities (Yang & Kayaardi, 2004; Yaacob et al., 2014). Religion is also a factor. Bosetti (2004) found that low-income families in Canada choosing private schools were more likely to choose a religious school, whereas high-income families were more likely to choose a non-religious school. Parents choosing private schools were more likely than parents choosing public schools to focus on the extent to which a school would meet the individual needs of their child.

Many parents in East Asian countries pay for private tutoring to supplement state schooling (Stevenson & Baker, 1992; Heyneman, 2011; Chan & Bray, 2014; Koh, 2014). Bray and Kwok (2003) reported that about half of all school children in Hong Kong were receiving private tutoring at any one time, while Dang and Rogers (2008) reported that nearly one-third of university students in Japan had received private tutoring to help them cram for entrance examinations. Private tutoring also appears to be growing in some countries in Europe and North America (Aurini & Davies, 2004). Levels of private tutoring are much lower in the UK. Nonetheless, Ireson and Rushforth (2011) found that 27 per cent of the students in English secondary schools they surveyed had received private tutoring at some point in time. Pearce and colleagues (2017) found that just under 15 per cent of Welsh secondary school students had received private tutoring at some point. Evidence from the UK, as elsewhere, finds that private tutoring is associated with preparation for high-stakes testing that governs entry to the next stage in a student's education. Dang and Rogers (2008) concluded from a review of international evidence that private tutoring does improve academic attainment, although they note that studies have found it very difficult to take full account of selection bias.[5] They cited one programme in Israel through which remedial education was provided to students judged to be making slower than expected progress. The programme cost $1,100 per student (40 per cent of the annual cost of state education) but it increased the probability of securing a baccalaureate certificate (entry to the next educational stage) by 12 percentage points. Gurun and Millimet (2008) found that relatively high expenditures on private tutoring by parents of students in Turkey were positively associated with success in securing entrance to universities. Unsurprisingly, students from higher SES households are more likely than others to receive private tutoring in any of these countries (Buchmann et al., 2010).

A survey carried out in England and Wales for the Sutton Trust (2014) found that children from 'more affluent families' (judged by consumer spending) were almost twice as likely as children from less affluent families to receive private tutoring to supplement their regular schooling. Tansel and Bircan (2006) found a similar strong positive correlation between household income and use of private tutors in Turkey. There is consistent evidence that income constrains household educational choices during the pre-school and 'compulsory' schooling years. These results are consistent with the value that parents attach to the consumption of schooling and the role of schooling in preparation for adulthood *beyond* the labour market.

Post-compulsory education is more strongly associated with preparation for the labour market, leading to the prediction that credit constraints will be unimportant in the demand for higher education. Of course, there is a strong positive correlation between household income and participation in higher education. Rice (1987) found a strong relationship between household income and female (but not male) participation in post-compulsory education in the 1970s in the UK. Carneiro and Heckman (2002) reported that in 1998 the proportion of male high school completers in the USA who enrolled in college was 80 per cent for the top half of the income distribution range but only 50 per cent for the bottom quartile of the income distribution range. However, this does not mean that higher current income causes higher demand for post-compulsory education. For example, current household income will be associated with accurate expectations of future income if there is a meaningful positive association between the income of a parent and the income of the child. In these circumstances (as asserted by Rational Action Theory), the well-informed rational student from a low-income background will expect a lower return than a student from a high-income background from further participation in education (Breen & Goldthorpe, 1997).

Numerous studies have provided little support for the belief that demand for higher education is meaningfully constrained by current income. However, there is evidence that graduate personal debt is affected by current household income (Keane & Wolpin, 2001) and this affects subsequent career choices as students with higher debt seek employment with high-income rewards rather than public service (Christie & Munro, 2003; Rothstein & Rouse, 2011).

Given the assumption of self-interest, private demand will focus exclusively on benefits *households* will receive and this will be reflected in the price they are willing to pay. But what if *other* people enjoy benefits and incur costs as a result? Benefits and costs which fall upon others are referred to as positive (benefits) or negative (costs) externalities in economics.[6] Education generates *production* externalities which are *outcomes* of education and *consumption* externalities which are consequences of the *process* of education. As discussed in Chapter 3, these externalities contribute to the value of education in terms of economic output, cultural development and social integration. Therefore, private demand will undervalue education from a social perspective.

Rational and well-informed demand for education from governments

Although governments step in to demand education on behalf of the community they serve, the perspective in this section assumes that they will actually be driven by self-interest when they do so. This means that decisions will be directed by implications for future employment and esteem for members of the government. This perspective has been expounded through the public choice critique of government intervention in any sphere (Buchanan & Tullock, 1962) and has been applied, with considerable impact, to education (Chubb & Moe, 1990). This section examines ways in which three dimensions of self-interest are constrained (Table 4.2).

When politicians are driven by a desire to be re-elected (Table 4.2, row 1), they are constrained by voters' enthusiasm for (1) public spending on education, and (2) paying taxes to finance that spending. Two main models have been developed to analyse these relationships: the 'median voter theorem' and the 'ends against the middle' theorem.

The 'median voter' theorem suggests that governments will focus on the median voter who will be the critical factor in determining the outcome of the next election. This idea has received plenty of media attention during election campaigns as political parties and commentators have tried to draw up an identikit profile of the median voter.[7] Public spending on education depends on taxation, so the willingness of voters to vote for 'higher tax, more education' policies is critical to government perception of the demand for education (see e.g. Rubinfeld & Shapiro, 1989). Much of the research on voters' willingness to pay for more education through taxes has been carried out in the USA. This research has been facilitated by the dependence of local state spending on variable local rates of taxation. Meltzer and Richard's (1981, 1983) Median Voter model suggests that as wage inequality increases there is more incentive for the median voter to vote for higher taxes on the basis that the tax burden will fall disproportionately on those with high incomes.

An alternative theory of the relationship between support for higher taxes for education and household income has become known as the 'ends against the middle' model. Following Benson (1961), Epple and Romano (1996) presented a model suggesting that households at the top and bottom of the income distribution will prefer low tax and low education spending for different reasons. Households at the top of the distribution will opt for private schools, while households at the bottom will prefer personal consumption (on the basis of rational choice theory). Households in the middle of the income distribution will prefer higher taxes and higher education spending. In a similar fashion, localities with a higher proportion of over-65-year-olds are more likely to vote against policies that do not favour the elderly (Poterba, 1997). It is difficult to make a definite judgement between the two theorems from current evidence. National- and state-level comparisons (e.g. Goldin & Katz, 1997) have suggested a positive relationship between income equality and support for education spending (in line with the ends against the middle theorem). Analysis of patterns at district level (e.g. Corcoran & Evans, 2010) tends to suggest a negative relationship between income equality and education spending (supporting the median voter theorem). Therefore, the spatial level at which education spending decisions are made may have substantial implications for public education spending in relation to income inequality. Education spending does not usually feature prominently in national elections, but overall taxation almost invariably does.

The second row in Table 4.2 highlights career prospects as a motivation of self-interested politicians and public officials. Public choice theory has tended to focus this line of critique upon public officials. The idea has been popularised recently through images such as 'the swamp' or 'the blob'.[8] Creating a monster with whom to do battle is a useful political device. The critique of public officials is based on the assumption that public officials will be constrained by the views of professional colleagues who will control possibilities for promotion. Senior colleagues will have established current practice and could be undermined by challenge to the status quo. Innovation is likely to be restricted to following fashions to convey an aura of 'being at the cutting edge'.

This line of critique is equally pertinent to politicians. Voters are not the only people who matter for political careers in democratic countries. Political leaders are also constrained by the preferences of members of the party they represent, especially when party governance confers considerable power to party members. As outlined by the law of curvilinear disparity, these circumstances may result in the preferences of the median voter being outweighed by the preferences of party members (Kitschelt, 1989; Norris, 1995). For a governing party, this state of affairs is more likely to occur in relation to an issue which will not be a determining factor in a forthcoming election. Politicians foster their careers by claiming credit for change that appeals to the political constituency from which they gain their support and which is able to enhance their prestige within their party (Crisp et al., 2010). These forces have tended to exert more influence over how governments spend money on education rather than the total amount of money spent.

For example, Anthony Crosland enhanced his reputation in the Labour government in the UK in the 1960s through championing comprehensive education. But 50 years after (in the words of Price (1999, p. 67)), Crosland's 'accidental appointment' to an 'unsought post', becoming Education Secretary was a potential route to party and national leadership.[9] As globalisation reduced the scope for action by national governments, the post of Education Secretary provided many opportunities for keeping a politician's name in the headlights through initiating 'bold reforms'.

The third row of Table 4.3 views politicians as visionaries rather than as headline stalkers. Once we regard self-fulfilment as a particular manifestation of self-interest, then a politician's pursuit of a particular vision for education is consistent with public choice that is self-interested, well informed and consistent. The careers of Anthony Crosland and Michael Gove may also be read in this way (Finn, 2015). Before becoming Secretaries of State for Education, both had articulated beliefs about how the reorganisation of education could improve what they regarded as productivity and growth, equal opportunity and intergenerational mobility, and being a 'well-informed, active and fulfilled citizen'. Any politician can claim to be acting as a custodian of public interest. But if they are responsible for an area of government policy which does not tip elections they have considerable scope for acting on a personal vision of education that is shared by only a minority of voters. It is, then, much more important to offer a vision that is attractive to party members and key opinion formers associated with the party.

Summary

If we assume that actors are all self-interested, consistent and well informed, *and* that the only benefit of education to the individual and the country is the effect of education on an individual's productivity and future income, then there is a prima facie case for relying on private demand. All individuals can use future income as security for loans to pay for their education. Why should others pay so that I can earn more? However, as soon as we admit other benefits from education – to the individual as well as to society – there is a case for government stepping in to demand education on behalf of citizens. This has always been the rationale for compulsory education funded by government. It still applies if we accept the assumptions about actors which have been made in this section (Friedman, 1955). There is a rationale for treating post-compulsory education (such as higher education) in a different way if we think either that future income is the only benefit from higher education or that non-income benefits are relatively unimportant when we judge the outcomes of higher education than it is in compulsory education. It would *not* be reasonable to base a difference in approach to higher education on a judgement that non-income benefits are hard to measure. The measurement problem applies equally to compulsory education.

Moreover, it is hard to discern a case for private demand for pre-school education once a case for government demand for compulsory education has been accepted. The existence of private demand for pre-school education implies (given the assumptions in this section) that pre-school has a positive impact upon subsequent progress in compulsory education. Given that the argument for public demand for compulsory education rests on the existence of non-income benefits, it is difficult to see how these would be unaffected by pre-school education.

Demand for education when actors are rational but lack information

The arguments considered in this section treat actors as self-interested and 'rational' (making coherent decisions in their best interests), but prone to bad educational choices as a result of inadequate information (Helburn & Howes, 1996). This gives rise to 'bounded rationality' (Simon, 1955; Conlisk, 1996) which has been used to frame analyses of private choices of schooling (e.g. Bell, 2009) and higher education (e.g. DesJardins & Toutkoushian, 2005; Mangan *et al.*, 2010b). Government demand for education has also been subject to this critique (see e.g. Keep, 2005). Limited information adds to the constraints upon choice. Choosers may be able to make a reasonable judgement about the limitations of their knowledge. The better their information, the better their judgement will be about the value of education. However, choosers may also misjudge the quality of their knowledge. It is perfectly possible to be confident but wrong. Males tend to be more confident than females about their economic understanding (Davies *et al.*, 2005), the accuracy of their predictions about their future academic achievements (Perry *et al.*, 2017) and their predictions about the financial benefits of graduating (Davies *et al.*, 2017).

Private demand with partial information

Most of this section addresses the consequences of partial information for individuals and households. The final part looks at the consequences of partial information for banks which are considering lending to finance education. If individuals and households make 'bad choices' because they have incomplete information, this can provide a justification for government intervention. Musgrave (1957) introduced the term 'merit goods' to refer to situations in which the state might be justified in overriding private preferences on the grounds that individuals (parents and their children) would make 'bad' choices[10] (Besley, 1988).

A first information problem makes it difficult to predict the qualities of an educational experience. Choosing a school or a university is not a 'repeat purchase', so parents and students have to rely on evidence beyond their personal experience. There is also a problem with incentives for those who do have information about the qualities of educational institutions to share this information with parents and students. The 'principal–agent' perspective (Davies *et al.*, 2005; Wohlstetter *et al.*, 2008) suggests that teachers have an incentive to withhold information about their classroom teaching from their school leaders, let alone people beyond the school who may affect the school's fortunes. Educational institutions also have strong market incentives to present their characteristics in a favourable light (Lubienski, 2007; Johnsson & Lindgren, 2010). While these problems are certainly not unique to education, the complexity of education (the range and uncertainty of its outcomes) makes it difficult to encapsulate 'educational quality' in simple metrics for public judgement.[11]

A second problem is that popular schools and universities are able to choose who they will admit. The likelihood of securing a place depends on the popularity of an institution and the criteria used to select among applicants. An experiment conducted in the USA by Hastings *et al.* (2007) showed that providing parents with admission rates as well as school average test scores affected their choice of school.

A third information problem arises from the 'transaction costs' which make it difficult to switch away from a school or university once it has been chosen (Mangan *et al.*, 2001). Parents usually choose a school for their child to attend for many years. The quality and character of a school may change over that time. The 2013/2014 annual report of the school inspectorate in England (OfSTED, 2014, p. 8) reported that "Thirty five per cent of secondary schools that were previously good or outstanding declined to 'requires improvement' or 'inadequate' compared with 24% in 2012/13. For primary schools, that proportion was 30%." Moreover, analysis of English schools' value-added performance shows substantial fluctuations from year to year (Leckie & Goldstein, 2011; Allen & Burgess, 2013).

These information problems create 'search costs' for parents and students: they can search for information which will help them overcome gaps in their knowledge but this takes time, and time spent searching for information comes at the cost of not using time for other things. Renfrew and colleagues (2010) asked final-year school students in England[12] to rate the importance of each of 54 pieces of information which might be considered relevant to higher education choices. Fewer than half of the students reported that they had looked for any of ten pieces of information ranked most highly by all respondents. Between a quarter and a half of respondents who rated a factor 'very useful' indicated that they had not attempted to look for information on that factor.

A bounded rationality approach suggests that decision makers will adopt a heuristic or 'problem-solving rule' that will lead them to a decision on the basis of the limited information they have collected. An effective heuristic will enable a decision maker to make a wise choice even though they have limited information (Levin, 1991; Schneider *et al.*, 1999). So, what kind of heuristics do educational decision makers use? We might expect heuristics to be framed by the context in which choices are made. For example, university applications in England are coordinated through a national admissions process, undergraduate degrees do not include a foundation year so that specialisation occurs at point of entry to HE, and each university sets tuition fees and eligibility criteria for bursaries vary among universities. Freedom for universities to set tuition fees and bursary criteria were introduced to encourage price competition among universities. Mangan and colleagues (2010b) found that school students in England adopted a 'sequential choice' heuristic when making choices about higher education. In this heuristic they only considered eligibility for financial aid after they had completed decisions in the following sequence: (1) whether to go to university; (2) which subject to study, and (3) which university to attend. Therefore, regardless of the actual extent of fee and bursary levels, this did not enter students' decision making until it was too late. There is substantial evidence that low-income families face greater search costs because their social networks have less rich information about education institutions and systems (Bell *et al.*, 2009; Slack *et al.*, 2014; Beal & Hendry, 2012). It has been widely argued (e.g. Ball *et al.*, 1995, 1996) that the social networks of middle-class parents possess more social capital in relation to school choice than the networks of working-class parents. Education professionals are generally from middle-class backgrounds their communications are more readily understood by middle-class parents who then share their knowledge with other middle-class parents in their friendship groups (Power *et al.*, 2003). Social networks also appear to be important in choice of higher education in England. Slack and colleagues (2014) asked final-year school students to indicate whether they had used each of 12 different sources of information and how useful they had found each source. 'Family and friends' came second after information provided by individual universities. While nearly three-quarters of students reported that they had gathered information from their social networks, less than a quarter reported that they had gathered information either from 'Student Voice' websites or from the national careers advice service. School students relied most heavily on whatever information individual universities used to portray themselves and their courses. The literature on search costs (e.g. Holzer, 1986; Mincer, 1991) indicates that education reduces search costs through two mechanisms. First, more educated people (who are likely to be higher earners) are more likely to be part of networks which will yield useful information at low cost. Second, more education should enable individuals to choose effective heuristics which will minimise search costs relative to the value of information obtained.

In the absence of government intervention in the provision of loans to students, banks would also face an information problem when assessing applications for loans. The scale of these problems is likely to be even higher than the scale of the problems facing students and households. Individuals will possess information which banks do not possess (e.g. information about their previous and future engagement with education which is material to interpretations of their grades and future work ethic). Therefore, we should expect banks to use heuristics to guide their assessment of the risk that an applicant will default on their repayments. Any information about the income of an applicant's parents, judged from address and school attended, could reasonably affect a bank's decision. This gives rise to a prediction that students from lower income households will face a credit constraint, restricting their capacity to demand higher education. However, controlling for parents' attributes and children's achievements in secondary school in the 1980s in the USA leads to the conclusion that there was only a slight relationship between current household income and children's higher education (Carneiro & Heckman, 2002; Cameron & Taber, 2004). More recent evidence from the UK (see Chevalier *et al.* (2013) for participation in 16 to 18 education and Chowdry *et al.* (2013) for participation in higher education) suggests a similar conclusion. However, Belley and Lochner (2007) provided evidence that credit constraints in post-compulsory education started to grow stronger in the 1990s in the USA as fee levels rose. Moreover, Lovenheim (2011) found that greater household wealth was positively associated with college attendance in the USA after controlling for household income.

Public demand with partial information

The existence of information problems for individuals and households per se is insufficient to justify government intervention. Markets adapt to certain information problems as intermediaries[13] set up to broker individuals' choices, although markets may rely heavily on information which governments either produce themselves or require providers to publish (Davies, 2012). The question is whether governments are likely to be better informed than individuals or more likely to use information in a way that is more strongly in the public interest.

Governments have enormous resources to deploy in gathering data on the inputs to, and outcomes of, education (Orcutt, 1970; Ozga, 2009). Thus we might expect them to be well informed about the costs and benefits of compulsory education and the distribution of benefits from non-compulsory education (Boe & Gilford, 1992; Hordósy, 2014). However, a government's data collection is likely to reflect its perspective on the relative importance of different educational outcomes and a perception of the proper role of government in education. Data collection in England has been impressive in terms of longitudinal samples (e.g. through the National Child Development Study and the Millennium cohort study) but it has focused on relationships between education, health, income and consumption.

The Westminster government is unlikely to learn much from these datasets about the outcomes of education for citizenship, social inclusion and cultural appreciation. Moreover, given the time it takes to collect and analyse these data they necessarily provide information about educational experience of several years earlier. Since the pattern of education has tended to change relatively rapidly over time, caution is needed when seeking answers to current questions in historic data.

Governments also have the resources to undertake large and systematic investigations of the views of parents, students and employers.[14] Governments gather evidence of employers' demand for education through formal and informal liaison bodies at national, regional and industrial sector levels (Payne, 2008). But the role of formal bodies varies among countries and over time, reflecting the organisation of, and relationship between, schooling and training systems. 'Dual' education systems in which students choose whether to follow vocational or academic schooling during secondary school have generally been accompanied by stronger employer engagement than comprehensive school systems in which vocational education tends to be marginalised and treated as 'second best' (OECD, 2009; Steedman, 2010). Dual systems appear to provide greater opportunities for employer engagement and stronger salary incentives for young people (Bennett *et al.*, 1995; Eichhorst *et al.*, 2012). They are not, however, without their problems. Employers only have sufficient incentive to engage with these coordinating bodies if governments are ready to meet the full costs of this engagement and to surrender power to judge the demand for education – as suggested by Sung's (2010) study of the Netherlands. However, successive reports in England have lamented the consequences of the low profile of vocational education and employer engagement (Moser & Moser, 1999; Leitch, 2006) in schooling and post-compulsory education. Commentators have long argued that this has left governments with inadequate information on which to judge the employment-derived demand for education below graduate level (Keep, 2005; Wolf *et al.*, 2010; Waite *et al.*, 2014). When governments do engage in 'public consultation' this is usually (1) to gauge reaction to a proposal generated by government; (2) to seek reaction to a single proposal rather than offering a range of options; (3) low cost in relation to the expenditure implications of the proposal, and (4) conducted in a way that favours response from larger organisations and those who are strongly committed to expressing their views to government. This behaviour could be justified by the argument (see the previous section) that private demand is too 'biased' to provide an adequate guide to public interest. In addition, the long history of compulsory schooling is predicated on the assumption that individuals do not know what is best for them, let alone what is best for their country. Nonetheless, policies sometimes seem to make arbitrary assumptions about when governments know best and when parents know best. For example, current policy in England assumes that parents know which school is best for their children but do not know how long their children should spend in education or which subjects they should study up until age 16.

But just because governments collect vast amounts of data does not necessarily mean that policies are based on careful analysis of the information they have to hand. In fact, when we examine the education they do provide, it appears that governments are driven more strongly by their values and beliefs than they are by the data they collect. This contention may be illustrated by reviewing the answers which governments have provided to the following questions:

1   At what age should children start formal education?
2   How long should children remain in compulsory education?
3   Should schools and universities provide a common education for hetero-geneous or distinctive forms of education for different homogeneous groups of students?
4   What should a common core look like?

As shown in Figures 3.1 and 3.2, governments in OECD countries have arrived at wildly different answers to Questions 1 and 2. It is far from obvious that the benefits of early education and post-compulsory education differ among countries to the extent suggested in these figures. It would appear that these huge inter-country variations in spending are rooted somewhere else.

Education systems may be designed on the basis that it is better for schools to have a heterogeneous or homogeneous intake. Countries have pursued different approaches to Question 3 and successive governments in the same country have shifted between common and differentiated schooling. These differences seem to be chiefly informed by the social and institutional histories of countries and the values of different governments. To the extent that information has played a role, it has been through accumulating evidence of sources of dissatisfaction with a previous system, rather than evidence that the new policy will change things for the better. In the 1960s and 1970s governments in OECD countries tried to restructure the provision of schooling to improve equality of opportunity. Comprehensive schools were introduced in Ireland in 1963 (Clarke, 2010). The incoming Labour government in the UK in 1964 required local authorities in England and Wales to accelerate a switch to a comprehensive school system (Rubinstein & Simon, 1969). During this period, similar changes were made in the schooling systems in Scandin-avian countries (Johannesson et al., 2002). Desegregation measures (including busing Black students to suburban schools) were introduced in US states to reduce imbalance in racial representation in schools (Clotfelter, 1976). Observable effects on social mobility were disappointing (as noted in Chapter 3), but subsequent reversals of these policies seem to have been directed by politicians' beliefs and values rather than by new information which demonstrates the superiority of one system over another.

Throughout the past half-century OECD countries have also differed in their provision of academic and vocational pathways within formal education. While there has been a general drift towards more children following an academic pathway, some countries have offered separate academic or vocational schools, some have offered vocational tracks within common schools and a few have all but removed vocational tracks from compulsory schooling (Raffe, 2003). Austria, Germany and

Japan provide different types of schooling (academic or vocational) which are intended to prepare young people for different occupations (LeTendre *et al.*, 2003; Hoeckel, 2010). The USA has opted for a system which effectively creates tracking within schools (Lee & Ready, 2009). In 1998, 12 per cent of secondary US students reported that they were following a vocational track within their school with the proportion nearly twice this level for the lowest SES quartile (Zemsky *et al.*, 1998). Australia has some secondary school students studying in vocational institutions and some students following vocational tracks within schools (Ryan, 2009). Vocational education in England has been subject to frequent change in recent decades (Wolf, 2011). However, despite a substantial increase in the proportion of 16-year-olds gaining a vocational qualification since 1990, pupils have not been following a distinctive vocational track within their schools, and a report for government (Wolf, 2011) concluded that their vocational qualifications yielded little benefit.

The case for separate vocational schooling rests on transition to the labour market. Comparative studies (e.g. Deissinger, 1994; Deissinger & Hellwig, 2005; Brockmann *et al.*, 2008) suggest that the successes of the French and German systems result from partnerships between vocational schools and industry and a strong emphasis on apprenticeships to develop technical expertise which is grounded in strong scientific knowledge. This system emphasises industry-specific prepara-tion for the labour market. Employers know what they need and are given the power to shape training routes in the light of that knowledge. But the system is facing challenges from change in industrial structure. The German dual system has been criticised (Hannan *et al.*, 1996) for lacking flexibility, locking individuals into employment in a particular industry, leaving individuals and economies exposed when industrial structure changes. Tracking in the USA and elsewhere has also been criticised for being a mechanism by which children from disadvantaged back-grounds are guided towards jobs with low prestige and modest earnings (LeTendre *et al.*, 2003; Crul & Schneider, 2009; Lee & Ready, 2009; van de Werfhorst & Mijs, 2010).

The fourth question is 'Are governments well informed about what to include in the core curriculum?' It is more or less ubiquitous for countries to have a common core curriculum up until the age of 14 (Dupriez *et al.*, 2008; Kauppinen, 2008), with numeracy, literacy and science as taken-for-granted cornerstones (Sundberg & Wahlström, 2012). This emphasis has reflected the PISA programme for inter-national comparison of students' achievements in mathematics, science and literacy, and acceptance of the case that higher average achievement in these cognitive skills increases economic growth (OECD, 2010). So, in this case, there is a clear relation-ship between systematic data collection which has been paid for by governments and policy design. This process is, however, open to the criticism that curriculum design is being directed by whatever is easy to test.

One challenge is that the definition of the common core ignores non-cognitive skills for employment that are harder to assess, especially on a reliable international basis. But can we be sure that they are less important for future productivity? Surveys of employers in the UK always suggest that schools should be doing much more to improve soft skills like teamwork and resilience. A survey of large employers in the UK (Confederation of British Industry (CBI)/Pearson, 2016) claimed that the attributes they most wanted schools to develop in students was 'attitude to work' and 'aptitude for work'. The skill which most large employers (69%) wanted to see schools improve was 'business and customer awareness' (CBI/Pearson, 2016). In a similar vein, a survey of small to medium-sized businesses in the UK (The British Chambers of Commerce, 2014) reported that 88 per cent believed that school leavers were not 'prepared for work'[15] and the most commonly identified deficiencies lay in communication, teamworking and resilience.[16] There is an accumulating body of evidence showing the importance of non–cognitive attributes for success in the labour market. Moreover, these attributes may be identified and assessed, and formal education can make a difference (Heckman & Kautz, 2012). Five attributes frequently identified[17] (Agreeableness, conscientiousness, extraversion, neuroticism and openness to experience) seem relatively consistent with reporting from employer surveys.

Beyond mathematics, literacy and physical science, governments have taken very different approaches towards education for citizenship in the core curriculum (Kerr, 1999). Sometimes the curriculum explicitly encourages a particular sense of identity. The Scottish curriculum for social science uses the word 'Scotland' 17 times to emphasise the expected focus of teaching and learning. The German regional government for Baden-Württemberg requires teaching "to awaken in young people the consciousness of a European identity; to prepare them to be aware of their responsibilities as citizens of the European Community" (Faas, 2011, p. 475). Changes in government can be accompanied by radical shifts in the curriculum. Ahonen (2001) described how the history curriculum in Estonia changed from normalising belonging to the Soviet Union before 1990 to normalising a belief in Estonia as an independent nation.

Governments also differ in whether this part of the curriculum is treated as a set of distinct subjects (as in England) or gathered under a broad umbrella of social studies. Scotland and Sweden adopt a social studies approach which emphasises preparation to debate current issues. Government guidelines for geography in the Swedish curriculum expect children in grades 1 to 3 to study "life issues of importance for pupils, such as good and evil, right and wrong, comradeship, gender roles, gender equality and relationships".[18] The descriptors of achievement in the curriculum for social studies in Scotland include "evaluates the effectiveness of responses to tackle inequalities of selected groups" and "gives critical accounts, supported by case studies, of the ways in which the media can influence citizens and decision makers".[19] In contrast, the National Curriculum for history in England concentrates on teaching subject knowledge with the requirement that "pupils should know, apply and understand the matters, skills and processes specified in the relevant programme of study". The programme of study for history[20] for pupils aged 11 to 14 requires them to study topics such as "the development of Church, state and society in Britain 1509–1745". The English government specifies what pupils aged 14 to 16 should study in history through requirements for examination specifications at age

16. These requirements[21] set out expectations in terms such as (pupils should demonstrate) "understanding of the key features and characteristics of the periods studied in relation to second order historical concepts of continuity, change, cause, consequence, significance and similarity and difference within situations".

These stark differences exist despite similarities between the social and political challenges faced by OECD countries such as: (1) the development of the 'knowledge society' (Hargreaves, 2003); (2) ethnic diversity and population movement (Olsen, 1994); (3) tensions between productivity growth, employee protection and welfare (Pierson, 1998; Bassanini *et al.*, 2009), and (4) climate change (Kagawa & Selby, 2010). To these we might now add a rising tide of alienation among electorates. The benefits and costs of globalisation and the financial crash of 2008 have not been evenly distributed. Moreover, globalisation has increased the distance between economic and political power and the mass of the electorate. Thus far, protest from the left of the political spectrum has had little discernible impact, despite moments of high visibility through the occupy movement (van Gelder, 2011; Byrne, 2012; Langman, 2013). However, discontent from sections of the population who have borne more than their fair share of the costs without getting a fair share of the benefits has been making itself felt more effectively in different directions. Support for Britain's exit from the European Union was stronger in those areas more affected by Chinese imports (*Economist*, 2016). This is consistent with broader evidence that regions throughout the USA and Europe with industrial structures more exposed to competition from Chinese imports have become increasingly supportive of protectionist policies (Colantone & Stalig, 2016). It is natural to look for governments to respond to voter alienation through redistribution policy. But voters in Wales voted to leave the EU despite the substantial level of EU funding received by the principality.[22] It may also be that education can – in the words of one chief inspector of schools in England[23] – act as the glue in society. Education may discourage belief in simplistic and divisive nostrums which populist politicians use in their bids for power (Davies, 2006, 2015).

To sum up on Question 4: (1) OECD governments can make a reasonable case for being well informed about the employment benefits of literacy, numeracy and scientific knowledge; (2) lack of attention to soft skills in the core curriculum is difficult to justify on the basis of being 'evidence informed'; and (3) governments routinely use the core curriculum to normalise particular ways of understanding the world – and this flows from the presumptions and values of those in government rather than any information they may have to hand.

Therefore, although there are good reasons to believe that governments have far greater capacity than individuals to be able to make 'well-informed' choices about education, it is far from clear whether they actually do so.

Demand for education when actors are non-rational

This section has a slightly different structure from the previous two. When we move from a world of limited information to a world of uncertainty we leave the possibility of calculated rationality behind. If we face genuine uncertainty we cannot estimate reasonable probabilities for different possible future outcomes. This has driven characterisations of choice under uncertainty in economics as well as sociology towards collective rather than individual choice. Demand is *born* in networks rather than individual preferences, regardless of whether it is expressed through markets, hierarchies or networks. Therefore, the first task in this section is to explain how this works in the context of demand for education. The first subsection on private demand under uncertainty addresses this task and prepares for the second section on demand for education from networks. The final subsection examines government's demand for education under uncertainty.

Private demand for education in the context of uncertainty

Demand may be described as non-rational when it is not based on reasoned calculation of net benefits. The existence of non-rational demand may be inferred from the consequences of policy changes which replace choice with no choice (or no choice with choice). Studies of this kind of policy change allow us to judge whether private choices are shown *ex post* to have been in the best interests of the choosers (although we cannot be sure that choosers have not tried to make reasonable calculations). For example, raising the minimum school-leaving age removes a choice and offers an opportunity to examine outcomes for individuals who indicated they wanted to leave school, but were then prevented from doing so. Two studies of raising the school-leaving age in England in 1947 (Oreopoulos, 2006; Devereux & Hart, 2010) found that boys who were forced to stay on for an extra year earned more in later life than boys who left school early before the change in the law. These results, identifying a causal effect of compulsory education, have subsequently been endorsed (Davies *et al.*, 2017) using biobank data. There have also been opportunities to observe whether educational choices conform to the predictions of rational choice theory. For example, undergraduate students in the Netherlands faced a choice between prolonging their studies while working part-time or completing their degree earlier while not giving up time for part-time employment. The rational choice is to borrow money and finish one's degree earlier because full-time graduate pay would more than compensate for the cost of borrowing. However, Oosterbeek and van den Broek (2009) found that students chose part-time employment even though they knew that if they finished their degree more quickly they would be able to get a better job and their lifetime earnings would be higher.

So how can we make sense of non-rational choice? Economic analysis of financial markets sometimes treats behaviour as driven by gut instinct. Keynes (1937) famously referred to 'animal spirits'[24] and later writers (e.g. Lux, 1995) have referred to 'herd behaviour'.[25] These perspectives retained the notion that individuals are fundamentally trying to maximise personal benefit, but they get swept along by the crowd because this is the best information they have. Conversely, consumers may seek to distinguish themselves from others through what they buy (Leibenstein, 1950). In either case, it is the behaviour of others that directs demand.

Alternatively, demand may be viewed as a reflection of a concept of 'how the world works'. Investment in education depends on a view of long-term consequences of the level and type of education. Even when parents seek a school in which their child will be happy they enact beliefs about what makes children happy. Our implicit and explicit concepts of an uncertain world provide a basis for action, But what is the relationship between these concepts and how the world actually works? It is well known that everyday concepts typically portray the world in more simple, less contingent terms than 'scientific' accounts[26] of those phenomena and that these everyday concepts are frequently impervious to contradiction (Vosniadou, 2013). Casting aside a simplistic concept implies that previous actions have been based on ignorance and this admission is rarely made lightly. The idea that individual choices are framed by (mis)conceptions of the world has attracted some economists (e.g. Shackle, 1974; Lewis, 2016) through the decades without managing to penetrate mainstream discourse in the subject. Aside from the challenges of turning these ideas into mathematical models, there is also a question of where these concepts come from.

The conceptual change tradition finds an answer to this question in the philosophy of science. According to Thomas Kuhn (1962), different ways of understanding the world are framed by different (academic) communities not only to make sense of evidence but also to fulfil aspirations for position and power. Concepts impose a social order through the way they make sense of the world. Therefore, everyday concepts of education are formed by communities to make sense of their shared experience of formal and informal education. This idea provides a basis, *inter alia*, for expecting parents' experience of education to play a strong role in the formation of their demand for education on behalf of their children. Graduates are more likely to see participation in higher education as normal for their children. Parents who have attended a private school are more likely to see private education as normal for their children.

The remainder of this subsection examines the effect of uncertainty on demand for education by returning to the case of an individual considering higher education and whose valuation of education is based solely on its impact upon future earnings. This allows the implications of uncertainty to be illustrated through a simple case. There are two prediction problems: (1) predicting future earnings for all graduates; and (2) predicting my earnings if I graduate. These prediction problems would be greatly reduced if I could assume that all graduates will earn the same. But of course, this is not true, and school students are perfectly aware that it is not true. Moreover, they are aware that the spread of earnings for graduates in any particular subject is greater above the median than below the median.[27] Expectations of one's graduate earnings depend on expectations of the distribution of earnings for all graduates, but they also depend on expectations of the position in that distribution that one is likely to occupy. This implies an expected distribution of personal earnings which is superimposed upon the expected distribution for graduate earnings as a whole.

For the moment we will focus on the average in this personal distribution which will be positioned at some point in the expected distribution for all graduate earnings. This relationship was explored in the project 'Labour market expectations, relative performance and subject choice' (Appendix 4.1). Students aged 15 to 16 were asked about their expectations of earnings for all graduates and their expected earnings at age 30 if they graduated in each of several subjects. Table 4.4 presents an analysis of students' expectations for history and mathematics.[28] The constant shows that, although the sample in this study had higher average attainment than the national average (Davies *et al.*, 2014), students expected to earn well below the average for each subject. Males expected substantially higher earnings than females, with the average difference being quite close to the raw difference in graduate pay by gender reported by Chevalier (2007). Attending a state or private school was unrelated to personal expected earnings relative to the mean. Beliefs about relative performance were strongly related to personal earnings expectations (as shown by the coefficients on expected grades).

The positive association between relative performance and expected personal earnings is explored further in Table 4.5. This table contrasts students' beliefs about personal earnings in subjects they did not intend to study with expectations for subjects they did intend to study. Females as well as males expected to earn higher than the average in the subjects they intended to study. These students believed that choosing their 'best' subject would make a massive difference to future earnings. Taken together, Tables 4.4 and 4.5 indicate substantial optimism bias in students' beliefs about the effect of choosing their best subject. One possibility is that students base their judgement on a comparison between themselves and their peers in school. They may reason that this comparison shows that their performance in their chosen subject is above average, but it ignores the behaviour of other university applicants who share the same pattern of reasoning. Faced with a complex prediction problem,

TABLE 4.4 Expectations of graduate earnings: relationships between expectations of labour market distribution and personal earnings

| | Expected graduate earnings mean (£'000s) | | | |
| | History | | Mathematics | |
	B	p	B	p
State school (= 1)	−0.33	0.46	−0.15	0.80
Gender (male = 1)	2.56	<0.001	4.96	<0.001
White (= 1)	0.22	0.64	−1.25	0.05
Graduate father (= 1)	−0.16	0.74	−0.65	0.31
Graduate mother (= 1)	0.13	0.79	−0.72	0.25
Cultural capital	0.16	<0.001	0.02	0.61
Expected English grade at age 16 (GCSE)	1.70	<0.001	−0.28	0.45
Expected maths grade at age 16 (GCSE)	−0.53	0.05	2.52	<0.001
Constant	−18.30	<.001	−18.57	<0.001
R^2		0.25		0.29
n		2,197		2,197

TABLE 4.5 Expectations of own salary by intention to study subject (£'000s)

	Females					Males				
	Average graduate salary	Intending to study subject?				Average graduate salary	Intending to study subject?			
		Yes		No			Yes		No	
		Av.	(%) diff	Av.	(%) diff		Av.	(%) diff	Av.	(%) diff
Art	27.9	28.7	2.9	21.7	-22.4	27.1	30.5	12.6	22.2	-18.2
Business	36.2	37.4	3.3	32.2	-11.1	36.5	48.9	34.0	39.2	7.3
History	31.9	33.4	4.8	26.6	-16.7	31.4	36.1	15.0	27.4	-12.7
Languages	33.5	35.7	6.6	28.4	-15.3	31.8	37.0	16.4	26.1	-18.0
Maths	38.2	38.4	0.5	33.3	-12.9	39	45.9	17.7	36.3	-6.8
Physics	38.7	41.7	7.7	35.6	-8.1	39.2	43.6	11.3	35.4	-9.7

Note
diff = percentage difference between actual and expected salaries.

students may tend to use peers as a reference point. In this case, these comparisons systematically bias expectations.

Returning to the probability distribution of expectations of personal earnings illuminates another issue. Figure 4.1 presents hypothetical expectations probability distributions for three students. The thick vertical line in each diagram indicates an expected graduate premium of 0. Students (A) and (B) face easy decisions. Student (A) predicts that they are very unlikely to improve their lifetime earnings by going to university, whereas Student (B) believes it is almost certain that they will improve their earnings by going to university. Student (C) faces the difficult decision. Uncertainty is concentrated on the marginal students.

The choices of these students are wide open to effects of their beliefs about the consequences of personal debt and their beliefs about their future earnings. Individuals who are debt averse will be reluctant to incur substantial levels of debt, even if this would increase their lifetime income (Davies & Lea, 1995; Callender & Jackson, 2005; Eckel et al., 2007; Oosterbeek & van den Broek, 2009). Optimism bias will encourage some individuals to overestimate their grades and to overestimate the effect of their grades on future earnings (Perry et al., 2017; Davies et al., 2017).

But what leads a student to the belief that they are unable to predict the impact upon future earnings of going to university? Table 4.6 presents results from a logistic regression which examined the likelihood that students in the labour market expectations, relative performance and subject choice study expected the graduate premium to be 5 per cent or less. Standard measures of socio-economic background were not associated with expectations of a low graduate premium. In fact, only three factors were significantly associated with pessimism about the graduate premium. After controlling for general academic achievement, students who were less sure about the graduate premium were more likely to believe that the graduate premium was very low or negative.[29] Moreover, belief that the graduate premium was low was inversely associated with the proportion of peers declaring that they

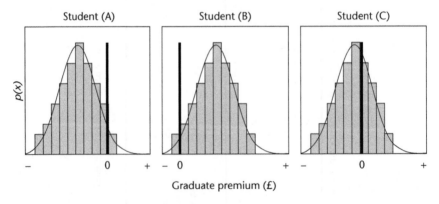

FIGURE 4.1 Probability distributions for the graduate premium expectations of three students.

TABLE 4.6 Likelihood of predicting a graduate premium of 5 per cent or less (logistic regression)

	B	p
State school (= 1)	−0.24	0.21
Gender (male = 1)	−0.14	0.29
White (= 1)	0.09	0.62
Graduate father (= 1)	−0.24	0.12
Graduate mother (= 1)	0.02	0.88
Cultural capital	−0.01	0.27
Expected grades at age 16 in maths and English	−0.18	<0.001
Confident about prediction of the graduate premium	−0.68	<0.001
% at school definitely going to HE	−0.02	<0.001
Constant	2.01	0.001
Log-likelihood		1,805
n		2,965

Source: Labour market expectations, relative performance and subject choice study.[30]

were definitely going into higher education. Beliefs about the personal value of going to university were related to the intended behaviour of others.

Non-rational demand for education through networks

The previous sub-section led to the conclusion that choice under uncertainty encourages a view of collective rather than individual demand for education. Each collective may be described as a network: a web of informal and formal relationships and allegiances that encourages shared conceptions, norms and interests which in turn create shared demand. One advantage of demand from a network is that it manages individual demand into a single, coherent, story. It also acts to conserve culture and heritage, helping education to play a role in nurturing appreciation of a particular culture and a particular way of life. However, these advantages also harbour problems with network demand: a tendency towards conservatism and parochialism. Networks also act to protect the interests of network members against the powers of other networks.

Demand for education may emanate from any of four types of network: households, professional groups, not-for-profit or commercial organisations. Most of the literature on network demand for education has focused on networks of households, with particular reference to social class, religion or race. The main themes in this literature have been the formation of shared preference for one type of education through norms (Reay, 1998) and cultural capital (Noble & Davies, 2009), sharing of information about opportunities for education through social capital (Coleman, 1988; Manski, 2000) and conflict between networks/communities over the nature of, and access to, common education (Ball et al., 1996; Power et al., 2003). Systemic problems arise when one network gains control over common education and is able to impose its preferred type of education upon everyone. Conversely, if each network is able to secure the type of education it desires to nurture its culture and continued existence, then education may entrench divisions and hostilities in society.

Demand for education may also come from professional networks. Universities in Europe were established by powerful communities to provide a flow of educated priests and lawyers to serve the changing needs of church and state (Scott, 2006). Communities of scholars within universities have determined what it means to be educated in particular subjects and they have also acted to maintain the status of certain subjects relative to others (Kuhn, 1962; Becher & Trowler, 2001). School teachers in England no longer have scope to act in this way. However, before the introduction of a National Curriculum they also acted through subject communities to determine the nature of school subjects and to protect the status of their own subject (Goodson, 1993). The argument for professional control of the demand for education derives from the idea of education as induction into an academic community. Students are not only learning *about* a subject, they are also learning to *become* a member of an expert community. This emphasis has recently been articulated through the idea of threshold concepts (Land *et al.*, 2005; Davies & Mangan, 2007) which are critical ideas that need to become embedded as organisers in a student's thinking if they are to graduate to membership of the community. Ideally, this knowledge-creating community generates new possibilities for society and members of this community will know best what education new members need. Problems start to appear as academic communities distance themselves from the needs of the societies they purport to serve. Sunk human capital motivates teachers and academics to cling on to subject knowledge that has lost its relevance for the world beyond.[31]

Demand for education may also come from not-for-profit and for-profit organisations with a stake in either the provision or the outcomes of education. Church Sunday schools were established in England in the late eighteenth and early nineteenth century to promote the kind of social order desired by the established church (Sturt, 1967). Employer networks have struggled with professional networks for control over the demand for education. Bowles and Gintis (1976, pp. 192–193) provided an account of efforts by the National Association of Manufacturers in the USA to introduce vocational education in order to impose a new order upon their own workforce. The Confederation of British Industry (1989, 1993, 2016) in the UK has also consistently lobbied to increase and shape the profile of vocational education in schools. These examples show employer networks seeking to influence government's demand for education, but without any stake in the supply of education. Not-for-profit and for-profit networks may also seek to shape demand for the education services they provide. Providers of financial education have lobbied strenuously for government to extend the requirement for schools in England to provide financial education to primary- as well as to secondary-age students (APPG, 2016). Any form of collaboration by providers which aims to manage demand for their services has been viewed with suspicion by mainstream economics. Terms such as 'cartel' and 'collusion' have been coined to capture the risks to efficiency and welfare (Connor, 2006). Taking this argument further, Ball (2012b) detected a coordinated international attempt by private providers to promote market conditions in which they will gain at the expense of others. This analysis highlights a recurrent theme in network demands for education: a perpetual battle among networks to gain sufficient power to shape the demand for education.

Non-rational government demand for education

Policy borrowing (Phillips & Ochs, 2003; Lingard, 2010) offers governments the prospect of cutting through the complexity of the demand for and supply of education by copying what has been done elsewhere. In principle, we may regard this behaviour as a state equivalent of 'herding' effects at the individual level. Charter schools from the USA, Free schools from Sweden and maths teaching from Shanghai have turned up in other locations around the globe. England has tried them all, being heavily dependent on imports and exports of education as it is in other spheres of the economy. Policy borrowing is an example of a bandwagon effect (Leibenstein, 1950) in which the effects of national context are ignored. This pattern may be observed at a deeper level in governments' acceptance of political discourse about education. The profile of human capital theory in international discourse about the role of governments in global competition has encouraged politicians to focus on increased productivity as the sole outcome of education, to regard increasing participation in higher education as essential for national well-being, and to privilege science, technology, engineering and mathematical (STEM) subjects. As noted in Chapter 3, the value of education may be judged in other ways besides its contribution to the formation of human capital.

Governments are also susceptible to non-rational judgements as a consequence of the bias to which they are prone. Optimism bias is notable here. Governments justify their existence by doing things and Ministers of Education promote their profile through action. This imperative encourages belief in the efficacy of government intervention. Reforms have to be made to work. But optimism bias also has a more personal source. Senior politicians have usually experienced considerable success in education and they are prone to relying on this experience in advocating 'what will work for everyone'. According to Graham and Tytler (1993), this shaped the Conservative government's design for the National Curriculum introduced in England and Wales in 1988. In 2016, Prime Minister Theresa May asserted that "politicians [...] have for years put their own dogma and ideology before the interests and concerns of ordinary people".[32] This assertion came in a speech in which Theresa May, a former grammar school pupil, announced a programme to expand grammar schools.

Bias in governments' judgements about the demand for education may also occur through the civil service. The status of a department for education within government depends partly on its size and there is an incentive for career civil servants to increase the budget for education to raise the profile of their department and to enhance the career prospects of those working in that department. There is a risk of this bias being compounded when different responsibilities for education are split between different parts of government. For example, in the 1980s in England, the Manpower Services Commission (a quasi-non-governmental organisation) pursued a more vocationally orientated view of the curriculum than the Department for Education (Evans, 1992). Since that period, the responsibilities of local government in England have been steadily reduced but also redirected (Payne, 2010). Dislocation and competition among arms of government can lead to policy fracture as different parts of government disagree about education needs (Davies & Hughes, 2009). One way to combat the problem within central government is through high mobility of civil servants among departments (Bekke & Meer, 2000). However, this mobility comes at the expense of the development of bureaucratic expertise in a particular field (such as education) (Gailmard & Patty, 2007).

Finally, if government policy were truly rational, the policies of successive governments would interpret available evidence in a similar way. In 1999 the government in England began piloting an Educational Maintenance Allowance (EMA) which provided a means-tested bursary to 16- to 17-year-old students who participated in full-time education. An evaluation of the early implementation of the EMA (Dearden *et al.*, 2009) found that it increased participation in post-compulsory education by between 4 and 5 percentage points and that about half of additional participation resulted from individuals who switched from inactivity to education. While the policy inevitably meant that some individuals received EMA even though they would have participated in education without this incentive, economists (e.g. Machin & Vignoles, 2006) generally judged the policy as providing good value for money. In 2007 the Labour government also announced plans (DfES, 2007a) to raise the minimum school-leaving age to 18 by the year 2015. This announcement came following a review (Spielhofer *et al.*, 2007) of the potential benefits and costs of this policy commissioned by the government's Department for Children Schools and Families (DCSF). This review had concluded that existing research evidence was not able to provide a convincing prediction, a judgement later echoed by Brunello and De Paula (2013) in a report to the European Commission. A new government in 2010 scrapped the EMA and shelved plans to raise the school-leaving age as part of its strategy to reduce public spending in the wake of the 2008 financial crisis. The rationality of government policies on education is not always easy to detect.

Conclusion

This chapter has examined private and public demand under three conditions: perfect knowledge and rational self-interest; limited knowledge but rational calculation; and uncertain, non-rational judgement. Each position carries different implications for the demand for education, yet it would be imprudent to rely on only one of these positions as a basis for policy formation. Within each position there are good reasons to regard private or public demand as imperfect. Thus policy-makers face awkward choices based on very limited knowledge of the likely outcomes. Despite these problems, major shifts in the public demand for education have produced encouraging outcomes. Raising the school-leaving age raised the earnings of students who thought there was no point in them staying on at school (sentiments that were probably echoed by a number of their teachers). Substantial subsidisation of participation in higher education was associated with a huge growth in participation and a stable graduate premium (despite the worries about over-education). Subsidisation of pre-school education has been strongly associated with female employment and pupil progress. We cannot be sure in all cases that public demand has not crowded out private demand – but we can in some cases (e.g. raising the school-leaving age). So the broad-brush case for public demand looks strong relative to private demand.

Appendix 4.1 Labour market expectations, relative performance and subject choice

Since the quality of educational outcomes is crucial for future prosperity and well-being, the subject choices made by students are 'high stakes' for others as well as for themselves. This project, funded by the Nuffield Foundation, evaluates the effects of providing 15- to 16-year-old students in England with information about the differences between earnings of graduates from different subjects.

Early specialisation remains a distinctive attribute of the English education system, but concern is frequently expressed that specialisation within formal schooling produces too few graduates in certain subjects: notably in science, technology, engineering and mathematics (STEM) subjects and modern foreign languages. A recent report for the Nuffield Foundation (Hodgen *et al.*, 2010) has highlighted comparatively low rates of post-16 participation in mathematics education in the UK.

Information and guidance currently available to students encourages them to choose the subjects they enjoy and the subjects they think they are good at. This advice is uncontroversial and students do choose subjects in which they have a relative advantage. However, a system which requires early specialisation needs students to have accurate expectations about the labour market implications of their choices.

This research focused on 15- to 16-year-old students choosing subjects to study in the sixth form (Year 12). It used an intervention through which students were provided with information about graduate earnings. The effect of this intervention was then evaluated using a randomised controlled trial and the effect of the intervention measured through students' preferences towards subjects before they start Year 12 and the actual courses they are studying in Year 12. Students who received information about the average salaries of graduates in different subjects were significantly more likely than other students to subsequently study mathematics.

Further information is available at www.birmingham.ac.uk/schools/education/research/cheea/research/subject-choice.aspx.

Notes

1 Although, strangely, a similar approach has not been taken to the more fundamental questions 'How much education?' or 'What kind of education?' Governments have been more ready to extend than to reduce the years of compulsory education and have been reluctant to relax control of what is studied in schools or to inform students about the relative benefits of studying different undergraduate subjects.

2 And also on supply, as will be seen in Chapter 6.

3 This position has been elaborated through the public choice critique (Buchanan & Tullock, 1962; Chubb & Moe, 1990).

4 At first sight it may appear odd that income appears in both columns of Table 4.2. The extent to which income constrains demand for income is a major source of debate which is addressed later in this section.

5 Parents who are willing to pay for private tutoring are likely to be committed to supporting their child's progress in other ways and their children may be motivated by a responsibility to justify their parents' commitment.

6 The argument that the state should take responsibility for education because others in society benefit from the education of an individual has been referred to as a 'public good' argument (e.g. Lauder, 1991; Wells *et al.*, 2002). This use of the term 'public good' emphasises the role of education for the 'public good' in the same way that Dewey (1939) used the term 'common good'.

7 In its popular guise, this can reduce the fate of a nation to a slug-it-out contest between cartoon characters such as 'Worcester Woman' and 'White Van Man'. 'Worcester Woman' was invented in 1997 by the Conservative Party in England (see also www. independent.co.uk/news/uk/politics/worcester-woman-is-unimpressed-and-may-not-be-voting-at-all-116881.html). 'White Van Man' appeared a little later and was viewed by some as critical in the 2015 UK election (www.telegraph.co.uk/news/general-election-2015/11536776/White-van-man-is-at-the-wheel-in-this-election.-But-which-way-will-he-turn.html).

8 The 'Drain the swamp' of the Donald Trump election campaign was applied to the whole of the 'establishment' but was also referred to in commentary on education policymakers (see e.g. www.breitbart.com/big-government/2017/01/09/mitt-romney-betsy-devos-will-challenge-education-establishment/). The term 'blob' was used by Michael Gove, Minister for Education in England between 2010 and 2014 (see e.g. Nelson, 2014). The Blob gobbled up Michael Gove – now it's coming for David Cameron. *Daily Telegraph*, 12 December 2014 (www.telegraph.co.uk/education/11288932/The-Blob-gobbled-up-Michael-Gove-now-its-coming-for-David-Cameron.html).

9 As observed in the leadership bid by former Education Secretary Michael Gove (see e.g. www.bbc.co.uk/news/uk-politics-36671336).

10 The term 'merit good' is also sometimes used to refer to goods and services that individuals deserve to have regardless of income and social position (see e.g. Bergmann, 2004; Rauh, 2011). For a discussion of Musgrave's concept of merit goods and debate about the relationship between merit goods and public goods see Ver Eecke (2003). Grace (1989, p. 219) calls education a 'public good' because it "potentially enhances the person (regardless of the social status of that person) for the full realisation of all their abilities and competencies". Using this construction he slips from a definition of what counts as an 'educated person' to an assertion that governments should take responsibility for this definition. This elision side-steps the crucial question of why we should believe that a government should take this responsibility out of the hands of its citizens.

11 Lubienski (2007) distinguishes between goods and services according to whether they are 'search goods', 'experience goods' or 'credence goods'. He argues that market incentives face greater challenges in providing adequate information to customers for experience and credence goods – such as education.

12 After excluding students who declared that they were not considering higher education, they had a total sample of 1,926 respondents (Renfrew *et al.*, 2010, p. 28).

13 See e.g. the *Good Schools Guide* in England (www.goodschoolsguide.co.uk/advice-service/london-school-service?gclid=CMTf6srQts0CFZAW0wod8SgEYA).

14 See e.g. the consultation document from the Department for Education in England (DfE, 2016), proposing an extension of the role of private schools in state-funded schooling and an extension of selective education, interestingly entitled 'Schools that work for everyone'.

15 This viewpoint is routinely offered by businesses in Britain. See e.g. a report of a survey carried out in 2016 by the Chartered Institute of Management Accountants (CIMA) (www.bbc.co.uk/news/business-37824641).

16 This evidence shows what employers thought schools should be doing (i.e. employers' voice demanding a particular kind of education). Heckman and Kautz (2012) summarise the case for believing that schools can change 'soft skills' sufficiently to make a difference to children's futures in the labour market.

17 See Heckman & Kautz (2012).

18 From the Swedish National Agency for Education (2011), 'Curriculum for the compulsory school, preschool class and the leisure-time centre 2011', p. 151 (http://malmo.se/download/18.29c3b78a132728ecb52800034181/1383645293487/pdf2687.pdf).

19 See guidelines for progression and achievement in social studies published by Education Scotland (2016) (www.educationscotland.gov.uk/Images/SocialStudiesGrid_tcm4-832619.pdf).

20 The Requirements for the National Curriculum for History in England were retrieved from www.gov.uk/government/publications/national-curriculum-in-england-history-programmes-of-study/national-curriculum-in-england-history-programmes-of-study.

21 Requirements are published by the Department for Education. At the time of publication the most recent requirements were dated 2014 and were accessed at www.gov.uk/government/uploads/system/uploads/attachment_data/file/310549/history_GCSE_formatted.pdf.

22 Some details are available at www.walesonline.co.uk/news/politics/heres-how-much-money-wales-11527889.

23 Speaking in 2016 the Chief Inspector of Schools in England claimed that "Schools provide the glue that helps hold our society together" (Wilshaw, M. (2016) *Sir Michael Wilshaw's Speech at the FASNA Autumn Conference*, 2 November, 2016 (www.gov.uk/government/speeches/sir-michael-wilshaws-speech-at-the-fasna-autumn-conference).

24 See also Akerlof & Shiller (2010).

25 Or 'bandwagon effects' in the language of Leibenstein (1950).

26 Which are themselves incomplete ideas that may be overthrown at some future point.

27 This is shown in the data gathered for the project 'Labour market expectations, relative performance and subject choice' described in Appendix 4.1. Students aged 15 to 16 in England expected the standard deviation above the mean to be approximately twice the standard deviation below the mean. Students were asked to indicate their expectations for the median, lower quartile and upper quartile in the wage distribution. This enabled a comparison of expectations of 'median – LQ' and 'HQ – median'.

28 The results in Table 4.4 are for a 'complete case' analysis. Analyses conducted with these data have consistently found no substantive difference between complete case analyses and multiple imputation results (see for e.g. Davies et al., 2014; Davies et al., 2017b).

29 This result echoes that found by Davies et al. (2009b).

30 This study was conducted at the University of Birmingham, UK, and funded by the Nuffield Foundation. For details see www.birmingham.ac.uk/schools/education/research/cheea/research/subject-choice.aspx.

31 A sentiment famously articulated in 1976 in a speech by British Prime Minister James Callaghan (1976) at Ruskin College and echoed by subsequent Ministers of State (see e.g. http://dera.ioe.ac.uk/26176/1/The%20importance%20of%20the%20curriculum%20-%20Speeches%20-%20GOV_UK.pdf).

32 From a speech on 9 September 2016, 'The great meritocracy', announcing the introduction of new selective grammar schools (www.gov.uk/government/speeches/britain-the-great-meritocracy-prime-ministers-speech) (accessed 11 April 2017).

5

PROVIDING EDUCATION

Productivity, cost, efficiency and equity

Introduction

Chapters 5 and 6 examine how we should judge the use of resources in education. This turns out to be quite problematic. According to the Audit Commission in England (Davidson *et al.*, 2008), we can use 'value added per pound of expenditure' to judge value for money. This view was later endorsed by the Department for Education (2013b). But, even leaving aside the challenges of interpreting value-added measures (Perry, 2017), 'value-added per pound of expenditure' ignores outcomes of education other than progress in core academic subjects. As noted in Chapters 2 and 3, this encourages a rather narrow view of the value of education. Moreover, 'value added per pound of expenditure' ignores inputs "contributed by clients and volunteers" (Barnett, 1993, p. 95). The outcomes of education depend partially on the efforts and self-direction of students, the influence of peers, and the support and engagement of parents and carers (see e.g. Feinstein & Symons, 1999; Todd & Wolpin, 2003).

Chapters 5 and 6 divide the analysis of providing education into three parts using terms from economics: technical efficiency, X-inefficiency and allocative efficiency. Technical efficiency focuses on relationships between inputs and outputs. If all providers of education had perfect knowledge we could reasonably expect them to choose a way of providing education that was ideal in terms of inputs and outputs: any given output would be provided at the least cost. Chapter 5 examines arguments and evidence largely in relation to technical efficiency: the size of educational institutions, the input mix, and the roles of parents, peers and pupils in 'co-production' and (social) reproduction in education. The chapter reviews what is known about inputs and outputs in education and the implications of defining inputs and outputs in different ways. The chapter concludes that current knowledge is partial: there are some things we have a fairly clear idea about, some things that are visible but hazy, and others that are difficult to judge. One response to uncertainty about what is known is to define the problem more narrowly to make it possible to say 'we know this'. This is technically helpful, but problematic as a basis for policy. An alternative approach is to say 'we know next to nothing because each school, classroom, teacher and pupil is different'. But this simply sets policy-making free from evidence. This chapter tries to steer a course between these two positions. It also prepares the ground for Chapter 6 which considers the con-sequences of limited information and uncertainty for private and public sector supply of education. Chapter 6 examines X-inefficiency and allocative efficiency. This involves relaxing assumptions about motivation and knowledge, raising the question of how governance systems may affect motivation and knowledge. However, before proceeding with the detailed analysis we must pause to clarify some language issues.

The language of production, efficiency and value for money

The language of production, efficiency and value for money causes problems for two main reasons. First, it is sometimes taken to imply that education should be regarded as *just the same* as the production of cars or beans. Some researchers perceive the language of production as necessarily imposing an alien discourse upon educa-tion to normalise some policies while casting others into the wilderness. There is force in these concerns and the first part of this section sets out the way in which the language of production is used in this chapter. The second problem is confusion: different meanings are given to the same word and different words are used to mean the same thing. These confusions discourage researchers from learning from work in other traditions and this gets in the way of building a stronger, shared basis for sens-ible policy. The second part of this section addresses the confusion problem.

Production, co-production and reproduction

The standard use of the term 'production' in economics implies that various inputs (such as teachers, ICT and buildings) are used to transform raw materials (unedu-cated children) into outputs (educated adults). This does capture a dimension of what happens in schools and universities, but it cannot stand as the only story. Figure 5.1 tries to distinguish between different ways of thinking about educational 'production'. A substantial proportion of the economics literature treats the process of education as a black box (Figure 5.1[a]). Large datasets are used to analyse rela-tionships between the quantity of one input and one output (usually academic achievement in mathematics, science or languages) while holding other inputs con-stant. This approach to analysing production examines variations in the amount of an input (and therefore its cost) or variations in the effort applied by teachers (which may or may not be related to cost).

Figure 5.1[b] allows the effect of an input to depend on the way it is deployed. If we make an a priori assumption that a school or university will always choose the

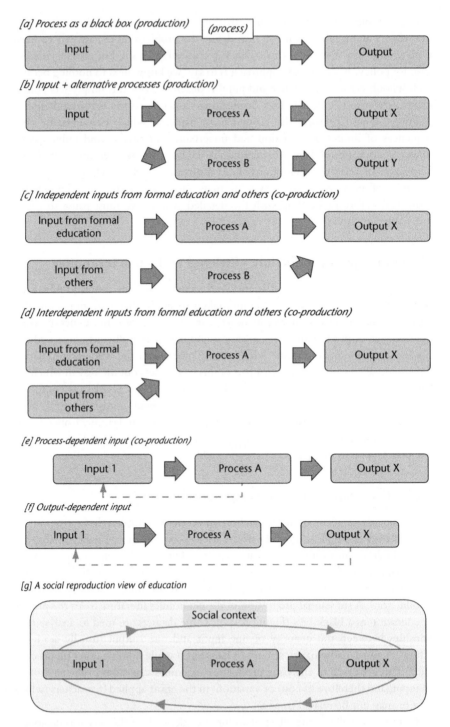

FIGURE 5.1 Different concepts of the production of education.

optimal way of deploying resources, then we do not need to worry about taking account of resource deployment. However, as soon as we accept that information and incentives are insufficient to make 'optimal use of resources' likely, then it becomes important to take account of educational processes which may lead to different outputs from the same input.

Figures 5.1[c] and [d] portray perspectives which will be referred to in this book as 'co-production'. This term has been used to describe and analyse circumstances in which the people who benefit from a good or service contribute to the production of that good or service (Becker, 1965; Kiser, 1984; Ostrom, 1996).[1] In education this includes parents, pupils and their peers. Figure 5.1[c] envisages independent effects. For instance, we may think of parents' role in helping pre-school children to develop. Figure 5.1[d] portrays an interaction between formal education and others. This may take the form of parents' engagement with school. These figures treat learners as more than 'materials' to be improved by the way that educational organisations use resources to make them more valuable. Learners play a critical role in shaping their own education through their efforts, attitudes and ideas.

Figures 5.1[e] and [f] develop this theme by representing ways in which the experience of education feeds back into the nature of inputs from students, parents and teachers. For example, psychologists have examined ways in which students' 'academic self-concept' is developed through comparisons with their immediate peers in school (Marsh *et al.*, 2008a) and how university students' 'approaches to learning' are shaped by the nature of teaching (Biggs, 1996). These feedback mechanisms affect what students put into their learning. Teachers' development is affected by the opportunities they have to reflect on and learn from their experience in teaching (Hatton & Smith, 1995). Figure 5.1[f] depicts ways in which the *outcomes* from education feed back into future learning (which is, after all, a long-drawn-out process). For example, a large body of evidence points to the impact of a sense of achievement (from outputs) upon students' readiness (self-efficacy) to attempt further tasks (Bandura *et al.*, 1996, 2001). Parents may also adjust their input into children's education in the light of deviations of their children's performance from what they expected (Okagaki & Frensch, 1998).

Finally, Figure 5.1[g] sets all of these possibilities within a social frame. The nature of the inputs, the processes in which these inputs are deployed and the outputs which arise are now seen as social processes rather than workings of a particular school or university, or co-production among particular schools, parents, peers and students at a particular time and place. This view is most associated with the term 'social *re*production', in which the key points at issue are how output will be distributed between students and the tendency of social systems to use education to re-create an existing order in which privilege and disadvantage is passed from one generation to the next. Even advocates of a traditional curriculum (e.g. Cox & Dyson, 1969) cast their arguments in terms of preserving a cultural heritage. For others (e.g. Ball, 1992, 2003a; Welch, 1998), education frequently reproduces the distribution of power and privilege. In either case, education is something that happens through, and to, societies.

This chapter is organised into three sections: production, co-production and reproduction. Each section provides one way of looking at the provision of education. Although the perspective broadens through the chapter, this does not mean that we can regard any section as adequately subsuming what has gone before.

Efficiency, effectiveness and economy: different words in different places

The same words mean different things when used by auditors or economists. In their report for the Audit Commission, Davidson and colleagues (2008) define three crucial words in the following ways:

- *Economy:* Minimising the costs of resources used in the public sector, but having regard to quality.
- *Efficiency:* The relationship between output, in terms of goods, services or other results, and the resources used to produce them.
- *Effectiveness:* The extent to which objectives have been achieved. The relationship between the intended impacts and actual impacts of an activity.

The phrase 'having regard to quality' in the first definition is somewhat ambiguous, but it draws attention to key distinctions. Quality may be defined in terms of a technical measurement of a particular *output*. For example, it may refer to the proportion of students at a school who have attained a particular level of examination grades. It may refer to the proportion of students at a school who can swim 100 metres. Technical measures of outputs make no reference to the desirability of different outputs. Quality may also be defined in terms of desirable *outcomes*. School outputs may contribute to the achievement of desirable outcomes such as 'educated citizens who are able to actively contribute to their society', 'fit and healthy individuals' or 'productive workers'. Markets measure the relative desirability of different outcomes through prices. When the state provides, it has to impose its own judgement about the relative desirability of different outcomes. Minimising resources used in producing a given output is referred to in economics as 'technical efficiency'. Minimising resources in producing what is most desired (either by markets or by states) is referred to in economics as 'allocative efficiency'.

A definition of each way of looking at efficiency is presented in Table 5.1. Technical efficiency assumes that each resource is being used in the best way. The term X-efficiency was coined by Leibenstein (1966, 1978) to refer to situations in which an organisation fails to make the best use of its resources as a consequence either of lack of knowledge or lack of motivation to use the knowledge that is available. Research on the provision of education quite frequently contributes to analysis of technical and X-inefficiency. For instance, the literature on teaching assistants comments on the number of teaching assistants who are employed and the way in they are deployed. In order to analyse particular issues (e.g. the employment of teaching assistants) the section on the input mix in this chapter also refers to

X-inefficiency. An educational organisation or system may be technically efficient and may avoid X-inefficiency while still being allocatively inefficient. It may simply provide the wrong kind of education. Of course, an assessment such as this must rely on a subjective judgement of what is the right kind of education. Table 5.1 exemplifies how each of these definitions may be applied in the field of education.

TABLE 5.1 Sources of efficiency failure and their relationship to definitions of efficiency

Efficiency failure	Example	Relevant definition of efficiency
1 Organisation is either too large or too small	A small secondary school has high administration costs per pupil and very small classes in the sixth form.	Technical efficiency
2 Using a sub-optimal combination of resources (input mix)	A school employs a higher ratio of support teachers to teachers than would be required to maximise pupils' achievement.	
3 Poor deployment of resources	A university allocates teaching to academics who are weak teachers because it wants to employ them for research.	'X' inefficiency
4 Using ineffective methods to provide the service	Academics run undergraduate seminars like 'mini-lectures' with little interaction between teacher and students.	
5 Paying more than necessary for inputs	A school pays 'above the odds' for administration supplies and catering when other suppliers would charge less.	
6 Disorganisation and lack of incentives leads to 'organisational slack'	Some teachers' efforts are misdirected due to lack of organisational clarity about shared objectives and other teachers' effort is reduced by confusion and lack of reward.	
7 Producing the wrong combination of outcomes	A school system fails to develop 'soft skills' which are valued in the labour market.	Allocative efficiency and equity
8 An undesirable allocation of the benefits of education between different individuals	Given a desire to give students of the same ability an equal opportunity to progress to university, students from some backgrounds are less likely to do so for reasons that are beyond their control	

Davidson and colleagues (2008) give a different meaning to the word 'efficiency': the relationship between inputs and outputs. This relationship may be described in terms of the physical quantities of inputs and outputs (e.g. the number of teachers and the grades achieved by students). This has long been described by economists as '*physical* productivity'. Alternatively it could refer to the cost of an input relative to the value of the output (e.g. the total wage bill for teachers relative to the difference made to students' future earnings). This has been defined as '*value productivity*'.

Finally, their definition of effectiveness draws attention to the question of who decides when an organisation is doing a good job. Davidson and colleagues place that responsibility in the hands of the organisation which is managing the resources: Are we achieving what we wanted to achieve? This definition is quite different from the use of the term in the *school effectiveness* literature (e.g. Scheerens, 1990). Researchers in the school effectiveness tradition have placed themselves in the seat of judgement by choosing to decide whether schools are doing a good job on the basis of their choice of measurement (improvement in students' attainment). They have also judged effectiveness in terms of what *can* be achieved (judged on the basis of comparing schools) rather than what is *desirable* to achieve. When researchers choose the way schools (or universities) should be judged, they open themselves to critique that they have chosen a criterion which suits them rather than society. For example, Kelly (2012) points out that measuring a school's effectiveness through the average attainment of its students ignores that school's impact upon equity in society. Similar problems afflict analysis of how the gap between attainments of children from rich and poor backgrounds changes as they progress through the school system (Blanden *et al.*, 2012). The grading system on which National Curriculum assessments are based in England is designed (National Curriculum Task Group on Assessment and Testing, 1987, para 104) such that there will necessarily be a widening gap in achievement as pupils age.

We might also add that the standard approach to school effectiveness has ignored differences between schools in the quantity and quality of inputs they have used in producing their outputs. It has been routine to assume that schools have used the same level of inputs. This assumption has been reasonable in many comparisons of state schools but it is certainly not appropriate in comparisons of state and private schools[2] (whether undertaken in the name of school effectiveness or 'production function research').

This returns us to the definitions of technical and allocative efficiency used to organise this chapter. School effectiveness (and much production function) research has stuck with a 'technical efficiency' approach to judging schools. Schools have been compared in terms of their performance against an output measure that fits in with researchers' theoretical perspective. Generally, there has been an implicit assumption that all schools had the same inputs and technical efficiency was labelled 'effectiveness'. Allocative efficiency raises the question 'But what's worth producing?' This in turn raises the question 'Who decides?' Somehow, a judgement has to be made about which outcomes from education and which distribution of outcomes best serves the interests of society as a whole. As discussed in Chapters 2 and 3, this is a very difficult question to answer, but has to be acknowledged. This chapter examines relationships between inputs and outputs using definitions of efficiency that have been developed by economists. However, some of the characteristics of inputs and outputs in education mean that that this *does not* entail a routine application of economic analysis to a 'standard case'.

Cost-effectiveness

Although cost-effectiveness tends to be ignored in education evaluations (Levin, 2001; Hummel-Rossi & Ashdown, 2002), it has recently been included in the judgements of education interventions provided (Higgins *et al.*, 2013) for schools and teachers in England. For the UK, at least, this has been an important step forward, increasing the profile of cost assessment in educational evaluation. Their 'Teaching and Learning Toolkit' provides information about the impact of an intervention upon pupil attainment and the cost per pupil of providing the intervention. This information corresponds to rows 2 and 3 of Barnett's advice (Table 5.2) on how to conduct economic evaluations in education.

The effect sizes used by Higgins *et al.* (2013) are based on meta-analyses which compute weighted averages of effects reported in randomised controlled trials which pass the robustness tests used by the meta-analysts when selecting studies. Random allocation of students between a treatment group and a control group provides confidence that any difference in outcomes between the two groups is a fair indication of the differential effect of the treatment. The effect size is a measure of the scale of the average difference (per student) between the two groups. If there is considerable variation in outcome *within* the groups this will be reflected in a large confidence interval, which may mean that even a substantial difference between the treatment group and the control group may fall short of conventional criteria for judging statistical significance.

Within-group variation can become a severe problem when the effects of studies are combined in a meta-analysis. For example, one highly influential meta-analysis in education was conducted by Hattie and Timperley (2007). They examined the effect of feedback from teachers, parents and others on the educational performance of pupils. They identified several categorical differences between types of feedback, one of which being praise directed at sense of self. They concluded that this type of feedback was ineffective. One of the sources that features prominently in their study was an earlier meta-analysis conducted by Kluger and DeNisi (1996). This earlier meta-analysis included studies undertaken in a wide range of contexts. One of their selected studies of feedback as praise was adults' performance in an 'in-tray task' in a work setting (Earley, 1986). He found that US and UK workers responded differently to criticism they received when undertaking this task. Another was a study of the effect of praise on the performance of a hockey team (Anderson *et al.*, 1988). The study of the effect of praise on a hockey team was conducted twice, in successive seasons, and the researchers interpreted the difference between the two

TABLE 5.2 Steps in economic evaluation

1 Define the perspective of the analysis	Will costs and consequences be measured only for identified individuals or groups, or for society as a whole?
2 Conduct cost analysis	Identify and estimate the value of all resources used, including capital costs, and time contributed by clients and volunteers
3 Estimate programme effects	A strong underlying outcome study of programme impact is required. Impact studies should have a sufficiently large sample size, experimental design, broad perspective on the benefits measured, the ability to measure outcomes over a long period of time, and replication in multiple environments.
4 Estimate the value of outcomes	In cost-benefit analysis, the outcomes must be valued in monetary terms. It is important not only to include the cost savings to governmental programmes, but also to assign whenever possible a monetary value for outcomes such as level of productivity, effects on non-labour income and use of health services.
5 Account for the effects of time	Adjust for inflation and discount future benefits to current value.
6 Aggregate and apply a decision rule	Even when the costs and benefits of different outcomes are estimated for comparison, there is no single simple decision rule that may be applied in all circumstances, and decision-makers may need to consider more than this information in choosing a course of action.
7 Describe distributional consequences	Who gains and who loses under each option?
8 Conduct sensitivity analysis	Identify critical assumptions made in the analysis and explore the effects of reasonable variations in those assumptions.
9 Describe the qualitative residual	Describe the important programme impacts that cannot be monetarily valued or perhaps even quantified.

Source: Barnett, (1993, p. 95) from *The future of children*, a publication of the David and Lucile Packard Foundation from 1991 to 2004.

years in the effect of praise as reflecting the degree of sincerity in the praise offered by the coach of the team. If variation in the sincerity of praise makes a difference to the effectiveness of praise, perhaps the context in which the praise is given also makes a difference. If praise is perceived differently by people in different contexts and if different people respond to praise in different ways then a meta-analysis is not really combining tests of the same phenomenon.[3]

Once an effect of a type of intervention has been established it is then appropriate to ask how much it costs to achieve this effect. Advocates of cost-effectiveness evaluation (e.g. Barnett, 1993; King Rice, 1997; Levin & McEwan, 2001; Hummel-Rossi & Ashdown, 2002) have consistently argued that *all* costs should be included. That is, the cost calculation should be made in terms of opportunity cost: the value of all the resources used in the intervention judged on the basis of the value of the next-best alternative use of those resources. Of course, this approach assumes that all those resources would have been used to the maximum alternative benefit but for this intervention. This assumption is consistent with the standard approach to technical efficiency followed in this chapter, but relaxed in the next. Including all the resource costs of an intervention means that the cost of an intervention will typically be higher than the amount directly paid for the intervention (usually restricted fees for training, equipment and materials to external providers and additional labour costs such as supply teachers). Other costs will include 'activity switching' and additional workload. For example, an intervention may require teachers to switch their use of time for preparation and training away from another activity. An intervention may also increase teachers' workload. Teachers may feel obliged to commit this additional time or they may be sufficiently engaged by the intervention to volunteer time that they would otherwise have used for leisure.

A standard approach to these costs is to use a 'shadow price' (e.g. hourly rate of pay for teachers which captures the value of the resource that is used though not directly paid for; see e.g. Walker & Jan, 2005). Evaluations conducted for the Education Endowment Foundation in England have been gradually, though not always consistently, including an imputation of the cost of teachers' time through activity switching and additional workload.[4] Omission of the cost of activity switching or additional workload biases evaluations in favour of interventions which demand more activity switching and more volunteer time. This bias risks generating unsustainable pressure on schools and teachers. A further problem is that the observed effectiveness of an intervention may be related to the extent to which different schools facilitate switching of teacher effort away from another activity and the degree to which teachers volunteer their time. We may, therefore, expect that there will be a greater variation in the effect of interventions which require more switching or volunteer time, thereby reducing confidence in their effect.

Moreover, the 'cost of effect' analysis exemplified by Higgins *et al.* (2013) is different from 'cost-effectiveness' as defined by Levin (1983) (Table 5.3). Levin defines cost-effectiveness as the least cost method of achieving given educational outputs such as student attainment or retention. 'Cost of effect' analysis uses evidence from pragmatic RCTs. Participants allocated to a control group in these trials undergo 'normal practice'. There are two main problems with this evidence. First, the use of RCTs in medicine has long recognised that the measured difference between the treatment and control groups conflates the actual treatment effect with any 'well-being' effect which results from participating in the treatment arm of an experiment (Wood *et al.*, 2008; Treweek & Zwarenstein, 2009). Placebos are provided to blind participants to which arm of the trial they have been allocated.

The second problem may be even more serious, particularly from a cost-effectiveness perspective. Educational interventions may be divided into three categories for the purpose of cost-effectiveness analysis (Table 5.3). If a school is able to employ an additional teacher or to purchase a new set of computers it is conceivable that the additional resource will be deployed either in exactly the same way as

TABLE 5.3 Three types of educational intervention

	Type of intervention		
	Additional resources	Additional resource + method of deploying that resource	Change in method of deploying a resource
	(1)	(2)	(2)
Payment for additional resource	★	★	
Training costs		★	★
Cost of materials		★	★
Switching costs		★	★
Volunteer costs		★	★
Question answered by 'cost of effect' analysis	How much per pupil does it cost to provide additional resource X?	How much per pupil does it cost to provide additional resource X deployed in method B?	How much per pupil does it cost to deploy resources in method B?
Question answered by cost-effectiveness analysis	If we want to increase pupil attainment by one month's progress, what combination of additional resources will achieve this at the least cost?	If we want to increase pupil attainment by one month's progress, which combination of resources and deployment will achieve this at the least cost?	If we want to increase pupil attainment by one month's progress, which change in deployment will achieve this at the least cost?

the school's existing resources or in a way that was simply not possible before. In this case (Table 5.3, Column [1]), a comparison between outcomes for a school with the additional resource and a school without the additional resource would only be subject to the placebo problem. However, most interventions in education are not like this. They involve some redeployment of resources in which teachers or others are expected to do things differently. If so, a comparison between the treatment and normal practice is not a 0/1 comparison; it is an A/B comparison. This has implications for the calculation of the effect and the calculation of the cost.

At first sight it appears that there is no difficulty with the calculation in column (1). If we know how much it costs to provide a given additional resource X or a given additional resource Y it looks as though we can calculate the combination of additional resources which will achieve a given change in attainment at least cost. Table 5.4 presents some 'cost of effect' calculations using the data presented in the

Education Endowment Foundation Teaching and Learning Toolkit. The calculations are for a one-form entry primary school (200 pupils) with seven year groups. The costs are estimated on the basis of every child in the school benefiting from the additional resources. The toolkit suggests that reducing class size can achieve three months' additional progress in pupils' attainment, while teaching assistants can achieve one month's additional progress. The toolkit implies that it requires class size to be halved to achieve the three-month progress and it implies that teaching assistants achieve their effect when they work with small groups of children. To make a fair comparison we need to know how long a teaching assistant has to work with a small group of children. Row [1] in Table 5.4 shows that the figures suggested in the toolkit imply that on average halving class size costs £385 per month of pupil progress. Row [2] imagines that when one teaching assistant works with a class for a whole year, then the average benefit for children in that class is one month of progress. This might occur if the teaching assistant spreads their input over the whole class (although the EEF toolkit suggests this is unlikely to be effective). If the teaching assistant works exclusively with a small group of pupils, the average progress of one month could reflect a combination of TA-induced progress for the small group and the benefits of additional teacher time for the remainder of the class. Row [3] imagines a teaching assistant working for a whole year exclusively with a group of five students and that the benefits of the teaching assistant are restricted to those students. This arrangement entails the employment of 40 TAs to cover the whole school. Row [4] imagines that TAs are employed to carry out the role reported by Gorard et al. (2014), who evaluated a programme in which TAs provided 1:1 support over a three-month period at an intensity of 20 minutes per day.[5]

Comparisons of different options in terms of 'additional cost per child per month of progress' are necessary to judge cost-effectiveness. This is not straightforward when data are presented in a cost of effect format. When calculations are transformed into a cost-effectiveness format they also encourage the reader to consider whether the relationships are linear or non-linear. Would halving class size again achieve a similar three-month gain in average pupil attainment? The school's initial

TABLE 5.4 Costs per one month of pupil progress comparisons using EEF data

Who?	Annual pay	How many extra required?	Total additional cost	Months of progress	Additional cost per child per month of progress
Halving class size through additional teachers	£33,000	7	£231,000	3	£385
Teaching assistant (A)	£18,000	7	£126,000	1	£630
Teaching assistant (B)	£18,000	40	£720,000	1	£3,600
Teaching assistant (C)	£18,000	8	£144,000	4	£180

endowment of resources may well affect the extent of a change that will ensue from a given additional input of resources. Introductory textbooks in economics (e.g. Baumol & Blinder, 2016) routinely present non-linear effects of additions of a single input as a core assumption, following the principle of diminishing marginal productivity.

If the intervention involves some redeployment of resources (Table 5.3, columns [2] or [3]), the difference between cost of effect and cost-effectiveness analysis becomes more pronounced when evidence is gathered from pragmatic RCTs which compare an intervention with 'normal practice'.[6] A first problem concerns interpreting the effect size of the trial. It is very hard to be sure that 'normal practice' includes no element which is included in the intervention. For example, suppose an intervention requires teachers to adopt a particular approach to providing feedback. Normal practice will include some kind of feedback from teachers to pupils, so a pragmatic trial is really testing the difference between one approach to feedback and another approach to feedback, regardless of whether the school is participating in any other development programme. Since normal practice typically involves praising pupils for good work, any intervention which involves praising pupils would struggle to be sufficiently different from normal practice to show any substantial effect size. Moreover, since education has multiple outcomes (Chapters 2 and 3) it is possible that redeploying teaching time achieves a gain in one outcome at the expense of a loss in another.

Pragmatic RCTs also create problems for cost estimation. For example, it is unlikely that normal practice has developed without requiring the teacher to devote any time to its development: in preparing lessons and discussions with colleagues if not through formal training. Of course, for the teacher in question, these are 'sunk' costs, but a fair comparison of the cost-effectiveness of an approach should weigh the costs of implementing that approach with the costs of whatever it will replace. The difficulties in securing a reasonable estimate of the costs of developing normal practice mean that while we may know that ignoring these costs will cause upward bias in an estimate of the costs of an intervention, it will be very difficult to judge the scale of that bias. Nonetheless, bias from the omission of the costs of developing normal practice may just be counterbalanced by bias from omission of costs arising from activity switching and volunteer time.

The difficulties in making judgements about cost-effectiveness may partially account for its frequent absence in education evaluations. However, measurement of educational progress involves many other challenges which have received much more attention. Insufficient attention to cost-effectiveness runs the risk of introducing systematic bias in the development of a knowledge base about the implications of adopting different approaches to teaching and learning.

Production

The main body of this chapter focuses attention on two key questions: (1) What is the ideal size for an educational organisation?; (2) What is the ideal mix of inputs in the education process? The problems are framed in terms of 'input–process–output' and much of the literature treats the process as a 'black box' such that the evidence is in the form of associations between outputs and inputs. This task would be much easier if all children were the same but of course they are not. They bring very different attributes to the starting line of their formal education. Controlling for this variation is a key concern of empirical studies in this field.

This section focuses on schools while making passing references to higher education. The principles are largely the same for universities, but the role of universities in research and knowledge transfer introduces some different issues which are not addressed. Issues are illustrated through data on state school income and spending in 2014/2015 in England matched with other school-level data available from the Department for Education. Details are provided in Appendix 5.1 at the end of this chapter.

Cost and scale of the organisation

Costs and productivity must be analysed in terms of a 'production unit', which could be a single institution such as a school or a university, a collection of institutions such as a school district or a chain of academy schools, or a type of school (e.g. all state primary schools) within a country. State schools have traditionally been subject local governance. In 2011/2012 there were 98,328 state schools in the USA organised into approximately 13,500 school districts.[7] Local governance in the UK has organised schools into somewhat larger units managed by local government (local authorities). State schools in Scotland are governed through 32 local authorities. However, the role of local authorities in funding education has steadily declined in England (Belfield & Sibieta, 2016). By 2010/2011 only 10 per cent of per-pupil funding was controlled by local authorities and even this was constrained by central government direction. When per-pupil spending depends on local tax income social inequality is compounded, as much less is spent on the education of disadvantaged pupils. This has long been an issue in the USA where dependence of district spending on local taxation has been greater than in England (Condron & Roscigno, 2003). A new form of collective organisation for state schools has emerged recently. 'Academy chains' are groups of schools (known as academies) which are funded directly from central government, independent of local authorities while sharing a common governance structure. This section begins by examining the costs of individual schools before turning to the implications of organising in schools in districts or chains.

The relationship between school costs and pupil enrolment depends on short-term capacity utilisation and long-term economies of scale (Riew, 1986). In the short term, the school's physical estate, including the number and size of classrooms, sets a limit on the number of pupils who can be enrolled. Local authorities in England have a responsibility to assess the physical capacity of each state-funded school on the basis of the number and size of the teaching spaces within that school.[8] Schools which are well under capacity still have to pay for the upkeep of the whole building and may be overstaffed for the number of pupils as they try to retain their capacity to recruit more students the following year. To some extent this may be illustrated through data on schools' spending. The caveat is that since state schools are not-for-profits they have limited incentive not to spend grant money they receive. Keeping this caution in mind, Table 5.5 presents descriptive data on the spending and characteristics of state schools in England. On average, state secondary schools were operating at 83 per cent of capacity and there was substantial variation in capacity utilisation among schools.

Table 5.6 presents results of a multivariate regression which examines the association between spending per pupil and capacity utilisation while controlling for a range of factors that affect the grants received by schools. The higher per-pupil spending on schools with high proportions of disadvantaged pupils reflects the funding formula used by central government in England.

TABLE 5.5 Descriptive statistics for spending per pupil and school characteristics (state schools in England, 2014–2015)

	Primary schools			Secondary schools		
	n	Mean	Std. Dev	n	Mean	Std. Dev
Spending per pupil	16,296	4,967	1,182	3,317	6,239	2,833
Pupils on roll	16,406	262	147	3,317	950	412
% of capacity filled	16,378	94	16	3,288	83	19
% pupils statement or EHC	10,802	1.9	2	3,054	2	1.5
% pupils with SEN statement	16,158	13	7	3,242	13	8
% pupils with SEN supported	16,405	15	12	3,313	15	11
% eligible for free school meals	16,347	15	21	3,265	15	20
% with English as a second language	16,315	0.60	1.7	3,248	0.6	1.3

TABLE 5.6 Factors related to spending per pupil (state schools in England, 2014–2015)

	Primary schools		Secondary schools	
	B	p	B	p
Constant	6,047	<0.001	8,391	<0.001
% pupils with SEN statement	89	<0.001	241	0.466
% pupils with SEN supported	18	<0.001	30	<0.001
% eligible for free school meals	25	<0.001	33	<0.001
% with English as a second language	2	<0.001	−0.7	0.815
% Black[9]	35	<0.001	96	0.024
Academy school (=1)	−197	<0.001	108	0.253
London school (=1)	841	<0.001	1,384	<0.001
% of capacity filled	−21	<0.001	−40	<0.001
R^2		0.33		0.19
n		10,621		2,986

Combining the data in Tables 5.5 and 5.6 shows that primary schools with capacity utilisation one standard deviation below the average spent 6 per cent more per pupil and secondary schools with capacity utilisation one standard deviation below the average spent 12 per cent more per pupil. Thus capacity utilisation appears to matter for the cost of state education. Competitive school markets require potential for schools to grow and to shrink, and this implies substantial variation in short-term capacity utilisation. The costs of change are not always factored into policy decisions, even when they are not hard to measure.

The analysis of capacity utilisation in Tables 5.5 and 5.6 treats the outcome of education simply as the number of pupils educated. Most studies of the optimum size of schools have focused on the relationship between school size and pupils' achievement. These studies aim to reveal the ideal size for schools in the long term when all inputs may be varied (the capacity of a school may be changed). However, they have usually not had access to data on school capacity, so the effects of short-term fluctuations are embedded in the data they use.

There are several reasons why we might expect pupil achievement to rise (and the cost of securing a particular level of pupil achievement to fall) when the size of a school increases in the long run. As the number of pupils increases the school is more able to organise teaching to reduce the diversity of needs in each classroom. Primary schools can teach children aged 5 to 6 in a different class from children aged 7 to 8. Secondary schools can organise some classes so that the pupils in each class are broadly ready to make similar progress. There are some powerful arguments for mixing children by age and ability, but teaching is easier when the diversity of demand is lower. Second, larger schools have more scope for making good use of specialist inputs (teachers or equipment). For example, larger secondary schools will be more able to employ science teachers with expertise in different scientific disciplines and language teachers who are specialists in a particular language (Kuziemko, 2006). They will also, therefore, be able to offer a broader curriculum for pupils to study. Third, larger schools offer more opportunities for promotion to posts with greater responsibility. This helps a school attract and retain good teachers.

Conversely, there are reasons to believe that smaller schools have advantages over large schools. A smaller school is able to offer a more secure environment because teachers and school leaders are more able to gather and share knowledge about their pupils (Lee & Smith, 1997). Pupils who feel they are known are more likely to feel they belong, and it is easier for teachers to take collective action in a small school (Leithwood & Jantzi, 2009). Behaviour problems should be reduced and pupils' motivation increased. Therefore, there are some a priori grounds for expecting that while costs per level of pupil attainment will fall up to a point, there is an optimum size beyond which costs per pupil attainment will start to rise. These arguments also imply that small schools and large schools are likely to offer a different mix of educational outcomes. Large schools are likely to be better at providing curriculum breadth and opportunities for specialisation, with the attendant risk of compounding stratification and social inequality. Small schools are likely to be better at providing a safe environment which helps children's sense of well-being.

We now turn to attempts to estimate ideal school size in the long run on the basis of data on school inputs and outputs. These studies may be divided into two categories: (1) those which focus on productivity (how school size is related to the quality of school outcomes), and (2) those which focus on cost (how the cost of a given outcome varies with size of school). Productivity studies face three main challenges.

The first of these challenges is how to define the outcomes of schooling. Most studies have focused on academic attainment. Data are more easily available on this outcome which is also given policy salience in an era of 'high-stakes' testing. Some studies have used achievement levels at the end of schooling (e.g. Bradley & Taylor, 1998), while others (e.g. Lee & Smith, 1997; Foreman-Peck & Foreman-Peck, 2006[10]) have also controlled for prior achievement. Controlling for prior attainment offers the prospect of a 'value-added' measure which shows the difference the school has made. However, grading systems are typically constructed in a way such that there is a strong correlation between prior attainment and progress, so the difference between these two approaches to measuring attainment is not always as great as may be expected. One further problem is which subjects to include in the outcome measure. Measures of academic attainment that are restricted to a few core subjects benefit small schools which offer a smaller range of subjects. When pupils are able to specialise within a wide course choice they do tend to choose the subjects in which they have a relative advantage (Davies et al., 2009a), and this is an advantage of large secondary schools. A review of research (Leithwood & Jantzi, 2009) did identify some studies (e.g. Friedkin & Necochea, 1988) of the relationship between school size and inequality. The consistent message is that students from disadvantaged backgrounds benefit from attending smaller schools and this appears to be associated with higher levels of pupil engagement in smaller schools. The expectation that smaller schools will reduce alienation from the education system is upheld by Bloom and Unterman's (2014) evidence that US pupils attending smaller schools were more likely to graduate to a four-year college. However, Leithwood and Jantzi's review does not cite any studies of the relationship between school size and either character or citizenship.

A second challenge is distinguishing between pupil-level and school-level effects. This problem may be addressed (as in Lee & Smith, 1997) by using a hierarchical linear model. Bradley and Taylor (1998), who only have school-level data, attempt to circumvent the problem by grouping their dependent variable (the percentage of 16-year-old pupils in England achieving five grades A*–C in GCSE examinations) into quartiles and using an ordered logit model.

The third problem is the most serious. While school size may affect school outcomes, school outcomes may also affect school size. This endogeneity arises because schools in which pupils achieve relatively high grades are likely to attract parents, increasing the size of the school. Foreman-Peck & Foreman-Peck (2006) try to address this endogeneity problem by lagging their school size variables (number of pupils) by one year so that it becomes 'predetermined'. However, 16-year-old pupils taking public examinations (as in Wales where Foreman-Peck and Foreman-Peck conducted their study) have attended the school for five years, so we should expect school size throughout this period to affect outcomes. More seriously, there is a high correlation between enrolment at each school in one year and enrolment in that school the following year. In the data for English schools used in this chapter the correlation between enrolment in 2013/2014 and enrolment in 2014/2015 was 0.99 for secondary schools. Kuziemko (2006) attempted to address endogeneity by focusing on shocks to school enrolment such as school mergers. He recognised that a negative association between school size and pupil achievement associated with mergers may be due to the disruption for pupils and teachers created by a merger. He claimed that the negative association with school size is not entirely a product of the disruption because his data show that the negative effect is strengthened after two years into the merger. This explanation is problematic because in the first year after the merger the majority of the school effect on the students taking public examinations will have occurred prior to the merger. Disruptive effects of a merger would take two years to become evident in achievement measures. Bloom and Unterman (2014) adopted a more compelling strategy. They compared outcomes for students who were successful or unsuccessful in gaining entry to small schools through lotteries in the USA. They found no effect of school size on achievement.

The diverse results from studies searching for an ideal school size (see Newman et al., 2006) may then be a consequence of difficulties in separating long-term relationships between school size and school outputs from short- to medium-term dynamic changes in school size reflecting school popularity and/or local bureaucratic decisions on school places. This conjecture is consistent with a study by Schwartz et al. (2013), who found that while old small schools had relatively low levels of pupil achievement, new small schools had high levels of achievement.

The measurement problems may be illustrated through analysis of school-level data for English secondary schools in 2014/2015. This analysis follows the modelling strategy of Bradley & Taylor's (1998) study of the size of English secondary schools. They used the proportion of 16-year-old pupils achieving five or more GCSE grades at A*–C. They converted these data into a categorical variable which separated schools into four quartiles and used an ordered logit model to examine the relationship between school size and pupil achievement. Models (1) in each of Tables 5.7 and 5.8 broadly replicate the specification used by Bradley and Taylor (1998). The results in Tables 5.7 and 5.8 are somewhat similar to Bradley and Taylor's, although the coefficients are smaller and the coefficient in the analysis of 11 to 16 schools on the squared school size is not significant.[11] Models (2) in Tables 5.7 and 5.8 include an extra variable for the percentage of school capacity utilised. This variable may be interpreted as an indicator of school popularity. Popular schools will be under pressure to expand beyond their notional capacity while unpopular schools will struggle to fill their capacity. Therefore, this variable captures the relationship between pupil achievement and school size. We can see

TABLE 5.7 Pupil achievement as a function of school size and other characteristics: English secondary schools for 11- to 16-year-olds

Control for prior attainment?	No				Yes			
Control for capacity utilisation?	No		Yes		No		Yes	
Model	(1)		(2)		(3)		(4)	
	B	p	B	p	B	p	B	p
Lowest quartile GCSE	-7.23	<0.001	-6.20	0.001	31.03	<0.001	31.82	<0.001
Second quartile GCSE	-2.77	0.12	-1.67	0.36	36.08	<0.001	36.95	<0.001
Third quartile GCSE	-0.36	0.84	0.80	0.66	38.93	<0.001	39.85	<0.001
Key Stage 2 average point score					1.43	<0.001	1.42	<0.001
% eligible FSM	-0.15	<0.001	-0.14	<0.001	-0.09	<0.001	-0.08	<0.001
% White British	-0.04	0.001	-0.03	0.003	-0.03	0.01	-0.024	0.03
% English second language	-0.03	0.02	-0.03	0.03	-0.01	0.42	-0.010	0.48
% SEN statement EHC	-0.05	0.33	-0.08	0.17	0.05	0.41	0.025	0.67
% SEN supported	-0.05	<0.001	-0.05	<0.001	-0.02	0.08	-0.023	0.07
Pupil–teacher ratio	0.01	0.87	0.01	0.76	0.01	0.75	0.023	0.62
% teachers without QTS	0.02	0.14	0.014	0.26	-0.002	0.86	-0.006	0.67
% teachers part-time	0.008	0.43	0.01	0.54	0.01	0.38	0.007	0.51

	Model 1		Model 2		Model 3		Model 4	
Total non-teaching staff	-0.07	<0.001	-0.05	0.001	-0.04	0.03	-0.027	0.12
Pupils at school/100	0.41	0.004	0.10	0.54	0.27	0.07	-0.028	0.87
Pupils at school^2/100	-0.00008	0.28	-0.00004	0.63	-0.00007	0.37	-0.00004	0.61
Pupils relative to capacity			0.030	<0.001			0.03	<0.001
Academy school	0.34	0.03	0.24	0.13	0.56	.0001	0.46	0.007
Faith school	0.81	<0.001	0.59	0.009	0.46	.05	0.25	0.29
Girls-only school	2.35	<0.001	2.17	<0.001	1.89	<0.001	1.76	<0.001
Boys-only school	0.13	0.82	0.04	0.95	-0.46	0.47	-0.57	0.38
Selective school								
Secondary modern	-1.12	0.02	-1.09	0.022	-0.51	0.28	-0.47	0.33
n	740		736		740		736	
Pseudo R^2	0.49		0.51		0.60		0.61	
Log-likelihood	1,308		1,281		1,161		1,140	

Note

Pupil achievement measured as % of pupils aged 16 achieving five or more GCSE grades, including maths and English at grades A★–C).

TABLE 5.8 Pupil achievement at age 16 as a function of school size and other characteristics: English secondary schools for 11- to 18-year-olds

Control for prior attainment?	No		Yes			
Control for capacity utilisation?	No		Yes		No		Yes	
Model	(1)		(2)		(3)		(4)	
	B	p	B	p	B	p	B	p
Lowest quartile GCSE	-4.64	<0.001	-3.192	0.014	37.051	<0.001	36.268	<0.001
Second quartile GCSE	-1.05	0.405	0.476	0.712	41.339	<0.001	40.595	<0.001
Third quartile GCSE	1.29	0.307	2.913	0.024	44.265	<0.001	43.579	<0.001
Key Stage 2 average point score					1.616	<0.001	1.561	<0.001
% eligible FSM	-0.12	<0.001	-0.116	<0.001	-0.060	<0.001	-0.061	<0.001
% White British	-0.03	<0.001	-0.022	<0.001	-0.004	0.466	-0.003	0672
% English second language	-0.02	0.018	-0.015	0.058	0.020	0.019	0.019	0.021
% SEN statement EHC	-0.01	0.733	-0.040	0.346	0.079	0.084	0.058	0.207
% SEN supported	-0.02	0.010	-0.021	0.011	-0.002	0.839	-0.002	0.817
Pupil–teacher ratio	-0.11	.001	-0.130	<0.001	-0.066	0.070	-0.079	0.034
% teachers without QTS	0.03	0.001	0.031	0.002	-0.015	0.148	-0.015	0.164
% teachers part-time	0.02	0.014	0.015	0.023	0.003	0.714	0.002	0.822

Total non-teaching staff	-0.04	0.000	-0.028	0.001	-0.026	0.003	-0.017	0.058
Pupils at school/100	0.35	0.000	0.006	0.949	0.157	0.059	-0.052	0.581
Pupils at school^2/100	-0.00006	0.056	-0.00003	0.321	-0.00002	0.500	-0.00003	0.327
Pupils relative to capacity			0.044	0.000			0.026	<0.001
Academy school	0.31	0.006	0.246	0.031	0.391	0.001	0.355	0.003
Faith school	0.63	<0.001	0.434	0.002	0.301	0.041	0.191	0.201
Girls-only school	1.47	<0.001	1.291	<0.001	0.867	0.001	0.783	0.003
Boys-only school	0.72	0.008	.612	0.026	-0.105	0.717	-0.196	0.502
Selective school	3.87	<0.001	3.582	<.001	-0.829	0.439	-0.886	0.407
Secondary modern	-1.30	<0.001	-1.436	<0.001	-0.432	0.117	-0.552	0.046
n	1,525		1,519		1,525		1,519	
Pseudo R^2	0.51		0.53		0.65		0.66	
Log-likelihood	2,754		2,671		2,323		2,288	

Note
Pupil achievement measured as % of pupils aged 16 achieving five or more GCSE grades, including maths and English at grades A★–C).

that when this variable is introduced the coefficients on the school size variable are reduced and they lose their statistical significance. The impact of the percentage utilisation of capacity variable is more dramatic than the impact of controlling for prior attainment. Models (3) and (4) also control for pupils' attainment at the point of starting secondary schooling (Key Stage 2 average point score). This reduces the coefficient on the school size variable (comparing equations [1] and [3]), but makes no difference to the interpretation of school size once we take account of capacity use. Adjusting for prior attainment does strengthen the coefficient on the 'academy school' variable while slightly reducing the strength of the 'girls-only' variable.

Overall, the results in Tables 5.7 and 5.8 are consistent with the results of Bloom and Unterman's (2014) study and the conclusions of reviews by Newman *et al.* (2006) and Luyten (2014) that school size is not likely to have a strong effect on academic outcomes. A further test restricting the sample to schools in the top quartile for percentage of pupils eligible for free school meals also found no association between school size and academic outcomes for pupils at school level. Those studies that have suggested substantive school size effects have not managed to find a convincing way of dealing with the endogeneity problem.

The optimal cost-effective size of a school has been estimated using the notion of 'economies of scale', defined by Bowles and Bosworth (2002, p. 290) as "the effect of changes in the scale of production on per-unit costs, holding all other factors constant". They estimated the relationship between school size and cost per pupil in 17 districts in Wyoming using a model presented in Equation 5.1.

$$\ln(\text{Cost}_i) = \alpha_o + \alpha_1\text{Scores}_i + \alpha_2\text{Salary}_i + \alpha_3\text{Income}_i + \alpha_4\ln(\text{Size}_i) + \alpha_5\text{Schooltype}_i + \varepsilon_i \qquad \text{[Equation 5.1]}$$

Cost per pupil and school size are transformed into natural log variables (ln) to take account of possible non-linearity. This also provides a convenient way of interpreting the results, since if α_4 equals 0.2 (as in Bowles & Bosworth's study) it means that a 1 per cent change in school size is associated with a 0.2 per cent change in cost per pupil. Scores_i is a school-level measure of pupil achievement so that the relationship between school size and cost is calculated for a given level of pupil achievement. Average teacher salaries are included in the equation to take account of possible variation in input prices. The income variable refers to average income in the school district, since this affects the amount of money made available to state schools through the collection of local taxes. Since income of state schools in England is largely determined by a national funding formula for the distribution of government grants, the appropriate variables to include for English data are the school characteristics which determine the distribution of funds. Finally, schooltype is a vector of dummy variables capturing types of school which may have different costs per pupil. Results from using this model with data for English secondary schools in 2014/2015 are presented in Table 5.9. Four variables regarding pupil intake (FSM, English as a second language and two for SEN) are included to reflect

TABLE 5.9 The relationship between (log of) cost per pupil and school size

	Age 11–16 schools				Age 11–18 schools			
	B	p	B	p	B	p	B	p
(Constant)	9.578	<0.001	9.340	<0.001	9.296	<0.001	9.006	<0.001
Best 8 value-added/100	−0.047	0.008	−0.032	0.075	−0.026	0.077	−0.006	0.681
Average teacher salary/1,000	0.006	0.001	0.006	<0.001	0.008	<0.001	0.007	<0.001
% eligible FSM	0.007	<0.001	0.006	<0.001	0.006	<0.001	0.006	<0.001
% English second language	0.001	0.004	0.001	<0.001	0.001	<0.001	0.001	<0.001
% SEN statement EHC	0.014	<0.001	0.015	<0.001	0.011	<0.001	0.011	<0.001
% SEN supported	0.001	0.056	0.001	0.049	0.001	0.137	0.001	0.072
London school	0.152	<0.001	0.152	<0.001	0.074	<0.001	0.076	<0.001
Academy school	−0.018	0.018	−0.016	0.034	0.018	0.004	0.016	0.007
Faith school	−0.044	<0.001	−0.031	0.004	0.002	0.837	0.008	0.285
Log of pupils on roll	−0.128	<0.001	−0.093	<0.001	−0.124	<0.001	−0.097	<0.001
% of school capacity used			−0.001	<0.001			−0.001	0.002
n	856		850		1,608		1,603	
R^2	0.59		0.60		0.53		0.55	

the funding formula. London schools also received additional funding and two further variables are included to capture differences in school type.[12]

Table 5.9 shows that costs per pupil in English secondary schools changed by about 1 per cent for each 10 per cent change in the number of pupils enrolled. When capacity utilisation is also included in the model there is a slight fall in the coefficient on school size, but it still rounds to 1 per cent and remains strongly significant.

Tables 5.7, 5.8 and 5.9 indicate that while increasing school size was not associated with academic outcomes for pupils it was associated with a fall in costs per pupil. One possible explanation for this would be that the smaller schools have to carry a proportionately heavier load in non-teaching expenses. We created a variable for the proportion of school-level spending on premises, back office and other staff. There was an approximate −0.2 correlation between this percentage and school size for each of 11 to 16 and 11 to 18 schools.

Size of operating unit for schools: from self-management to chains

Schools may operate as single, autonomous, 'stand-alone' units or they may belong to a group of schools which is managed as a unit by a school district, local authority, a not-for profit organisation or a for-profit business. The arguments in favour of local school autonomy have been marshalled variously in the names of 'the self-managing school' (Caldwell, 2005, 2008), 'site-based management' (Odden & Busch, 1998) or 'school autonomy' (Clark, 2009; Hanushek *et al.*, 2013). These arguments have been very influential in the policies of some governments (e.g. in England), while being resisted elsewhere (e.g. in Scotland).

Some commentators have argued that single autonomous schools will be more efficient in their use of resources because they will be able to exploit local knowledge of input prices and the forms of teaching and organisation that will work best with the kinds of students they enrol (Wohlstetter & Chau, 2004). References to 'self-managing schools' and 'site-based management' typically emphasise this argument which claims that giving control to school managers will reduce costs and add value. An alternative argument is more associated with the term 'school autonomy'. This argument claims that giving control to the market will create incentives which will constrain school managers in a way that forces cost reduction and adding value. According to this reasoning, individual schools will have insufficient power to resist market incentives created by parental choice. Advocates of 'school *self-management*' may oppose policies that increase parental choice (Caldwell, 2008). Advocates of school *autonomy* assert that parental choice is essential to create the conditions in which school self-management will improve efficiency and welfare.

Advocacy, critique and discussion of school self-management (e.g. Smyth, 1993; Caldwell, 2008; Hopkins *et al.*, 2014) has made little mention of economies of scale which might favour larger operating units. When schools are grouped in larger units they may share costs of administration, leadership and specialist professional services (such as educational psychologists, education welfare and professional training). A small organisation may, of course, 'contract out' some of these services and buy from specialist providers. However, the price at which they buy will generally have to cover the transaction costs for the provider that has to market its services and charge a fee which covers the uncertainty in securing business.[13] One transactions cost problem is the difficulty of preparing contracts that are sufficiently detailed to cover the contingencies which the purchaser wishes to be covered. A government which contracts a self-managing school to educate a representative range of children may pay a premium rate for children enrolled who have special educational needs and children who are disadvantaged by socio-economic background. But it is very difficult for a government to monitor exactly how the money is spent or to specify a sufficiently detailed set of required outcomes that cover the range of children educated in an inclusive school.

Researchers have found little evidence of an effect of local school management on outcomes for pupils (Leithwood & Menzies, 1998; Maslowski et al, 2007). This may be due to the difficulty of distinguishing between causal mechanisms, since there has been no random assignment of autonomy to schools. Despite their optimism about the effects of autonomy on school performance, Machin and Vernoit (2011) noted that a substantial proportion of improved performance in academy schools was attributable to a change in their intake: more pupils with high prior attainment at point of enrolment, at the expense of other local schools. They also noted that the performance effects seemed to be concentrated in early switchers to academy status which might indicate a selection bias problem. Clark (2007) claimed to overcome this through a regression discontinuity design which compared schools that either just succeeded or just failed to secure autonomy through a ballot of parents in England. However, subsequent analysis (Allen, 2013) suggests that Clark's result was an artefact of the measures used. There is also, as yet, insufficient evidence to judge the effect of 'school-based management' on costs per pupil. There are plenty of claims (e.g. Leithwood & Menzies, 1998, p. 236) in the literature about the effect of school-based management on per-pupil costs, but there is insufficient evidence to judge.

A simple descriptive comparison of spending by local authority-controlled and academy secondary schools in England is presented in Table 5.10. The percentage point difference is barely affected if we control for a wide range of school characteristics.[14] A comparison of the proportion spent on different inputs provides some indication of ways in which schools have used increased freedoms over their budgets.

TABLE 5.10 Proportion of spending on educational support, back office and professional services: local authority and academy schools in England (2014–2015)

% of total spending on	Local authority controlled schools	Academy schools
Back office (%)	7.8	12.9
Professional services (%)	4.4	1.8
Educational support (%)	10.5	6.5

Since increasing local school autonomy involves a shift of responsibility for 'back office' services from a central authority to a local school, the difference in percentage spent on back office is unsurprising, though we cannot tell from these data whether this increases or decreases total spending on back office (since the central spending does not appear in the table). The table does suggest, however, that schools with more autonomy choose to spend less on professional services (which would include educational psychology and speech and language therapy). They also choose to spend considerably less on educational support. This could mean that they took more notice than local authority schools of evidence questioning the impact of teaching assistants upon children's achievement.[15] It could mean that they were more reluctant to devote resources to children with special educational needs whose achievements would have little impact upon key market indicators.

One of the interesting features of school systems that have encouraged schools to break free of local government control is the development of school 'chains'. Between 2000 and 2008 approximately one-third of primary school children enrolled in private (voucher) schools in Chile attended a franchise school belonging to a chain (Elacqua et al., 2011). By 2008, the for-profit organisation Edison Schools was running more than 250 schools (Marsh et al., 2008a). By 2014/2015 62 per cent of English secondary schools were 'academies' and, of these, 41 per cent belonged to an 'academy chain' in which the leadership and administration was at least partially shared in common across the schools.[16]

Should the spread of school chains be interpreted as an indication of the natural capacity of 'free systems' for developing organisational forms which increase efficiency? There is no easy answer to this question. It depends, in part, on the form that these chains take. If they are loosely coupled networks (loose-knit communities in Bauman's[17] terms), then individual schools may retain substantial autonomy. But if they are offering a common brand (tight-knit communities in Bauman's terms), then individual schools may have even less freedom in their resource decisions than local authority-controlled schools. From the perspective of the 'local school management' argument this appears to be a backward step. From the perspective of the 'autonomy' argument it may not be a problem. This argument was based in Public Choice Theory (Buchanan & Tullock, 1962), which regarded local (state) authorities as slow, self-serving bureaucracies beyond the reach of market incentives which would instil efficiency. As long as school chains remain subject to market pressure, the school autonomy argument prefers these schools to those under local authority control. Even when a school chain seems to be controlling a large proportion of a local market this may not be a problem for the school autonomy argument. The necessary market incentives depend on the possibility of competition, not simply on the existence of competition. As long as a market is 'contestable' a school chain has reason to fear that if it slips into inefficiency it will lose its market share (Baumol et al., 1982). However, school chains which combine secondary schools with their 'feeder' primary schools (vertical integration) and schools which are able to shield themselves from competition through their chain's local market share look like backward steps from a school autonomy perspective.

Even so, threats to efficiency from school chains' market power may be more than offset by economies of scale. There is, after all, a substantial body of evidence suggesting that there are significant economies of scale when local authority schools are organised in larger groupings. Comparison of the total spending of local authorities in England (which vary greatly in size) has suggested substantive economies of scale for larger authorities (Andrews & Byrne, 2009). Several studies have investigated the relationship between the size of US school districts (in terms of number of pupils or schools) and costs per pupil. These studies (e.g. Duncombe et al., 1995; Chakraborty et al., 2000; Duncombe & Yinger, 2007) consistently report economies of scale. Studies (such as Chakraborty et al., 2000) which examine school and district costs find economies of scale at both levels.

Data on school spending in England enable a comparison between schools which are single academies and those which belong to multi-academy chains. On average, single academy schools spent £174 more per pupil than multi-academy schools. After controlling for other school characteristics,[18] this difference increased to £750 per child. It is tempting to infer that this difference was due to lower 'back office' costs in multi-academy schools which were able to share these costs across schools, reaping economies of scale. Indeed, a review of the early development of academy chains in England (Hill et al., 2012, p. 10) asserted that the growth of chains was driven in part by a search for "a cost-effective operating model with enough academies contributing to the funding of the central support functions of the chain". The same study concluded that academy chains did benefit from economies of scale. However, in 2014/2015 multi-academy schools actually spent a significantly[19] higher proportion (13.3 per cent compared to 12.7 per cent) on back office costs. This may reflect the costs of collaborative working. The big difference in spending lay in educational support. Whereas single academy schools reported spending 9 per cent on educational support, multi-academy schools spent only 3 per cent. This difference was not simply attributable to differences in intake. After controlling for school and pupil characteristics single-academy schools spent £477 more per child on educational support than did multi-academy schools.

One possible interpretation of these data is not very encouraging. The shift in control of resource decisions from local authorities to 'self-managing' or single autonomous schools involved some loss of economies of scale and was accompanied by a reduction in spending on educational support. The latter may reflect better decision making with local knowledge and the incentives that resource control entails. It may also reflect a weakening of concern for outcomes (e.g. in relation to inclusion) which are not rewarded by headline indicators in local markets. A shift back towards groups of schools, this time organised into not-for-profit or for-profit chains, may yield some benefits from economies of scale. However, the headline spending figures also suggest that chains may not yet be large enough to secure these economies of scale while incurring additional back office costs in 'chain management'. Perhaps, more worryingly, schools in chains spend even less than single academies on educational support. Does this mean even greater efficiency or greater neglect of the social good beyond the immediate interest of the school as an organisation? We need stronger research evidence to begin to answer these questions.

Summary

Once appropriate account is taken of endogeneity (the effect of school grades on school popularity) there is, so far, insufficient evidence of a substantive association between school size and academic outcomes for pupils. There is, however, evidence of greater pupil engagement in smaller schools and this may mean that smaller schools are more pleasant working environments for pupils and teachers. Some studies have reported higher attainment for disadvantaged pupils who attend small schools, although it was not possible to detect evidence of this effect in the school-level data analysed in this chapter.

However, there is evidence of economies of scale in larger state schools. The data on English schools reviewed in this chapter suggested that a 10 per cent increase in school size is associated with a 1 per cent fall in cost per pupil. It appears that smaller schools have to carry proportionately greater non-teaching costs. Therefore, public funders of schools face an incentive to provide larger rather than smaller schools in addition to an incentive to allocate pupils so that schools are close to capacity. These incentives conflict with policies that offer parents freedom to choose between schools. Parental choice encourages variation between schools in the extent to which capacity is utilised. In the data on English secondary schools analysed in this chapter, 84 per cent were below capacity. Moreover, the average capacity utilisation of schools with below 100 per cent capacity utilisation was 80 per cent, while the average capacity utilisation of schools reporting above 100 per cent capacity utilisation was 104 per cent.

The average size of private schools in England is much smaller than the average size of state schools.[20] In 2014/2015 the average size of state schools with pupils aged 11 and pupils aged 16 was 962, while the equivalent figure for private schools was just 331.[21] At first sight this looks curious, given the evidence about cost-effectiveness and size of school. If economies of scale operated in the private sector in a similar way to the state sector we might expect market-constrained private schools to be more cost-efficient and therefore larger than state schools. Moreover, since the proportion of disadvantaged pupils is much higher in state schools than in private schools, any benefits of small schools for these pupils should lead to state schools being smaller than private schools. A plausible answer is that parents who pay to send their children to private schools place a high value on small schools and small classes. This is consistent with the evidence that pupils are more engaged and less alienated in small schools. If parents are prepared to pay for these benefits it makes sense for private schools to keep their size below the level that would minimise costs per pupil. Nonetheless, the difference in average size of school is very striking.

Cost and the combination of inputs

How do schools spend the money they receive from government or secure through their own efforts? Table 5.11 shows that just under half of the total spending of state-funded schools in England is devoted to employing teachers. The size of the standard deviations relative to the means in most rows indicates that the variation in distribution among schools is relatively large. However, Table 5.11 needs to be read with caution, as academies, schools in London and primary schools are different from other schools in ways that may affect the distribution of their funding. Academy schools are more likely to be secondary schools (and therefore they are larger) and they have a smaller percentage of children awarded statements of special educational needs. The proportion of Black children in London schools is nearly eight times the proportion in non-London schools. The proportion of children with English as a second language (44%) is four times the proportion in non-London schools. Compared to the average secondary school, the average primary school has one-third of the number of pupils on roll.

Therefore it is useful to see how the distribution of spending varies once background characteristics of pupils are taken into account. This is shown in Tables 5.12 and 5.13.

Schools with higher proportions of children eligible for free school meals, Black children, children with English as a second language and children with a statement of special educational needs spend slightly proportionately less on teachers and more on educational support (e.g. teaching assistants). London schools spend more on teachers and supply teachers and less on educational support. Academy schools spend much less on educational support learning resources and more on back office and capital financing. Primary schools spend proportionately less on teachers and back office and more on educational support and other staff. Some of these differences may be interpreted as consequences of the circumstances that schools face:

TABLE 5.11 How state-funded schools in England allocated their spending in 2014/2015

	All schools		Academies		London		Primaries	
	%	s.d.	%	s.d.	%	s.d.	%	s.d.
Teaching staff	45.8	(7.3)	48.5	(10.1)	44.4	(8.1)	45.1	(6.0)
Supply teaching	3.5	(2.7)	3.1	(3.7)	4.4	(3.7)	3.6	(2.5)
Educational support	15.1	(7.0)	7.5	(6.7)	15.4	(7.0)	15.5	(5.6)
Premises	9.4	(3.5)	10.7	(5.8)	9.4	(3.8)	9.6	(3.1)
Back office	7.3	(3.9)	12.6	(4.9)	7.4	(4.1)	6.6	(3.2)
Other staff	7.7	(3.2)	6.3	(4.2)	7.4	(3.2)	8.4	(2.6)
Learning resources	10.8	(4.6)	8.8	(5.7)	11.2	(5.1)	10.9	(4.2)
Capital financing	0.5	(2.2)	2.5	(4.5)	0.4	(1.9)	0.3	(1.7)
n	19,861		3,770		2,311		15,705	

Source: Department for Education school-level data for 2014/2015.

TABLE 5.12 Associations between school characteristics and distribution of spending (1)

	Teachers		Supply		Support		Back office	
	B	(p)	B	(p)	B	(p)	B	(p)
(Constant)	51.8	(<0.001)	22.8	(<0.001)	9.1	(<0.001)	9.01	(<0.001)
FTE	0.003	(<0.001)	-0.001	(<0.001)	0.002	(<0.001)	-0.002	(<0.001)
% eligible for FSM	-0.10	(<0.001)	0.02	(<0.001)	0.02	(<0.001)	-0.001	(0.68)
% Black pupils	-0.29	(<0.001)	0.03	(0.05)	0.08	(0.003)	0.03	(0.05)
% English second language	-0.05	(<0.001)	0.01	(<0.001)	0.03	(<0.001)	0.01	(<0.001)
% pupils statement or EHC	-0.10	(<0.001)	-0.004	(0.03)	0.20	(<0.001)	-0.03	(<0.001)
% pupils SEN supported	-0.03	(<0.001)	0.01	(<0.001)	0.04	(<0.001)	0.001	(0.74)
London or not	0.88	(<0.001)	0.77	(<0.001)	-1.25	(<0.001)	-0.14	(0.12)
Academy	0.84	(<0.001)	-0.13	(0.03)	-7.60	(<0.001)	5.94	(<0.001)
Primary school	-5.18	(<0.001)	0.36	(<0.001)	5.91	(<0.001)	-2.75	(<0.001)
Faith schools	0.91	(<0.001)	-0.02	(<0.001)	-1.00	(<0.001)	0.22	(<0.001)
R^2	0.33		0.07		0.52		0.48	
n	13,879		13,879		13,879		13,879	

Source: Department for Education school-level data for 2014/2015.

TABLE 5.13 Associations between school characteristics and distribution of spending (2)

	Premises		Other staff		Learning resources		Capital financing	
	B	(p)	B	(p)	B	(p)	B	(p)
(Constant)	10.4	(<0.001)	5.46	(<0.001)	11.95	(<0.001)	-0.61	(<0.001)
FTE	-0.002	(<0.001)	-0.001	(<0.001)	-0.001	(<0.001)	0.001	(<0.001)
% eligible for FSM	0.02	(<0.001)	0.02	(<0.001)	0.03	(<0.001)	0.002	(0.22)
% Black pupils	-0.02	(0.20)	0.05	(0.003)	0.12	(<0.001)	0.002	(0.88)
% English second language	-0.003	(0.04)	-0.001	(0.49)	0.01	(0.005)	0.002	(0.02)
% pupils statement or EHC	-0.03	(<0.001)	0.002	(0.33)	-0.035	(<0.001)	0.006	(<0.001)
% pupils SEN supported	-0.03	(<0.001)	-0.01	(<0.001)	0.02	(<0.001)	0.001	(0.67)
London or not	0.13	(0.19)	-0.22	(0.013)	0.07	(0.003)	-0.25	(<0.001)
Academy	1.45	(<0.001)	-0.47	(<0.001)	-2.58	(<0.001)	2.55	(<0.001)
Primary school	-0.20	(0.09)	2.98	(<0.001)	-1.54	(<0.001)	0.41	(<0.001)
Faith schools	-0.51	(<0.001)	0.12	(0.031)	0.30	(0.001)	-0.02	(0.56)
R^2	0.06		0.22		0.07		0.33	
n	13,879		13,879		13,879		13,933	

Source: Department for Education school-level data for 2014/2015.

academy schools have to undertake back office duties that local authorities deal with for other schools. London salaries and living costs are higher and this is reflected in teachers' pay rates, though not, it would seem, in rates of pay for educational support assistants. London schools also face more difficulties in recruiting teachers and this is reflected in higher spending on supply teachers.

Governments and schools face tough decisions in their choice of combination of inputs. They may spend on new buildings as well as on different types of staff, maintenance and learning resources. State schools which do not own their own buildings generally have to pay for maintenance of their premises, but they are not responsible for financing capital.

The distribution of spending by state secondary schools in England in 2014/2015 is shown in Table 5.14.

The sizes of the standard deviations indicate that schools vary in their choice of input mix. Some of this variation is attributable to governance. Academy schools (or their sponsors) have ownership of their own buildings and, consequently, have to devote part of their budget to repaying debts on capital (shown as capital financing). Other differences (e.g. in the proportion spent on educational support) reflect variations among schools in the characteristics of pupils on roll. Nevertheless, the figures indicate that schools did exercise different judgements about the mix of inputs that would best meet their needs. This section examines the rationale for the mix of inputs.

TABLE 5.14 The proportion of spending on different inputs by state-funded secondary schools in England (2014–2015) ($n = 2,945$)

	Mean	Std. deviation
Teachers	52.6	7.6
Supply teachers	2.6	2.7
Educational support	8.2	4.4
Premises	9.5	4.5
Back office	10.7	4.8
Other staff	4.7	3.2
Professional and community services	2.9	4.0
Capital financing	1.5	3.7
Non-ICT learning resources	6.6	3.4
ICT	0.9	1.0

Source: Department for Education school-level data for 2014/2015.

Note
372 schools that had reported spending figures which implied that in one or more category they had negative spending were excluded from this analysis.

Buildings

Government spending on buildings for educational institutions forms part of capital spending which has been constrained by three forces. First, government spending on capital projects has been easier to cut than current spending and has less immediate effect on voters. This makes it attractive to governments wanting to cut overall spending in the short term (De Haan et al., 1996). Second, pro-market discourse has declared that governments tend to make poor investment decisions and government capital spending crowds out private sector investment.[22] Third, increasing globalisation has put downward pressure on taxation, reducing the scope for large-scale capital initiatives by governments (Garret & Mitchell, 2001). These forces have affected all OECD countries, so we might anticipate relatively low levels of spending on capital in education throughout these nations.

However, OECD[23] data show that this has not been the case. In 2013, spending on capital comprised 7 per cent of total spending on secondary schools and 13 per cent of total spending on tertiary education in OECD countries. In the UK those figures were 2 to 3 per cent for secondary education and 6 per cent for tertiary education. While the figures for the USA and Australia were close to the OECD average, the variation across countries was striking. Government decisions about capital spending in education appear to have been directed more by national politics and norms than by economic argument and evidence. Moreover, a review by Woolner et al. (2007) found little evidence of an effect of learning environments (buildings and equipment) on outcomes for students.

Relatively low capital spending in education in the UK was nothing new. To address a perceived long-standing problem in the quality of school buildings, the Department for Schools, Children and Families in England announced a massive building programme for secondary schools in England (NAO, 2009). The plan was to completely rebuild half of all secondary schools, 'structurally remodel' 35 per cent and refurbish the remainder. The funding commitment was huge: £10.3 billion by 2011, with 40 per cent of this sum being raised through 'private finance initiatives'.

A strategy of relying on private finance to fund building improvements in education was far from unique to England, but the scale of plan was ambitious by international standards. It did receive some positive responses. Beneficiaries in newly built or refurbished schools were, unsurprisingly, pleased with the results (Kakabadse et al., 2007). In addition, as pointed out by Mahoney and Hextall (2013), schools serving disadvantaged communities were more likely than other schools to benefit from the policy. They argued that the policy, therefore, served an objective of increasing social equality, insofar as modern buildings are more pleasant for pupils and they also tend to encourage engagement with schooling.

However, as in other countries[24] (English & Guthrie, 2003; Reeves, 2008; Cruz & Marques, 2012), there were problems in drawing up rigorous and effective contracts. The private companies contracted to build the schools were far more familiar with the contracting process than the local authority and school representatives purchasing their services (Keenan & McCabe, 2010). The fundamental issue, though, was cost. Private finance initiatives meant that the immediate cost to government was greatly reduced but only at the cost of an increase in long-term debt. In an era of very low interest rates that would not appear to be so great a problem, but the new Coalition government in 2010 quickly brought the scheme in England to an end.

The Coalition government in the UK also substantially cut capital grants to HEIs following its electoral success in 2010 (Frontier Economics, 2015). This change in policy reflected the government's expectation that universities would use part of their additional income from increased tuition fees to finance their capital programmes. By 2014/2015 30 per cent of universities' capital expenditure was financed through earnings and 40 per cent through loans taken out on the security of expected future earnings (Universities UK, 2015a). Newspapers have regularly featured university expansion and building plans financed through loans.[25] Some HE marketing studies have encouraged the belief that campus quality is a key factor in student choice. However, this stance does not always convince. Price and colleagues (2003) found that four of the top six factors influencing students' choice of university were facilities related, but then their survey offered students 16 items, 12 of which were related to facilities.

Number of teachers

At the end of the twentieth century the primary pupil–teacher ratio (PTR) in England was about half of what it had been 100 years earlier (Bolton, 2012). During the past 30 years[26] the continuing decline in PTR has been more marked in private schools where the pupil–teacher ratio fell from 14.4 to 9.6.[27] Over the same period the PTR fell in state primary schools from 22.1 to 20.9 and in secondary schools from 16.2 to 15.5.[28] Between 1990 and 2007 the PTR in state schools in the USA fell from 17.6 to 15.8 (US Department of Education, 2010). In Australia between 2001 and 2016, the PTR in state primary schools fell from 17.5 to 15.6, while the PTR in non-government primary schools fell from 18.2 to 16.1.[29] As income per person has risen, the PTR has fallen. Moreover, parents paid higher fees to send their children to schools with lower PTRs (Davies & Davies, 2014). Undergraduates also tend to prefer smaller classes, as judged by the ratings they give in student evaluations (see e.g. Fernandez et al., 1998; Bedard & Kuhn, 2008). Consumers prefer institutions with fewer students per teacher.

Schools with a lower PTR have more teacher time at their disposal. This time may be used in different ways. A survey of classroom teachers' self-reported workload in state schools in England (Deakin et al., 2010) found that primary and secondary teachers spent one-third of their working time in 'class contact', one-third in preparation and assessment and one-third in other duties. So a fall in PTR could be used to reduce class size or to provide teachers with more time for preparation, assessment and improving their capacity as teachers. While the importance of preparation, assessment and professional development has been widely extolled, there is little evidence about the resource implications. The evidence base concentrates on the option of reducing class size.

Reducing the number of students in a class could help their learning for several reasons. It could make it easier for the teacher to manage students' behaviour so that students' learning is not disrupted by others. It could also make it easier for the teacher to interact with students' ideas. Being taught in a smaller class could also affect students' engagement through building their sense that the teacher knows them. Students who have less capacity to direct their behaviour may also benefit more than other students from being taught in a smaller class in which they receive more support and direction from the teacher.

Empirical studies face several challenges when trying to identify effects of smaller classes. First, school-level data combine effects of class size and teachers' preparation and assessment time. Second, students who are judged to have problematic behaviour and students judged to be less capable of directing their own learning are more likely to be educated in smaller classes. In 2014/2015 there was a modest (0.3) negative correlation between the pupil–teacher ratio in secondary schools and pupil attainment (at Key Stage 2) on entry to the school.

Third, the extent of variation in class size in state schools is generally relatively small once relevant student characteristics have been taken into account. Some indication of this variation may be gathered by the comparisons of PTR in Table 5.15. These suggest that while there is substantial variation by school type, there is a small variation in PTR in each type of school. Fourth, an effect which operates through teachers' interaction with students will only be observed when teachers choose to take advantage of the opportunities provided by smaller classes.

While many studies have reported estimates of the effects of reduction in class size, few have managed to come close to providing convincing ways of dealing with the measurement problems. Three studies stand out: Angrist and Lavy (1999), Finn and Achilles (1999) and Blatchford et al. (2002, 2003). Each of these studies reported substantial positive effects of lower class size on pupil attainment. Angrist and Lavy (1999) used a regression discontinuity design which exploited policy restricting class size in Israel. Finn and Achilles (1999) used a randomised controlled trial in schools in Tennessee in the USA. Blatchford and colleagues (2002, 2003) gathered detailed evidence of classroom process which enabled them to control for

TABLE 5.15 Pupil–teacher ratios by school type in England

	Lower quartile	Median	Upper quartile
State primary schools[‡]	18.1	20.3	22.5
State secondary schools[‡]	13.7	15.0	16.3
Private schools sampled by Davies & Davies (2014)[†]	6.3	7.7	9.1

Notes

[‡] Data for 2014–2015 – see Appendix to this chapter.

[†] This sample was restricted to schools with sixth forms which featured in a newspaper league table of the 'best independent schools'.

within-class variation in a way that went well beyond previous studies. They found that in smaller classes primary school teachers (1) organised children into smaller groups; (2) spent more time on teaching and less on organisation, and (3) spent more time interacting with individual children. They also found that children in smaller classes were more attentive and less prone to challenging behaviour. In the reception year, Blatchford and colleagues (2002, 2003, 2011) reported that a reduction in class size from 30 to 20 resulted in a 0.25 standard deviation increase in mathematics attainment. They also found that while children from all backgrounds had higher literacy attainment in small reception classes, children who started with a lower initial level of literacy benefited the most. Browning and Heinesen (2007) used a regression discontinuity design (similar to Angrist and Lavy) and found a significant positive effect of smaller classes on the attainment of secondary students.

Teachers' pay

Rather than recruiting more teachers, a government or a school could aim to improve schooling outputs by paying higher salaries to all or some teachers. The argument is outlined in Figure 5.2. The case for raising teachers' salaries rests partly on the observation of a positive correlation between average teacher pay and the academic credentials of entrants to teaching (steps [1] and [2] in Figure 5.2). For example, Figlio (1997) observed an increase in relative qualifications of entrants to teaching in the USA following an increase in relative teacher pay in the 1990s. A small survey of undergraduates at one university (Kyriacou & Coulthard, 2000) found that, of those considering teaching, two-thirds were more likely to apply if pay was higher and working conditions were better. These results do not require salary to be the dominant motivation for the majority of applicants to teaching. They are, therefore, consistent with survey results such as those provided by Moran et al. (2001), who found that most of the applicants in their sample claimed that their dominant motivations were 'love of children', 'sense of vocation', 'intellectual fulfilment' and 'desire to serve society'.

However, the dominant trend in recent decades has been a steady decline in the academic credentials of teachers relative to other professionals in the USA (Corcoran et al., 2004; Eide et al., 2004; Hanushek & Rivkin, 2007), Australia (Leigh & Ryan, 2008) and the UK[30] (Nickell & Quintini, 2002). Bacolod (2007) relates the

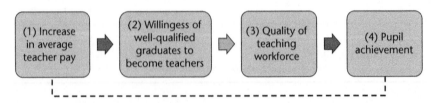

FIGURE 5.2 The pattern of causation presumed by the argument that raising average teachers' pay would improve pupils' progress.

decline in average grade point score of female entrants to teaching in the USA to the way in which alternative professional opportunities have expanded over time. This trend has been related to who leaves the profession as well as who joins. Murnane and colleagues (1991) found that better qualified teachers in North Carolina were more likely than others to leave the profession.

There is also strong evidence of the effect of teacher quality on pupil achievement (steps [3] and [4] in Figure 5.2). Teacher quality may be measured through the value-added of the students they teach. Analyses of pupil level value-added which control for students' background and school effects have consistently reported that individual teacher effects on pupil progress are greater than school-level effects (e.g. Nye *et al.*, 2004; Kane & Staiger. 2008; Slater *et al.*, 2012). One problem with this evidence is the difficulty researchers face in fully controlling for non-random assignment of teachers to classes. If some teachers are more likely to be assigned to classes with initially higher achievement, correlation between prior achievement and progress will bias estimation of teachers' value-added. A second problem is that teachers' effects on immediate performance may be weakly related to long-term impacts. Teacher effects may be expected to decay over time as other factors come to the fore. More critically, short-term performance may be boosted by 'teaching to the test' or intensive teacher input. Either of these approaches to teaching could undermine the development of students' input into learning: their self-regulation and self-determination, and this could damage longer term achievement and capability. Rothstein (2010) found only a modest correlation between short- and long-term teacher value-added. However, even after taking account of Rothstein's concerns, Chetty *et al.* (2014, p. 2633) estimated that 'replacing a teacher whose VA is in the bottom 5 percent with an average teacher would increase the present value of students' lifetime income by approximately $250,000 per classroom'.

Finally, there is also international evidence of a correlation between teachers' relative pay and pupil achievement (shown by the dotted black line in Figure 5.2). Dolton and Marcenaro-Gutierrez (2011) included 39 countries in their study and concluded (p. 35) that a 5 per cent increase in the relative position of teachers in the salary distribution would increase pupil performance by between 5 and 10 per cent.

Despite the strong evidence for accepting steps [1] to [2] and [3] to [4], and the correlation between [1] and [4], the weakness of Figure 5.2 lies in the relationship between steps [2] to [3]. Hoxby and Leigh (2004, p. 236) take this link as self-evident in their assertion that "Logic suggests that a teacher's value-added is related to her academic aptitude". However, using academic credentials as a measure of teacher quality is problematic for several reasons. First, degree classifications in some countries (notably the UK) are very broad, and cross-sectional analysis (Slater *et al.*, 2012) has not detected a firm positive relationship between degree classification and pupils' value-added in England. Second, even a fine-grained and reliable measure of academic achievement at university would provide an incomplete picture of the qualities that schools seek in teachers. The quality of teaching is affected by individuals' perception of children's needs and selection of instructional techniques,[31] as well as by their knowledge and understanding of the subject they are teaching (Baumert *et al.*, 2010). Third, since teachers have a high degree of autonomy in their work there is a moral hazard problem in recruitment: schools need recruits who can be trusted to put the interests of children before their own interests, but self-interested applicants may be attracted by freedoms they will exploit. Evidence on the recruitment process suggests that schools regard this as a major issue (Davies *et al.*, 2016). Schools want Knights not Knaves (LeGrand, 2010). Finally, supplementary tests at point of recruitment have not overcome the problem. Angrist and Guryan (2008) found no association between teacher quality and the use of such tests in the USA. Therefore, Figure 5.2 provides an incomplete account of causation and there is a possibility that the correlation between steps [1] and [4] is a consequence of other processes.

Moreover, recruits to teaching who are extrinsically motivated (by external incentives such as pay) are less likely to intend to stay in the profession than those who are intrinsically motivated (by their commitment to the job). This finding has been consistently reported by surveys in Australia (Watt & Richardson, 2007, 2008), the Netherlands (Bruinsma & Jansen, 2010), Turkey (Eren & Tezel, 2010) and the USA (Thomson *et al.*, 2012). Retention is a substantial problem in many countries, with 30 per cent of teachers in Australia leaving the profession within five years. In summary, we can group factors in teacher quality into three dimensions: academic grasp of what is to be taught (content knowledge), understanding of children and teaching (pedagogic content knowledge), and motivation to serve the interests of children. Higher average pay attracts applicants who are better qualified but it also attracts individuals who are less motivated to serve the interests of children. Both of these factors interact with teachers' understanding of children and teaching but we do not know how much.

An alternative argument on teacher pay is that the average teacher salary is less important than *which* teachers get paid more. One part of this argument is that teachers' pay in the public sector is compressed by the efforts of teacher unions. This has the consequence that graduates with modest academic records can expect good pay in teaching relative to what they could earn elsewhere, while highly qualified graduates will not be able to earn the higher salaries that their talents would bring them in other occupations (Hoxby & Leigh, 2004). In England, graduates in education who have relatively low A-level grades have relatively high earnings compared to graduates in other subjects. Conversely, graduates in education with relatively high A-level grades have relatively low earnings compared to graduates in other subjects (O'Leary & Sloane, 2011). The Department for Education in England (2011) has responded to this situation by targeting an increase in the proportion of recruits to teaching who have higher grades at degree level (classifications 2i and 1). However, rather than seeking to attract recruits by raising average teacher pay or by raising maximum teacher pay, they have relied on marketing and regulation of training providers.[32] These providers have responded by recruiting more graduates with first-class or upper second-class degrees, but without expressing any confidence that they are thereby recruiting individuals who will become better teachers (Davies *et al.*, 2016). This scepticism is in line with available evidence about teacher quality in England (Slater *et al.*, 2012).

Higher pay may also be awarded to some, but not all, teachers through performance-related pay (PRP). A survey of teachers in England found that younger teachers were much more supportive than older teachers of the introduction of such a scheme (Tomlinson, 2000). This supports the conjecture that a pay structure which offers greater opportunity for teachers to influence their final reward will be attractive to potential recruits. Gerhart and Fang (2014) identify three design features that may distinguish one PRP scheme from another: (1) performance measured in terms of results or behaviours; (2) performance measured at individual, group or organisational level, and (3) intensity of the reward for higher performance. Implementation of PRP in education reflects this diversity (see e.g. Eberts *et al.*, 2002), but most schemes have aimed to reward individual teachers on the basis of the performance of their pupils in attainment tests.

This kind of PRP scheme has been criticised on the basis that technical problems preclude accuracy in ascribing children's progress to teachers, groups of teachers or schools (Ball, 2003b; Mahony *et al.*, 2004). PRP systems which reward groups of teachers (such as a subject department in a secondary school) do not overcome this problem. Telhaj and colleagues (2009) compared the performance of geography and history departments in English secondary schools. If, in a given school, the geography department performed better than the history department one year, the probability that it would also be better the following year was no greater than tossing a coin. However, the degree to which a PRP system accurately identifies and attributes pupils' progress to individual teachers is irrelevant to the short-term effectiveness of the system. What matters is whether teachers *believe* that greater effort will receive rewards which interest them. A system which inaccurately measures teacher effects could be effective in the short run, but teachers may then become disenchanted on discovering that their expectations were not fulfilled. Therefore, any evaluation of a PRP system should wait a few years for a system to become embedded in schools' practice. In the short term at least, the size and timing of the potential reward may be more important than the accuracy of the attribution of teacher effects. Fryer Jr. and colleagues (2012) compared two designs of PRP. In one arm of a field experiment teachers were paid a bonus up front and were required to pay back the bonus if they did not meet the performance target. In a parallel arm of the experiment teachers were told they would receive a bonus if they met the performance target. Students' achievement in mathematics rose by more than one standard deviation in the 'up-front payment' arm of the experiment.

Evaluations of performance-related pay schemes in the USA and England have generally reported substantive improvements in performance measured by the target rewarded by the scheme. Ladd (1999) found that seventh-grade children's achievements in mathematics and reading had improved in PRP schools relative to other schools in Dallas. Dee and Keys (2004) found that a merit pay scheme in Tennessee, USA resulted in a three-percentage point improvement in mathematics achievements of primary school children but no significant difference in reading. Atkinson and colleagues (2009) found that teachers eligible for a new PRP scheme in England increased students' performance by the equivalent of 40 per cent of an examination grade.

A performance-related pay scheme may improve measured performance for any of several reasons. Teachers may increase their effort, working longer hours. Teachers may change instructional methods having been motivated to find out how to improve their work and to act upon advice. Teachers may also switch their effort from other educational objectives in order to increase their performance on the target that will be rewarded. Since performance-related pay schemes assume that teachers are self-interested maximisers of personal earnings we should expect them to exhaust 'effort switching' before considering any option that requires them to expend additional effort. Evidence of PRP effects on teachers' effort is mixed. Yuan and colleagues (2013) reviewed evidence collected through three RCTs of performance-related pay schemes in the USA. Fewer than half of the teachers reported that the incentive pay scheme had energised them to improve their teaching and there was no evidence that teachers had increased their hours of work. There is some evidence that PRP encourages teachers to switch their effort towards the PRP target. Eberts and colleagues (2002) found that a PRP scheme which rewarded teachers on the basis of pupil retention had a positive impact upon pupil retention at the expense of pupil performance. An underlying fear is that by encouraging teachers to respond to extrinsic rewards, PRP undermines intrinsic motivation (Firestone, 2014). This is one possible interpretation of Belfield and Heywood's (2008) finding that PRP had simultaneously increased teachers' pay and decreased their job satisfaction. Therefore, while there are good grounds for believing that it is possible to design a PRP scheme that will improve students' examination grades, we do not yet know whether this is offset by losses in long-term teacher motivation or student capability.

Teaching assistants

Since 1997 there has been a dramatic increase in the number of teaching assistants employed in primary and secondary schools in England (Figure 5.3). Additional teaching assistants were employed to work alongside rather than to replace teachers. The number of teachers employed by primary schools and secondary schools also increased slightly over this period. In 2014/2015 in the state sector the average pay of teachers was approximately double the pay of the average teaching assistant.[33]

This section considers why this happened and how it is affecting outcomes for students. Explanations for the rise of the teaching assistant are divided into the proximate and the underlying.

The rise in the number of teaching assistants in state schools has been a direct consequence of government policy in the USA (Gerber et al., 2001) and in England.[34] The rapid increase in England was associated with government policy to 'remodel the workforce'. This started with a 'pathfinder' project (Thomas et al.,

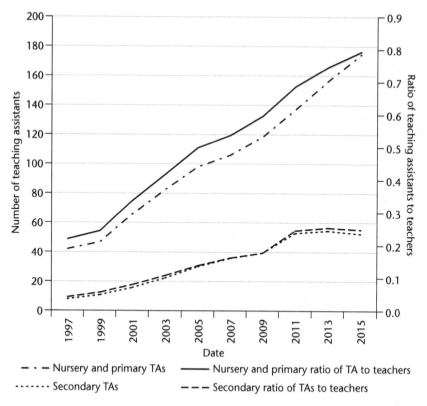

FIGURE 5.3 The number of teaching assistants in primary, secondary and higher education: England.

Source: Data from the Schools Workforce dataset, Department for Education, England.

2004) and was cemented through an agreement with the trade unions (DfES, 2003). The aim was to reduce the amount of time teachers spent on administration and to provide additional support for managing pupils' behaviour. These changes were expected to have two consequences. First, it would reduce teachers' workload and stress, thereby increasing the retention of teachers (DfES, 2003). Second, it would increase the amount of time teachers spent in classroom interaction and, in particular, in preparation and assessment: activities that were directly related to pupils' learning. In the early years following the Workforce Modelling Agreement, schools concentrated on reallocating administrative tasks from teachers to teaching assistants (OfSTED, 2005).

Similar increases in the employment of teaching assistants in other countries such as Scotland (Warhurst *et al.*, 2014) suggest an underlying cause prompting policy change. Workforce remodelling in schools may be understood in the contexts of the challenges governments have faced in recruiting and retaining teachers while reducing teachers' professional freedom and increasing public accountability. According to Baumol's Cost Disease, governments in countries with increasing income per head would be experiencing these problems, regardless of any perceptions that the job was becoming less attractive. As households' income increases they want more education: they want to stay in education for longer and they want smaller classes. The demand for teachers increases, but how can they be attracted unless through offering relatively higher salaries either for all teachers or at least for 'high-performing' teachers? Increasing teacher pay means higher government spending and, *ceteris paribus*, higher taxes. Teaching assistants offer a way out of this problem if either (1) teacher retention is improved by reduced workload, or (2) teachers spend more of their time teaching and less of their time in administration.

Baumol's Cost Disease anticipates an even more severe problem for higher education. Between 1995 and 2011 the rate of participation in tertiary education in OECD countries increased on average by 50 per cent (OECD, 2014a). Yet between 1999 and 2007 OECD countries managed to hold the ratio of students to teachers more or less constant (UCU, 2010). The traditional job description in higher education has demanded that teachers also be able to conduct high-quality research. Increasing demand for this pool of specialised individuals must increase relative salaries. Therefore, it would not be surprising to find universities turning to a new type of employee (individuals who teach but do not research), as well as making increasing use of graduate teaching assistants. However, the publicly available information only permits glimpses of graduate teaching assistants within a broader trend in the employment of teachers in higher education.[35] These glimpses[36] suggest that there has been a trend towards greater reliance on part-time teachers, graduate teaching assistants and lecturers on 'teaching-only' contracts in countries such as Australia, the UK and the USA.

What effect, if any, have these changes had on outcomes for learners in schools and higher education? In reviewing the evidence it is important to remember that teaching assistants in schools have been employed *in addition to* teachers but employment changes in higher education have switched teaching responsibilities from staff on one kind of contract to staff working under different contractual arrangements or under no contract at all.

Studies of teaching assistants working alongside teachers in the classroom to provide 'learning support' have reported zero or negative impacts upon attainment. Evaluations of the Tennessee Project STAR (Gerber *et al.*, 2001), and the early years of the 'workforce remodelling' strategy in England (e.g. Muijs & Reynolds, 2003; Blatchford *et al.*, 2007) found no evidence of an effect on pupils' attainment. Blatchford and colleagues (2012) found a negative association between pupils' progress and the intensity of support from teaching assistants. They attribute this effect to displacement of teacher–pupil interactions when teaching assistants help in the classroom. Nonetheless, they found positive effects on teacher satisfaction with teachers reporting reduced workload and reduced stress, thereby meeting one of the objectives of the workforce remodelling policy. When teaching assistants are given careful training and implement interventions targeted at individual pupils or a small group the results have been more positive. A review (Farrell *et al.*, 2010) of the impact of teaching assistants who were specifically trained and assigned to pupils with identified learning difficulties reported attainment gains when intensive support was provided. Gorard and colleagues (2014) conducted a randomised controlled trial of an intervention in which teaching assistants were provided 1:1 support for pupils' reading and found a 0.24 effect size improvement in reading. But this way of using teaching assistants is expensive. In this three-month programme each participating pupil received 20 minutes' input per day from a teaching assistant at an estimated cost per pupil of £627 (using direct salary costs rather than full costs of employment). Using the same method of calculation the average annual cost per pupil of employing a teacher was £1,865 in a primary school and £2,487 in a secondary school. Schools may be interested to know whether ten minutes of input from a teacher would have been more or less effective than 20 minutes from a teaching assistant,[37] since this is the kind of resource choice they have to make.

The impacts of graduate teaching assistants (GTAs) may be detected in comparisons of the progress of undergraduates taught by tenured staff with the progress of undergraduates who have been taught by 'contingent' or 'adjunct' non-tenured staff. Contingent or adjunct staff are cheaper to employ and they allow institutions to avoid long-term employment commitments. Graduate teaching assistants in the UK are paid an hourly rate which does not include 'on-costs' such as contributions to pensions. However, in contrast to the teacher–teaching assistant relationship in schools, GTAs take responsibility for whole classes which would otherwise be taught by a salaried academic. So, do GTAs and other part-time and non-tenured staff have a negative impact upon undergraduates' experience? Bettinger and Long (2010) found that first-year undergraduates who were taught by adjunct staff were more likely to choose to study a major in that subject. Figlio and colleagues (2015) found no difference between the value-added scores of first-year undergraduates taught by the best 75 per cent of tenured academic staff and those of first-year undergraduates taught by the best 75 per cent of 'contingent' staff (including part-time staff and graduate teaching assistants). They did, however, find that undergraduates made better progress when taught by one of the 25 per cent least effective part-time staff than they did when they were taught by one of the least effective tenured staff. They attributed this difference to the stronger motivation of contingent staff to do a good job which might affect their prospects of further employment.

Thus, while there are some interesting similarities between the use of 'supplementary' teaching staff in higher education and schools, there are, perhaps, even more interesting contrasts. In both sectors we may observe increasing use of supplementary staff in a way that is consistent with Baumol's Cost Disease. Schools have struggled to find ways of using teaching assistants that are cost-effective in terms of pupils' attainment, although there is plenty of evidence that teaching assistants have made schools easier to manage and more pleasant places to work (Blatchford et al., 2012). HEIs have faced greater challenges in coping with increased participation and have reduced teaching costs through supplementary staff instead of permanent salaried staff. Happily for students and HEIs this appears to have been achieved with no loss of quality in teaching. Of course, this situation may have arisen because the quality was not all that high in the first place. There is little evidence that lessons learned in one sector are influencing the other. Perhaps they could.

Professional development

The steps in the argument for an effect of teachers' professional development on pupils' attainment (Figure 5.4) somewhat echo the arguments about teachers' pay. It is convenient to see the two options as alternatives. Through professional development a school may try to improve the teachers it has rather than going to the trouble of recruiting better teachers or increasing teachers' effort through PRP. Each strategy presumes a different problem. Raising salaries suggests that ability to teach is an innate characteristic and you have to pay more to recruit individuals with higher innate ability. Introducing PRP suggests that the problem is that teachers have not been working hard enough or that teaching needs to be made more attractive to more talented individuals. Providing professional development suggests that teachers did not previously have sufficient understanding or skill. None of these suggestions is attractive for teachers, and this partly accounts for the popularity of self- or mutual help for teacher development.

While much of the literature agrees on using standardised tests of academic attainment to measure the final step shown in Figure 5.4, there is considerable variation in the construction and description of each of the preceding three steps. Formal support for teachers' professional development may be provided outside the school, within the school or through collaboration between teachers and outside 'experts'. Widespread acceptance in teaching of the ideas of 'reflective practice' (Schön, 1987) and 'professional learning communities' (Lieberman, 1995; Stoll et al., 2006) has encouraged schools to regard professional development as something best accomplished 'in-house'. This has the added attraction of reducing cost through limiting reliance on outside experts. While there is plenty of support in the literature for positive relations at each step from [1] to [2] (Garet et al., 2001; Desimone et al., 2002), [1] to [3] (e.g. Thoonen et al., 2011), and [3] to [4] (e.g. Hattie &

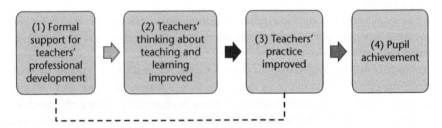

FIGURE 5.4 The pattern of causation presumed by the argument that professional development for teachers will improve pupils' progress.

Timperley, 2007) there is very little evidence of a positive association between professional development in general and improvements in pupils' attainment in public examinations. Hanushek and Rivkin (2006) summarise studies which found no association between possessing a Masters' degree and pupil attainment. The vast amount of literature on 'reflective practice' and 'professional learning communities' as vehicles for teacher development offers little systematic evidence of effects on student attainment (Muijs & Lindsay, 2008; Guskey & Yoon, 2009).

Failure to find convincing positive associations between professional development and students' attainment in public examinations may reflect the problems that typically beset research in education. First, teachers who enrol on Masters' degrees may not be representative of all teachers. There is an incentive for teachers with weaker first-degree qualifications to improve their credibility by gaining a postgraduate qualification. Masters' courses in education may be designed to develop teachers' capacities in ways (e.g. for inclusive education) that are not designed to improve headline measures of pupil attainment. Second, given the small amount of resources devoted to professional development it will be difficult to detect associations between professional development and student attainment in large, national, datasets. In 2014/2015 the proportion of spending on professional development by state secondary schools in England was just under half of 1 per cent. Even if all of this was spent on professional development for teachers it would amount to about £1 for every £100 in salary costs. This problem is aggravated by the variation in forms of training, targeted change in teachers' thinking and targeted change in teachers' practice.

There is an increasing chance of detecting associations and effects in more fine-grained comparisons. For example, Antoniou and Kyriakides (2011) compared the effect on student attainment of two approaches to professional development for teachers. Both approaches entailed the same external resource input (largely in expert time) and the same internal resource input in teachers' time. The cost of this resource input was not reported. The researchers found substantive change in teaching skills and student attainment for one-third of the teachers experiencing professional development that was designed according to the authors' analysis of teaching skills. In their review, Vescio *et al.* (2008) report positive associations between specific interventions and student attainment in fairly small-scale studies. Papay and Johnson's (2012) work on the impact of a peer evaluation programme remains a rare example of a study attempting to follow through each step shown in Figure 5.4 and then to estimate costs and benefits of the programme. They concluded that this form of professional development had substantial net financial benefits. Nonetheless, for an aspect of teacher and school improvement that has commanded huge attention over a long period there is still only a small evidence base from which to judge the wisdom of devoting resources to teachers' professional development.

Information and communications technology

Technological advances have created many new opportunities for teaching and learning: increasing speed of access to information and debate; providing interactive simulations of technical processes; and enabling teachers to review their work using an online platform to reflect on videos of their teaching and the teaching of others. Unsurprisingly, therefore, recent decades have witnessed many optimistic forecasts (e.g. Kent & McNergney, 1999) of the impact of information and communications technology (ICT) upon education. These forecasts looked plausible enough given the evidence of the transformative effect of new technology on many other areas of production (e.g. Mitra & Chaya, 1996). ICT may change the input mix in any of three different ways. This section examines each of these in turn.

First, ICT may be used as an alternative to face-to-face contact with teachers, notably in the case of distance learning. Rumble (2003) and Jung (2003) provide careful accounts of how cost-effectiveness analysis of online and distance education should be carried out. However, the number of studies that have systematically followed such guidelines is relatively small. Studies (e.g. Allen *et al.*, 2004; Euzent *et al.*, 2011; Driscoll *et al.*, 2012) have typically reported no statistical difference between the achievement of students who have received face-to-face instruction and those who have received online instruction. The implication is that if an online education programme costs less than a face-to-face programme it makes sense for HEIs to substitute ICT for teaching staff.

However, there are reasons to be cautious about these results. Critically, these studies have struggled to address problems of selection bias, since students are typically given an option of choosing to study online or face-to-face. This could create a disadvantage for online instruction if the students who opt for that route are less interested in the programme, have lower prior attainment or spend more time in paid employment. For example, Driscoll *et al.* (2012) found that undergraduate sociology students who opted for an online route expected to do more paid work and expected lower grades (GPA) than students who opted for face-to-face instruction. Once they took account of students' expected GPA the difference between the performance of online and face-to-face students was reduced. The lower performance of the online students was no longer sufficiently precisely measured to be claimed to be statistically significant. The researchers claimed that students' estimates of their GPA reflected their academic ability. However, these estimates may also have reflected their expectations of the effectiveness of online and face-to-face instruction. Another difficulty was that the students who opted for the online route were, on average, older than those who opted for the face-to-face route. Mature students tend to be more likely to adopt a deep approach to learning, to be more strongly engaged with their studies and to achieve higher grades than younger students (see e.g. Davies *et al.*, 2012). Omission of this factor also undermines confidence in results reported by studies (e.g. Cheng *et al.*, 1991), including the meta-analysis conducted by Allen *et al.* (2004). One group of researchers (Bernard *et al.*, 2009, 2014) who have been very active in this field concluded that there was simply too much variation within face-to-face instruction and within online education for comparisons of the two to contribute to improving teaching and resource use. As in other aspects of educational research, there is a great need for studies in which the variation between conditions is tightly controlled. Pragmatic RCTs are not sufficient for this task.

Alternatively, schools or universities may secure ICT hardware or software to use in addition to their teaching staff. Schools have typically used ICT as a supplement to other resources. Legal responsibilities to look after their students preclude asking them to work off-site during normal school hours. If we assume that schools will tend to exploit additional resources to improve students' attainment we would expect that schools will improve student attainment when they have more computers. However, Angrist and Lavy (2002) found that a national programme in Israel which provided many elementary and middle schools with substantially more computers had no effect on pupils' attainment in maths. As Miller and Olson (1994) showed, adding computers into the classroom does not necessarily change the way in which teachers conduct their lessons.

In a third option, additional ICT hardware and software is accompanied by a specific teaching strategy and training on how to make good use of the technology. A review of meta-analyses of the impact of the use of ICT in schools (Higgins et al., 2012, p. 14) concluded that "how (or how well) technology is used is the important consideration rather than the choice of a particular technology or a particular approach". Nonetheless, based largely on this meta-analysis the Education Endowment Fund[38] concluded that using digital technology had an indicative effect size of 0.28 or four months' progress. Compared to other possible interventions this places digital technology in the middle rank of effective strategies for schools and teachers. In contrast, the most recent (and among the most robust) meta-analysis (Cheung & Slavin, 2013), included in the review by Higgins et al. (2012), estimated an effect size of 0.15 (or two months' progress). Even at the level of meta-analyses the variation in estimated effects is relatively large.

Moreover, as noted in the earlier discussion about cost-effectiveness, the way in which experiments deal with the control condition substantially affects the interpretation of the results. Meta-analyses in education (e.g. Cheung & Slavin, 2013) have not set 'uses a placebo' as a condition for inclusion. Interventions which replace 'traditional teaching' with an experience in a computer lab might reasonably be considered at risk of a Hawthorne effect. Furthermore, the meta-analyses reviewed by Higgins et al. (2012) include composite ICT interventions (e.g. Nunnery & Ross, 2007; Barrow et al., 2009) which combine the use of technology with a particular method of teaching. Although the ICT provides a different way of implementing an approach to teaching, there are few approaches to teaching which could not be operationalised either with or without using ICT. Therefore, it is difficult to judge whether an effect size from a composite ICT intervention reflects the effect of the ICT or the effect of the approach to teaching. A meta-analysis of feedback using ICT (Kleij et al., 2015) claims similar average effect sizes to those reported in Hattie and Timperley's (2007) general review of feedback.

Only a minority of the studies included in the meta-analyses (e.g. Fletcher *et al.*, 1990) explicitly compared a particular teaching approach (in that case, 'drill and practice' in mathematics) with and without ICT.

The EEF summary estimates the per student capital cost at £300 plus a further £20 per pupil cost of training teachers to achieve an average of 4 months' progress (£80 per month of pupil progress). This contrasts with the approximate cost of $20 per month of pupil progress which Fletcher *et al.* (1990) estimated in their study of computer-aided instructed in the USA. Many factors combine to make estimates of average cost-effectiveness of ICT a matter of conjecture: issues in RCT design (relating to choice of control); variation in technologies and strategies for teaching, and paucity of studies including cost data.

Co-production and reproduction in education

This section considers the roles of parents, peers, parents and the students themselves in the production process. This contribution which students make to their own education is shaped by peers and parents, while parents may also influence a student's peer group beyond and within a school. Figure 5.5 builds on Figure 5.1 to outline the roles of parents, peers and pupils in relation to formal education.

Figure 5.5 distinguishes between direct effects (shown in the dark straight arrow) which operate directly on pupils' development, and indirect effects (shown in the light curved arrows) which operate through interactions with others. Direct and indirect effects may be abstracted from social context and viewed as co-production, or may be viewed as socially embedded. The term 'social reproduction' views the 'co-production' relationships in Figure 5.5 as embedded in social contexts where outcomes for individuals and society as a whole are reproduced by intergenerational transmission shaped by power relations.

Input from parents

According to Carneiro and Heckman (2002, p. 75), "families are just as important as, if not more important than, schools in promoting human capital". Parental support for their children's progress in education has implications for the possible impact of government intervention. Parents who regard education through the lens of human capital may see government intervention as a substitute for their own efforts. The more government does, the less they have to do. Conversely, parents who believe that education is a zero-sum game may be galvanised by state intervention to devote even more of their resources to creating advantages for their children.

This section begins by looking at direct effects of parental inputs. The second half of the section examines indirect effects.

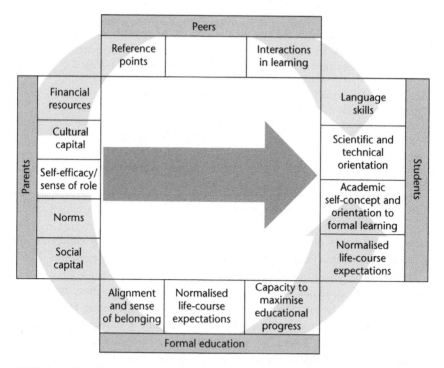

FIGURE 5.5 Parents, peers and pupils in the co-production and (social) reproduction of education.

Direct effects of parental inputs

First, we summarise how parents directly influence children's educational progress through what they do. This prepares the ground for examining (in the light of Figure 5.5) how parental behaviour is influenced by the resources they have.

The amount of time parents spend engaging with their children has been associated with the development of a range of children's subsequent aptitudes (Bronfenbrenner, 1979; Bryant & Zick, 1996; Lam et al., 2012). Parents' interaction with their children through play and reading stories influences their early literacy and preparation for reading and participation in school environments (Baker et al., 2001; Leseman & Jong, 1998; Davis-Kean, 2005; Saracho & Spodek, 2010; Pillinger & Wood, 2014).

More broadly, Melhuish et al. (2008) distinguished between home-related activities that were or were not positively related to numeracy and literacy at age 5. Evidence from this research is summarised in Table 5.16.

Parents also influence their children through the ways in which they develop the child's sense of self-worth and their capacity for independent action and reasoning. Steinberg and colleagues (1992) defined three dimensions of parenting (parental acceptance or warmth; behavioural supervision and strictness, and psychological autonomy granting or democracy) as 'authoritative parenting'. They found that

TABLE 5.16 Home environment activities related to numeracy and literacy at age 5

Home environment activities unrelated *to numeracy and literacy at age 5*	*Home environment activities* positively *associated with numeracy and literacy at age 5*
Eating meals with family	Being taught letters
Playing with friends at home	Being taught numbers
Playing with friends elsewhere	Going to the library
Regular bedtime	Painting and drawing
Shopping	Parent reading to child
Visiting relatives/friends	Playing with numbers
Watching TV	Songs/poems/rhymes

Source: Evidence presented in Melhuish *et al.* (2008).

these characteristics of parenting were positively associated with children's subsequent achievement in school. Children's capacity for self-regulation (taking control of their own learning) in formal education has also been associated with previous parent–child interaction (Grolnick & Ryan, 1989; Grolnick, 2009).

We now turn to the question of the dependence of parenting behaviour on parents' resources. Financial resources affect the amount of time parents devote to their child's education. Given the risk of stigmatising particular lifestyle choices or families facing challenging circumstances, studies of this phenomenon bear an intensified responsibility in adequately controlling for confounding factors associated with students' attainment in schools. Low-income families experience emotional and mental stress which can impair parent–child relations with negative consequences for the role of parents in supporting learning (Dahl & Lochner, 2012). Parcel and Dufur (2001) reported that US children whose mothers were not in paid employment had higher school achievement. Astone and McLanahan (1991) found that children growing up in one-parent families were more likely to show early disengagement in school and were prone to later drop-out. Downey (1995) examined the dilution model which suggests that children with more siblings receive less attention from their parents. He found strong support for the model which was partly mediated by economic resources such as access to a computer and the ability of the family to provide financial support for attending college.

Parents can also use their financial resources to provide a richer learning environment for their children (e.g. through paying for books, visits to places of cultural interest and early education).

Parents' capacity to support their children's literacy and cultural capital is also affected by their own cultural capital (Sullivan, 2001). Table 5.17 summarises three definitions of cultural activity and ways in which the capital possessed by the parent influences what they are able to offer their children. A traditional formulation regards cultural capital in terms of knowledge and participation of the '*beaux arts*' (Table 5.16, row 1) (Bourdieu, 1973). This definition of cultural capital treats awareness of highbrow art, music and theatre as a set of indicators of social status which will be used to secure successful passage towards positions of power and prestige in society.

TABLE 5.17 Dimensions of cultural capital

		Dimensions of cultural capital		
		Attitudes and interest	*Knowledge*	*Language fluency*
Activity focus	1 Highbrow culture (*beaux arts*)	e.g. interest in famous art and music	e.g. knowledge of famous books and plays	e.g. awareness of allusions to great art and literature in modern and colloquial texts, ability to deploy phrases with allusions to highbrow culture.
	2 Scientific, technical and media oriented framing	e.g. positive attitude towards science, interest in current affairs	e.g. knowledge of famous scientists, current affairs events and issues	e.g. familiarity with scientific and current affairs terms and idioms.
	3 Parent–child dialogue (which develops ready-for-school language codes and registers)	e.g. positive attitude towards literacy, teachers and schools	e.g. knowledge of school conventions	e.g. ability to read and ability to interpret teacher language and non-verbal communication.

Source: Adapted from Davies *et al.* (2014, p. 806).

A second formulation (Table 5.16, row 2) of cultural capital argues that interest in, knowledge of and capacity to talk about the language of science and technology are now more important than *beaux arts* to participation in 'educated society' (Prieur & Savage, 2011). The final dimension (Table 5.16, row 3) locates cultural capital in the development of language and language registers which characterise 'educated society' (Bernstein, 1982; Lareau, 1987; Farkas *et al.*, 1990). Since formal education is carried out through the medium of language, language skills are critical for educational progress. Parents' interactions with their pre-school children (e.g. in reading and talking about stories) affect progress in literacy in school (Leseman & de Jong, 1998). Studies in the USA (McNeal, 1999; Bodovski, 2010) and the UK (Sullivan, 2001) have found positive associations between parents' socio-economic status, 'highbrow' and 'parent–child dialogue' cultural capital and attainment in schools. De Graaf and colleagues (2000) found that subsequent attainment in Dutch schools was positively associated with 'parent–child dialogue' rather than *beaux arts* transmission of cultural capital.

The third way in which Figure 5.5 suggests that parents shape their children's educational progress is through their influence on what their children take for granted: norms which reflect the key relationships in which an individual's identity is embedded (habitus). These norms include life-course expectations (and the role of formal education in the fulfilment of those expectations), accepted forms of social behaviour and how these should vary between contexts, and self-regulation (Reay, 2015). Family members' employment and educational experience provide reference points for children's expectations (Pimlott-Wilson, 2011). Status attainment theory (Kerckhoff, 1976) offers a formal exposition of normalisation in relation to education and employment. According to this view, children will aim to achieve at least the same educational and employment status as their parents. Therefore, parents affect children's motivation to achieve at school through the reference points they provide. The process of familial normalisation has been detected through detailed qualitative research (e.g. Reay, 2004), but it is more difficult to establish in quantitative analysis. If habitus is treated as a mechanism distinct from cultural capital we should observe associations between attainment and each of parental expectations, parental education and parental occupation after taking account of cultural capital. Roksa and Potter (2011) reported a positive association between children's attainment and parental expectation that their child would graduate from higher education (after taking account of cultural capital). However, Sullivan (2001) found that that when she included a measure of cultural capital which included cultural knowledge and vocabulary associations became parental occupation and education and children's attainment at age 16 became non-significant.

Parents' capacity to directly support their child's education is also affected by their belief in their ability to provide this support and their concept of the role of a parent. Hoover-Dempsey and colleagues (Hoover-Dempsey & Sandler, 1997; Green et al., 2007) developed and exemplified a model of parent–child interaction in which parents' self-beliefs and concepts played critical roles.

Indirect effects of parents through peer groups

As described in Chapter 4, parents' demand for education is an important factor in determining the peer group with whom the child is educated. But the benefit a child gains from their peer group is shaped by their capacity to interact constructively with their peers. This capacity is developed in part through the way in which mothers and fathers interact and play with their children in their early years (Mac-Donald & Parke, 1984).

A learner's peers (the other students with whom the individual is educated) may affect their progress in several ways: providing role models; collaborating in learning, and affecting teachers' expectations and the effectiveness of teaching through the classroom learning environment (Barnes, 1976; Mouw, 2006; Calvó-Armengol et al., 2009). One private, not-for-profit university in the USA has established itself on the premise that learning entirely from peers is a sufficient basis for a commercial operation.[39] Empirical studies of the role of schools in pupils' attainment can incorporate peer effects as if they were a separately identifiable part of the school's production. The influence of peers on a child's attainment may be measured through the average and variance in peers' prior attainment (e.g. Feinstein & Symons, 1999;

Vandenberghe, 2002). Estimates by country show that the distribution of peer effects among the sectors affects the relative performance of private and public schools (Zimmer & Toma, 2000; Bertola & Checchi, 2013). Unsurprisingly, when private schools in a country attract a disproportionate number of children with high prior achievement they appear to be relatively more effective than in countries where private schools tend to attract students with lower levels of achievement whose parents are viewing private schools as a way of trying to catch up.

Therefore, the critical issue for a comparison of public and private schools is that models of private competition predict a strong segregation of children by ability (Adnett et al., 2002; Epple et al., 2004). This has substantive consequences for attainment and equity in the school system. Lower stratification within schools and more mobility between tracks is associated with higher average achievement (Gamoran, 1992; Buchmann & Park, 2009), while tracking between and within schools increases social inequality in achievement in Germany (Maaz et al., 2008). International comparisons also suggest that greater tracking between schools is associated with greater inequality by social class in early earnings (Brunello & Checchio, 2007). Critical responses (e.g. Grice, 2016) to Conservative government proposals to increase selection by ability in the English schools system (Riley-Smith, 2016) were based largely on this expectation.

The extent to which segregation in private markets is an argument for government supply depends on the process used by government to allocate children to schools. Governments usually rely on neighbourhood allocation such that children attend the school that is geographically nearest to where they live. Since poor and rich families tend to be concentrated in different neighbourhoods, allocation to school by neighbourhood is a powerful source of segregation. Burgess and Briggs (2010) estimated that, compared to children from non-poor families, children from poor families in England have half the chance of attending a 'good' school. Historical patterns in the distribution of housing are compounded by the willingness of some parents to pay a premium for a house that is close to a high-performing school (Black, 1999; Gibbons & Machin, 2008).

Governments have tried to combat this problem in different ways. Buses may be used (as endorsed by the US Supreme Court in 1971) to transport children to schools beyond their neighbourhood (Borman et al., 2004). Although racial segregation among schools in states such as Florida decreased in the 1980s, busing travelled along a one-way street: children from disadvantaged neighbourhoods were bused to schools in advantaged neighbourhoods (Shircliffe, 2002). Alternatively, children may be allocated to schools through a lottery. However, examples of a pure lottery are very rare. One local authority in England introduced a partial lottery allocation to schools in 2007 which, being partially constrained by catchment areas, did not lead to a more equitable distribution of children among schools (Allen et al., 2013). Finally, parents may be given limited freedom to choose between schools. Freedom of parental choice is limited by the capacity of schools to expand. Popular schools are, by definition, over-subscribed and must use some rules to determine which parents succeed with their choice and which parents fail. Proximity to the school typically features strongly in these rules and the scope for over-subscribed schools to use other selection criteria tends to leave the segregation problem broadly unchanged (Gorard *et al.*, 2002; West *et al.*, 2004). While we cannot judge from this evidence the extent to which state provision affects segregation between schools, we can see that governments find it very hard to sustain reductions in between school segregation.

Indirect effects of parents through educational institutions

Parents influence their child's education through interacting with their child about school or university and through interacting with educational institutions about their child's progress (Steinberg *et al.*, 1992; Izzo *et al.*, 1999; Gutman & McLloyd, 2000). However, Eccles and Harold (1993) found that both parents and schools reported that they wished parent–school engagement was more intense. How could this state of affairs arise? Schooling is largely conducted through the language of the managerial and professional (middle) classes and teachers are drawn predominantly from this social class background. Therefore, parents with the cultural capital and academic achievements that are prized by the school system have an advantage in their interactions with schools (Lee & Bowen, 2006). The role of shared values, expectations and beliefs between schools and parents has been widely cited as a reason for the success of faith schools where a large proportion of pupils have been drawn from a particular faith community (Coleman & Hoffer, 1987; Vella, 1999; Pugh *et al.*, 2006).

This has prompted proposals to change the outlook and practice of schools to address the unequal starting points for parents seeking to engage with schools to support their children. Some researchers have suggested that the problem with schools lies in what they believe about their capacity to make a difference. Hoy and colleagues (2006) have found a positive association between what they call 'academic optimism' (of schools and teachers) and the achievement of pupils, particularly those from disadvantaged backgrounds. Others have focused on schools' practices in engaging with parents. Epstein (2001) has suggested six ways in which schools could help parents support their child's learning (Sheldon, 2007, p. 268): (1) parenting: helping all families establish supportive home environments for children; (2) communicating: establishing two-way exchanges about school programmes and children's progress; (3) volunteering: recruiting and organising parent help at school, home or other locations; (4) learning at home: offering information and ideas to families about how to help students with homework and other curriculum-related materials; (5) decision making: having family members serve as representatives and leaders on school committees, and (6) collaborating with the community: identifying and integrating resources and services from the community to strengthen school programmes.

Efforts to implement this agenda have been channelled through movements for 'full-service' or 'extended' schools. These programmes have been high-cost and evaluators have claimed substantial benefits (Grossman *et al.*, 2002; Cummings *et al.*, 2007), while acknowledging that their evaluations have been commissioned before it was possible to reach firm judgements about these benefits. The scope of these schools (in terms of range of educational and social aims) and the variety of initiatives in which they have engaged has also made the task of evaluation very complex (Kalafat *et al.*, 2007). It is somewhat easier to identify relationships between practice and outcomes when the scope and methods of the intervention are more tightly defined. For example, Sheldon (2007) found a small difference between the attendance of children whose parents had attended a school–parent initiative based on Epstein's framework and children attending schools which had not participated in the scheme. Since attendance at school is positively associated with pupil per-formance, the association gives some grounds for believing that parents' engage-ment with school matters and that the behaviour of schools and parents can be changed.

Input from students

Students can affect their own educational outcomes through their levels of parti-cipation, engagement and learning strategy. This section examines each of these processes in turn. Engagement is treated largely as an outcome of alignment between students and formal education, participation as an interaction between structure and agency, and learning strategy as largely a reflection of learners' agency.

Students' engagement with education has often been related to the alignment among cultural norms, home background and the nature and conduct of schooling. This broad argument has taken several different forms according to the dimension of social life on which researchers have focused. A long-standing critique of 'common education' (e.g. Willis, 1977; Weis, 1990) is that it turns out to be heavily biased towards indigenous, middle-class students, leaving working-class and minority students marginalised and alienated. Critical race theorists (e.g. Ladson-Billings & Tate, 1995) and others have argued that endemic racism biases the education system against the interests of African-American students. Academic success in Catholic schools has been attributed (Coleman & Hoffer, 1987; Pugh *et al.*, 2006) to home–school alignment in social capital.

The relationship between participation and educational outcomes returns us to the debate regarding human capital, sorting and credentialism reviewed in Chapter 3. While human capital theory treats attendance as continuously and positively related to educational outcomes, sorting and credentialism assume that 'just being there' does not make any difference to an individual's readiness for paid work. Sorting and credentialism treat change in knowledge and understanding as out-comes of maturation: a pure development model in which individuals accumulate knowledge and expertise through physiological development and everyday experience.

However, it is the work of psychologists, rather than economists or sociologists, that has most to tell us about relationships between teaching and learning and, therefore, the consequences of 'being there'. Students do develop understanding on the basis of everyday experience and never arrive in formal education as 'blank sheets'. One line of argument (diSessa & Sherin, 1998) suggests that everyday experience develops a jumble of embryonic ideas which education can build on and develop into more integrated and powerful modes of thought. A contrasting argument (Vosniadou & Brewer, 1992) is that everyday experience builds up misconceptions that are powerfully framed as 'common sense' and which teaching has to challenge and refute before offering a more 'scientific' way of understanding the world. Both arguments portray teaching as changing knowledge and understanding, in which case being there matters. As exemplified by Clark and Linn (2003), limited study time reduces integration and understanding of complex ideas.

Students may spend more time in education through the number of years they spend studying or through the intensity of study in any given week. Since Chapters 2 and 3 examined the impact of the number of years spent in education, the focus here is on the intensity of study. Students in some parts of the world which have been identified as 'high-performing' spend many hours a day studying. School students in Shanghai have been reported (Tan, 2012) to study on average for 13 hours a day and to be assigned 13.8 hours of homework a week (compared with about six in the USA and Australia and about five in the UK: OECD, 2014c). There is also a firm positive association between undergraduates' self-reported hours of academic work and their subsequent achievement (Stanca, 2006; Davies et al., 2012).

But it is quite hard to isolate the effects of attendance on educational outcomes. A choice not to attend formal education is associated with other factors that may affect outcomes. It may reflect challenges in the home environment or peer relations that make learning more difficult. It may reflect a lack of engagement with studying or alienation from formal education. Therefore, isolating attendance effects requires control for students' circumstances and engagement. Only a few studies manage to get close to this ideal (Cooper et al., 2006). However, these studies (e.g. Gottfried, 2010) do suggest that more study time leads to higher grades, perhaps with a non-linear relationship. Studies of undergraduate attendance which manage to deal with the selection bias problem (e.g. Marburger, 2006; Newman-Ford et al., 2008) tell a similar story. Lengthening the school day seems to have a similar effect (Bellei, 2009). Effect sizes are small ($d = 0.1$ or below), but meaningful.

Students affect the outcomes of their education through the way in which they approach and conduct their studies. School students with higher self-efficacy and students who believe that 'knowledge is uncertain' achieve higher grades (Bandura et al., 1996, 2001; Stankov & Lee, 2014; Trautwein & Lüdtke, 2007). Undergraduate students who adopt a 'deep approach' to their learning achieve a higher grade point average than those who adopt a 'surface approach' to their learning (van Rossum & Schenk, 1984; Meyer et al., 1990).

While this evidence has important implications for the conduct of teaching it also has implications for the design of school systems. This is because of the relationships between students' efforts, attitudes and beliefs and their sense of identity as a learner. Psychologists (e.g. Bandura et al., 2001; Deci, Koestner & Ryan, 2001;

Presley *et al.*, 2010[40]) have paid close attention to the formation and role of self-concepts in directing students' efforts and choices in formal education. These theorists identify two related strands in goal-directed behaviour: a desire for competence and a desire for self-determination, each framed by social contexts.

The desire for competence has been investigated in the context of narrowly defined tasks (self-efficacy: what I can do) and broad domains (self-concept: the kind of person I am). The prediction of these theories is that higher self-efficacy and higher self-concept motivates resilience and effort. The theory of self-efficacy (Bandura *et al.*, 2001; Presley *et al.*, 2010) suggests that goals are formed on the basis of experience of success or failure in specific tasks and that an individual's sense of success is shaped by significant others (notably parents and teachers). Theories of self-concept (e.g. Marsh *et al.*, 2008b) suggest that goals are framed by students' success relative to their peer group. This gives rise to a so-called 'Big-Fish-Little-Pond' effect: a higher achieving young person will develop a stronger self-concept if they are educated with low-achieving peers than if they are educated with high-achieving peers. Both theories predict that working-class children will be discouraged from achievement goals favouring academic subjects. Given that higher cultural capital enables early achievement in school (Sullivan, 2001), middle-class children are likely to develop stronger self-efficacy and self-concept in relation to academic subjects.

Cognitive Evaluation Theory (Deci *et al.*, 2001) asserts that a drive for competence intertwines with a drive for self-determination. To some extent this theory may be read as combining the core elements of 'Rational Action Theory/Relative Risk Aversion' with 'Self-efficacy/Self-concept' theory. This combination of supposed causal mechanisms is frequently referred to in terms of students' aspirations (Ashby & Schoon, 2010): students form concepts of the kind of person they aspire to be and this concept interacts with their achievement in schools with important consequences for their goal-directed behaviour. This analysis aligns students' self-directed efforts in learning with the extent to which they believe that their school will help them fulfil their life ambitions.

School and university funding typically reflects student inputs that are regarded as structurally determined while ignoring pupil inputs which are believed to be under the control of the students themselves. Table 5.18 shows how the total funding received by primary schools in England is related to factors that are included in the government's formula for allocating funds to schools. A core-per-pupil allocation of approximately £3,000 (row 1) is supplemented by additional funds according to an assessment of resource needs for children from financially disadvantaged backgrounds (row 2), children with modest (row 3) or more substantial special needs (row 4) and children with English as a second language (row 5). Schools also received additional funds if they were located in London (row 6) or had opted out of local authority control (row 7). Schools that are aiming to equate income and expenditure will find ways to spend the total income they receive. Since the factors in Table 5.18 account for 95 per cent of the variance in total income, they will also account for nearly all of the variation in spending.

TABLE 5.18 Factors associated with total government grants received by primary school children in England (2014–2015)

	Government grants (total)	
	£	p
1 Pupils on roll (school size)	2,989	<0.001
2 Pupils eligible for free school meals (number)	4,168	<0.001
3 Pupils receiving support for special educational needs (number)	830	<0.001
4 Pupils with statement of SEN or EHC (number)	11,072	<0.001
5 Pupils with English as a second language (number)	886	<0.001
6 London school (= 1)	288,644	<0.001
7 Academy school (= 1)	62,460	<0.001
8 Constant	101,777	<0.001
n		10,697
R^2		0.95

Source: Department for Education school-level data for 2014/2015.

This kind of funding system explicitly assumes that the cost of education is inversely related to the input from pupils. The additional funding may be interpreted and used as compensatory finance, making good some initial deficit. Alternatively, it may be understood and used to build students' capacity to direct their own learning. Given the evidence (e.g. Hattie & Timperley, 2007) of the positive impact of teaching which explicitly aims to build capacity for learning, it is important to judge the use of resources in education in terms of how they change learners' capacities and not only how they change short- and medium-term outcomes.

Summary

If education were like any other good or service we could be confident that encouraging competition among schools and among universities would benefit parents and students. However, co-production means that the productivity of schools is partially shaped by the efforts of students and parents – and by students' and parents' capacities to direct their efforts effectively. This means that schools and universities have powerful incentives to enrol students whose efforts and capacities will boost the results achieved by the school or university. Moreover, parents have strong incentives to choose a school that they believe will be attended by other students who will provide a good learning environment for their children. Economic models which add co-production to otherwise make standard assumptions (e.g. Adnett *et al.*, 2002; Epple *et al.*, 2004) predict that schooling will act powerfully to segregate children by ability and social class.

Conclusion

So what do we know about the cost of providing education (in schools)? Table 5.19 summarises the evidence reviewed in this chapter. The items that are 'known' are hugely important for the allocation of resources to schooling, but they leave vast scope for disagreement about the quantity and types of resources schools need.

Even what we know presents some challenges for policy. Bigger schools cost less, but parents prefer small schools. Headline-grabbing changes in policy have frequently fallen into the third column. The evidence we have for these policies indicates that it all depends on how the resources are deployed. Spending more on information and communication technology can make a difference, but only if it is used in particular way. Moreover, the evidence on the items in this column suggest that changing the quantity and deployment of one resource only becomes effective when combined with a change in the quantity and/or deployment of another resource. The impact of ICT and teaching assistants is contingent upon teacher development that promotes effective interaction among different inputs to education.

Since home background and pupil effort and engagement are so strongly related to students' progress and outcomes, the interactions among school resources, parents and students are probably very important, but we do not know for sure at this point in time. What we can be sure of is that estimates of the effects of a change in the quantity of one resource are unlikely to be very accurate if they either (1) use a

TABLE 5.19 What do we know about the cost of providing education through schools?

Known	Fuzzy	Matter of judgement (great variation within category)
1 Teaching and teacher quality is the most important resource for schools	Students make better progress in smaller classes	Information and communications technology
2 Home background is very strongly related to progress as well as levels of attainment	Outcomes are greater when there is closer alignment between school and home values and beliefs about education	Teachers' pay
3 Student effort and learning strategies make a meaningful difference to outcomes	Schools can make a difference to students' capacity for learning	Teaching assistants
4 Bigger schools cost less per student (economies of scale are quite large)		Teacher development
5 Parents prefer smaller schools and smaller classes		The effects of school size and buildings on attainment

narrow definition of school outcomes; (2) ignore variation in inputs from pupils and parents, or (3) ignore interactions between inputs or outcomes.

This creates uncertainty about providing education, which is a major problem for policy. Who is most likely to have the best grasp of what is known and what is not? Who is likely to make the best use of the knowledge that is available to them? Governments? Schools and teachers? Parents? Given the limited knowledge we currently have, it is also important to know who is best placed to add to knowledge and who is best placed to disseminate knowledge to others. These questions are addressed in Chapter 6 where we relax assumptions about providers' knowledge and motivation.

Appendix 5.1 Analysis of school income and expenditure data

The dataset for the analysis of school income and expenditure in 2014/2015 was created by combining records from publicly available Department for Education datasets. Income and expenditure data are provided on separate data tables for local authority and academy schools. These data were combined with data tables and include fields for eligibility for free school meals, racial mix of pupils, pupils with special educational needs and school capacity. Data were matched using the unique reference number for each school. Data on eligibility for free school meals were missing for approximately 140 schools, but in most of these instances it was possible to locate these data on a school-by-school basis using Edubase. Just under 5 per cent of records included a negative figure for one or more fields of income or expenditure. These cases could indicate instances where a correction is being made to income following previous overpayment or where a source of revenue is being set against expenditure. Alternatively they could simply be errors that occurred during data collection or reproduction. Each of these 1,007 records was removed from the dataset, since they generated peculiar patterns (e.g. where subcategories of spending were more than 100 per cent of total spending). This left a total sample of 19,983 schools, of which 15,814 were primary schools, 2,945 were secondary schools and 1,224 were either special schools or pupil referral units.

Notes

1 This definition excludes 'multi-agency' provision (Edwards, 2005; Siraj-Blatchford *et al.*, 2007) which involves joint inputs from different professional services but excludes inputs from those who directly benefit.

2 The story tends to be very different for public/provate comparisons in OECD countries compared to similar comparisons in developing economies. Average spending per pupil in private schools in England is about twice as high as average spending per pupil in state schools (Davies & Davies, 2014). In contrast, Cox and Jimenez (1991) found that teachers' salaries in Colombia were twice as high in state schools as in private schools.

3 Hence the scepticism of Levin and McEwan (2001) towards the usefulness of cost judgements based on meta-analyses of educational outcomes.

4 The technical guidance on costs provided by Higgins *et al.* (2013) makes no explicit mention of imputing a cost for activity switching or additional workload. A report on

the Durham Shared Maths project in July 2015 referred to a calculation of imputed teachers' time but did not state the rate. Likewise, a report on Project-based Learning in November 2016 referred to an imputation of cost of teacher time but showed no calculations. A report on the Oracy Curriculum, Culture and Assessment Toolkit (June 2015) is opaque regarding whether its cost items were fee only or included the cost of teachers' activity switching and additional workload. A report on ReflectED (November 2016) made no mention of imputed cost for teacher time. A report Shine on Saturday teaching (June 2015) assumed that there were no related coordination costs for the school.

5 Their evaluation reports the effects of the intervention on the students who received the input from the teaching assistants.

6 Four of the RCTs testing feedback which have been funded by the Education Endowment Foundation in England have this design. See a study of a maths intervention (https://educationendowmentfoundation.org.uk/public/files/Projects/Evaluation_ Protocols/EEF_Project_Protocol_ICCAMS_University_of_Manchester_March_2016. pdf); a study of a formative assessment intervention (https://educationendowment foundation.org.uk/public/files/Projects/Evaluation_Protocols/EEF_Project_Protocol_ EmbeddingFormativeAssessment.pdf); a study of self-regulation (https://education endowmentfoundation.org.uk/public/files/Projects/Evaluation_Protocols/EEF_ Project_Protocol_Calderdale_effectiveness_protocol.pdf), and a study of digital feedback in maths (https://educationendowmentfoundation.org.uk/our-work/projects/digital-feedback-in-primary-maths/). In contrast, the final project related to feedback funded by the EEF is a multi-arm trial which compares different ways of communicating research findings to teachers (https://educationendowmentfoundation.org.uk/public/files/Projects/ Evaluation_Protocols/EEF_Project_Protocol_TheLiteracyOctopusActiveTrial.pdf).

7 Data from the US Department of Education retrieved from https://nces.ed.gov/ programs/digest/d12/tables/dt12_098.asp.

8 See a publication from the Department for Education (2002), *Assessing the Net Capacity of Schools. DfES/0739/2001REV.* London, Department for Education and Skills.

9 The standard deviations for this variable are low and the distributions are heavily skewed towards zero. For secondary schools the standard deviation was only 1.3 percentage points. Thus the large coefficients on this variable must be interpreted with this small variation in mind.

10 Foreman-Peck and Foreman-Peck (2008) use achievement at age 14 as their control for prior achievement, although they are estimating the effects of the size of schools for pupils 11 to 16 or 11 to 18.

11 Notwithstanding the p score on the quadratic term in equation [1], the coefficients for equation [1] could be used to calculate an 'optimal school size for pupil attainment' figure: this quadratic would be $0.41P/100-0.0008P^2/100$ which when differentiated gives $0.41P/100-0.00016P/100$ and set to zero to find the maximum solves for $P\star = 0.41/0.00016$. This gives an optimal school size of 2,563 which is clearly very large and not reliable because we have no schools of this size, so it is an 'out of sample' estimate (I am grateful to Marco Ercolani for this suggestion).

12 Virtually all 11 to 16 schools were comprehensive in their intake, although a substantial minority of 11 to 18 schools were selective. We may expect selective schools to have lower costs because they do not have to cater for such a large range of pupils. Although a simple t-test comparing costs per pupil was lower in selective schools, a dummy variable for selective schools was not significant in the multivariate analysis.

13 The existence of transaction costs has long been held by institutional economics as the *raison d'être* for organising production in firms (Coase, 1937).

14 Controlling for whether a school is: in London; a faith school; single or mixed sex; total pupils on roll; total pupils on roll squared; percentage of capacity used; percentage of pupils achieving five or more grades A$\star$ to C at GCSE; percentage of pupils eligible for free school meals; percentage of pupils who are White British; percentage of pupils with English as a second language; percentage of pupils with a statement for SEN, and percentage of pupils receiving support for SEN.

15 The evidence publicised by the government-financed Education Endowment Fund suggests that teaching assistants are relatively expensive and have little impact upon achievement (https://educationendowmentfoundation.org.uk/resources/teaching-learning-toolkit).

16 See Hill *et al.* (2012) and Chapman (2015) for detailed descriptions of policy and practice in academy school chains in England.

17 Bauman (2001).

18 Using an OLS regression with spending per pupil as the dependent variable and controlling for: whether the school was a London school, a faith school, a single sex school, a selective school; GCSE results (percentage achieving five grades A* to C, including English and mathematics); percentage of pupils eligible for free school meals; percentage of children of White European ethnic background; percentage of pupils for whom English is a second language; percentage of statemented SEN pupils, and percentage of pupils receiving some support for SEN.

19 Judged by a simple t-test.

20 This is the case even without adjusting for the fact that private schools tend to cater for a wider age range.

21 Figures calculated from the tables provided by the Department for Education for 2014 to 2015 (January 2015) with the sample restricted to schools attended by 11-year-olds and 16-year-olds.

22 Although the 'crowding-out' hypothesis is challenged by evidence that public spending on infrastructure benefits the private sector (referred to as 'crowding in'), see e.g. Argimon *et al.* (1997).

23 Data from the OECD publication *Education at a Glance 2016*, Paris, OECD.

24 The references are to studies of PFI initiatives in schooling in Australia, Ireland and Portugal.

25 For example, in 2012, the *New York Times* ran a feature entitled 'Building a showcase campus, using an I.O.U.' (www.nytimes.com/2012/12/14/business/colleges-debt-falls-on-students-after-construction-binges.html?pagewanted=all&_r=0). On 28 April 2016, The Financial Times ran a feature headlined 'UCL to borrow record £280 million to expand' (www.ft.com/content/ee759cbe-0c6f-11e6-b0f1-61f222853ff3).

26 Between 1984 and 2014.

27 Data for private schools affiliated to the Independent School Council which accounts for the majority of private schools. Private schools not affiliated to the ISC tend to be relatively small and more recently established. The ISC provides data on its members through an annual census.

28 Data from Department for Education statistical releases on schools, teachers and pupils.

29 Data accessed 18 September, 2017 from the Australian Bureau of Statistics, Schools, Australia, 2016 (www.abs.gov.au/AUSSTATS/abs@.nsf/DetailsPage/4221.02016?OpenDocument).

30 For males but not for females.

31 Often referred to as 'pedagogical content knowledge' after Shulman (1987).

32 By using 'percentage of recruits with degree classifications first or upper second' as a criterion to judge the quality of provider of initial teacher education. These judgements affect subsequent allocation of government grants to providers.

33 Data for teachers' pay drawn directly from Department for Education statistics on the School Workforce. These statistics did not contain information on the pay of teaching assistants. Average teaching assistant pay was estimated from the data provided by the Department for Education on school income and expenditure. These data include a figure for school expenditure on 'educational support'. Since this figure includes spending on staff who were not teaching assistants we cannot simply divide it by the number of teaching assistants. Therefore, regression was used to identify the average association between the employment of one FTE additional teaching assistant and school spending on educational support. Comparison with other sources (suggested as averages of advertised pay) suggests that this figure is a realistic estimate.

34 It is difficult to compare trends in the state and private sectors due to accessibility of data on the latter. Davies and Davies (2014) reported that, in 2008, the ratio of non-teaching to teaching staff in the sample of private schools they studied was 0.63. However, 'non-teaching staff' in private schools include staff members who were not teaching assistants, so this figure is not directly comparable with the data in Figure 5.3. The ratio of non-teaching staff to teachers in England in 2014/2015 was 1.25 in state primary schools and 0.79 in state secondary schools.

35 For example, the Higher Education Statistics Agency only began distinguishing between 'teaching-only' and 'teaching and research' contracts in 2003 and its reporting of higher education teaching staff does not include graduate teaching assistants.

36 Brown and colleagues (2010) interpret evidence from Australia as revealing a growing 'casualisation' of the teaching workforce in higher education which includes the increasing use of part-time contracts and graduate teaching assistants. Between 1975 and 2011 the percentage of US HE faculty members on part-time contracts increased from 30 to 51 per cent. Evidence from the USA suggests a stronger tendency towards the use of part-time contracts in community colleges and other teaching-intensive institutions and a stronger tendency towards the use of graduate teaching assistants in research universities. Kirshstein (2015) claimed that by 2013, 48 per cent of instruction in research universities in the USA was carried out either by part-time staff or by graduate teaching assistants, although the US Bureau of Labor Statistics reported in 2015 that graduate teaching assistants accounted for 4 per cent of the total workforce in US colleges, universities and professional schools. In the UK, academic staff under the age of 25 are largely employed on part-time contracts and there has been a slight shift towards part-time employment over the past decade (Universities UK, 2015b). The proportion of academics on teaching-only contracts in UK HEIs also rose from about 20 to 25 per cent in the decade after 2003. An indication of casualisation in the UK was also provided by one-third of postgraduate students (who were employed as graduate teaching assistants) who indicated through survey responses that they had no contract (NUS, 2013).

37 Given that average teacher pay was approximately double the average teaching assistant pay.

38 The Teaching and Learning Toolkit provided for schools in England by the government-funded Education Endowment Fund aims to promote 'evidence-based practice' by summarising research evidence and making it accessible to schools and teachers (https://educationendowmentfoundation.org.uk/resources/teaching-learning-toolkit).

39 A university, named '42' and located in California, dedicated to the development of workers in the IT industry, was established by a French billionaire (www.42.us.org/).

40 Bandura coined the term 'self-efficacy' to refer to the effect of success in particular tasks on future readiness to attempt similar tasks. Deci and Ryan developed a 'Cognitive Evaluation Theory' which predicts that goals will be directed by the combination of a desire for competence and a desire for self-determination. Ajzen's (1991) Theory of Planned Behaviour suggests that intentions to behave in particular ways can be predicted by attitudes, subjective norms and perceived behavioural control.

6

SUPPLYING EDUCATION

Choosing a system

Introduction

This chapter changes the focus from the choices faced by an individual provider of education to the implications of providing (supplying) education through one system or another. Since we spend so much on education, the question is: 'Which provider system will deliver the best value?' The chapter follows Chapter 4 in distinguishing between three types of system: markets, hierarchies and networks. That chapter concentrated on judging systems in terms of implications of how demand is identified: for total public welfare and the distribution of benefits between individuals and groups. This chapter concentrates on judging systems in terms of the supply of education: Do they coordinate providers in a way that leads to efficient provision of education? The analysis is organised in terms of three coordination mechanisms highlighted by Hirschman (1970): exit, voice and loyalty.

Each system coordinates providers by creating and distributing knowledge about what to provide and how to provide it. Markets do this through prices (exit). Hierarchies do this through bureaucracies which gather information for chains of command (voice). Networks do this through establishing normalised patterns of behaviour and by sharing experience within the network (loyalty). That is, we may think of knowledge as embedded in a system of supply as well as knowledge being held by individual providers. But the coordination provided by each system also depends on the ways in which providers are motivated to act upon the knowledge they have. Markets reward self-interest. Hierarchies reward subservience and 'following the book'. Networks reward loyalty to the interests of the group. It is not self-evident that any of these systems encourages motivation which is unambiguously in the public interest. Following the analysis in Chapter 5, we can judge the advantages and disadvantages of any system on the basis of how it will cope with the incomplete information and uncertainty that will affect any way of providing education. The chapter divides these knowledge problems into two: 'using know-ledge' and 'having, creating and disseminating knowledge'. The first problem focuses on what we should assume about providers' motivation and the ways in which this motivation is directed and altered by the system. The second problem focuses on the way in which the system encourages providers to improve what they do through learning from their experience and the experience of others.

Different disciplines in social science have developed modes of analysis that con-centrate on one mechanism (voice, exit or loyalty) with the consequence that other mechanisms, and systems that prioritise other mechanisms, appear inherently suspect. Economists have frequently portrayed government hierarchies and profes-sional networks as threats to markets offering the best hope for efficiency and equity. Sociologists have portrayed markets and hierarchies as threats to professional networks that will naturally serve the public interest. As indicated in the Introduc-tion, this book tries to set out the rationale for, and limitations of, competing ways of understanding systems for providing education. In practice, education, like most other services, is provided through a combination of markets, hierarchies and net-works. Changes in policy in OECD countries alter the combination of governance through markets, hierarchies or networks; they do not shift governance entirely from one system to another.

Therefore, the main purpose of this chapter is to identify the strengths and weaknesses of each system as a prelude to the closer examination of particular policy combinations in Chapter 7. First, it examines ways in which each system addresses the challenge of how providers use what they know. Next, it considers the ways in which each system deals with the second knowledge problem: having/creating/disseminating knowledge. Although both of these sections refer to the provision of education, they concentrate on arguments that are pertinent to the provision of any good or service. The fourth section considers arguments that education is different from other goods and services. This section also examines how these arguments affect the way in which general characteristics of markets, hierarchies and networks bear upon the provision of education. The chapter ends with a short summary which prepares the ground for Chapter 7.

Using knowledge

What will providers do with the knowledge they have? One way of looking at this problem treats 'having information' as the same as 'knowing'. This is the approach of mainstream economics which is consistent with the 'information-processing' view of learning. The principal concern is that one of two parties to a transaction may have better information than the other: there is assymetric information. If we assume that all individuals seek to maximise their personal benefit, then whenever someone has an information advantage they will use it to benefit themselves at the expense of others. Alternatively, if we assume that an individual is motivated by 'public service', they will use their information advantage to benefit others (Crewson, 1997; Francois, 2000). Another way of looking at the knowledge/

information problem is to say that individuals have to interpret any information they possess and this interpretation will be based on their pre-existing way of understanding the world (Vosniadou, 2013). Two people may see quite different things in the same information if they interpret that information through different frames of reference. This is the perspective taken by theories of learning that are commonly described as 'constructivist'. According to this view, data do not speak for themselves. This perspective invites us to consider the likelihood that any system for supplying education will encourage individuals to interpret information through a more sophisticated frame of reference. How might each system encourage reappraisal of ways of interpreting information? A third perspective treats knowledge as a social rather than as an individual entity. Individuals come to know things as they participate in the activities and shared assumptions of particular groups or communities. Thus the 'using knowledge' problem takes on a different complexion depending on which of these three perspectives is taken. The first (information-processing) perspective is optimistic about the impact of new information upon an individual's knowledge. The second and third perspectives are sceptical about the likelihood that information will make much difference to what a person believes they know. The exposition in this section tries to highlight the perspective on knowledge and learning that is most usually taken for granted in analyses of the 'using knowledge' problem in markets, hierarchies and networks.

Using knowledge: private sector supply through markets

Analysis of markets usually defines the 'using knowledge' problem in terms of assymetric information. This problem comes in two forms: what providers do with knowledge they have about benefits that their consumers are unaware of or have no interest in, and what managers and front-line workers do with knowledge they possess but which the owners of the business do not. The second is commonly referred to as the 'Principal–Agent problem' (Davies et al., 2005; Wohlstetter et al., 2008).

The first problem in private supply is what providers will do with any knowledge they have about benefits to education that do not accrue to the households of the individuals they educate. According to the theory of 'for-profit' supply, providers have *no* intrinsic interest in what is being produced. Yet they will be constrained to provide what consumers want at the least possible cost by the threat of competition. Any provider in a free market that ignores information they could use to improve what they provide will lose out to other providers. Therefore, the main concern for public welfare lies in the existence of viable competitors. As long as a provider's position is contestable (Baumol et al., 1982) we should expect them to use information in the public interest. But this threat also provides an incentive for private providers to secure some room for manoeuvre by protecting themselves from competition. This may be achieved either by making their position more dominant in a market or by seeking to create their own market. Dominance may be achieved by taking over or colluding with other providers. The internationalisation of higher education appears to make this prospect unrealistic for universities.

However, universities operate simultaneously in many markets. Even in a crowded and competitive market such as undergraduate education in the UK, one research-intensive university often offers the only option for undergraduates who want to live at home while attending a research-intensive university (Mangan *et al.*, 2010a). Local school chains or federations (Arreman & Holm, 2011; Chapman, 2015), especially where these include several secondary schools and their 'feeder' primary schools, may also achieve a sufficiently dominant position to achieve substantial freedom from local competition.

For-profit organisations will also be expected to ignore any information about the benefits of education of which individuals are unaware, or about which they do not care. Whatever satisfies consumers will be good for providers and free markets will not provide incentives for producers to worry whether consumers know what is best for them or whether consumers make well-informed choices. They will therefore disregard externalities. Not-for-profit providers, however, will take account of these benefits insofar as they fall within the scope of the organisation's mission. A 'not-for-profit' charity has a mission to provide a particular kind of service which the founders and supporters of the charity believe is intrinsically valuable. Once we allow for households to have limited knowledge of school and university quality we also open the door to institutional branding which enables a provider to attract students at a cost that is lower than the cost which would be necessary to attract students through quality improvements (Wæraas & Solbakk, 2009; DiMartino & Jessen, 2016). The appearance of quality may be easier and less expensive than quality itself.

As discussed in Chapter 4, a government may try to overcome knowledge problems in market supply by stepping in to demand the service on behalf of households. The argument here is that a government can act on behalf of all of its citizens, taking account of benefits that do not accrue to those who are receiving the education. A government may also claim to have better knowledge than households regarding the quality which each provider offers. However, the government will want to tie the provider down through a contract that fully specifies what the government expects. The problem is that detailed contracts are expensive to prepare and they still cannot foresee all eventualities; nor can they specify outcomes in complete detail. This leaves the private supplier with a certain amount of 'wriggle room'. What can we expect them to do with this freedom? Market analysis anticipates that for-profit organisations will exploit this freedom to advantage themselves. This is known as 'quality shading': cutting corners to reduce costs. Not-for-profit organisations will be less prone to quality shading insofar as quality of service falls within their mission (Hart *et al.*, 1997; Ben-Ner, 2002; Dollery & Wallis, 2003). Nonetheless, a not-for-profit provider that has been established to serve the needs of a particular community within a broader society will only be expected to pay attention to benefits which accrue to that particular community.

Organisation leaders also face information problems through the separation of owners (or principals) from front-line staff (or agents). The principals may not know exactly how agents are using their time. Since agents are assumed to be rational and self-interested they are expected to exploit any opportunity they get to pursue their own interests rather than those of the organisation they are working for or the people whose needs they are meeting (Levačić, 2009).[1] The standard exposition[2] of this idea assumes that principals and agents *do* know perfectly well how best to provide a service. The problem lies in the willingness of staff to do what they should and, from this perspective, unionisation of front-line staff is regarded as necessarily against the public interest (Hoxby, 1996).

However, this view of the relationship between school leaders and front-line staff treats the question of trust in an organisation as unidirectional: it ignores the extent to which agents can trust principals (McCauley & Kuhnert, 1992).[3] Incomplete contracts may benefit the employer more than the employee. Given the power relationship between employers and employees, incomplete information may offer more scope for principals to demand additional duties from agents than it offers agents opportunities to avoid duties that are not specified in the contract. To overcome the assymetric information problem, we may expect owners to (1) prepare contracts for teachers which define teachers' duties in a relatively detailed way so that they can be held to account; (2) monitor teachers' behaviour through classroom observation and students' achievements, and (3) provide incentives (such as performance-related pay) to encourage teachers to stick to 'effective methods' and to work hard while doing so.

Using knowledge: public sector supply through a hierarchy

Public sector hierarchies face the same use of knowledge problems as markets. This section first considers providers' use of knowledge about the benefits of education before turning to the principal–agent problem. In both cases, much turns on whether we regard public sector workers as completely self-interested (as is assumed in mainstream economic analysis of markets). The alternative is to regard public sector workers as people who take account of public welfare as a result of their 'public service motivation' (Crewson, 1997; Francois, 2000). However, predictions of public sector behaviour also depend on whether we treat knowledge as the same as having information (as in analysis of assymetric information). This has particular resonance in analysis of government behaviour, since governments usually have access to far more information than they can handle and because political decision making often appears to highlight the way in which interpretations of data are framed by prior concepts.

Public sector decision making is often viewed as taking account of broad public interest rather than the immediate self-interest of the decision maker. There is a long history of economic analysis of externalities, public goods and equity (e.g. Pigou, 1920; Samuelson, 1954) which sets out how governments should behave. Governments employ plenty of skilled analysts to advise them on how to interpret their data in the light of these arguments and they occasionally commission expert reports (e.g. Elton, 1989; Dearing, 1997; Browne, 2010) which are intended to supplement the advice of civil servants. We may, of course, wonder about the extent to which governments create contexts which make it likely that they will hear advice that is music to their ears. They can, and sometimes do, ignore advice they don't like. Politicians who have formed a view that public administrators are a barrier to their sense of mission may also credit themselves with a uniquely true perception of what a nation needs.[4]

But politicians are often quite complex characters trying to speak simultaneously to mutually exclusive constituencies. In 2012 the UK Minister for Education (Gove, 2012) declared that "governments are notoriously flat-footed when it comes to anticipating and facilitating technical change". In the same speech he also declared: "I've been lucky enough to see first hand in Singapore how brilliant lessons can be delivered through a mixture of on-line and teacher-led instruction." Two years earlier (DfE, 2010) he had announced a long-term plan for government funding of systematic research into teaching interventions that would raise children's attainment. Following in the footsteps of some previous Secretaries of State for Education, Mr Gove found that commitment to small government and reducing bureaucracy should not be allowed to translate into a lower public profile for the minister. While globalisation has diminished the scope of some government ministries, the post of Minister for Education offers a brief in which a politician can pursue a career-enhancing programme of vigorous action and public profile (Wolf, 2001; Clarke, 2004). This does not mean that they do not have a genuine personal sense of mission. It does mean that others may find it difficult to read it that way.

When decisions about what kind of education to provide are devolved to schools within a hierarchy, we face the question of whether centrally gathered information about educational benefits for public welfare is shared and whether schools will interpret the information in the same way. One problem may be that governments are prone to *not* sharing the rationale for advice to schools. The promotion of Citizenship Education in English schools is a case in point. Curriculum guidance, resources and training were provided to schools at government expense. Schools were free to interpret and respond to this advice as seemed best to them. The government did little to enable schools to review the arguments for devoting time and effort to Citizenship Education. Reflecting on his initiative when Minister for Education, David Blunkett (2014) later wrote:

> Above all, as the evidence from National Foundation for Educational Research (NFER) and elsewhere shows, we did not collectively reach head teachers and persuade them that engaging young people in this way improved their wider engagement and yes, their attainment levels in other mainstream subjects.

When responsibility for taking account of social benefit is devolved to schools the outcome depends on teachers' frame of reference: What do they think that schooling is for? Traditionally this question has been answered by (1) recruiting individuals who have a strong predisposition towards 'the public good', and (2) enculturating them into a set of professional values which will frame new teachers' concept of the public good and their role in promoting it (Hoyle, 1982; Matthews, 1991). Even in England, where the context for initial teacher education has been described as threatening teaching as a profession, schools as well as universities have remained focused on recruiting individuals who are committed to the public good (Davies *et al.*, 2016).

If we could assume that every teacher, lecturer and organisational leader in education was motivated by public service, the assymetric information problem would be substantially diminished: we would only have to worry that teachers' views about public welfare may be clouded by misconceptions. Any suggestion that public sector employees can be trusted to act in the public interest is explicitly rejected by the 'public choice critique'. The critical idea was expressed by Tullock *et al.* (2002, p. 55): "Government bureaucrats are, in this respect, much like private-sector executives in that they will attempt to maximise the well-being of their employer, the state, only if it pays off for them." This assumption leads to some strong, negative predictions about public sector supply when public sector employees: (1) are necessarily employed on 'incomplete contracts' because the complexity of the work makes it impossible to pre-specify responsibilities in fine detail; (2) gain no direct personal benefit from reducing costs, and (3) are protected from competition by a state monopoly. Without competition and autonomy there is insufficient incentive to control costs, leading to a waste of resources through 'X-inefficiency' (Haskel & Sanchis, 1995). Moreover, middle managers will benefit from increases in public expenditure which expand the scope of their professional responsibility and status (Schwartz, 1994) with the consequence that public spending on inputs will bear little relation to the quality of outputs (Hoxby, 1996; Hanushek, 2003). Finally, public supply will become cautious and rule-laden as promotion depends more on being a 'safe pair of hands' than being an innovative risk-taker (Buchanan & Tullock, 1962; Chubb & Moe, 1990).

The public choice critique has had a powerful effect on policy-makers' perceptions of what they must do to avoid schools and teachers exploiting assymetric information. On the one hand they have strengthened top-down, hierarchical information control. On the other hand they have offered schools more autonomy and relied on market competition to control the use that schools and teachers make of what they know. It is not obvious why simultaneous use of both policy mechanisms makes sense. Yet both were combined under the banner of 'new public management' (NPM) (Gruening, 2001; Bach & Kessler, 2011) or, in the language of critics, 'the curse of performativity' (Ball, 2003b; Lingard, 2010).

The 'tighter hierarchical control' arm of NPM has been pursued in education through monitoring the outcomes of education *and* by monitoring the process of education. In principle, either one of these should remove the need for the other. Doubling up the scrutiny betrays a lack of confidence in either approach.

The outcomes of educational institutions may be monitored either by exit credentials (exam results) or by the subsequent trajectories of students once they have completed their time at that institution. Since universities award their own degrees, any comparison of outcomes by degree levels or 'grade point averages' requires a heroic assumption about equivalence among institutions. Outcomes of higher education may also be judged by graduates' subsequent status in the labour market: by employment, status of employment or pay. There are two main problems. First, we know that students do not judge the benefits they expect from higher education purely in terms of future employment and certainly not simply in terms of higher pay (Davies *et al.*, 2013). We also know that graduates display a range of characteristics that are commonly regarded as serving the public interest (see Chapter 3). Second, given the need to take account of variation in graduate income by subject study, sample size problems make it difficult to identify meaningful differences in labour market outcomes by individual institutions (Davies, 2012).

Thus monitoring educational outcomes has focused on the school sector in Australia (Rowe, 2000), England (Allen & Burgess, 2013) and the USA (Eisner, 2001). Wherever state involvement in education is justified by human capital theory, absolute achievement (measured by examination grades) is not enough. It is important to know whether schools and teachers have improved students' capacities (Ladd & Walsh, 2002). Measures of raw achievement and decontextualised value-added measures have been criticised for attributing variation in students' achievement to schools which simply reflect students' prior achievement and factors beyond the school that affect students' progress (Goldstein & Spiegelhalter, 1996; Wiggins & Tymms, 2002; Leckie & Goldstein, 2011). But contextualised measures of students' achievement have also been criticised for failing to distinguish among schools and for attributing school effects to non-school factors (Wilson & Piebalga, 2008).[5]

The problems with outcome-based measures encourage reliance on measures of adherence to 'best practice'. As observed in Chapter 5, claims to know what constitutes 'best practice' at any level of education are undermined by our current state of knowledge. While there is plenty that we *can* claim to know, the visible scope of our ignorance seems greater. It is therefore unsurprising to find instances where national inspection systems have strongly promoted practices that have been subsequently shown to run counter to evidence. For example, OfSTED inspectors in England went through periods when they encouraged schools to pay close attention to children's learning styles[6] and awarded better grades to schools with more computers (Hurd *et al*, 2005). Limitations in current knowledge also mean that problems with holistic professional judgements from trained inspectors cannot be overcome by detailed observation schedules (de Wolf & Janssens, 2007). A newly appointed Chief Inspector of Schools in England summed up the problem with the phrase, "the illusion of objectivity is death by tick box" (quoted in Baxter & Clarke, 2013, p. 703). In addition to these problems with the validity of judgements on educational process there are also some challenges with reliability. The reliability of inspectors' judgements is put at risk when there is a difference between what schools do before and during an inspection (Ouston *et al.*, 1997). When schools have substantial advance notice of an inspection they can prepare a 'good show'. When they do not have notice the additional stress may impair teachers' performance. More generally, treating teachers as entirely selfish and devious workers in need of careful monitoring may turn them from 'knights' into 'knaves' (Broadbent *et al.*, 1996; Levačić, 2009). A Benthamite/Foucauldian/Orwellian option would be to observe teachers continually through video technology – an option which is now technically feasible. Alternatively, the unannounced entry of observers may be deemed a sufficient threat. Nonetheless, there is evidence to inspire some confidence in the reliability of national inspection systems (Matthews *et al.*, 1998; Hussain, 2012).[7]

The 'market incentives arm' of NPM has relied on parent and student choice to put pressure on suppliers of education to use their information to benefit learners. Policy changes in Australia, England, New Zealand and the USA during the 1980s and 1990s (Whitty & Edwards, 1998; Adnett & Davies, 2002) increased opportunities for parents to choose a school outside their local area. Since this system maintained a 'no fees' policy, schools could only affect their popularity through the quality of the achievements and experiences of their pupils. Perhaps the greatest challenge for this system lies in the scope schools have for improving their performance by enrolling pupils with higher prior achievement and greater likelihood of making strong progress. If parents believe that their children have much to gain from being educated with more able peers then the system will encourage 'cream-skimming': deepening stratification among schools (Adnett *et al.*, 2002; Epple *et al.*, 2004).

Measurements of the relationship of competition between schools to pupil achievement have to find a way to gauge the strength of competition among schools. The neoclassical theory of the firm predicts that competition will be positively associated with the number of firms in the market and this provides a rationale for measuring competition through the number of schools within easy access for parents. Some studies have used the Herfindahl or Herfindahl-Hirschman Index (HHI) (Rhoades, 1993) to measure the strength of competition in line with this theoretical perspective. This index is calculated by summing the squares of the market shares of the firms in the market: it takes account of the relative size as well as the number of firms. US studies reviewed by Belfield and Levin (2002) indicated no substantive association between the HHI and school-level achievement. It should be noted, however, that the HHI has been criticised on the grounds that it does not sufficiently reflect observable competitive behaviour in other industries (Matsumoto *et al.*, 2012). UK studies (e.g. Bradley *et al.*, 2001; Gibbons *et al.*, 2008) have tended to use a simpler measure: the number of alternative schools within a given radius of a school. The choice of radius reflects a judgement about how far parents are willing for their children to travel to school. These studies have either found no association or a weak, positive association between the number of local schools and pupil achievement. Gibbons and colleagues (2008) found that after endogeneity issues were accounted for there was no association. This conclusion is in line with a subsequent review of studies undertaken for the OECD (Waslander *et al.*, 2010). One study with a contrasting message (Bradley & Taylor, 2002) used the past performance of local schools as its measure of competition. They regressed change in secondary school performance in England between 1993 and 1999 on the change in exam performance of other schools in the district between 1992 and

1998. They found a strong positive association after controlling for intake characteristics and inferred a causal effect from quasi-markets to school performance. The problem with this result lies in the general rise over time in pupil achievement. Between 1992 and 1995 alone the percentage of 16-year-old pupils achieving five GCSE examination grades at A★ to C rose from 38 to 43 per cent (Coe, 1999).

Some underlying challenges with defining local school markets have made it difficult for researchers to identify whether or not there is a meaningful association between competition and pupil achievement in schools. First, the intensity of competition may be affected by stratification in the local market. Suppose there are three schools in a local market. If each of these schools offers a similar type of schooling to a similar group of households there is good reason to expect them to compete with each other for enrolments. However, suppose one school has a long record of high (absolute) pupil achievement and attracts a very large proportion of pupils from high socio-economic status households, whereas another has a long record of low (absolute) pupil achievement and attracts a very high proportion of pupils from low socio-economic status households. In this case schools have evolved to serve different constituencies within the local market and the scope for competition is less. Second, the school effect on pupil achievement is more strongly associated with variations among teachers than with variations among schools (Nye *et al.*, 2004; Slater *et al.*, 2012). Therefore, the scope for competition effects on pupil achievement lies chiefly in competition among schools to recruit talented teachers and competition within schools to encourage teachers to make best use of what they know (Adnett & Davies, 2005; Davies *et al.*, 2009c). Third, local school markets are essentially oligopolistic in nature: there are relatively few players and the consequences for any school of its own actions depend on how other schools will react (Davies *et al.*, 2002). Competition in a local market will be greater if one school is willing to act as a 'first-mover', regardless of the actual number of schools in the local area. A study of secondary schools in England (Levačić, 2004) reported a very weak (0.2) correlation between the number of schools in a local area and headteachers' perception[8] of the intensity of competition. The number of other schools that schools believe they are competing with may matter more than the actual number of schools in a local area. Using PISA data for Italy for 2006, Agasisti and Murtinu (2012) found a modest, positive association between schools' self-reported number of competitors and school performance.

Using knowledge: networks

Analysis of 'use of knowledge' in networks of workers is typically quite different from the analysis used in the previous two sections examining the use of knowledge in markets and hierarchies. Critically, knowledge emerges from practice rather than the other way round. Analyses of networks emphasise tacit knowledge arising from adjustments workers make when doing the job (Lam, 2000). Tacit knowledge may subsequently become 'reified' through articulation in formal documents or taken-for-granted ways of describing and judging practice. If actions precede knowledge there can be no question of workers *choosing* to use their knowledge to act in the interest of others or themselves. Analysis of networks also typically assumes that practice and knowledge are socially constructed and exist as social rather than as individual properties (Emirbayer & Goodwin, 1994). Moreover, workers are intrinsically motivated by job satisfaction and the extent to which the workplace provides space for 'belonging and becoming'. Thus the broad equivalent of the 'principal–agent' problem in a network system is when workers use taken-for-granted knowledge that conflicts with the available knowledge about the best way of providing education. A judgement about whether workers' knowledge serves the public interest rests on an account of how practice has developed. Is it steadily evolving as workers discover ways of improving their efficiency and responding to public needs or is it enmeshed in workplace traditions?

The answer to this question depends on how the collective agency of workers and organisations interacts with the contexts for their work. These contexts have been defined in terms of: (1) the immediate physical and social constraints in which they are working; (2) the positioning of their work in a broad social and economic context; (3) the history of that workplace and the way this has shaped conventions, and (4) the prior experience and cultural norms of the workers. The 'communities of practice' literature (e.g. Wenger, 1998; Cobb & McClain, 2010) tends to focus on the first of these strands, while the 'cultural and historical activity theory' literature (e.g. Engeström, 2001) emphasises the final three. Doubts about the use of knowledge in networks centre on what we may call the 'insider/outsider problem'. The rationale for a network means that it includes some people and organisations while excluding others. If we look exclusively at the outcomes for those inside the network it may look good,[9] but if we look exclusively at the outcomes for those outside the network it often looks bad. Worker networks in the form of trade unions have been criticised for promoting restrictive practices that resist opportunities to increase productivity in order to protect job security and maximise 'organisational slack' (Nickell & Nicolitsas, 1997). There is a short-term incentive for a network of workers to resist change that will be costly for them. Teachers' unions in the USA have been accused of resisting change to the detriment of productivity (Hoxby, 1996; Lieberman, 2000). However, when a network of workers (or organisations) takes a long-term view it will also be concerned about the impact of practices upon the positioning of the network within society and the economy. This provides a countervailing incentive for embracing change. Machin and Wadhwani's (1991) analysis of union activity in the UK since the 1980s found no clear evidence of damage to productivity growth.

The process of 'reification' (articulating and crystallising work practices through words and codes) may also be interpreted in a positive or a negative light. Reification may be regarded as enabling collective action: helping a group work consciously towards a shared objective to the benefit of all (Denis *et al.*, 2011). Alternatively, it may be viewed as a mechanism for preserving the mystique of the network, excluding others from access to the privileges bestowed by network membership and network knowledge (Dika & Singh, 2002). Analysis of the exclusive nature of the language codes developed by networks of education providers has drawn substantially upon Bernstein's socio-linguistics (Hoadley & Muller, 2010). This perspective has been used in critiques of teacher education (Popkewitz, 1985) and higher education (Becher & Trowler, 2001).

The literature extolling the virtues of provider networks inclines towards an optimistic view of the readiness of providers to change their practice for public benefit. Literature on communities of practice in commercial organisations (e.g. Koliba & Gajda, 2009; Denis *et al.*, 2011) has echoed the belief of the 'quality circles' literature in a natural commitment of workers to improving what they do. A similar assumption underpins the expectations that communities of professional practice in schools (Stoll & Louis, 2007) and higher education (Sherer *et al.*, 2003; Cousin & Deepwell, 2005) will foster effective practice. Some support for this position may be found in a survey of the beliefs about professionalism held by school teachers in England (Swann *et al.*, 2010). In successive surveys ($n = 2,383$, $n = 5,340$) the factor accounting the highest proportion of variation in their data was a belief in 'teaching as constructive learning'. The caveat to this evidence is that it could simply reflect how teachers have learned to describe what they do. It is possible that teachers' practice is somewhat stuck in received ways of working reflecting socio-economic and historical influences that are rarely foregrounded in the community of practice literature. In contrast, researchers using cultural historical activity theory aim to make workers in education aware of this problem and to be ready to consider other possibilities under the influence of outsiders: from academia or other professions (Edwards, 2005).

Beyond education, networks among organisations have been described as *the* model of governance for the information age (Castells, 2010). Networks of workers within organisations and networks among organisations are portrayed as inevitable forms of governance to enable exploitation of the opportunities created by information technology.

Having, producing and sharing knowledge

What it means to 'have knowledge' about how to provide education is far from clear-cut. Having knowledge is not the same thing as having information. Information may be misinterpreted or ignored. Thus any system for providing education faces challenges not only to equip providers with information but also to make it likely that information will be recognised and interpreted appropriately. Another issue in 'having knowledge' is the degree to which knowledge about providing education is generalisable or localised. The more we regard knowledge of local contingencies as critical for educational provision, the more we will prefer to place decisions about supply in the hands of local providers. This kind of approach does not rule out some role for hierarchy, as reflected in the idea of emergent strategy expounded by Mintzberg and Waters (1985). A third issue in 'having knowledge' is the accuracy of what providers think they know. A persistent critique of the claims for local knowledge in schooling has been that schools serving disadvantaged communities develop low expectations on the basis of false beliefs about what is possible. In a similar vein, lecturers in higher education have been criticised for believing that they know that didactic teaching is best.

The conditions for 'producing knowledge' also depend on the extent to which we believe that knowledge about providing education is generalisable. Local providers may produce the knowledge that is most relevant for their contexts, but generalisable knowledge will require substantial resources to serve the knowledge needs of the whole system. The production of knowledge also depends on beliefs about the current state of knowledge. Local or national providers who believe they already know what is best will be less inclined to engage in the production of new knowledge. Finally, how will new knowledge get to those who need it? This question sits more comfortably with perspectives that accept the existence of at least some generalisable knowledge. If we believe that knowledge about providing education is entirely locally specific, then what remains to be shared is knowledge of how best to develop and use capacity to produce local knowledge.

These questions are closely related, since the production and dissemination of knowledge determine who has knowledge. Collectively, they delineate the coordination problem facing any supply system: How will the activities of myriad providers be coordinated to achieve the best outcome for society – however this 'best' (see Chapters 2 and 3) is defined?

Having, producing and sharing knowledge: markets

In a market system, knowledge about the best methods to use in providing education will come from three sources: the price of resources, innovation by the provider, and information about the methods being used by successful providers.

The theory of market supply treats knowledge about how to provide services as generalisable and located in the market rather than in the individual provider.[10] This is because price adjustment in response to supply and demand reflects the relative value of different resources and the benefits for providers of using those resources in one way rather than another. Providers who ignore this information go out of business. Survival of the fittest preserves better knowledge. Private providers will have an incentive to change their input mix as relative prices change. For example, we are living in an age when the cost of IT is falling relative to the cost of teachers and lecturers. We should expect providers to exploit this change by switching their input mix. Two major problems stand in the way. First, an increasing role for IT in education is likely to involve some trade-offs between cost and personalisation and between reliability and standardisation. Yet, as we have seen, parents want their children to have more teacher time in school, not less. Markets create incentives for providers to respond to what consumers believe is the case, whether or not these beliefs are correct. Thus the scope for substituting IT for teacher time is probably greater in higher education. Second, existing providers have sunk capital into their existing resource mix and the reputations they have established in the market. Changes in resource mix are likely to be concentrated in new entrants to the market. These new entrants will take time to build reputations which will help them take a larger slice of the market (as predicted by Christensen and Eyring's (2011) forecasts for higher education in the USA).

If market prices do not reflect the relative cost to society of different resources, then the 'knowledge' provided by the market will be wrong. This concern underpins attacks on collective bargaining and other market regulation (e.g. Hoxby, 1996) perceived as distorting signals required for efficiency.

Markets also rely on the profit motive as a stimulus for entrepreneurial activity which will yield better ways of providing education (Kirzner, 1997). All providers will face an incentive to discover better ways of providing education, since these will offer competitive advantage in the market. The standard exposition of this principle refers explicitly to for-profit organisations. However, even in the private sector, the majority of schools and universities in OECD countries are not-for-profits with charitable status. The owners of these organisations stand only to gain from innovation insofar as this promotes realisation of the core mission of the organisation. This may prove difficult to judge, since 'remaining true to the original mission' may well encourage a conservative attitude towards innovation (Walford, 2002).[11] For not-for-profits and for state schools operating in quasi-markets the incentive for innovation is concentrated in schools struggling for survival (Adnett & Davies, 2003). This means that incentives are most strongly felt by schools that have the most limited capacity to respond. Successful schools have the capacity to innovate but their market position provides little incentive (Lubienski, 2003),[12] and research has questioned whether market incentives have prompted innovation by charter schools (Lubienski, 2003; Preston et al., 2012).

While for-profit organisations face strong market incentives to copy successful rivals, successful organisations have reason to keep their knowledge to themselves. Despite this, knowledge does leak out, but it does so imperfectly (Rogers, 2003). Using a huge global study of citation of patents, Peri (2005) found that knowledge of innovations spread beyond the (within-country) region of origin in only 20 per cent of cases, although diffusion of new ideas was much more widespread in the information and communications technology industry. The benefits of adopting an innovation are also unevenly spread (Silverberg et al., 1988). Early adopters face challenges in the application and refinement of the innovation and later adopters can learn from, and avoid, earlier mistakes. This makes it rational for providers to be cautious about change even when they believe knowledge of production processes is generalisable. The major issue for the diffusion of innovations through markets for education is the extent to which schools, universities and teachers *believe* that practice is transferable. Notwithstanding the substantial education literature asserting that knowledge for teaching is localised, changes in practice have spread across the private school sector in the UK over recent decades (Peel, 2015). As the number of UK boarding pupils has declined, schools have adapted to serve an increasing international demand. Use of price discrimination[13] to attract able students from households with more modest incomes has become increasingly sophisticated and class sizes have decreased (Davies, 2011). Evidence of change in teaching methods is too limited to allow an overall judgement. Nonetheless, while the spread of innovation may be slow, it has been discernible.

Having, producing and sharing knowledge: hierarchies

Large organisations may be found in the public or the private sector. In either case they will use some form of hierarchy to govern internal operations and this gives rise to common information problems.

These problems stem largely from hierarchies' need for standardisation. Common definitions, norms and procedures bring coherence and manageability to a large organisation. They are essential in enabling organisational leaders to see what is happening as well as helping workers understand and respond to each other's practice. Requirements for feasibility in a large organisation provide a necessary and sufficient explanation of standardisation (Thompson & Alvesson, 2005). This vision of the operation of large organisations has been frequently associated with the terms 'Fordism' and 'Taylorism'[14] and the division of labour in a quest for higher productivity (Rosenberg, 1965). The standardisation and associated visibility of 'what workers do' has also been read as a requirement for power relations in a capitalist system.[15] On this view, standardisation is an ideological imperative to impose control over the population while preserving privilege for the few (Davies & Guppy, 1997; Lemke, 2012). Control is exercised through setting standards, getting workers to internalise these standards, normalising the view of humanity from which these standards have been developed and encouraging effort through comparison of performance. This combination of practices has been named 'performativity' in many analyses of education policy (e.g. Ball, 2003b; Perryman, 2006; Burnard & White, 2008; Lingard, 2010). The standard exposition of this idea (e.g. Peters, 2002; Ball, 2012a; Jankowski & Provezis, 2014) frames it as a consequence of the effect of neoliberalism on education. That is, performativity is treated as a consequence of making education more subject to market forces. One difficulty with this perspective arises from the case of Alexey Stakhanov (Siegelbaum, 1990). Stakhanov was a miner in the Soviet Union who was made famous in the 1930s on account of his prodigious productivity. From a Foucauldian perspective his identity was constructed by the Communist Party to create a standard for workers' performance which would be internalised by the populace. The Soviet Communist Party at that time was not noted for its strong neoliberal credentials. That is, not only are many of the elements of performativity visible in the performance measurement of Taylorism in the early twentieth century (Radnor & Barnes, 2007), but subjectification (or internalisation) in performativity is also evident in the history of the Soviet Union. It may be sufficient to regard standardisation of knowledge and its association with control mechanisms as a characteristic of hierarchy in large organisations.

Whichever way you look at it, standardisation and top-down information management in hierarchies leads to taken-for-granted beliefs about the organisation of work. Performance standards need to be set, workers need to be held accountable and incentives are needed to drive and direct workers' efforts. As hierarchies have strengthened their roles in education in recent decades, they have assumed that measures to ensure accountability and incentives are natural and essential. Three examples illustrate the story. First, the National Curriculum introduced in England and Wales in 1988 provided a standardised template to direct teachers' work while also creating an assessment regime designed for comparisons of school and teacher performance (Perryman, 2006). League tables based on pupils' examination results were gradually internalised by teachers as benchmarks for professional esteem (Davies *et al.*, 2005). National government also introduced a new regime of school inspection (Fitz-Gibbon & Stephenson-Forster, 1999), signalling that it did not believe that the National Curriculum and league tables would provide sufficient control. Second, the legislation for the No Child Left Behind (NCLB) policy in 2002 pushed federal influence over school education in the USA in the same direction that had been previously pursued in England (Cooper *et al.*, 2009; McDonnell, 2005): placing 'high-stakes testing' at the centre of an accountability regime for schools. Third, accounts of the largest private sector organisation (Edison Schools) running state schools in the USA paint a similar picture of hierarchical control. The organisation has rigorous processes in place to implement the same curriculum, emphasises analysis of performance data, engagement with parents and high contact hours across all of its schools (Gill *et al.*, 2005, Saltman, 2005; Zimmer & Buddin, 2007; Marsh *et al.*, 2008b). An emphasis on centralised control and brand management has also been observed in multi-academy chains in England (Chapman & Salokangas, 2012).

So what are the problems?

First, the 'performativity critique' treats the subjection of workers in a hierarchy and their subjectification (formation of their identities once they internalise the norms promoted by the hierarchy) as necessarily injurious to the identity and well-being of those workers. Hierarchies take freedoms away from individuals. This critique raises the question of how much weight should be given to the well-being of workers. If there were no transactions costs in moving between occupations (perfect mobility), it would be reasonable to assume that workers will gravitate towards employment that provides the best overall package of satisfaction. The high rate at which teachers leave the profession (Borman & Dowling, 2008; House of Commons Education Committee, 2017) implies that mobility is not a problem. The problem appears to be that the high rate of teacher turnover disadvantages pupils (Ronfeldt *et al.*, 2013).

Second, the association of knowledge with power and control privileges communication flows from the top to the bottom of an organisation and discourages flows of information from the bottom to the top. The organisation's knowledge is restricted to the convictions of those at the top (Nutley *et al.*, 2002). These convictions are found in two kinds of knowledge. One kind of knowledge belief is 'how the system should be judged'. Organisational leaders are drawn to observable indicators of the unobservable outcomes of education which they believe are desirable.

Students' grades in public examinations (Wilson & Piebalga, 2008), levels of undergraduate satisfaction with teaching (Renfrew *et al.*, 2010) and the proportion of undergraduates from disadvantaged backgrounds (Moore *et al.*, 2013) are cases in point. The use of these indicators is threatened by 'Goodhart's law': "When a measure becomes a target it ceases to be a useful measure" (Goodhart, 1989). This is exemplified in education by problems of grade inflation and 'teaching to the test'. The incentives for teachers, lecturers and schools are very clear. Student satisfaction ratings in higher education are positively correlated with expected grades (Greenwald & Gillmore, 1997; Eiszler, 2002; Centra, 2003). A second kind of knowledge belief is 'how the system should be configured'. The UK Prime Minister Theresa May's (2016) espousal of grammar schools in England illustrates the point. A position of power will encourage a leader to believe that they already know what is best regardless of information that may have been collected by the organisation (see Morris & Perry, 2017).

Third, decision making at the top of hierarchies about what type of education to provide has knock-on effects for the way the service is provided. One line of critique suggests that purpose and clarity of vision get lost at the top of public hierarchies as politicians and civil servants wrestle for control. Wilson (1989) contrasted the very limited time spent discussing organisational direction and strategy by the CEO of an energy company with the preoccupation of the Director of the FBI with negotiations with politicians. On the basis of evidence collected on a wide range of public bureaucracies in the USA, he concluded (p. 31):

> In the United States, high-level government executives are preoccupied with maintaining their agencies in a complex, conflict-ridden, and unpredictable political environment, and middle-level government managers are immersed in an effort to cope with the myriad constraints that this environment has imposed on their agencies.

In a similar vein, critics of federal government direction of education policy (e.g. Darling-Hammond, 2007; Berliner, 2011) have argued that removing control over curriculum decisions from teachers diminishes their capacity to do a good job. Their argument assumes that teachers work better when they are driven by personal mission and responsibility rather than by adherence to organisational objectives. This argument is pertinent to beliefs about how teachers will use what they know, so empirical evidence will be reviewed later.

Fourth, accountability and incentive policies focus teacher appraisal and the curriculum on what may be easily measured. This has led to widespread criticism of 'high-stakes testing' narrowing the curriculum (Amrein & Berliner, 2002; Darling-Hammond, 2007; Berliner, 2011). 'High-stakes testing' regimes divide curricula into the accountable and the unaccountable. There are obvious consequences in organisations driven by accountability and incentives. The quality of provision beyond the 'high-stakes' curriculum is entirely dependent on providers being motivated by public service rather than by self-interest. Yet accountability and incentive systems assume that providers *are* driven by self-interest. Dee and Jacob's (2011) carefully designed study of the impact of NCLB provides good evidence of the consequences of a strong accountability and incentives regime in education. They found a substantial improvement in the maths achievement of primary pupils in the USA, but no improvement in reading and no closing of the achievement gap between high and low achievers. Moreover, the absence of measurements of other educational outcomes means that we cannot know whether the improvement in maths achievement came at the expense of weaker progress in other educational outcomes.

Fifth, a top-down approach to knowledge isolates the organisation from its environment. Whatever front-line staff learn, through implementing procedures and through contacts with customers, will have little value within the organisation. Moreover, much of the knowledge developed by front-line staff will be tacit: embodied in their learned responses to different kinds of situation (Nonaka, 1994; Cowan & Foray, 1997; von Krogh *et al.*, 2000). There is a problem of knowledge mobilisation within the organisation and a whole field of 'knowledge management systems' has developed to analyse the resulting challenges for organisational efficiency (Alavi & Leider, 2001; Goh, 2002). Isolation from the external environment reduces the organisation's capacity to respond to external change. Past practice benefits from a radiant halo of the normal order. The National Curriculum introduced in England in 1988 bore a remarkable resemblance to the list of largely academic subjects in the 1904 government prescription for schooling (Goodson, 1993). Despite a flirtation with encouraging 'specialist' schools (Davies *et al.*, 2004), subsequent revisions (see Oates, 2011) have pared away even the inclusion of technology and information technology to leave the core curriculum in England remarkably traditional and academic. Government responses to globalisation and international comparisons of educational performance have concentrated this conservatism (Kamens & McNeely, 2010). Many voices (e.g. Jacob, 2002; Goldin & Katz, 2007) have argued that schooling and higher education have struggled to adapt sufficiently to changing industrial structure. This conservatism in the provision of education has also been attributed to the power of social class structure, preserving a curriculum that helps enshrine middle-class privileged and disadvantaged children from other backgrounds (Apple, 1993). Isolation from the external environment also gets in the way of the organisation's knowledge of the effect of variation between local contexts on the best way of providing education. Standardisation assumes that knowledge of how to provide a service is generalisable: what works here will also work there. However, learners in one locality may have capabilities, approaches to learning and expectations that make them different from learners in another locality (Dahlin & Watkins, 2000).

One response to these problems with 'top-down' knowledge management in hierarchies has been to advocate 'evidence-based policy and practice'. There is plenty of evidence of national governments and universities trying to gather 'third-person' knowledge of educational processes (Cooper *et al.*, 2009). 'Third-person' knowledge (Winch, 2008) is gathered through observation of patterns of behaviour and outcomes attributable to that behaviour. Governments have implemented school assessment regimes to tell them something about school and teacher performance and they impose inspection regimes which tell them about the extent of school and teacher adherence to processes that governments believe improve educational outcomes. Given the resources they are able to deploy, governments are well placed to gather and systematically analyse these data. They are also able to commission systematic reviews of research evidence and to commission their own evaluations. A 'third-person' approach has been promoted in recent decades under the banners of 'evidence-based policy' and 'evidence-based practice'. The profile of 'evidence-informed policies' in England increased dramatically following the election of the New Labour government in 1997, and espousal of this approach to policy-making spread quickly to Australia (Marston & Watts, 2003). However, even once there is political espousal of a commitment to evidence, the challenges for implementation are huge. Nutley, Davies & Walter (2002) suggest that the first of these is 'deciding what counts as evidence'. Governments are awash with information about education and they have to decide what new information to gather (Perri, 2002; Hordósy, 2014). We might add that they also have to interpret the information on which they choose to focus. Moreover, even a genuine desire for evidence-informed policy has to contend with political imperatives to act and to be seen to be acting.

In 2011 the Coalition government in the UK set aside £125 million for randomised controlled trials to be commissioned by the Education Endowment Foundation. This has yielded a substantial flow of evidence about the practice of teaching in schools (albeit with the caveat of the doubts noted in Chapter 5 about pragmatic RCTs that focus on specific practices). Given all these data it may be reasonable to suppose that the national government in England knows far more about the process of schooling and teaching than any individual (private or public) school or teacher.

For some critics of evidence-based practice (e.g. Biesta, 2007a) the interactive[16] nature of education means that it cannot be understood as a causal process that may be revealed through RCTs. This critique parodies evidence-based practice as suggesting that intervention X *always* leads to outcome Y. However, the whole point of RCTs is to provide evidence of the size of the *average* effect of an intervention. There is a compelling case for using an intervention with a very large average effect. It won't work for all children or for all classes or all schools, but it will probably work better than 'normal practice'. The problems with evidence from pragmatic RCTs lie elsewhere. One problem (as discussed in Chapter 5) lies in the way in which 'pragmatic' RCTs compare an intervention with 'normal practice' (National Research Council, 2002; Ainsworth et al., 2015). 'Normal practice' is neither a fixed benchmark nor necessarily known, making it difficult to interpret the difference between the 'treatment' and the 'control'. This problem could be addressed by designing RCTs that compare two interventions which differ only in the way they aim to activate a known underlying principle in teaching and learning.

However, this would still leave a problem for policy in how to interpret and act upon variation around the average effect of an intervention. Teaching and learning are complex activities. The consequences of any particular act of teaching for learning depend not only on the characteristics of the learners, but also on learners' beliefs and the interaction between different principles in teaching and learning. Students' response to any particular type of feedback they receive will depend on their self-image as a learner (Ryan & Deci, 2000), their disposition to understand (McCune & Entwistle, 2011), their epistemological beliefs (Trautwein &Lüdtke, 2007), their trust in the teacher (Olson, 1981), the way their current understanding is framed (Caravita & Halldén, 1994), their capacity to go beyond their current understanding (Tharp & Gallimore, 1988), their interaction with peers (Marsh *et al.*, 2008b), and the way in which the feedback deploys variation and sameness to highlight the point (Marton, 2014), etc. This complexity undermines expectations that practice can be easily improved through 'best practice manuals' for teaching. Critics of evidence-based practice in education (e.g. Sanderson, 2002, 2003, 2009; Biesta, 2007a) have good reason to worry that policy-makers might imagine that improvements in education involve straightforward application of 'best practice' by technicians who have become proficient at their craft. This is a seductive delusion for a politician who would prefer to pay for a less expensive and more easily judged craftsperson than a more expensive and more independent professional capable of making complex judgements in a range of contexts.

Conversely, teachers have an incentive to exaggerate the uniqueness of the contexts in which they operate. Claims for the uniqueness of particular educational contexts provide natural defences against external scrutiny. But I have yet to meet a teacher who believes that learners' responses to their teaching are entirely unpredictable. All teaching presupposes some implicit or explicit theories about how teaching affects learning. In fact, we do know quite a lot about teachers' beliefs about what they do (e.g. Wood, 2000; Fives & Gill, 2014). This means that there is scope for *informing* teachers' thinking and practice with a reasonable expectation of improving what teachers do. However, the study of hierarchies tells us that accumulating knowledge at the top of a hierarchy to become useful in the daily front-line activity of an organisation is challenging (Huberman & Miles, 1984; Fullan, 2000). But it is possible. Despite critics' doubts (e.g. Wyse, 2003) about the evidence base for the National Literacy Strategy introduced in England in 1998, a comparison of schools participating in a pilot programme for the National Literacy Strategy in England (Machin & McNally, 2008) found a substantive and cost-effective gain for those schools participating in the intervention. The evaluators of the National Literacy and Numeracy strategies (Leithwood *et al.*, 2004) claimed that the effectiveness of the strategy was contingent upon whether schools exercised 'transformative' (as opposed to transactional) leadership. However, it is possible that this observation may have been tinged by the evaluators' previous advocacy of 'local school management' and 'transformational leadership' which sought change through engaging and developing teachers rather than through programme implementation and incentives.

An alternative response to the problems of 'top-down' knowledge management in hierarchies has been to advocate delegation of responsibility to lower levels of management: requiring them to act as leaders rather than as implementers. This tradition values 'first-person' (Winch, 2008) knowledge: the beliefs developed and espoused by those who are directly engaged in an activity. The doctrine of 'emergent strategy' (Mintzberg, 1979; Mintzberg & Waters, 1985) declares that organisations should delegate their decision making closer to their front-line staff who will possess more accurate knowledge than it is possible to gather at the centre of the organisation. Collaborative work groups or 'quality circles' enjoyed a short period of high popularity in for-profit companies in the early 1980s (Lawler & Mohrman, 1984). In essence, this trend aimed to create network processes within a hierarchical structure. Enthusiasm for 'quality circles' then became subsumed, or perhaps submerged, in the fashion for 'Total Quality Management' (TQM). Total Quality Management combines traditional elements of control in a hierarchy (such as benchmarking) with organisational characteristics associated with quality circles (e.g. open culture, empowerment of workers). One widely cited review of the implementation of TQM (Powell, 1995) concluded that where it was successful this was due to openness of culture and worker empowerment rather than formal processes such as benchmarking. Practices associated with 'quality circles' have survived in organisations committed to network structures (see e.g. Forcadell & Guadamillas, 2002). While there has been plenty of advocacy of TQM in education (e.g. Kanji *et al.*, 1999; Sallis, 2014), there is more evidence of TQM practices (such as a 'balanced score card' approach to benchmarking: see Chen *et al.*, 2006), which align with traditional organisations in a hierarchy, than with characteristics associated with quality circles.

These ideas about how to organise supply within a hierarchy found their shape in education in advocacy of 'local school management' (see e.g. Caldwell, 2005) and 'distributed leadership' (Harris, 2004; Spillane, 2005). According to Caldwell, local management of resources will only generate benefits when schools also have control over the curriculum and methods of teaching. This version of local school management presumes that the best information about teaching and learning, curriculum needs and the organisation of resources is held locally by senior managers and teachers in schools. Caldwell's position treats knowledge itself as situated within local contexts and local heads. As well as suggesting that 'what works here will not necessarily work there', this view emphasises the importance of actors' belief in knowledge (Hargreaves, 2003): teachers will only try to make an intervention work if they really believe in it, and their belief will depend on the extent to which they think that the knowledge is rooted in their place of work, 'places like here'. Chapter 5 reviewed evidence for the 'local school management' assertion which was judged 'unproven'. The evidence on distributed leadership is similarly ambivalent (e.g. Harris, 2004).

In many ways it is unsurprising to discover that the evidence is so mixed. It is gathered from confusing policy contexts. For example, school policy in England has simultaneously pursued: (1) a strong accountability and incentives regime;

(2) top-down information management through national programmes (such as the National Literacy Strategy) and government-funded RCTs (through the Education Endowment Foundation); (3) delegation of governance and decision making to schools (Gibb, 2015), and (4) espousal of distributed leadership in schools (e.g. National College for Teaching and Learning, 2014). Since schools are left with the job of trying to pick a way through these contradictory stances on knowledge management it is unsurprising to find that it is tricky to infer much from what they actually do.

Having, producing and sharing knowledge: networks

While networks have always played some role in providing education, academic interest and policy changes have pushed network governance into greater prominence over recent years. Networks[17] are collaborations between providers. This could entail collaboration between organisations or collaboration between individuals. This section focuses on three kinds of networks in education: between parents and teachers, between professional educators, and between educational institutions. Before looking at each kind of network the section offers brief summaries of some critical features of networks: the nature of transactions; tensions between preserving and creating knowledge, and different reasons why networks may come into being.

The key mechanism in a network is reciprocity: I help you, you help me. Networks have two major advantages over barter systems when it comes to reciprocity. The first is that reciprocity may be deferred and indirect. I can help you and expect that at some later date someone else in the network will help me. The 'social contract' within the network is implicit and open. Therefore, trust is essential to prevent the network from breaking up (Schweers Cook, 2005). Second, belonging to a network surrounds one with the collective power of the network. I can enjoy the strength of the network, negotiating on my behalf with the rest of the world. The size of the network, the status of its members and the willingness of its members to act as one are critical to the strength of its collective benefit. A key problem for any network is that these two benefits live uneasily together. As a network grows it becomes harder to maintain openness and mutual trust and there is a tendency for the network to drift towards a hierarchical structure.

Networks also experience tensions between preserving knowledge and creating new knowledge. Networks provide secure environments in which individuals can participate in received ways of doing things. New ideas risk destabilising relationships within the network. Moreover, the network benefits members by championing the importance to society of the received knowledge and expertise of the network. So where is the impetus for knowledge creation and how can tensions between new and old knowledge be resolved? One possibility is that the network has a core belief in the value of progress in knowledge. Educational, and especially academic communities, find natural appeal in this idea. Kuhn's (1962) idea of paradigm shifts provides one way of resolving the tension between an inherent desire to increase knowledge with social constraints on knowledge formation in networks. The critical notion here is that the network will spend most of its time tidying things up within strong conventions of how things should be done and what we know. Periodically, a sufficiently large proportion of the network will see advantage in pursuing a radically different perspective. A second possibility is that a network will be forced to change its way of thinking and acting as a consequence of competitive pressure from other networks. This has been observed (e.g. Thorelli, 1986) in the behaviour of networks between for-profit businesses. This possibility also encourages an expectation of periodical, radical change rather than the gradual assimilation of new ideas. A third possibility is that new ways of seeing and acting will develop through interactions between one network and another. Theories of networks (Tonnies, 1957, Granovetter, 1973; Bauman, 2001) have distinguished between 'tight-knit' and 'loose-knit' communities. A loose-knit community has members who also belong to other communities and this facilitates cross-fertilisation of ideas. This idea suggests a gradual infiltration of new ideas from elsewhere, provoking new hybrid ways of seeing and acting.

Before turning to different kinds of network in the provision of education we also need to consider reasons why a network may come into existence. Muijs and colleagues (2010) offered a categorisation of different types of institutional networks in education and this is a useful place to start. They suggested four reasons for the emergence of a network: (1) shared resources through social capital; (2) a community of practice; (3) a shared moral imperative, or (4) a place to belong.[18] In common with much of the literature on school-to-school networks (see e.g. Hopkins & Jackson, 2002; Stoll et al., 2006), this list is largely restricted to benign reasons for the emergence of networks. Critically, it omits (5) sharing physical and human capital, and (6) collusion to secure power and status. Mainstream economics has traditionally viewed collusion as a threat to competition and a source of welfare loss (e.g. Maudos & de Guevara, 2007), while Goodson's (1993) narratives of subject histories provide accounts of professional alliances in search of power and resources.

Household/teacher networks have been analysed chiefly in terms of social capital and a sense of belonging. The social capital literature emphasises the resources (in knowledge, expertise and time) available in the community upon which members could draw (Lin, 2002; Schweers Cook, 2005). The benefits to members of the community depend not only on the nature of the resources held within the community but, crucially, on the relationships within the community (Coleman, 1988). Once we acknowledge the roles of households as well as formal education providers as co-producers of education, we may then ask whether households and formal providers are embedded in the same community. Research on Catholic schools (e.g. Coleman et al., 1982; Neal, 1997; Pugh et al., 2006) has suggested that they benefit from social capital shared between parents and schools. However, the process of education is also affected by community boundaries drawn in terms of social class (Power et al., 2003). Relationships observed between parents and schools (Lareau, 1987; Lareau & Horvat, 1999) revealed patterns of education that disadvantaged Black and working-class children. White middle-class children and their parents possessed cultural capital which was similar to that possessed by teachers, enabling them to establish household–school relationships that constituted social capital and gave them better access to the formal schooling process. Differential rates among ethnic groups and social classes in applications to higher education have also been attributed to social and cultural capital (Perna & Titus, 2005; Noble & Davies, 2009). Alignment of cultural capital between households and educational providers creates advantage and non-alignment creates disadvantage. Recruitment of new teachers and lecturers may aim to address this problem either through achieving fair representation of different social groups or by fostering a commitment to the needs of all social groups and an appreciation of the cultures they bring to educational contexts.

Networks of professional educators have been chiefly analysed in terms of communities of practice and, to a lesser extent, in terms of social movements. The earlier literature on communities of practice (Lave & Wenger, 1991) emphasised 'ways of doing things' and the habits and thinking that underpin those practices. While professionals in education settings tend to believe that what they do is necessarily for the public good (Tierney, 1988), it is far from clear that received procedures, habits and culture are a 'good thing'. In fact, practices in schools have been frequently criticised (e.g. Blanchett, 2006; Auwarter & Aruguete, 2008; OfSTED, 2015) on the grounds that they have disadvantaged one type of student or another.[19] Moreover, professional networks in education have frequently been accused of acting in defence of received practice in order to serve the interests of professionals rather than those whom the profession is meant to serve. Insofar as teacher unions have been able to exert power, they have naturally done so in order to serve members' interests, leaving the impact upon children open to debate (Steelman *et al.*, 2000; Kleinhenz & Ingvarson, 2004; Karseth & Nerland, 2007). Teachers' practice, especially in higher education, has frequently be accused (e.g. Reimann, 2004) of ingrained conservatism.

Later applications of 'communities of practice' in commercial settings (e.g. Wenger *et al.*, 2002) have focused on achieving change within organisations through groups of workers constituted as 'learning communities' with strong echoes of the earlier literature on 'quality circles'. Applications in education have largely followed this approach, concentrating on change through teachers learning together in 'networked learning communities' (see e.g. Katz & Earl, 2010). This literature (e.g. Hargreaves, 1999; Buysse *et al.*, 2003; Vescio *et al.*, 2008) typically assumes that knowledge for teaching is local to particular contexts: in which case the imperative is to make sure that all teachers are constantly improving their local knowledge.[20] Talk of dissemination makes little sense. The 'professional learning communities' literature assumes that teachers have a natural desire to improve their practice through creating new knowledge. There are scant references in the professional learning communities literature to challenges faced in motivating teachers to seek change. However, as noted earlier, this may be a reasonable assumption given that teaching is likely to be attractive to individuals who enjoy and value learning. The real difficulty comes in explaining how the tension between existing practice and a desire for change is resolved. An assumption that teachers naturally desire improvement could be resolved by a Kuhnian espousal of 'paradigm shifts', largely assigning professional learning communities to the task of 'tidying up'.

Paradigm shifts are more likely to be associated with what have been dubbed 'new social movements' (Klandermans & Oegema, 1987; Rao et al., 2000). These are networks that have been formed to change society in one particular way or another. For example, networks of academics and teachers promoted inclusive schools (Thomas, 2013) and equality of opportunity for girls in schools (Francis, 2000). However, it is possible that the likelihood that education professionals will act in this way depends on the degree of autonomy they are granted. Numerous commentators within education (e.g. Talbert & McLaughlin, 1994; Carr & Hartnett, 1996; Hargreaves, 2000; Wilkinson, 2007) have claimed that when teachers were given more autonomy they exhibited a 'service ethic' which drove them to seek educational change for the benefit of society.

Networks of educational providers are a relatively recent phenomenon.[21] The Ivy League of US colleges was formed in 1954, the Russell Group of research intensives in the UK was formed in 1994[22] and the 'Group of Eight' leading universities in Australia was formed in 1999. Elsewhere in the market for higher education in England, partnerships have developed between universities and colleges of further education (Parry & Thompson, 2002; Robinson et al., 2006). The first example is a case of a horizontal network: partnership between providers offering similar services at the same stage in the education process. The second example is a case of a vertical network: partnerships between providers offering different services at different stages in the education process. These are examples of networks aiming to promote the interests of one group of educational institutions relative to others (although this is relatively less important in the case of the Ivy League).

The promotion of school networks has been a central feature of government policy for schools in England since 2010 (Greany, 2015). The incoming government announced the creation in England of 'Teaching School alliances' in 2010. These alliances were to act as hubs for initial teacher education and continuing professional development, led by an 'outstanding school'. By 2012 one in eight pupils in England was taught in a school belonging to one of these alliances (Matthews & Berwick, 2013). By early 2016 the majority of secondary schools were designated as academy schools: free from local authority control. Two-thirds of these belonged to 'multi-academy trusts' (MATs) (Andrews, 2016), although the majority of these networks were very small. These school networks could also be categorised according to their governance structure. Chapman and Muijs (2014) distinguished between soft and hard federations. Schools in soft federations preserve their independent governance. The federation may be understood as a form of network. Schools in hard federations share a common governing body and are therefore best understood as a hierarchy rather than as a network (as in the case of the ARK federation described by Junemann and Ball (2013)).

The emergence of these networks in schools and in higher and further education may be understood through the lens of the long-standing literature on networks of firms. These may be divided into literatures on collusion (Jacquemin & Slade, 1989), supply chains (Fiala, 2005), external economies of scale (Krugman, 1991) and cooperatives (Restakis, 2010). Economists have referred to networks of providers offering the same product as collusion: making deals which benefit providers at the expense of customers who are denied the fruits of competition. However, networks of firms occupying different positions within an industry have received more mixed reviews. The supply chain literature analyses relationships between companies where one company supplies inputs (e.g. components) to another. A long-term relationship between a firm and a supplier enables both parties to become familiar with the needs and constraints of the other. This knowledge can help both to become more efficient and means that fewer resources have to be set aside for contingency planning and unforeseen circumstances. However, while this security can foster innovation tailored to the needs of both companies it can also encourage complacency. External economies of scale are cost savings that accrue to each of a group of firms that benefit from close proximity in a locality. Specialised expertise is attracted to the area, firms hear quickly about the innovations of others and geographical proximity fosters collaboration (Hanson, 2001). Universities (Quintas *et al.*, 1992) and governments (OECD, 1997) have sought to exploit possibilities for external economies of scale through science parks and 'business incubators'. There are good reasons for expecting cooperatives to be inefficient (Ferrier & Porter, 1991). Action depends on agreement among members of the cooperative and this will often take considerable time and resources to achieve. Moreover, monitoring members and avoiding 'free-riders' is made difficult when the members are stakeholders in the network. There will also be a tendency to remain below the optimum size for the cooperative because members' influence will be diluted as the cooperative grows. Nonetheless, cooperatives account for a substantial proportion of economic activity in some sectors and some economies (8 per cent of the Swedish economy, according to Nilsson (2001)). The existence of cooperatives has been explained (Nilsson, 2001; Golovina *et al.*, 2013) as a consequence of market failures associated with declining long-run average cost and transaction costs. This is an argument for networks rather than for markets: on the basis that when small suppliers work together they are able to reduce their costs, counteract market volatility and negotiate with powerful buyers. The largely unexpressed implication is that cooperatives will work better than a hierarchy for the same reasons that prompted the move towards quality circles within hierarchies.

Vigorous advocacy of school networks (e.g. Hargreaves, 2003) has echoed this argument: coordination through networks beats coordination through a hierarchy because (1) the knowledge that is critical for success is located in practitioners on the spot; (2) workers will be more committed to improving what they do when they also believe they are stakeholders in the service (Bartunek *et al.*, 1999); (3) workers in education have a natural desire to learn and to improve what they do, and (4) when schools collaborate they share their collective knowledge about teaching to provide a stronger basis for improving practice (Muijs, 2015). The final argument suggests that a school-to-school network creates new relationships between teachers, thereby increasing social capital. Hargreaves (2003, p. 30) approvingly quoted a passage from a policy document from an initiative to improve schools in London:

> We want to free schools to innovate, taking advantage of the nationwide deregulation of the system and new legislative freedoms. The length of the school day, the type of lessons, the patterns of the timetable, partnerships with business, the involvement with parents, the ethos of the schools, the recruitment and retention of teachers, ways of making good behaviour the norm and bad behaviour unacceptable, use of classroom assistants, the shape of the curriculum – all these are ready for reform school by school.

But what does it mean for a school to innovate? The scientific and business literatures (e.g. Marchetti, 1980; MacDonald, 2004; Gokhberg & Meissner, 2013) suggest distinctions between discovery, invention and innovation. Underlying principles are discovered. Inventions apply a combination of principles in a new way of doing things. Innovation exploits an invention: making it feasible to use the new way of doing things in one setting or in a range of settings. A change in practice could be simply a shot in the dark. Deregulation opens the gates to change: but opportunity to change offers no guarantee of innovation, invention or discovery. The concept of innovation as applied invention requires knowledge of the combination of principles embodied in the invention as well as knowledge of the feasibility constraints in the context where the innovation will be introduced.

However, if knowledge for teaching is regarded as completely situated[23] there are no general principles to consider, and teachers and schools have to work out a *modus operandi* for their unique situation. It seems unlikely that the only learning teachers undergo when they move from one school to another is how to make sense of the new place. Given that analysis of teacher effectiveness (e.g. Clotfelter *et al.*, 2007) shows that they do not go back to ground zero when they move schools, we know they must take something. As Fenstermacher (1994) pointed out, the great challenge for any teacher is how to develop a coherent account of general principles, their local knowledge and the local knowledge of others.

The case for network supply of education rests on a judgement about three key tensions. A first tension is between the benefits of being included in a network and the costs of being excluded. A network cannot include everyone, so someone must get excluded. A second tension is between the extent to which a network acts to preserve knowledge and the extent to which it creates knowledge. A third tension is between resources released in the form of social capital relative to the resources consumed in maintaining the network. Much of the recent wave of literature on networks in education has provided valuable evidence of the benefits of networks, but less evidence of the drawbacks or how networks are recognising and resolving these tensions. Conversely, the literature on policy networks in education (e.g. Mintrom & Vergari, 1998; Ball, 2012b) has tended to place relatively more emphasis on the drawbacks than on the benefits.

Providing education: something distinctive or just like any other good?

The language of production and supply encourages us to view the provision of education in the same way that we might view the provision of any good or service. There are some advantages in doing this, because it means we can draw upon a vast amount of analysis that has been developed to judge the qualities of different supply systems. However, looking at education in this way will encourage us to ignore any distinctive characteristics. At the very least, it makes sense to consider whether education is distinctive and what the implications of ignoring distinctiveness may turn out to be. This section considers six lines of argument that are sometimes used to claim distinctiveness for the *provision* of education.[24]

'Public' and 'toll' goods

Education has been frequently referred to as a 'public good' (Grace, 1989; Schneider *et al.*, 1999; McNeil, 2002; Carnoy *et al.*, 2014). An unqualified assertion that education should be provided by the public sector because it is a 'public good' does not move us beyond a tautology. So what does it mean? The term 'public good' was introduced by economists (Samuelson, 1954; Buchanan, 1965) to distinguish between goods according to whether they are 'non-rival' and 'non-excludable'. A good is non-rival when one person's consumption does not interfere with another person's consumption of the same good. This can only be the case if once something is provided to one person it costs suppliers nothing more to provide it for the next person. The additional (marginal) cost of providing the good to one more person is zero. A good is non-excludable if, once it is provided for one person, it will unavoidably be enjoyed by others. Street lighting and national defence are frequently cited as fulfilling both conditions (e.g. Stiglitz, 1999; Deneulin & Townsend, 2007). The benefits of national defence provided for one citizen will be enjoyed by others without diminishing the benefits to the first person. These benefits cannot be withheld from others who live in the country. Ostrom (2010) suggested that instead of these two criteria being treated as dichotomous variables it would be more useful to distinguish between goods according to whether they were low or high on each dimension (Table 6.1).

If a low-excludability good is left to pure private provision there is a risk that rivalrous goods will be over-consumed and non-rival goods will be under-supplied. If a toll good is left to pure private provision there is a risk that a pure monopoly will charge prices well above the marginal cost of providing the good. There is a prima facie case for arguing that the supply of a public good is best left to government. Imagine a charge for using street lighting. One more person can walk down

TABLE 6.1 Four different types of goods

		Rivalry	
		High	Low
Excludability	High	Private goods: exemplified by agricultural and manufactured products, traditional forms of schooling and higher education.	Toll or club goods[25] such as digital recordings of films and music, online educational resources.
	Low	Common pool resources: exemplified by natural resources such as fish stocks which can suffer from the 'Tragedy of the Commons' when property rights are not enforceable.	Public goods such as national defence and street lighting.

Source: Ostrom (2010).

a well-lit street at no extra cost to the supplier (zero marginal cost/non-rival) and gains a benefit from doing so. Public welfare is therefore increased. But a private supplier cannot make a profit if their price is equal to the marginal cost. If a charge is introduced and the supplier could exclude non-payers, some people would use a different route and would lose benefit. The cost of supply would not fall, so net public benefit would be lower. If a private supplier cannot exclude non-payers, then there would be no supply at all.

However, education has traditionally satisfied neither the condition of non-rivalry nor the condition of non-excludability. Of course, if one new child starts attending a school they can be accommodated by a small increase in one class size and the teacher's job may even grow easier if this new child is very good at cooperating with others in their learning. But once a school is at the limit of its capacity it cannot take on more children without more teachers and more build-ings. At a national level, policies such as raising the school-leaving age cannot be implemented without incurring substantial additional costs. Students may also be excluded from a school or any other educational institution.

Online education which does not involve tutors in feedback or summative assessment is 'non-rival', since additional views do not add to the costs for the sup-plier. Online education may take the form of instructional television (Seels *et al.*, 2004), including the many YouTube videos providing guidance on how to carry out statistical procedures. It may also take the form of online platforms for peer-to-peer interaction through handheld mobile technology (Wang *et al.*, 2009; Sharples & Pea, 2014). However, although online education may be provided free at point of use, the technology makes it perfectly possible to exclude viewers by requiring a password. Therefore, this form of online education is better described as a toll good than as a public good (Rauh, 2011). Online courses have been growing rapidly in higher education and new 'for-profit' entrants to this market have responded strongly to the opportunities this creates.[26] A survey conducted in the USA for organisations providing distance education (Allen & Seaman, 2011) and their sponsors reported that annual growth in enrolments in online courses (10%) was far exceeding growth in enrolments on traditional courses.

Nonetheless, beyond the fee-based online courses there has been rapid growth in OERS (Open Educational Resources) and MOOCs (Massive Open Online Courses). These developments have drawn attention to the scope for 'non-exclusion' in the provision of online education. As yet, MOOCs appear to be viewed by institutions and students chiefly as supplements to fee-charging programmes on which students are enrolled (Zheng *et al.*, 2015). The costs of course development are borne by the institution on the basis of promoting the university's brand and attracting new students (Leeds & Cope, 2015). Non-rivalry is kept to a minimum when students only receive automated formative and summative assessment. Thus it appears that the scope for this method of supplying education depends critically on the alignment between automated assessment and educational objectives. If the objective is to develop a particular skill (e.g. how to carry out a particular statistical test or technical procedure) there is great scope for open access online education. If the objective is to enable a student to develop a more complex and coherent understanding of a field of study, the scope looks small. Open access online courses of any form have also suffered from high drop-out rates (Downes, 2010; Clarke, 2013), and an evaluation of online education for secondary school students in South Carolina (Rauh, 2011) found that students from lower income families were less likely to complete. Nonetheless, all forms of online education are experiencing rapid growth. Low or even zero marginal costs make this way of providing education very attractive to suppliers and also offer huge benefits to any supplier that can secure a large slice of the market. The inherent problems with 'toll goods', therefore, loom very large indeed. A private supplier that can secure a near-monopoly in providing a particular kind of education would be able to exploit this position at great welfare loss to society. This analysis underpins anxieties about the prospects for international trade agreements (such as TTIP) limiting the public role in education (e.g. Fritz, 2015; Williams, 2015).

Sorting and the positional good argument

Education is sometimes (e.g. Marginson, 2006; Brennan & Naidoo, 2008) referred to as a positional good and elsewhere (e.g. del Mar Salinas-Jiménez *et al.*, 2011; Van der Werfhorst, 2011) is referred to as a partly positional good. The term 'positional good' was introduced by Hirsch (1977) who also described education as a 'partly positional good'.

What does this mean? Hirsch (1977) combined three themes in his account of a positional good. The first theme is 'fixed supply'. Hirsch illustrated this point using the example of the painting *Mona Lisa*. Since there is only one *Mona Lisa*, an increase in demand to own the painting can only result in its price going up. It is a zero-sum game in which the winning bid takes all. If more money is spent on securing ownership of this painting the only thing that changes is who gets to see the painting. The distribution of benefits can be changed but not the overall level of benefits. A typical application (e.g. Marginson, 2006) of this idea treats education as an investment in which the benefits of education are located in jobs, status and earnings. Hirsch argued that the number of 'top leadership jobs' is fixed and that demand for education is driven by a desire to secure these jobs. However, even when 'top jobs' are narrowly defined it is difficult to interpret evidence about the number of executives, millionaires and billionaires as showing a static pool of jobs (Petras, 2008; Keeley, 2015). Moreover, in the USA at least, the typical profile of leaders of top companies changed substantially between 1980 and 2001 (Cappelli & Hamori, 2005). It is, perhaps, more relevant to look at the number of high-status professional jobs in OECD countries. The economic indicators provided by the World Bank show that between 1981 and 2011 the number of physicians per 1,000 people rose from 1.5 to 2.5 in the USA and from 1.3 to 2.8 in the UK. At any one point there is a fixed number of 'top jobs', but this number changes over time (see also Green et al., 2002). Moreover, changes in the proportion of jobs requiring more education occur throughout the labour market. A survey of employers in the UK conducted by the employers' organisation the Confederation of British Industry (CBI/Pearson, 2016) reported that 77 per cent of firms expected to require more workers with higher level skills and only 3 per cent expected to employ more workers with lower level skills. As noted in Chapter 3, the balance of evidence suggests that a high proportion (perhaps 50%) of the additional earnings of more educated people *does* reflect greater productivity. Labour markets, like any other market, do change over time in response to shifts in supply. If we accept (see Chapter 3) that the benefits of education also include harmony in society and the appreciation of culture this further reduces the scope for positional effects in the provision of education

Hirsch's second theme was negative production externalities. He noted that economic growth may be accompanied by negative externalities (e.g. pollution and congestion) such that measured income may rise while the welfare (or happiness) of people declines. The scale of production externalities from education is disputed, but they are always assumed to be positive. His final theme ('relative consumption': see Frank, 1997) relates to demand rather than to supply and was reviewed in Chapter 2. If happiness is related to relative rather than absolute income, then education (like anything else) cannot increase total happiness through increasing incomes: one person's gain is another person's loss (Easterlin, 2005; Hagerty & Veenhoven, 2003; Clark et al., 2008).

In summary, even if we restrict the outcomes of education to effects on income and labour market status, education is not a zero-sum game. The significance for education of the standard positional good argument is further diminished once we accept that education should be valued for social, aesthetic and character benefits to the individual and to society.

Goods and services which form identities and attitudes

Standard economic theory treats an individual's tastes and preferences as given, but the value of education in a society derives partly from its role in developing identities and shaping attitudes (as discussed in Chapters 2 and 3). In the late nineteenth century, Welsh schools were required by the UK state to suppress the Welsh language (Cummins, 1997) but by the late twentieth century promotion of the Welsh language in Welsh schools had become a major force for reinvigorating Welsh identity (Jones, 1992). This is a story with echoes around the globe (Hornberger, 1998; Fierman, 2006) as communities and ethnic groups redefine their shared identity within a globalising context. In 2014 the British Prime Minister, David Cameron, spoke about his "uncompromising stance on requiring schools to teach *British* values". In these cases, governments have been seeking to use education to influence individual allegiance to a national community. Conversely, private education providers may explicitly aim to serve the needs of communities *within* a nation state. This is exemplified by private Catholic schools in the USA (Coleman & Hoffer, 1987) and Australia (Vella, 1999; Rymarz & Graham, 2006). The introduction of 'free schools' in England has also led to a growth in small schools committed to the values and beliefs of particular faith communities (Higham, 2014; Morris, 2014). Private schools in England also define their missions to appeal to the values, beliefs and expectations of parents from particular sections of society. The following are two extracts from 'mission statements':

> To develop a strong character, boys are encouraged to adopt a robust moral code and to embrace wholeheartedly all that Harrow has to offer. Our busy, structured and purposeful environment produces young men who are confident, creative and better team players – be it in the form room or the board room, these are things that really count.[27]

> To promote the spiritual, moral, intellectual, physical and social development and to extend the awareness of all students so that they will successfully integrate into British society. [...] To nourish the seed of Islam in their hearts.[28]

The broad thrust of these statements is similar to the declarations of many state schools. Few would quibble with a desire to develop individuals who are 'confident, creative and better team players' or a desire for successful integration into British society. Thus these private schools express unambiguous commitment to a cohesive society. However, they also have particular ambitions that are signalled in Harrow's reference to 'the board room' and Al-Burhan's reference to 'nourishing the seed of Islam'. One question for a society is whether private provision can adequately balance competitive pressures to meet parents' preferences for particular types of schooling against shared ambitions for a harmonious and just society. Another question is whether a state education system has any advantages in addressing this problem.

Schools like Harrow and Al-Burhan have been established to serve the needs of particular communities and they only benefit from the way in which they develop characters and preferences through nurturing societies which are likely to demand their services in the future. However, they are small organisations and, despite their reputations, they have quite limited market power. Large multi-product companies such as Pearson Education may turn out to be more typical of a well-developed fully private system of education (Mansell, 2012). This large multinational owns one of three examining boards setting public examinations in England and also publishes a wide range of teaching resources for schools to use as they prepare pupils for those examinations. Organisations with a large share of a market and interests in different stages of education (vertical integration) have more capacity and incentive to operate against the public interest. Many banking organisations include the development of financial literacy in schools as part of their commitment to community development (England & Chatterjee, 2005; APPG, 2016). But their work in defining the nature of financial literacy problems and solutions leaves them open to the criticism that they are tacitly developing consumers to suit their organisational interests.

Conversely, governments could exploit monopoly power over the curriculum to indoctrinate young people into taking a particular view of the world for granted (Apple, 2000). This kind of behaviour is generally associated with non-democratic government (see e.g. Yuen & Byrom, 2007), and there is strong institutional and cultural resistance in OECD countries when governments are perceived as overreaching their democratic authority. Government influence on the teaching of English and history through the introduction of a National Curriculum in England provoked public debate as well as protest from teachers (King & Protherough, 2006; Jones, 2000). Nonetheless, one reading of this episode is that after overcoming this resistance, government in England has normalised its interference in the curriculum so that subsequent ministerial intervention has been seen as less contentious. An alternative reading is that the episode has served as a reminder to government that citizens will expect it to avoid partisan changes to identity formation through schooling.[29]

Government exploitation of power over education may be regarded as more problematic in OECD countries when it is exercised less bluntly. For example, the European Commission programme on education and training has a strong theme of common European benchmark and shared practice in line with overall goals for European 'harmonisation'.[30] Citizenship education is largely promoted as preparing young people to accept a given definition of rights and responsibilities. National strategies in the field of financial literacy encourage young people to adopt 'responsible behaviours' in relation to personal finance rather than enabling a capacity to evaluate what politicians say about government finances or the proper role for government in relation to financial services (Pinto, 2013; Davies, 2015).

These dynamics position education as a place where tensions between the role of governments and markets and tensions among communities, nations and regional groups of nations are played out. National governments are, therefore, placed in an awkward position. The problem looks like this: (1) the role of government relative to markets and the role of national governments relative to diverse communities within the nation and other nations are matters of ongoing national debate; (2) education is a site for citizen formation: citizens who will be expected to express their views regarding the role of government and the nation state (Davies, 2006, 2015); (3) thus, on what grounds can national governments determine how education will prepare citizens to participate in decisions about the future of national governments?

Co-production and social reproduction

The previous chapter examined the extent to which the provision of education depends on inputs from parents and students. This makes a difference to the analysis of the supply of education, since the beneficiaries of education are also providing inputs to the process. Co-production has been identified as a feature of the provision of a number of services that often fall within the public domain (Parks *et al.*, 1981; Aligica & Tarko, 2013). Inputs provided through formal education may be considered as substitutes for input from parents and pupils. For example, parents may take on more paid employment when formal education for their children is extended. Alternatively, the effect of inputs from formal education may be regarded as contingent upon inputs from parents and pupils.[31] For example, pupils' effort could be galvanised by the efforts of schools and teachers either because of a role model effect or because they believe that their effort will have a higher pay-off when the efforts of schools and teachers are greater.

This introduces two new knowledge problems. One problem is that neither party to the bargain (parents or pupils on one side and schools on the other) knows the extent of the interdependence of formal and non-formal inputs into education. But even if formal providers, parents and pupils knew the extent of the interdependence of their inputs they would not know how much input others will be willing to give. This problem is somewhat akin to the prisoner's dilemma, but in this context it creates difficulties for market and traditional public sector provision (Aligicia & Tarko, 2013).

When we observe what schools do, we can see that these problems exist in practice, not just in theory. High-stakes examination systems reward schools which enrol children who (together with their parents) will provide a high level of input into their own learning. Evidence from England (West *et al.*, 2004) suggests that when schools are given some freedom to decide who to enrol, they do take parent and pupil inputs into account.

Schools also spend considerable effort in trying to maximise what *students* put into their learning. This seems to operate on three levels: behaviour, engagement and self-regulation. If students are not attending to teaching then the prospects for learning are low. These prospects can be improved by increasing the extent to which students feel engaged with their learning and increased still further if students direct their efforts more effectively. Variation in the initial commitment of students to the kind of education a provider offers will, therefore, be very important to the outcomes for the students at that institution. Students with high commitment to the kind of learning offered by the institution present providers with a smaller information problem: there is less need to worry about effectiveness of the inputs provided by the school or university and less need to worry about how to increase the input from the learner.

Students attending public schools may be expected, on average, to have lower levels of commitment to their education. Parents who pay to send their child to private school and parents who choose to move their child to a charter school in the USA or a free school in England tend to report higher expectations of the outcomes of schooling and tend to become more involved with their children's schooling (Witte & Thorn, 1996; Yang & Kayaardi, 2004; Goldring & Phillips, 2008). Greater parental input may also be accompanied by expectations of greater effort from their children. This suggests that, on average, public sector schools will face greater challenges than private schools through being less able to rely on co-production from parents and students, and this will make them more reliant on inherently uncertain information about the effectiveness of their choice of organisation and approaches to teaching.

Opaque quality and high switching costs

Difficulties consumers have in securing information about the quality of supply (discussed in Chapter 4, pp. 69–77), the multiple outcomes of education (discussed in Chapter 2, pp. 23–24), the 'one-off' nature of education choices and the high costs of switching from one school to another combine to create opportunities that a supplier might exploit for their own benefit.

Adam Smith (1937) famously argued that private suppliers would be driven to meet the needs of consumers by pursuing their own interests in a market context. Neoclassical economics formalises this idea as 'maximising profit leading to maximising efficiency'. Two critical conditions are required. First, consumers must be able to observe variation in quality; second, consumers must have an option to switch to a similar service offered by another provider at a price which is not inflated by 'abnormal profit' or organisational inefficiency. In cases where it is difficult to observe quality there is an incentive for a new market to develop to provide consumers with the information they want. In cases where there is only one provider, the threat of a new provider moving in to offer the service may be sufficient to encourage the supplier to act as though consumers always had the opportunity to switch to a competitor (Baumol, Panzar & Willig, 1982). If both of these conditions are fulfilled there is no reason to worry about providers' motivation: maximisation of profit serves the public interest if private and social costs and benefits are the same.

However, if either condition is not fulfilled, then providers' motivation matters. If consumers cannot easily observe the quality of a service, producers have an incentive to change the way in which they provide the service for their own benefit. Workers have an incentive to increase 'organisational slack' or 'X-inefficiency'

(Vining & Weimer, 1990; Ruggiero *et al.*, 1995): concentrating on their own working conditions, prospects for promotion and the expansion of spheres of influence within the organisation. Owners of private suppliers have an incentive to 'quality shade': reducing their cost of production by 'cutting corners' and providing a lower quality of service (Hart *et al.*, 1997; Adnett, 2004). For instance, Lacireno-Paquet *et al.* (2002) reported evidence suggesting that charter schools in the USA were reducing costs by cutting services to students whose first language was not English and to students with special educational needs.

The extent to which service providers will exploit the opportunities created by consumer ignorance and inflexibility will depend on producers' motivation. The public choice critique (Buchanan & Tullock, 1962) assumes that all providers will be motivated by self-interest regardless of whether they are for-profit or not-for-profit, privately or publicly owned. This analysis suggests that quality shading will be a problem in private supply and X-inefficiency will be a problem in public supply. The complexity of education makes it difficult to test this proposition. For example, Waldo (2007) reported that the efficiency of Swedish schools improved following the introduction of a voucher system in the early 1990s. However, he used examination and progression results as the sole measure of educational output. Therefore, we cannot tell whether he has provided evidence of X-inefficiency in state-owned education or quality shading by private suppliers (who may have reduced inputs by cutting services which contribute to other educational outcomes such as the inclusion of children with special educational needs).

Francois (2000, 2003) offered a contrasting view, suggesting that public sector workers would be more likely than private sector workers to act in the public interest even when this conflicts with their self-interest. Survey evidence (e.g. Houston, 2000) does suggest that workers in the public sector are more likely than workers in the private sector to declare that they are motivated by commitment to their work: intrinsic motivation. Moreover, they are more likely to volunteer and donate blood and money. Nonetheless, Bright (2008) found no relationship between public sector workers' commitment to public service motivation and their intentions to stay in their current job. Moreover, a comparison between public sector and private sector workers conflates two factors: the public/private sector difference and differences in the nature of the work. Many public sector workers are involved with caring for individuals either in education, social services or in health. In addition, it is important to know whether public service motivation is fostered by the governance of an organisation or whether individuals with a disposition towards public service seek employment in the public or not-for-profit sectors. Gregg and colleagues (2011) found that care workers in not-for-profit organisations were more willing than workers in for-profit organisations to work additional unpaid hours. However, their comparison indicated that this difference was largely due to workers with high public service motivation seeking employment in not-for-profit settings.

Consumers' information problems in education encourage them to foreground institutional reputations in their choice of school or university. The importance of supplier reputation has long been recognised in the marketing analysis of consumer choices (Barich & Kotler, 1991), and it is routinely noted in analyses of higher education choices (Olssen & Peters, 2005; Kim & Lee, 2006). Reputation helps establish a hierarchy of providers which is sustained by the pattern of educational choice. An educational institution which has established a reputation for higher quality attracts more applicants and can select the most able: reinforcing its reputation through its selectivity and through the peer effect which should positively support students' achievements (Adnett et al., 2002; Epple et al., 2004; MacLeod & Urquiola, 2009).[32] The strength of reputational effects in sustaining hierarchies of educational suppliers mitigates the scope for competition. If educational reputation takes years to develop and it depends on attracting the most able students, contestability will be weak, though this is more apparent in higher education than in school education. The supply of education through schools and universities is characterised by strong hierarchies built upon institutional reputations. This is reflected in the variation in tuition fees charged by universities in the USA and private schools in the UK. Average tuition fees at US community colleges in 2014/2015 were a quarter of those charged by private colleges offering full four-year degrees.[33] Private schools in England at the upper quartile charged tuition fees that were 33 per cent higher than the median (Davies & Davies, 2014). To some extent these differences reflect the quality of experience and investment that institutions offer. Parents paying higher school fees in England secure smaller class sizes, more non-teaching support staff and a slight advantage in the value-added performance in the school (Davies & Davies, 2014). Graduates of elite schools and universities also signal distinctive qualities to employers which help them secure high salaries and prestigious positions in the labour market.

Contingency of effective provision on local conditions

Education policy in OECD countries frequently proclaims that knowledge about effective provision of education is completely generalisable across all educational institutions in all countries. Policy borrowing assumes that 'it works there, so it will work here'. This approach to the generalisability of educational knowledge focuses on practices (e.g. 'Shanghai Maths', 'Reading Recovery', or increasing the length of the school day). Randomised controlled trials are used to compare outcomes of using the practice with outcomes of not using the practice. Results of these trials are subsequently collated by meta-analyses which gather types of practice into broad categories.[34] This process distils large volumes of evidence into clear messages for policy and practice. This characteristic is very attractive for governments seeking justifications for national policy, and it is also useful for busy teachers and lecturers looking for 'ready-to-implement' advice on practice. If we can rely on the guidance offered by 'what-works' generalisations then providing education is much the same as providing anything else: we can shift modes of provision around the world as long as we can train workers up to implement the best practice. However, we noted in Chapter 5 some of the challenges facing the use of RCTs in education.

As the results of RCTs are gathered up by meta-analyses we also face the challenge of how to judge whether practices really belong to the same category (as illustrated in Chapter 5 in a discussion of interventions using information and communications technology).

A very different view of knowledge about providing education suggests that it is entirely localised. 'What works' for one teacher does not work for another. 'What works' in one school does not work in another. 'What works' with one class does not work with another. This view of educational knowledge portrays individual teachers and schools as generators of knowledge for their own situations (Carr & Kemmis, 1986; Gore & Zeichner, 1991; Sanderson, 2003; Biesta, 2007a). This view of the provision of education foregrounds co-production: what will work in any educational context depends on the goals and capabilities of each of the participants: school, community, teacher, pupil and parent. The assumption here is that the way any practice turns out will depend on how it is interpreted by each of the participants and the outcome will be contingent upon the interaction between these interpretations. Improvement depends on the capacity of teachers and schools to recognise causation within the pattern of daily work and to be ready to respond to the causation they observe. This perspective is perfectly compatible with a market approach to identifying and firing teachers who do not recognise and respond to patterns of causation in their classroom. It is not compatible with the advocacy of randomised controlled trials.

A third perspective on knowledge about providing education suggests that there are generalisable underlying principles, but the activation and interplay among these principles depends on the participants and the social and cultural history of the context.[35] This position may be illustrated through the following extended quotation from a study of the impact of reducing class size or providing teaching assistants:

> We have learned that small classes in the primary grades are academically beneficial (especially for students at risk), have positive impacts on student behavior, and have benefits that last through ensuing years. Adding a full-time teacher aide to a regular-sized class, in contrast, does not affect the academic performance of the class. A great deal remains to be learned. One question is paramount: Under what organizational and instructional conditions can the benefits of small classes be maximized? For example, are the benefits increased if small classes are employed in conjunction with other programs targeted to students having difficulty (e.g., preschool programs, full-day kindergartens)? We know that teachers tend not to change their fundamental teaching strategies when given a small class. However, should they change their approaches to classroom management and instruction to take best advantage of the opportunities a small class presents?
>
> *(Finn & Achilles, 1999, p. 106)*

The initial claim that pupil behaviour was better in small classes does not mean that Finn and Achilles found that the behaviour of *every* pupil in a small class was better than the behaviour of every pupil in a larger class. Their paramount question directs attention to the contingency of the benefits of small classes upon factors that are locally determined. Variations *within* any particular approach to teaching or school organisation appear to have substantial impacts upon effectiveness. These problems are exemplified in the evidence and debate concerning (1) how phonics are taught in school (e.g. Pressley *et al.*, 2001; Wyse & Styles, 2007; Johnston *et al.*, 2012); (2) the deployment of teaching assistants (e.g. Cremin *et al.*, 2005; Blatchford *et al.*, 2007), and (3) the use of collaborative learning in schools (e.g. Johnson *et al.*, 1981, 2000; Slavin, 1990).

Summary

If education was like other goods and services (e.g. newspapers or agents in the housing market) then we might expect market incentives to offer the best chance of getting close to allocative efficiency. This section has examined several reasons why we might believe that education is sufficiently different from other 'information' goods and services to justify government intervention. The heart of the matter is whether we treat education as something that happens to individuals or to society as a whole.

Education is frequently portrayed as something that happens to individuals: the language of randomised controlled trials even refers to the 'dose' that individuals receive from a 'treatment'. When education is treated as something that an individual receives it becomes easier to think of the supply of education in much the same way as we think of the supply of any good or service provided by markets. But education may also be thought of as something that a whole society does to equip itself for the future. The term 'educated society' conjures up an idea of collective behaviour and imagination, not simply a set of individuals who have received a given amount of education. A society may educate itself to tolerate some things and not others, to value and preserve some things and not others, and to foster common effort to achieve some things and not others. This second view of education shares agency in education between teachers *and* students, between schools *and* parents, and between individuals *and* communities. It is the cornerstone of arguments that it is better not to treat education as just the same as any other good or service. In a world where globalisation is perceived as eroding local identity and autonomy, reassertion of the collective role of education is long overdue.

However, the arguments about education being either a public or a positional good do not provide a sound basis for preferring government supply of education. Careful reasoning and mutual understanding is rarely served well by words used by different scholars to mean completely different things and this is palpably the case with the term 'public good'. Moreover, there is a hint of normalised circularity in claims that a service traditionally provided by the public sector is a 'public good' which, therefore, naturally belongs in the public sector. Education provided by schools and universities does not fulfil the criteria that economists use to distinguish 'public goods'. The relevant strand in Hirsch's positional good argument is whether education is fixed in supply. There is conclusive evidence that it is not absolutely fixed, though the sorting literature indicates that only half of the additional income gained through more education is attributable to increase in productive capacity. The positional good argument is the wrong place to look for concerns about inequality in the supply of education. The place to look is the role of parents, peers and children themselves in the co-production of education and the association between co-production and an exclusively individualistic perspective on the outcomes of education.

Finally, online education *is* 'non-rival' if it is not 'blended' with input from a tutor. The low or even zero marginal cost of this form of providing education is highly attractive to any private supplier who can exclude non-payers and secure a large monopoly market. In principle, ease of access to supply online education may encourage belief that competition would stop this happening. However, the emergence of huge and powerful software companies in the IT industry discourages this optimism. Since education is a formative good (shaping tastes and identity), the risks of private monopoly supply are severe and these two arguments provide a strong basis for some form of government intervention. There is a tension between governments' desires to use education to form coherent and fair societies and the fulfilment of values and aspirations in different parts of a society.

Some policy implications

This chapter concludes with a few observations on the implications of this analysis for education policy. The overall question for policy is to what extent it makes sense to pay for education through markets, hierarchies and networks in providing education. Chapter 7 follows up these observations by examining particular policy problems.

Treating the problem as markets versus hierarchies versus networks offers a more complete frame for analysis than treating the problem as 'public versus private sector'

Treating the policy problem as 'public or private sector provision' glosses over some important factors. First, it ignores the role of networks in providing education. Networks of individuals and organisations always play some role in providing education. The provision of education is influenced by the nature of networks that connect (1) parents, schools and teachers; (2) professional workers in education, and (3) educational organisations. Second, conflating 'public' with 'hierarchy' and conflating 'private' with 'market' detracts attention from interactive governance within the private as well as within the public sector. Large private sector organisations act as hierarchies: as described by the huge literature on the implications of organisational structure in the private sector.

It is useful to separate demand-side and supply-side arguments

Chapter 4 focused on implications of different governance systems for the demand for education, while this chapter has focused on the supply or provision of education. This distinction is clearly derived from economics. While the whole point of market analysis is that outcomes arise from the interaction between supply and demand, separate analyses of these two sides helps clarify the mix of ingredients involved in creating outcomes. Chapters 4 and 6 have extended this division to an examination of governance through hierarchies and networks as well as governance through markets. From a policy point of view this perspective means that government intervention may be justified in terms of the demand for education, the supply of education, or both. Many advocates of a greater role for market forces in the provision of education have accepted arguments for government intervention in the demand for education. They have accepted that market forces alone would create unacceptable inequality and would pay inadequate attention to the role of education in building a just, civilised and well-functioning society. Their arguments have largely focused on the rationale for encouraging governance through markets on the supply side.

Judgements about the best system for providing education rest heavily on prior assumptions about (1) the generalisability of knowledge about providing education, and (2) whether educators are self-interested or have public service motivation

Prior assumptions about the generalisability of knowledge in providing education and the motivation of workers have been referred to throughout this chapter. If knowledge about how to provide education is tacit and localised ('what works *here*'), then the people with the knowledge are the workers on the spot and it makes sense to leave the governance of education to networks which respond to the voices of these people. This argument underpins a diverse set of programmes in education: 'professional learning communities', 'distributed learning', 'academy' or 'charter' schools and 'free schools'. This chapter has examined how these programmes have mirrored, and in some cases directly borrowed from, developments in private sector organisations. However, if knowledge about education is entirely generalizable, then it makes sense to opt for a form of governance that will be most effective in generating and disseminating this knowledge and which will create conditions which more or less force workers in education to act in line with these known 'general truths'.

Arguments or policies that stick to either a stance of 'all knowledge is local' or 'all knowledge is general' can be outlined with clarity. This makes them attractive for academics and policy makers. However, either position looks simplistic in the context of what actually happens in classrooms or seminar rooms. Teachers follow some general principles *and* they adapt what they do according to their perceptions of particular classes, particular students and particular occasions. It is reasonable to judge teaching according to the way that general principles have been recognised and according to the way that teaching has responded to the here and now. The account provided in this chapter has reflected a belief that teaching at all levels is a complex activity because many principles are in play. The job of the school, university, teacher and lecturer is to frame practice in the light of a bagful of principles and to resolve the tensions among these principles. This necessarily entails some reliance on governance through networks on the spot, but it does not mean that there is no place for either hierarchies or markets.

The assumption that workers in the public sector are entirely motivated by self-interest has been highly influential in the design of education reforms in some OECD countries. This assumption is fundamental to the public choice critique of governance through (public sector) hierarchies and networks (Chubb & Moe, 1990). According to the public choice critique, competition is the only answer to the provider's self-interest. Therefore, market governance is required on the supply side in education, just like any other part of the public sector. If we assume the existence of 'public service motivation' in education, then the critical thing is to make sure that the governance of education fosters workers' intrinsic desire to do the right thing: to nourish the 'teacher's soul' (Ball, 2003b). The literature on both sides of this argument is among the most widely cited in the field of education. This, perhaps, is testimony not only to the salience of these arguments but also to the depth of conviction with which these arguments are held. But, as with the argument about the generality of knowledge, the clarity of the opposing positions is achieved at the expense of attention to the many sides of providers' behaviour. Studies of teacher motivation in the USA (e.g. Shann, 1998), the UK and Australia have reported what Day *et al.* (2005, p. 575) refer to as "strongly held purposes and principles of care and commitment to pupils' learning and achievement". Many teachers have reported readiness to work beyond allotted hours despite the stress this has caused them (Punch & Tuetteman, 1996; Jepson & Forrest, 2006). Yet, retention of teachers in challenging urban schools is a major problem (Quartz & TEP Research Group, 2003). Teachers do drift from tougher to easier environments in which to work. Like workers elsewhere, teachers are driven by a mix of motivations. Not all teachers have the same intrinsic motivation (Firestone, 2014). Moreover, teachers who have a strong public service motivation are not immune from self-interest.

The arguments for and against different provider systems apply in different ways according to the type of education in the spotlight

One of the key arguments for treating education as different from other goods and services is the role of education in forming individual (McClellan, 1999; Berkowitz & Grych, 2000) and collective (e.g. Kerr, 1999; Davies, 2006) identities. This theme is more prominent in literature on schooling than in literature on higher education, notwithstanding the association between participating in higher education and a range of behaviours (e.g. voting) that are commonly regarded as sources of public benefit (as noted in Chapter 3). It is understandable that expectations that education will play a positive role in forming character and citizenship will focus on compulsory schooling rather than higher education in which only a portion of each cohort participates. This chapter has outlined the hazards in relying on either markets or governments to shape education which will affect individual or collective identities. Even when a government takes control of the demand for education, it is extremely difficult to draw up contracts for providers that fully specify the education provided. Providers may ignore education for character and citizenship formation which does not affect how their performance is judged in the market and they may also aim to develop preferences and beliefs which will serve the interests of the provider organisation in the future. Even so, the choice between form of governance is not straightforward, since there are also problems for networks and (public) hierarchies. Even when members of a network have 'public service motivation', they may have a partisan concept of the public interest which favours one social class or one ethnic group. A public hierarchy may struggle to respect the interests of minority communities.

The 'toll-good' characteristics of online education apply differently in compulsory schooling and voluntary higher education. Since schooling has a dual role of educating and minding children in place of parents, there is currently little scope for largely replacing teachers with online education. However, there is considerable scope for online education in higher education, especially since online media already provide plenty of scope for online social interaction. With current technology, online courses offer a cheaper but educationally inferior experience with very high drop-out rates. There is considerable potential for online education to increase educational stratification with consequences for inequality in society. It is also worth noting that past science fiction imaginations of education through electronic media[36] assumed that such education would be provided by a state hierarchy. Dystopia wore a public face. But what if the face is private, driven by a profit motive?

The implications of governance for co-production may also change as students get older. One dimension of the problem is substitution of effort between the student, parents and educational institutions. A second dimension is the complementarity between the approaches to instruction and learning adopted by parents, students and educational institutions. A third dimension is the dependence of the student's capacity for learning on previous educational experiences. Although we know that each of these three dimensions creates challenges for any form of governance, there is no theoretically clear reason why one system should be better than the others and we do not currently have sufficient evidence to help us to judge.

Different forms of governance continually interact

Policy changes need to take account of interactions between forms of governance. Increasing the role for markets, hierarchies or networks is not a simple business. A change in the scope for one form of governance stimulates reactions by other forms of governance, and it makes sense for these to be taken into account before any change is initiated. There are continual processes through which markets erode hierarchies and networks, hierarchies erode markets and networks, and networks erode markets and hierarchies.

Even when education is provided through a state hierarchy, the policies announced by a central government are implemented through networks. Policies may be resisted or re-interpreted by workers as they are put into practice (Fullan, 2000; Ball *et al.*, 2012). Similar problems afflict government policy when it is enacted through markets for education. Since education is expected to provide a range of outcomes through complex processes it is impossible to draw up contracts for private suppliers that preclude providers' room for manoeuvre over the quantity and quality of what is provided. Moreover, networks and markets naturally seek to extend their influence to the formation of policy itself. Workers form professional associations to bargain with government and to foster support from individual politicians. Private providers try to achieve 'regulatory capture': where interaction between government regulators and private companies redirects the regulators away from the public interest and towards the interests of the organisations they are supposed to be regulating (Carpenter & Moss, 2014). Mintrom (1997) and Ball and Junemann (2012) have expanded the analysis of this problem as it affects education through their accounts of the behaviour of 'policy networks'.

Hierarchies erode networks through external and internal actions. First, government hierarchies will seek to capture networks by normalising ways of thinking (e.g. about education) which recruit networks to actions in line with government wishes (Lemke, 2012). Second, they reduce scope for action by networks through legislation limiting rights of association and through monitoring work practices. But networks are also eroded from the inside when they become like hierarchies: particular interest groups or individuals may secure the 'commanding heights' of a network, effectively disenfranchising members of that network. The loyalty of network members is maintained in these circumstances by the benefits of belonging to a large network and the expectation that a shift to hierarchical control will strengthen the network's ability to act decisively and coherently. Markets erode networks through tempting network members away with the prospect of higher personal gains if they trade on their own (Slaughter & Rhodes, 2004). Networks may be particularly vulnerable to market erosion during periods of substantial economic, social and technological change if markets respond more rapidly than networks.

Notes

1 As in McGregor's (1964) 'Theory X'.
2 Referred to by Sappington (1991) as the 'canonical' model.
3 It also ignores the possibility that (some) unions will negotiate with government to shape policy and working arrangements for front-line workers (Stevenson, 2007).
4 The arrival of Donald Trump in the White House gave this impression a substantial boost.
5 Since, according to Lavy (2007), valid and reliable value-added measures are essential for an adequate performance-related pay scheme, doubts over value-added measures undermine the incentive schemes discussed in Chapter 5.

6 Despite the lack of evidence to support the strategy of matching learning activities to 'learning styles' (Coffield *et al.*, 2004) it became routine for Ofsted inspectors to encourage this practice. It is still happening, as is apparent from recent reports complimenting schools on attention to children's learning styles (see e.g. the reports on The Loddon School (July 2015) and the report on the Oaklea Montessori (June 2015). The report on the Longdon Park School (April 2016) praised the school because "teaching staff give excellent attention to pupils' individual learning styles" (school inspection reports are available at https://reports.ofsted.gov.uk/). A summary of Ofsted reports in 2014 and 2015 prepared by Oxfordshire County Council stated that it was a requirement that there was "accurate assessment of children's development and learning styles so that children can be fully engaged in their learning" (www.oxfordshire.gov.uk/.../Themes_from_recent_Ofsted_inspections.pdf).

7 Some support for the reliability of school inspections in England has been suggested by the association between inspection grades and pupil performance (Hussain, 2012). However, since inspectors are required to take pupil performance into account when making their judgements this is hardly surprising.

8 Gathered through a survey. Nearly 90 per cent of schools in the UK and Australia taking part in the OECD-PISA survey of 2006 believed they were competing with two or more schools. The comparable proportions were just over 60 per cent in the USA and 40 per cent in Finland (Agasisti & Murtinu, 2012). While some of this variation will be due to differences among countries in the distribution of population, the comparisons across all countries suggests that this does not explain all of the variation.

9 Although this is not necessarily always the case. A network that takes the form of a closed or bonded community can become so isolated from the rest of the world that it turns into a powerless object of pity or wonder to those outside.

10 See Birchler and Bütler (2007, ch. 7) for a detailed exposition.

11 As Walford (2006, p. 20) comments, we might expect governing bodies of private schools who are typically alumni of private schools and not infrequently of the private school they now govern to have a somewhat conservative approach to change. However, from his own research Walford observes a willingness of governing bodies to embrace change, albeit somewhat slowly.

12 As noted later, incentives to innovate may still arise from positioning in networks, status within the profession and public service motivation. But these incentives arise beyond markets.

13 Price discrimination involves charging different processes (in this case tuition fees) to different consumers. This requires the provider to be able to separate out consumers into groups to determine eligibility for lower fees: in this case by household income, subject to very high prior attainment by the child.

14 After the industrialist synonymous with production line manufacturing and the inventor of 'scientific management' epitomised by time and motion studies.

15 This being a view derived from Marx as discussed, for example, by Timmermans and Epstein (2010).

16 Biesta (2007b) views education from the perspective of 'symbolic interactionism', since teaching and learning involves an interaction through the symbols embodied in the language and thought of the participants.

17 Throughout this section networks will be treated as synonymous with communities.

18 Muijs and colleagues (2010) label their four classifications 'constructivist organisational theory as a basis for networking', 'creating social capital as a basis for networking', 'creating networks as New Social Movements' and 'Avoiding organisational anomie as a basis for collaboration', and they ground each type in a theoretical literature.

19 Systematic evidence of the effect of teachers' expectations (Jussim & Harber, 2005) suggests that they do have an observable but small effect. It does matter if teachers systematically underestimate the potential of a particular group of students, but this only accounts for a small proportion of observed variation in performance among students from different backgrounds.

20 This concept of improvement in schools is very similar to Mintzberg's (1979) espousal of 'emergent strategy' in commercial settings.

21 Although there are earlier examples of collaboration between universities. Cantoni and Yuchtman (2014) have described the impact of a network of early universities in Germany upon economic organisation and trade in the late medieval period. Three universities in Northern England set up a joint entrance examination board (the Joint Matriculation Board) in 1902. There are some long-standing examples of private school groups (such as the Girls Day School Trust formed in England in 1872), but these have a single governing board and report their finances through a single annual statement, so they are better understood as a single organisation.

22 See http://russellgroup.ac.uk/about/.

23 The 'innovation as applied invention' perspective treats innovation as partially situated: contingent upon what is feasible in the context.

24 Education may also be distinguished from some other goods on the basis of *demand-side* factors such as the existence of positive externalities which were examined in Chapters 3 and 4. A free market would be expected to ignore positive externalities with the consequence that supply will be below the level that is best for society. This chapter focuses on distinctiveness which is associated with the *conditions* of supply rather than distinctiveness which is initiated by demand to which there will be a supply response.

25 Buchanan (1965) defined goods which could be shared within a limited group on a 'non-rival' basis as 'club goods', since non-members of the group could be excluded from the good.

26 This may be observed in the portfolios offered by recently established for-profit universities in the UK such as Arden and BPP. See https://arden.ac.uk/ and www.distance learningportal.com/universities/741/bpp-university.html.

27 From the Headmaster's welcome to Harrow School (www.harrowschool.org.uk/from-the-head-master).

28 From the 'Our missions, aim and values' on the website of Al-Burhan Grammar School (http://alburhan.org.uk/site/about-us/our-missions-aims-and-values).

29 As perhaps suggested by the readiness of a minister to revise proposed reforms to the history curriculum in 2013 (www.theguardian.com/education/2013/jun/21/michael-gove-history-curriculum).

30 See e.g. the statements on the European Commission website for Education and Training (http://ec.europa.eu/education/policy/strategic-framework/index_en.htm).

31 This process is referred to in the co-production literature as interdependence, but it may also be described as symbolic operations (see e.g. Biesta, 2007b), in that educational outcomes are products of interactions between teachers and students in the realm of ideas or symbols.

32 Giving rise to the 'cream-skimming' phenomenon.

33 See QS Top Universities website (www.topuniversities.com/student-info/student-finance/how-much-does-it-cost-study-us).

34 See e.g. the Teaching and Learning Toolkit provided by the Education Endowment Foundation in England (https://educationendowmentfoundation.org.uk/resources/teaching-learning-toolkit).

35 Broadly speaking, this is the position adopted by critical realism (see Maxwell, 2004; Scott, 2013).

36 As in, for example, Huxley's *Brave New World*, originally published in 1932, and Asimov's *The Naked Sun*, originally published in 1957.

7

POLICY QUESTIONS

Introduction

Two major questions for policy are how much to pay, and how to control the supply of what is paid for. Each question has a value-for-money dimension and a fairness dimension, as suggested in Table 7.1.

The first question (Row 1) focuses on the value of education to society. This is the demand question (examined in Chapters 2 to 4). Although the idea that 'people don't always know what is best for them' is troubling or even offensive to some (e.g. West & McKee, 1983), we know that even when education is free and will increase their future earnings, some individuals choose to drop out of formal education. This is demonstrated by comparisons of earnings of students before and after the raising of the school-leaving age in England. But the major arguments for government paying for education stem from benefits for society: productivity, cohesion, culture and equity. The fundamental problem here is that all these benefits are difficult to measure. It is hard for a government to justify how *much* it pays for education by referring to tables of statistics measuring the value of what it has paid

TABLE 7.1 Value for money and fairness in policy questions

	Value for money dimension	*Fairness dimension*
1 *How much to pay?*	Could social welfare be improved by expecting individuals to pay more?	How do government payments affect equity and social mobility?
2 *How to control supply?*	How does government intervention affect the costs of supplying education?	Can government intervention improve equity by changing the form of education that is provided?

for. Therefore, anyone who believes that governments will always waste money will believe that government has spent too much on education (see Craig, 2008; Grubb, 2009). Conversely, governments which base their appeal to voters on low taxation will have a strong political incentive to spend insufficiently on education. As incomes and demand for education rise, the pressure on education spending becomes hard for governments to handle. They look for ways of spending less and asking individuals to pay more. A decrease in public spending as a proportion of total education spending risks increasing inequality. It also implies that the social benefits of education are becoming less important at a time when private valuations of education are rising.

The second question (how to control supply) was examined in Chapters 5 and 6. Governments influenced by the public choice critique have tried to improve value for money by changing the conditions of supply (e.g. replacing government-owned provision by contracting private suppliers; encouraging competition between publicly owned schools and universities; reducing scope for professionals to determine what is provided and how it is provided; and providing information to students and parents in the belief that this will help them make better choices). A range of terms has been used to classify and analyse these changes. Since these terms have been used in different ways in different places it makes sense to pause and clarify how they may be used to avoid confusion.

First, the term 'public provider' (as in 'public' university) could usefully be restricted to cases where a provider is owned by the state. Many charities rely on being commissioned by the state to provide services. Some defence contractors rely heavily on the state buying what they produce. But we do not refer to these charities or defence contractors as being *public* organisations. Referring to a 'not-for-profit' provider as a 'public university' makes it more difficult to select appropriate analytical frames that have been developed to study the operation of different types of organisation. Second, the term 'privatisation' was coined to refer to instances where the ownership of an organisation changed from the public to the private sector. Gas, water and rail industries charged consumers for their services at point of use while they were owned by the government. Introducing a fee for use when previously there was none is not privatisation; it is something else. Third, marketisation is a useful shorthand for capturing a broad policy shift towards more reliance on market forces (e.g. Bartlett *et al.*, 2002; Lynch, 2006). It also guides us towards the implications of this policy stance for the distribution of benefits and inequality in society. But it is useful to distinguish between micro and macro aspects of this term. At the micro level it refers to the increasing exposure of an organisation to market forces (e.g. through competition) and it implies a reduction in the power of hierarchies and professional networks. At the macro level it refers to the extent to which markets determine the allocation of all goods and services, and the consequences for the fairness with which benefits are distributed. This theme has been highlighted by analyses of the 'labour share' of national income. This share has been declining in OECD countries (Karabarbounis & Neiman, 2013; Piketty, 2014; Piketty & Zucman, 2014; ILO/OECD, 2015) during recent decades when governments have been increasingly relying on governance through market forces. This trend has been attributed, at least in part, to long-term changes in industrial structure, especially the increasing importance of ICT. But government policies have also played a part. Figure 7.1 shows how the percentage of UK GDP (Gross Domestic Product) going to earners has changed during the stewardship of governments with different standpoints on market forces and social equality.

Finally, policy changes have often been described as making providers more accountable. This term conveys an impression of restraining selfish intentions: the assumption of 'principal–agent' analysis. But a provider can be held to account in different ways. Accountability can be increased by tightening hierarchical control. It can be increased by greater exposure to competition that offers viable alternatives to consumers. It can also be increased when professional networks become more tight-knit, increasing the benefits from sticking to the norm. In each case it is not self-evident that more accountability is necessarily a good thing. Moreover, accountability focuses attention on what may be measured: results in public examinations, international tests in 'core skills' or subsequent earnings. These measures do tell us a lot about the private benefits of education, but they do not tell us anything about the wider benefits of education for society. If we make schools and universities accountable for their performance in delivering private benefits we also discourage them from bothering about the wider benefits to society which justify the government spending in the first place.

This chapter uses the frame presented in Figure 7.2 to analyse policy options for controlling the supply of education. The contracting literature suggests that the main choice for governments is whether to provide education through organisations it owns or to commission private ('not-for-profit' or 'for-profit') organisations to provide education as specified in contracts that it prepares. Either alternative accepts that the analysis in Chapters 2 to 4 justifies governments in demanding

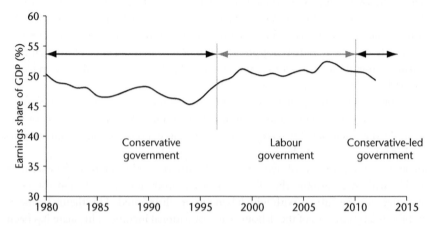

FIGURE 7.1 The share of earnings in UK Gross Domestic Product over time.

Source: Office for National Statistics on the share of earnings in GDP (time series).

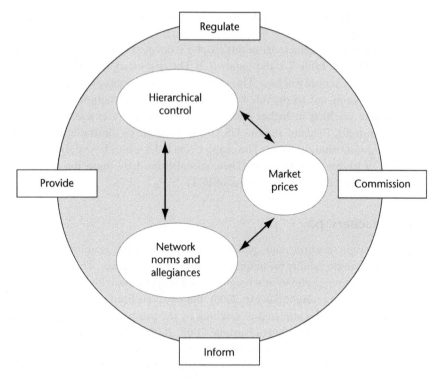

FIGURE 7.2 A frame for analysing policy options for government intervention in education.

education on behalf of their citizens. The answer to the 'provide or commission' question depends on judgements about the efficiency of different suppliers, and this, in turn, depends on judgements about motivation, incentives and norms. A government may also opt for a hybrid of 'provide and commission'. It may retain ownership of school properties while commissioning organisations to provide education using publicly owned facilities. This is a form of 'franchising' which is a common model in business (Gillis & Castrogiovanni, 2012).

The outer circle shown in Figure 7.2 indicates that governments may opt for regulation or information either as alternatives or supplements to providing or commissioning education. The chosen combination of provision, commissioning, regulation and information will frame policy which will be worked out through interactions among hierarchical, market and network governance (the inner part shown in Figure 7.2). Regulation may be conducted through inspection of educational establishments and threat of closure. It may also be exercised through price control, as in the case of a cap on tuition fees. Governments may try to inform students and parents by providing information about the qualities of different education providers and they may try to inform providers by disseminating advice and evidence. The choices a government makes about regulation and information interact with choices about providing and commissioning, and these interactions feed into the implementation of education policy through the combination of governance mechanisms.

The majority of the remainder of this chapter is devoted to analysis of two policy areas in the light of Table 7.1 and Figure 7.2. The first example is the problem of how much to pay school teachers. This case is chosen as an example of policy issues when governments opt to provide education. The second example is paying for undergraduate teaching in higher education. This example uses a comparison of policy in Australia, England and the USA. This comparison illustrates the options of providing and commissioning. The chapter concludes with a few speculations on the future of paying for education. These speculations draw upon the analysis in this book and they focus on the impact of ICT.

School teachers' pay

Getting the right quantity and quality of teachers is a big issue. Teachers are entrusted with responsibility for helping to create future societies. This includes the human capital narrative and so much more. Suitable applicants will only be attracted to teaching if the pay is right (Lazear, 2003), but pay is far from the only consideration. Individuals are also attracted to teaching by the prospects of helping children and nurturing society (Watt & Richardson, 2007, 2008). This is fortunate, because teaching is a complex job[1] and it is very difficult to continuously observe and check what teachers do. These characteristics suggest that teaching should be considered a 'profession' (Hoyle, 1974; Matthews, 1991) in which self-regulation and public service motivation play important roles. This creates a problem for governments that employ teachers. Governments that 'pay the piper' may like to call the tune, but the quality of a teacher's work depends on whether their heart is in it.[2] Paying for effective teachers also involves paying for their development at point of entry to the profession and later in their careers (OECD, 2011). This section examines three questions: How much should teachers be paid on average? Should local providers be allowed to vary teachers' pay? How should teachers' work be governed in order to secure good value for money?

Setting the level of average teacher pay

On average, teachers in OECD countries earn just under 80 per cent of the average pay of tertiary educated workers in those countries (OECD, 2017). A government may consider using this figure as a rough benchmark in setting teachers' pay. However, there is variation among countries: the UK and Australia are close to the OECD average but teachers in the USA have low relative wages compared to teachers in other OECD countries. This looks like bad news for students in the USA if we accept that there is a positive association between teacher pay and academic outcomes for pupils: the conclusion of a comparative study by Dolton and Marcenaro-Gutierrez (2011) using a sample of 39 countries, including several from outside the OECD. However, the importance of teachers' relative pay depends substantially on the reasons why people choose to become teachers and the reasons why they stay. If teachers accept lower average pay because the job offers security and a good pension, then the profession will attract cautious and risk-averse individuals. If individuals begin teaching because entry salaries are competitive, but leave because high performance and high responsibility are not rewarded very well, then there will be high rates of teacher turnover.[3] Either of these two arguments could explain the findings of Dolton and Marcenaro-Gutierrez (2011). However, if teachers accept lower pay because they are more driven than others by public sector motivation, then public welfare will benefit from teachers' altruism. An association between teacher pay and student performance does not necessarily mean causation. Finally, if teachers receive relatively low pay because they work in a female-dominated profession, there is a clear equity issue for public policy. The majority of teachers in state schools in England are female (85 per cent in primary schools, 62 per cent in secondary schools[4]). Some of the gender pay gap in European countries may be attributed to motivation, choice of subject of study and career (Chevalier, 2007). Some may be attributed to childcare policies (Blau & Kahn, 2003). But part is attributable to the pay disadvantage experienced by professions with a high proportion of female employees (Tomaskovic-Devey, 1993). It is not yet clear how far each of these factors affects average teacher pay.

There are also several reasons why pressure on teachers' earnings may change over time. First, there is evidence that demand for education grows as general prosperity increases (discussed in Chapters 2 and 3). Secular decline in pupil–teacher ratios (PTRs) may be interpreted in this light. For example, between 1984 and 2014 the average PTR in private schools in England fell from 15.2 to 10.9.[5] Market principles suggest that the relative pay of teachers would have to rise to attract more entrants into teaching. The alternative would be to accept entrants into teaching who would previously have been turned away. Second, fluctuations in birth rates and migration can lead to substantial changes in the school-age population. Between 2002 and 2016 the number of children in primary and secondary schools in Australia increased by approximately 1 per cent a year, but there were also fluctuations around this average. Between 2014 and 2015 the number of children in primary schools rose by 5 per cent and the number of children in secondary schools fell by just over 1 per cent.[6] Between 2003 and 2017 in England the number of children rose by an average of 0.6 per cent a year in primary schools but fell by an average of 0.25 per cent a year in secondary schools (Department for Education, 2017a). Table 7.2 shows the combined effects of secular rise in the demand for education (reflected in lower PTRs) and population changes. The growth in the number of teachers was much stronger in the private sector, primarily on account of the greater reduction in PTR.

The third factor affecting the demand for teachers in the state sector is the budgetary policy of central government. One traditional criticism of public sector ownership has been the susceptibility of spending decisions to the government's stance on fiscal policy. The consequences of the 2008 financial crash began to affect teachers' salaries after 2010. In 2011 central government introduced a pay freeze for

TABLE 7.2 Change over time in the number of pupils and teachers in state-funded schools in England

	1984	2014	1984–2014
State primary schools			
Number of pupils	3,765,845	4,416,710	17.3
Number of teachers	165,637	215,500	30.1
Pupil–teacher ratio	22.1	20.9	−5.4
State secondary schools			
Number of pupils	3,645,586	3,181,360	−12.7
Number of teachers	224,648	213,400	−5.0
Pupil–teacher ratio	16.2	15.5	−4.3
Private schools			
Number of pupils	421,520	511,928	21.4
Number of teachers	28,695	47,084	64.1
Pupil–teacher ratio	15.2	10.9	−28.3

Sources: Statistical releases on the school workforce from the Department for Education and the annual census conducted by the Independent Schools Council which accounts for more than 80% of private school enrolments.

public sector workers in England and from 2013 to 2017 this was superseded by a 1 per cent cap on pay increases. The OECD (2017) calculated that the real value of average teachers' salaries in England fell by 10 per cent between 2005 and 2015. Average real pay for all workers in the UK was the same in 2015 as it had been in 2005,[7] so the pay of teachers relative to other workers has also declined by 10 per cent.

In 2017 the National Audit Office (NAO, 2017) reported the results of a survey of school leaders they had conducted in 2015/2016. Only half of these school leaders reported that they had filled vacancies with teachers who had the required experience and expertise, and 97 per cent believed that cost was a barrier to improving their teaching workforce. Only one-fifth of those leaving teaching in 2015/2016 in England were retiring. Perhaps more worryingly, the rate at which teachers were leaving the profession increased substantially (by 2.1 percentage points) between 2011 and 2016. Over the same period the pupil–teacher ratio in secondary schools rose by approximately three-quarters of 1 percentage point. Moreover, in 2015/2016, the government allocated just 0.16 per cent (one-sixth of 1 per cent) of the £21 billion spent on employing teachers to improving teacher quality. Any government with some belief in the virtues of market forces would know that they were presiding over long-term damage to prospects for children and society.

Local variation in teacher pay

When teacher pay is set at federal or state level there are inevitable imbalances between supply and demand for teachers by locality and by subject. In 2017 the

House of Commons Education Committee worried (p. 7) that there had been (in England) "recruitment shortages of secondary teachers of physics, mathematics and design & technology for many years". Approximately 30 per cent of schools in outer London reported at least one unfilled vacancy in 2016 (NAO, 2017). This contrasts with vacancy rates in the same year in Scotland at less than 1 per cent in primary schools and 1.2 per cent in secondary schools (SPICe, 2017). Financial incentives for individuals to train to teach maths or science and extra pay for London teachers were clearly inadequate to deal with the problems. For Wolf (2010), the answer is clear: get rid of national pay bargaining in the public sector and let providers negotiate rates of pay in response to local market pressures. The feasibility of this option depends on what schools would do if they had freedom to set local pay scales.

Even when salary scales are negotiated nationally there is still some scope for schools to offer higher salaries through the number of posts with greater responsibility and through the number of posts awarded to newly qualified teachers. Table 7.2 shows that, in 2014/2015, schools in London spent just over £5,000 more per teacher than schools in the rest of the country. This partly reflects an additional salary allowance for teachers in London schools. In 2014/2015 this amounted to just over £5,000 for schools in inner London and just over £1,000 for schools in outer London. Given that the ratio of schools was 60 per cent in outer London and 40 per cent in inner London, Table 7.3 suggests that approximately half of the

TABLE 7.3 Factors associated with school spending on teachers[†] in state-funded secondary schools in England (2014–2015)

	B	p	mean	s.d.
London school	5,083	<0.001		
Not an academy school	37	0.808		
Not a faith school	−75	0.699		
Percentage of teachers qualified teacher status (certificated)	103	<0.001	95	7.5
School value-added (best 8 measure)	5.26	0.132	999	26
Percentage of pupils eligible for free school meals	83	<0.001	15	11
Percentage of Black pupils	87	0.253	0.63	1.3
Percentage of pupils with English as second language	−9	0.089	15	20
Percentage of pupils with statement of special educational needs	157	0.004	2	1.5
Pupil–teacher ratio	774	<0.001	15	2.4
Constant	19,098	<0.001		
R^2		0.50		
N		2,617		

Notes

† Spending per teacher (rather than total school spending on teachers) is greater than average salary, as it also includes employers' pension contributions and national insurance. It reflects the overall cost to a school of employing an additional teacher. Data obtained from school expenditure tables produced by the Department for Education.

higher teacher earnings in London schools were attributable to the London allowance. Given the challenges in recruitment for schools in outer London (NAO,
2017) it appears that they were trying to attract teachers through higher salaries.
Table 7.3 also shows that schools with higher proportions of pupils eligible for free
school meals (FSMs) were paying higher salaries. During that year secondary schools
received an additional £935 for each student eligible for free school meals. A school
of average size (950 pupils) with a proportion of children eligible for FSMs one
standard deviation above the average received close to £100,000 more income
than a school with the average proportion of children eligible for FSMs. Given that
the average school employed just under 70 teachers, the figures in Table 7.3 suggest
that using higher pay to retain valued staff was a major consideration in schools' use
of the pupil premium. After taking school characteristics into account, Table 7.3
also shows that some schools in England were willing to pay higher average salaries
while increasing average class size. However, there was no indication that academy
schools, which were given more budget flexibility, used this freedom to attract
teachers through higher pay. They did (as shown in Chapter 5), compared to other
schools, choose to employ more teachers relative to teaching assistants. Moreover,
private schools in England with greater income per pupil (through tuition fees and
endowments) employ more teachers and more non-teaching staff, but do not offer
higher salaries (Davies & Davies, 2014).

Therefore, there appears to be an asymmetry in schools' tendency to use higher
pay to attract teachers. The main driver seems to be desperation rather than capacity. Schools offered higher salaries when they had difficulty recruiting enough
staff. This supports Wolf's expectation that severe shortages of teachers in some
localities and severe shortages of certain types of teacher might be resolved by local
bargaining. However, schools which had greater financial freedom to attract higher
quality staff were not using salary incentives. Perhaps higher quality staff are more
attracted by the characteristics of the school and the quality of environment it offers
for teaching. Moreover, we do not know how much pay would need to rise to
attract sufficient teachers to outer London, or to attract graduates to teach mathematics or physics in secondary schools across the country. Nor do we know how
teacher productivity would be affected if teachers on the same scale earned much
more for teaching mathematics than for teaching English. The viability of the local
market solution depends on the size of pay differentials required to deal with shortages: and this cannot be inferred from comparisons with other countries.

Paying teachers and value for money

Improving the quality of teaching without paying more to employ teachers is obviously going to be attractive to a government. It is also attractive to those who
assume that increases in state spending will necessarily waste money (e.g. Grubb,
2009). The previous two sections have set out the case for believing that teachers'
pay does matter. But it is not all that matters. Once a teacher has been employed,
several factors will affect the quality of their work: how hard they work; what they

know and how this knowledge improves; their expectations of students; what they come to regard as normal patterns of teaching and teacher behaviour; their effect on what students and parents put into the process of learning, and their capacity to make wise judgements in complex situations. Each of these factors is affected by the way in which teaching and teachers are governed: the inside of the circle in Figure 7.2. This section examines three ways in which policy may seek to secure better value for money by changing the way in which teachers' work is governed: (1) through encouraging market forces; (2) through tighter hierarchical control, or (3) through professional norms and professional development.

The case for expecting market forces to drive improvement in the quality of teaching places considerable weight on a relatively tenuous sequence of cause and effect. It assumes that parents will choose schools on the basis of value-added school performance; this will drive schools to improve value-added; schools will identify teachers whose value-added needs to be improved, and schools will either find ways to improve these teachers or they will get rid of them. At best, the evidence of a positive association between competition among state schools and value-added performance may be described as mixed and rather modest (Bradley *et al.*, 2001; Gibbons *et al.*, 2008). The chain of argument seems to fall at the first hurdle given that parental choice of state schools seems to pay little attention to value-added (Adnett & Davies, 2002; Rothstein, 2006; Abdulkadiroglu *et al.*, 2017). However, it is also possible that schools respond to the existence of parental choice *as if* value-added affects their enrolment. Moreover, Davies and Davies (2014) did find a positive association between income per pupil and the value-added by private schools.

As observed in Chapter 6, tighter hierarchical control of teachers' work has been the driving force behind a great deal of policy reform in a number of OECD countries over recent decades. This is most obvious in the role given to inspection regimes. While there have been changes to the specification of teachers' contracts (Adnett, 2003), there is limited scope for controlling the complex activity of teaching in this way. The dominant modes of hierarchical control have been: dissemination of information about what the state believes 'good teaching' looks like; creating measurement systems to allow outcomes from teaching to be judged, and an intensive inspection system that holds teachers to account in relation to the process and outcomes of teaching (Smith, 2000; Luginbuhl *et al.*, 2012). This 'failsafe' system means that it is not enough for teachers to demonstrate acceptable outcomes; they also have to show that these are being achieved in 'the right way'. This policy approach aims to (1) raise teachers' expectations of pupils from disadvantaged backgrounds through comparison of attainment data; (2) make teachers work harder (through the threat of failing inspection), and (3) improve teachers' knowledge by making them responsive to information disseminated by government. The case for raising teachers' expectations of the attainment of pupils from disadvantaged backgrounds rests on long-standing evidence from a wide range of countries (e.g. Rist, 1970; Newmann *et al.*, 1989; Diamond *et al.*, 2004; Morris, 2005; Rubie-Davies, 2007). A plausible explanation for teachers' low expectations is that teachers usually come from white middle-class backgrounds and this frames their expectations of children from different backgrounds (Rubie-Davies *et al.*, 2012). According to MacLeod *et al.* (2015), government policy in England has succeeded in encouraging many schools to use data to adjust teachers' expectations for pupil attainment and some schools to take account of evidence about teaching disseminated by the government, not least through the work of the Education Endowment Foundation.

However, there are a few things to set against this optimistic judgement. First, the emphasis on measurable outputs in tight hierarchical control encourages teachers to game the system. Gaming may consist in 'teaching to the test' to the neglect of deep understanding (Popham, 2001) and/or ignoring any desirable outcome that will not be used to hold a teacher to account (Berliner, 2009). Second, by taking control away from teachers it reduces the scope for motivating teacher behaviour through a sense of mission. Replacing 'understanding how to make judgements in complex situations' with 'learning to do the right thing' also places a heavy burden on the accuracy of governments' knowledge and inspectors assertions. As discussed in Chapter 6 it is far from clear whether they can bear this weight. These concerns provide a backdrop to the policy of giving control back to schools that have demonstrated that they are doing a good job (Gibb, 2015, 2016). However, the idea of teacher and school autonomy within a strong accountability regime is difficult to pin down while government ministers continue to declare that they know exactly what good teaching looks like and they have seen it either in a school in China they visited or in a report on a free school in their own country.

Policy may also try to affect what teachers do through influencing professional norms and networking. Professional norms bear upon: expectations of children; the responsibility teachers take for affecting what students and parents put into the learning process, and the teachers' view of the purpose of education – the expected outcomes and the extent to which teachers regard good teaching as following rules or making judgements. There have been long-standing criticisms of teachers' expectations of students from working-class and (some) racial backgrounds, and failure to engage adequately with parents or with pupils' capacity to direct their own learning. This undermines the case for relying on unfettered professional norms as developed by teachers and professional associations. However, attempts by policy makers to address these concerns through strong hierarchical control have undermined teachers' readiness to be pro-active and their commitment to a broad range of outcomes of education that envisage their work as serving society and not just particular individuals. Every policy creates some problems while trying to solve others. Policy may also try to affect the way in which teachers and schools work together. Recent policy initiatives in England and the USA have encouraged the formation of school alliances (Wohlstetter *et al.*, 2005), school chains (Chapman, 2013) and 'school-to-school support' (Chapman & Muijs, 2014; Muijs, 2015). However, as noted in Chapter 6, the cost-effectiveness of conducting between-school collaboration for teachers has rarely been considered. Therefore, this section finishes with a brief consideration of different modes of governance for teacher development.

Teachers' professional development receives a very low profile in English schools. A report from the National Audit Office (2017, p. 11) is worth quoting at length on this point:

> Unlike many other professions, teaching does not set and regulate continuing professional development requirements. The Department has published guidance but schools do not have to follow it and there are no minimum expectations for teachers' continuing professional development. The Education Policy Institute reported that, on average, teachers in England spent four days a year on continuing professional development in 2013, compared with an average of 10.5 days across the 36 countries covered by its analysis.[8] In our survey, at least 94% of school leaders said that time and cost are barriers to improving the quality of their teaching workforce. The need for schools to make significant workforce efficiency savings is likely to make it more difficult for them to support teachers' development. Schools also struggle with finding training of the right quality, with no regulation of the wide range of external providers.

The theory of specific and general human capital offers one explanation of this state of affairs. An individual increases their specific human capital when their productivity in their current post improves in ways that would *not* be transferable to another employer. General human capital *is* transferable to other employers. Firms have an incentive to increase workers' specific human capital but face a disincentive to increase general human capital, since this makes it easier for their employees to get jobs elsewhere (Stevens, 2001). If, as in England, schools are allocated the money to spend on teachers' CPD we might expect them to be reluctant to spend on improving teachers' transferable, general, human capital. Even if teachers remain at the school after effective CPD, schools face a trade-off between supporting CPD and class size. An increase of six days per year in secondary teachers' CPD in England (from four to ten), while keeping overall spending the same, would require a 3 per cent increase in average class size.

The form as well as the quantity of CPD is likely to be important for teacher improvement. CPD may consist of 'on-the-job training', 'off-the-job training and education' or 'through the job collaboration between schools and external providers'. On-the-job training in education has tended to focus on 'how to do things' rather than on understanding underlying processes of teaching and learning (Darling-Hammond, 2000). However, simple accumulation of experience does make a difference. Ost (2014) found that primary school teachers' recent experience of teaching the same grade was positively associated with improvement in children's attainment in maths and reading. Off-the-job training may be provided by for-profit and not-for-profit organisations with some of these being commissioned by governments (NAO, 2017) and some being provided by HEIs. The claim for these courses is that they give teachers access to levels of expert knowledge and experience that are not available in their schools. The challenge for these courses is that the biggest problem teachers face is how to use principles in practice when a clutch of principles are always vying for the teacher's attention. This creates the risk that 'off-the-job' courses will add to head knowledge without affecting practice. In principle it appears that forms of CPD which combine direct experience with external input (e.g. Pang & Marton, 2003; Reeves & Drew, 2012) are likely to provide better value for money. However, headteachers in England claim that value for money is their least consideration when choosing between types of CPD (Muijs & Lindsay, 2008). This does not bode well for efficient use of resources.

Paying for participation in HE

This section is spilt into three parts. The first recaps the case for government paying part of the cost of teaching in higher education. The second focuses on whether the government should act as provider or commissioner. The third examines how much the government might pay and how these payments should be made.

The case for government paying part of the cost of teaching in higher education

As outlined in Chapters 2 and 3 we will divide the benefits from participating in higher education into those that accrue to the individual and those that accrue to society but not to the individual. Each of these two categories may be subdivided, as suggested in Figure 7.3. Benefits to the individual include human capital,

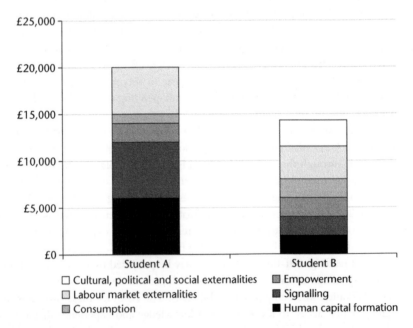

FIGURE 7.3 Valuing the benefits of participation in higher education for two students (net of forgone earnings).

signalling, empowerment and consumption. In addition, there are externalities for society in the form of labour market benefits and cultural, political and social benefits. The figure subsumes effects of graduation on inequality in the category 'cultural, political and social externalities'. Figure 7.3 imagines the sum of net benefits from participation in higher education divided by the number of years of study so that these benefits may be compared with the level of tuition. The total private benefit is £15,000 for Student A and £8,000 for Student B. If each student would have to pay £9,000 per year in tuition fees and both were certain about the future value of participating in HE, Student A would participate and Student B would not. In addition, participation by Student A would generate positive externalities of £5,000 per year of study, while participation by Student B would generate £6,300 of externalities per year of study. Even if we subtracted the signalling element[9] from the value of Student B's participation, the value to society of their participation in higher education is worth more than the £9,000 tuition fee. This externalities argument provides the main justification for governments paying at least part of tuition fees. The externalities generated by each student will be affected by their choice of subject and the use they subsequently make of their education through employment and participation in society. The higher education reform package introduced in Australia in 2017 was predicated on a belief that externalities contributed approximately half of the total benefits from an undergraduate education, with only modest variation between subjects (Australian Government, 2017, p. 10). A second argument was reviewed in Chapter 4: namely overcoming the uncertainty about future private benefits. The uncertainty problem is distributed unevenly among applicants (not least according to socio-economic background), creating the risk that government spending on higher education could increase rather than reduce inequality in society. Therefore, there is a case for targeting government financial support by subject and by student.

One further argument for governments to shoulder part of the tuition fee burden concerns intergenerational inequality and the challenges faced by younger adults in starting to accumulate capital which will provide them with a flow of income later in life. Higher education has been, and remains, a critical way for young people to position themselves among the 'well-off' (Dwyer et al., 2012). Being well-off in economies like the UK and USA means accumulating capital which provides financial support throughout the life cycle: through home ownership, pensions and other savings. This pattern of behaviour is encapsulated in the life cycle hypothesis of consumption and income (Figure 7.4). During the main 'earning years' an individual saves for their old age. In Figure 7.4 it appears that the excess of income over consumption during these years may be insufficient to cover spending during retirement. However, savings during the 'earning years' will accumulate in value through compound interest. Although the figures used to generate Figure 7.4 show a net accumulated surplus by age 65 of just under £400,000, if the interest rate during this period has been 2 per cent (in real terms), the individual will have accumulated nearly £550,000. But the critical factor will be the security of an expected graduate income enabling the purchase of a house which will accumulate in value over time.

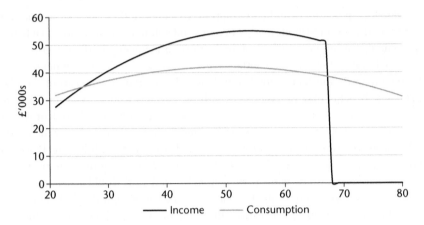

FIGURE 7.4 The life cycle hypothesis of income and consumption.

Emerging from university with a substantial student debt threatens the smooth transition towards accumulating financial assets. Andrew (2010) modelled the implications of student debt for home ownership and found not only that graduates were likely to delay buying a house, but they would also become more dependent on sources (notably parents) other than their own income when entering the housing market. Elliott and Nam (2013) paint a similar story for the USA. The rise in tuition fees and student debt in the UK has coincided with a steep rise in the ratio of average house price to average income: 3.6 in 1997, jumping to 7.6 in 2016 (ONS, 2017).

Should government act as provider or commissioner?

Looking at the histories of higher education in Australia, England and the USA, we may ask whether it makes much difference whether governments pay for higher education as providers or commissioners. Despite some references to 'privatisation of higher education' (e.g. Walford, 1988; Pick, 2006), elite universities in Australia (Harman & Treadgold, 2007; Forsyth, 2014), the UK (Dearlove, 1998) and the USA (Feldman & Desrochers, 2003) were founded to be independent[10] not-for-profit organisations and this is how they have remained. Governments have commissioned them to provide higher education. These institutions have owned their real estate and have been run by management groups following constitutions requiring that they were 'not-for-profits'. In some instances, endowment funds from property and alumni gifts considerably outweigh income from student fees.[11] However, the extent of government regulation of higher education has encouraged some commentators to refer to elite universities in Australia and England as 'public institutions' (e.g. Edwards & Radloff, 2013). In the USA, and in England up until 1992, higher education has also been provided through public sector institutions: state universities and community colleges in the USA and polytechnics and colleges of further education in England (Pratt, 1997; Parry, 2009). These institutions played strong roles in increasing participation in higher education in the latter part of the twentieth century in the USA (Brint & Karabel, 1989; Tollefson, 2009) and throughout Europe (Taylor *et al.*, 2008). In the half-century between 1965 and 2015, college enrolment in the USA increased from approximately 6 million to 20 million.[12] Public universities and colleges (e.g. state universities and community colleges) accounted for 67 per cent of enrolments in 1965 and 72 per cent of enrolments in 2015.

These figures may tempt speculation that governments have found it easier to increase participation in higher education through public sector HEIs. However, this overlooks the relationship between stratification[13] and increasing participation in higher education. Participation in HE in Australia, England and the USA has been achieved largely by extending access to HE to students with relatively lower levels of success in school exit examinations. Since there is strong stratification in the HE sector, this means that the effect of increasing participation is initially clustered in lower status institutions with a 'trickle-up' effect as other institutions try to maintain their market share while safeguarding their reputations. Between 1994 and 2011 the number of undergraduates in England increased by just under 90 per cent, but the Russell Group and Oxbridge only increased enrolment by 36 per cent.[14] The 'second tier' of universities expanded most rapidly, largely by taking over specialised, less prestigious institutions. Thus there is little evidence to suggest that choosing between provision and commissioning makes much difference to the achievement of national policies on increasing HE participation.

But does the choice between providing or commissioning affect value for money? The critique of public provision concentrates on inadequate incentives. To what extent may this be addressed through commissioning? The literature on contracting and the role of governments has concentrated attention on the challenges involved in preparing contracts that are sufficiently 'closed' to provide confidence that the provider will deliver what is wanted (DeHoog, 1990; Hart *et al.*, 1997) and the competitive conditions (van Slyke, 2006) which foster efficient contracting (See Chapter 6). There are two substantial challenges to framing higher education policy in these terms. First, since universities have the power to award their own degrees, comparisons of degree classifications or grade point averages (GPA) are problematic. One consequence is that market comparisons[15] of the 'quality' of HE providers rest heavily on the *prior* achievements of enrolled students. Moreover, with no discernible trace of irony, the UK government body which carried out a review of the higher education market (CMA, 2015, p. 3) argued that this market was "to a large extent already characterised by healthy competition between providers who compete with each other for *the best students*" (emphasis added). Second, since externalities loom large in the rationale for government paying part of the cost of higher education teaching we must be interested in how governments decide whether a university is delivering value for money in developing "qualities that also prepare graduates as agents of social good in an unknown future".[16] Remarkably, this is an issue on which HE policy documents in England (e.g. DBIS, 2013, 2016;

CMA, 2015) have been almost uniformly silent. If governments have no idea what they are trying to buy, how can universities compete to provide it?

Several measurement tools have been developed in the USA to address these challenges (e.g. the ETS Proficiency Profile,[17] the Collegiate Learning Assessment (CLA)[18] and the Collegiate Assessment of Academic Proficiency).[19] However, these measures have been criticised on grounds of validity and reliability. Three examples illustrate the challenges to validity. First, in abstracting from the curriculum these tests tend to miss what lecturers have been trying to teach. Second, 'critical thinking' tends to be prominent in these tests and the argument about the validity of a generalised construct of critical thinking is not yet settled (Moore, 2004). Third, assessment of attitudes which encapsulate a graduate's tendency to act on behalf of society are underdeveloped and therefore underrepresented.[20] These tests have also been criticised on grounds of reliability, not least because in an era of high-stakes testing, student motivation towards low-stakes assessment tends to be highly variable (Liu *et al.*, 2012).

By 2017, the UK government and the quasi-governmental body, the Higher Education Funding Council for England (HEFCE), were also working to address these challenges. In 2017 a new voluntary regime (the 'Teaching Excellence Framework') for regulating HE teaching was announced (Department for Education, 2017b) for HEIs in England. This regime comprised five main strands. Three focused on the process of teaching in terms of student satisfaction, the learning environment and observation of teaching. Two focused on outcomes in terms of the labour market and learning gains. To address the measurement of learning gains, the HEFCE commissioned 13 research and development projects. The evaluation of the first year of these projects (Kandiko Howson, 2017, p. 4) reported that these projects defined learning gain in terms of "a change in knowledge, skills, work-readiness and personal development". Reflecting a general tendency in development work on learning gains in HE, this neglects externalities, in particular those relating to civic responsibility. Thus, although governments have been commissioning HEIs for a very long time, exploration of what is being bought is still in its early stages.

This means that governments have had to rely on being able to trust the organisations they commission. Paying an organisation to educate an individual for two, three or four years and to allow that organisation to decide whether to award the student a degree at the end leaves HEIs with a lot of room for manoeuvre. As examined in Chapter 6, governments have had to decide what scope they will extend to professional networks, hierarchical management and markets in filling in the huge empty space left by the impossibility of drawing up contracts specifying detailed outcomes. Since about 1980 governments have adopted a similar stance towards HEIs in the public sector and HEIs they are commissioning: they cannot trust professional networks and they need to bolster market forces *and* encourage hierarchical management structures within organisations (Randle & Brady, 1997; Watson & Bowden, 1999; Watson & Crossley, 2001; Kezar & Eckel, 2004). They have brought about changes in the structure of the market by fostering mergers, closing institutions by withdrawing funding and by granting university status to new institutions (Meek, 1990). They have also laid down requirements for how universities operate as well as what they provide. This has been observed in dictation of management structures and processes which have shifted governance in university from professional networks to hierarchies (Shattock, 2004, 2013; Vidovich & Currie, 2011). This level of government intrusion goes well beyond what is typically discussed in the contracting literature. It is made possible by the extent of universities' dependence on government funding. This has encouraged HEIs to align themselves quite closely with government discourse: in van Slyke's (2006) terms, acting as stewards rather than as agents.[21]

Of course, loss of trust in professional networks and faith in markets and hierarchies is naturally unwelcome for the professionals whose freedom of action is curtailed. Professionals' assumption that they naturally 'do the right thing' is swept aside by politicians' assumptions that professionals naturally 'do their own thing'. The problem here is not that professional networks have been proven to be the best guardians of the public interest in higher education, but that evidence of the superiority of market or hierarchical governance is equally thin on the ground. Progress is more likely if proposals (such as those by Dill (1997)) for adjusting the interplay between market, hierarchical and network governance in higher education are carefully trialled and evaluated.

One further issue facing a commissioning government is whether to buy services from 'for-profit' as well as (or instead of) 'not-for-profits'. The argument here is that 'for-profits' will be more innovative and responsive to consumer needs: they will be sharper at exploiting opportunities because they will reap the financial rewards from doing so. However, dealing with an organisation that is good at exploitation may bring trouble for a government which finds it difficult to specify what they want in a market where consumers find it difficult to evaluate the choices before them. Thus far, for-profit universities have only occupied a small, and largely niche, corner of the HE market in Australia, England and the USA (Breneman *et al.*, 2006; DBIS, 2013; Shah & Sid Nair, 2013). They also appear more prone to 'quality shading' (Adnett, 2004): exploiting opportunities to reduce the quality of provision where this achieves cost savings. Governments in OECD countries have every reason to prefer to commission teaching in HE from not-for-profits.[22]

How much should government pay for teaching in higher education?

Governments can pay for undergraduate teaching in four main ways: (1) through a subsidy paid to the university; (2) through a grant paid to the student; (3) through a loan to the student, or (4) through a tax break offered to the household of the student. Although a £5,000 subsidy or a £5,000 student grant cost the government the same amount of money, they may have different impacts. Student grants and loans affect the demand for undergraduate education while subsidies affect the supply. Economic analysis of the options has generally preferred grants and loans to subsidies (St John & Asker, 2003). One reason for this preference is that grants and loans can be adjusted more easily than subsidies to take account of the household income of the student. This adjustment may also provide for some of the student's living costs. Moreover, by directing the money to the student, the government may hope to encourage institutions to improve what they offer in order to compete for students. Grants that cover some living costs may be particularly important to attract and reduce drop-out rates of students from low-income backgrounds. However, governments can reduce the burden on *their* finances by replacing grants with loans (Dynarski & Scott-Clayton, 2013). Students may be required to repay loans through (1) a fixed repayment system whereby the repayments are calibrated to the size of the loan; (2) an income-contingent loan, whereby the rate of repayment depends on the graduate's income, but the total sum to be paid is determined by the initial loan and the interest charged on that loan, or (3) through a graduate tax whereby the total amount paid as well as the rate at which they repay depends on their income as graduates. Income-contingent loans and graduate taxation provide more equitable ways of distributing the burden of student debt among graduates as well as reducing uncertainty about the affordability of loan repayments. The long-term cost of loans to the government depends on the interest rate that is charged and the level of defaults. Tax credits to students' households benefit middle- and high-income families, since these families pay more tax. Governments may also cap tuition fees: regulating the maximum tuition fee that can be charged. As with subsidies paid to universities, tuition fee caps may vary according to the subject studied. Finally, a government may also cap the number of student places for which they are prepared to offer financial aid. The alternative is to have a 'demand-led' system in which the number of places expands according to the number of students willing and able to take up places offered by universities.

All of this means that there are various ways of looking at what students pay for an undergraduate education. There is the gross tuition fee: the headline price for the course as advertised by the university. This is commonly (e.g. Heller, 1997; McPherson & Schapiro, 1999) referred to as 'the sticker price' following standard use of this term in the USA. There is the 'net price' which is the fee a student actually pays after taking account of all financial aid. Finally, there is the price of living on campus away from home. This price is the net tuition fee plus living costs. This section examines the policy options through recent practice in Australia, England and the USA. Governments in each country have been concerned about the implications of rising participation in higher education and rising costs of teaching for the demands on government budgets.

A review of higher education in Australia in 2008 (Department for Education, Employment and Workplace Relations, & Bradley, 2008) lifted a cap on student numbers eligible for financial aid to usher in a 'demand-led' system. Between 2009 and 2017 the cost to the government of providing financial aid rose at twice the rate of GDP, encouraging the government to introduce a further major reform in 2017. These reforms retained a system that combined subsidies paid to institutions (through a 'Commonwealth Grant Scheme' (CGS)) and loans to students (through a 'Higher Education Loan Program' (HELP)). The reforms aimed to reduce government contribution to tuition costs from 58 per cent in 2017 to 54 per cent by 2021 (Australian Government, 2017). The HELP scheme was linked to the Consumer Price Index, effectively providing students with loans at a zero real rate of interest. In 2016/2017 these loans had only been repayable when a graduate's income rose above A\$54,869. The new reforms reduced this threshold to A\$42,000. This figure was 62 per cent of average GDP per capita. The government also set maximum fee caps which varied by subject group (Table 7.4). The CGS subsidies to universities also varied by subject: A\$5,400 a year for a three-year arts course; A\$10,425 a year for a four-year teaching course; A\$17,600 a year for a three-year science course, and A\$22,883 a year for a six-year medicine course. These variations far exceeded the estimates of externalities cited by the government as a justification for government spending (Australian Government, 2017, p. 10). They were also quite different from variation by subject in graduate pay. Chia and Miller (2008) estimated differences between graduate starting salaries by subject after taking account of student and institutional characteristics. They found the following differences compared to the average science graduate: arts (+11%); computer science (+24%); dentistry (+104%); economics (+11%); engineering (+16%); law (+23%).

In 2009/2010 the UK government paid a subsidy to universities in England of £3,947 for each undergraduate enrolled on a course that did not involve laboratory or clinical work. These students also paid a maximum tuition fee of £3,225 (HEFCE, 2009). Ignoring all other grants[23] provided for teaching, the government contribution was 55 per cent. The new funding arrangements in 2012 raised tuition fees to a maximum of £9,000 and largely replaced the teaching grant to universities with a loan system. A residual teaching grant to 'high-cost' subjects (requiring the use of

TABLE 7.4 Maximum undergraduate tuition fees in Australia (2017)

Subject group		Maximum tuition fee		
		Australian A\$	% of Australia GDP per capita	US US\$
Band 3	Law, dentistry, medicine, veterinary science, accounting, administration, economics, commerce	10,596	19.0	8,440
Band 2	Computing, built environment, other health, allied health, engineering, surveying, agriculture, mathematics, statistics, science	9,050	16.3	7,200
Band 1	Humanities, behavioural science, social studies, education, clinical psychology, foreign languages, visual and performing arts, nursing	6,349	11.4	5,060

Source: http://studyassist.gov.au/sites/studyassist/helppayingmyfees/csps/pages/student-contribution-amounts.

laboratories and technical equipment) remained, and this amounted to £652 million in 2017/2018 (HEFCE, 2017). Under this new system the government contribution was 42 per cent (Belfield *et al.*, 2017). Although the government contribution reduced in terms of proportion, there was not a great deal of change in the absolute per-student contribution because the maximum tuition fee had almost tripled.

The maximum tuition fee was raised to £9,250 by 2017. The average tuition fee for an undergraduate programme was £9,048 in universities and £6,939 in Further Education Colleges (equivalent to TAFEs in Australia and Community Colleges in the USA) (OFFA, 2017). The average UK university undergraduate tuition fee was just under 50 per cent more than the maximum allowed in Australia for 'top band' subjects like medicine and law, and just under 150 per cent more than the maximum allowed in Australia for the lowest band of subjects. In addition, grants to students from disadvantaged backgrounds were abolished in 2015. The system now relied largely on income-contingent loans to address the problem of equity. In 2012 the threshold for loan repayments was set at an annual income of £21,000 (76 per cent of average GDP per head in 2012, 71 per cent of average GDP per head in 2016). Outstanding debt increased by the retail price index + 3 per cent during the period of study and between 0 and 3 per cent (income-related) thereafter. In 2017/2018 this meant that a student who was not earning saw their debt rise by 3.1 per cent (while average weekly earnings in the year to August 2017 had risen by only 2.1 per cent). According to Belfield *et al.* (2017, p. 17), "this has resulted in students from the poorest 40% of families graduating with the largest debts: around £57,000 on average, compared with around £43,000 for students from the richest 30% of families". Belfield and colleagues (2017) also calculated that subsequent adjustments to the student loan system had reduced the government share of the tuition fee burden to 34 per cent. Since policy statements over this period avoid any estimates of the value of externalities,[24] they leave the impression that policy was directed by a desire to reduce the government's financial commitments rather than an intention to achieve a socially efficiently solution to the problem. Although the government expected each change in the level of the tuition fee cap to prompt variation in tuition fees, this did not happen. The tuition fee paid by students did not reflect the modest difference in graduate premium attributable to the type of university attended (Hussain *et al.*, 2009) or the substantial difference attributable to the subject studied (Chevalier, 2011; O'Leary & Sloane, 2011; Walker & Zhu, 2011).

The role of government in US higher education has been somewhat different from that observed in either Australia or England. A move to shift the burden of higher education teaching costs from the state to the student began earlier in the USA (Berger & Kostal, 2002). This may well be due to participation rates during the 1980s and 1990s being higher in the USA than in Australia or England. Nonetheless, financial aid per student tripled in the USA between 1990 and 2010 (Dynarski & Scott-Clayton, 2013). In part, this rise was caused by the introduction of tax credits for families whose children went to university. By 2010 this form of federal aid had risen to more than half of the level of financial aid provided through federal grants (Dynarski & Scott-Clayton, 2013). This form of financial aid, which largely benefited middle-class families, was not provided in Australia or England. In addition, in contrast to Australia and England, most US undergraduates (73%) attend public universities. Of the remainder, 20 per cent attend not-for-profit private HEIs and 7 per cent attend for-profit HEIs. Private universities are free to set their own tuition fees, while public universities and community colleges are, at least nominally, constrained by state and district governments. Kim and Ko (2015) investigated the attempts made by US states to limit tuition fee increases in public universities offering four-year degree courses. They found that tuition fees rose more slowly when states linked tuition fees to financial aid available to students. Tuition fees rose faster at institutions which were given the freedom to set their own fees *and* in states which tried to control increases through tuition fee caps. One consequence of this system is that students from within the state are charged much lower fees than out-of-state students. Essentially, out-of-state students are treated in the same way that universities in Australia and England treat international students. This contrasts with the EU system in which applicants from other EU member states are charged the same fee as domestic students. Another consequence is that state (as opposed to federal) aid encourages students to attend public rather than private institutions within their home state (Long, 2004). Table 7.5 summarises US tuition fee differences by type of institution. The table shows the 'headline' or 'sticker price' tuition fee before any grants are taken into account.

Government funding in the USA continues, as in Australia, to be provided through a mixture of grants and loans. However, government provides only about two-thirds of the grants and loans available to undergraduates. This is shown in Figure 7.5. The grant element in Figure 7.5 means that the average (net) tuition fees actually paid by students are considerably lower than the 'sticker' price.

Current household income is negatively associated with expected (Kim et al., 2009) and actual (Paulsen & St John, 2002) college enrolment and also negatively related to college drop-out (Chen & DesJardins, 2008).[25] These relationships

TABLE 7.5 Tuition fees and enrolments in US HEIs (2017–2018)

University type	'Sticker price' US$	% of US GDP per capita
Public university two-year course (Community College)	3,570	6.9
Public university four-year course (state university) (in-state fee)	9,970	19.1
Public university four-year course (state university) (out-of-state fee)	25,620	49.1
Private university not-for-profit	34,740	66.6

Source: Figures from the College Board. Available at https://trends.collegeboard.org/college-pricing/figures-tables/average-published-undergraduate-charges-sector-2017-18.

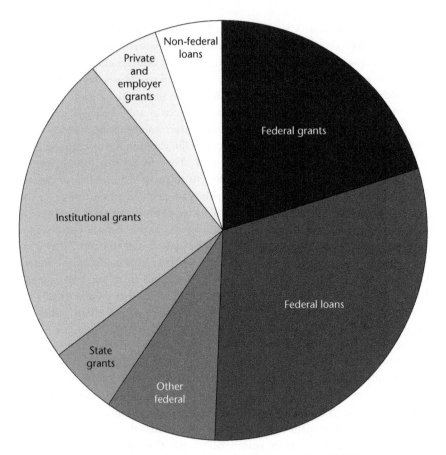

FIGURE 7.5 Sources of financial aid to US undergraduates (2016/2017).

Source: Figures from the College Board. Available at https://trends.collegeboard.org/college-pricing/figures-tables/average-published-undergraduate-charges-sector-2017-18.

strongly suggest the existence of substantial credit constraints Eligibility for most grants was strongly related to income, so that the average net tuition fee was considerably lower for applicants from low-income families. A quarter of all forms of financial aid to students is provided by grants from institutions. These are motivated by a mixture of institutional self-interest and desire to make access easier for disadvantaged students. HEIs face incentives to lower prices to talented students who will (1) boost the 'peer effect', but (2) would not be able to afford the 'sticker price' tuition fee.[26] Grants have been more effective than loans in encouraging applicants from low-income households (Heller, 1997, 1999). The availability of financial aid has also been more important to the college decision making of some racial groups (St John *et al.*, 2005).

Headline (or 'sticker price') tuition fees vary among institutions more widely in the USA than in Australia or England. Douglass and Keeling (2008) found little variation in tuition fees by subject in private sector institutions (a pattern that seems to be ongoing).[27] However, they did find a large variation in fees for public in-state students (fees for medicine 2.7 times the fee for theatre studies and the fee for law 2.3 times the fee for theatre studies). Table 7.4 shows the average 'sticker price' charged by each type of university.[28] The average actual fee paid by students was substantially lower. This 'net fee' was, on average, US$4,140 (8 per cent of US GDP per capita) for students enrolled on four-year courses at public universities (College Board, 2017).

A comparison of the systems for paying for undergraduate education in Australia, England and the USA prompts several questions. First, what proportion of the cost of undergraduate education should be borne by the state? The answers to this question have differed between countries and over time.[29] The proportion paid by the state has fallen over time as participation rates have increased. The Australian government is aiming for 54 per cent, while in England the aim seems to be for around 33 per cent. Of course, the implications of these percentages depend on the average level of tuition fees. Given that average fees in 2017 were much higher in England, and given the exchange rate at that time, the absolute government contribution per student was relatively similar in these two countries. Since GDP per head in 2016 was 25 per cent higher in Australia than in the UK, relative to average income the government contribution was greater in England. Governments do face a huge problem in the difficulty of quantifying the future value of externalities from higher education. Short-term fiscal pragmatism encourages them to reduce their contribution, while long-term vision encourages them to keep the contribution high. The student loan system in England has shifted the burden on government onto future rather than current budgets. In one way this may be viewed as a smart wheeze, as the cost of future social benefits is placed on future societies. Alternatively, this may be seen as a way of compounding the intergenerational problem. If graduates repay less than the full amount of their debt, the difference will be made up by taxation on the same generation.

Do caps on tuition fees help? The case for a tuition fee cap is that it helps widen participation and raise participation to a level that reflects the wider benefits of higher education to society (externalities). This presumes that the tuition fee cap is set below the price that would be charged in a free market. Students who would have been put off by a higher tuition fee now decide that it is worth participating in HE and this increases the proportion of disadvantaged students attending university. This argument does not work if we assume that HEIs are operating in a free competitive market. Supposing it costs the same to educate every additional student: if the fee cap is set below this cost, how could any provider break even? A more plausible possibility is that each additional student costs more to educate than students who are already participating.[30] In this case, a fee cap set below the market equilibrium would lead HEIs to reduce the number of students they are prepared to enrol. The general argument for price caps is that the market is not operating freely. Providers are able to charge higher prices because of their market power and a fee cap eats into the surplus they would otherwise generate. Three sources of market power may be identified in higher education. First, reputation developed through the institution's history may give the institution a brand advantage or disadvantage. Second, being educated with high-achieving students offers the prospect of a stronger signalling element from the degree and possible learning gains from being educated with more able students (as in the school effect in Epple *et al.*'s 2004 model). Third, endowments from benefactors and alumni may allow a university to offer the prospect of a greater resource input and more attractive environment. Therefore, the tuition fee caps in England and Australia may be read as indicating greater commitment to equality of opportunity than we observe in the USA. This impression is compounded by the use of tax credits in the USA but not in Australia or England.

Governments may also intervene so that some students pay less than others and they may also intervene so that students pay more to study one subject than others or so that HEIs receive more income from providing one subject than another. Grants distinguish between students according to their families' income. Income-contingent loans distinguish between students according to what they will earn later in life. The English system of income-contingent loans looks perfectly fair if we ignore differences between families' wealth. In terms of income, it may appear that uncertainty about future earnings is thoroughly dealt with: removing a potential barrier to HE entry. However, the size of a student debt and the speed at which it is paid off depends on the capacity of a family to transfer wealth from the older to the younger generation: a process in which home ownership plays a critical role. As shown by Belfield *et al.*'s (2017) calculations, students from low-income backgrounds end up with higher debts. Although these may eventually be wiped off, they may discourage graduates from low-income backgrounds from becoming home owners, reducing intergenerational mobility.

Governments may ensure that HEIs receive greater income for some subjects than for others by setting differential tuition fee caps (as in Australia) or by paying grants (or higher grants) for some subjects directly to HEIs (as in England). The espoused logic for this practice has been that HEIs need higher income for 'high-cost' subjects. This argument does not look strong. It would be perfectly possible to make a fine art degree cost as much to provide as a degree in medicine. It could require state-of-the-art technology, placements with leading art studios and site visits all over the world. It makes more sense for a government to base interventions to create differential HEI income by subject on the benefits that different courses have for individuals and society. A differential fee cap focuses on benefits to the student: they may be willing to pay more to study law than to study fine art because they know that, on average, law graduates are high earners. A differential fee cap should affect application rates to different subjects and, thereby, contribute to maintaining earnings differentials. The grant direct to universities in England has no effect on rates of application (since students face the same level of tuition fee whatever they study), but it does encourage HEIs to supply more places for those subjects than they would otherwise offer. The rationale for this practice must lie in believing that the externalities from these subjects are much greater than they are for other subjects. It is far from clear that this is the case.

One common theme in the funding of higher education in these three countries is the lack of regulation of the process of teaching. There have been some efforts to create 'benchmark' standards describing learning outcomes from degrees (Coates, 2010), but these are open to wide differences in interpretation that are not subject to tight government monitoring. Likewise, government intrusion into the process of teaching has been largely restricted to the introduction of student satisfaction surveys.[31] This contrasts with a school inspection regime in England[32] which includes unannounced school visits and classroom observations, a firm depiction of what counts as good teaching and the threat to close schools that do not measure up. Australian and English governments have been far more intrusive in how HEIs are run than in how they teach.

Possible futures

This chapter, and the book, concludes with some speculations about what the future holds for education: how much we pay for it and who pays.

Extrapolation from past trends suggests that OECD countries will steadily devote a higher proportion of their national income to education. This reflects Baumol's 'Cost Disease' argument. Education has traditionally depended on 'face-to-face' teaching. Even if class sizes stay the same, the cost of employing teachers rises to match increasing earnings elsewhere in the economy, created by increases in physical productivity.[33] If people want more education then the problem intensifies. As income has risen, this is exactly what has happened. People spend longer in education. Children go to universities when their parents did not. Children study for a Master's degree when their parents stopped after a Bachelor's degree. Students, parents and governments think that smaller classes are better than bigger classes.

Evidence of rising private demand for education is provided by trends in spending on private schooling. Increased demand for private schooling in Australia has been taken up by an increase in the proportion of children being privately educated (Beavis, 2004; Dearden et al., 2011). Figure 7.6 shows that, in the UK, the real level (after taking account of inflation) of tuition fees in private schools in the UK more than doubled over this 31-year period.[34]

The increase in public spending on education in the UK has been less steady, but it has been dramatic. Between 1955 and 2012 the proportion of national income spent on public education doubled. Figure 7.7 shows the pattern of UK government spending on education over this 60-year period.

Between the mid-1950s and the early 1970s, government spending on education accounted for a steadily increasing share of national income. This changed when Keynesian policies were rejected following the oil crises in the 1970s, and the Conservative governments between 1979 and 1997 steadily reduced government spending as a proportion of national income. The New Labour government from 1997 returned to a policy of increasing the proportion of national income devoted to education until a change in government in 2010 reversed this policy following the financial crisis of 2008. This follows a general pattern that centre-left

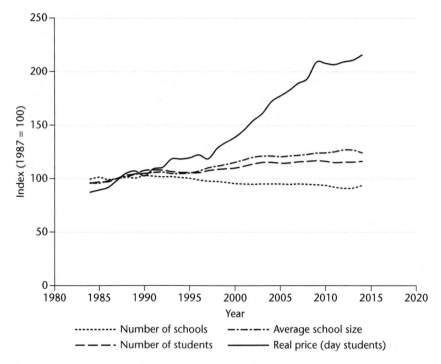

FIGURE 7.6 Private school trends in the UK (1984–2015).

Source: Independent Schools Council Annual Census and Office for National Statistics Price Index.

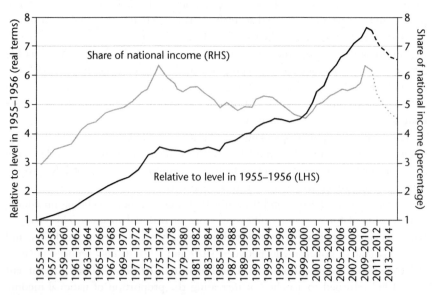

FIGURE 7.7 UK public spending on education between 1955 and 2014.

Source: Chowdry & Sibieta (2011, p. 3).

governments tend to spend more on education (Busemeyer, 2007; Ansell, 2008). Governments responded to the 2008 financial crisis in different ways. While most governments tried to protect education spending, there were real cuts in education spending in a minority of OECD countries between 2008 and 2011 (e.g. 3 per cent in the USA, 5 per cent in Russia and 11 per cent in Italy) (OECD, 2014a). In England the government initially planned 'efficiency savings' rising from £1.1 billion in 2016/2017 to £3.0 billion (equivalent to 8 per cent of the total budget) in 2019/2020 (NAO, 2017). This was subsequently revised in the face of political pressure and an additional £1.3 billion being allocated to schools from 2018 to 2020 without clarity on where the money was coming from. Fluctuations in public spending around a rising trend may be attributed to global financial events, political priorities and short-term political expediency. However, if we compare trends in private and public spending on education it appears that some governments tend to restrain overall spending on education, perhaps reflecting a desire to 'keep things as they are', thereby reinforcing 'traditional values' and inequalities in society.

Recent education policy in OECD countries has emphasised benefits from education that can be more easily measured, especially benefits that can be measured in terms of increased earnings. It has also encouraged a view of education as something that is *done to* people through institutions, and these institutions must be held accountable for what they do. These two ideas combine to offer a narrow and unhelpful view of the role of education. Education is a way in which a society creates its own future. This involves far more than formal institutions. They do their job in the context of what families and social networks see as *their* job in education. What happens in universities and schools also depends crucially on what students have learned to see as *their* job in learning, what they think learning is and what they think learning is for. Critics who have sought to remind policy makers of this broader view of education have sometimes, perhaps often, also tended to gloss over the cost of providing education. Criticism of this kind can descend into accusations being made between social scientists with different disciplinary loyalties. This book has assumed that a broad view of the role of education is necessary and that careful scrutiny of the level and use of resources in education is equally necessary. One implication is that scholars in different disciplines have equally important contributions to make. Another is that we are a long way short of a secure framework for handling the tensions between different insights.

These two speculations will be hugely affected by the role played by continuing change in information and communications technology. Earlier chapters have noted that expectations that ICT will create dramatic change in education have, so far, been largely unfulfilled. However, we are beginning to see some changes in higher education through the profile of online education.[35] There is potential here for Baumol's Cost Disease to be averted in education. Physical productivity in education could yet be increased through greater use of online systems. There are some substantial dangers lurking in the costs of e-learning. First, the quality of e-learning depends greatly on the resources allocated to designing the programme (Bartley & Golek, 2004). These are fixed costs, so the cost per student becomes much more competitive when the number of students enrolled is very high. Any organisation that can secure a very large share of the market could make a huge surplus, but this would give that organisation huge power over the nature of education that individuals receive. The cost per student of online education also depends greatly on the extent to which feedback is provided by lecturers. Thus there is substantial opportunity for market segmentation: low-price, low-feedback courses and high-price, high-feedback courses. Given what we know about the importance of feedback for learning, the growth in online education threatens to increase inequalities. Of course, technological change could yet enable drastic improvements in the quality of what is available and the speed of change in this industry has been astonishingly fast. It may happen, but we cannot see it yet. Some online education already uses social interaction rather than didactic instruction as the mode of teaching and learning, but the rules of social interaction and communication are different from those in face-to-face contact. We do not yet know how much cohesion in society is attributable to socialisation in school through face-to-face interaction with peers and the management of this interaction by teachers on the spot.

ICT has already created massive change in the nature and distribution of employment. This has changed the work for which people are being educated. What if the role of robots on production lines is extended to the service sector which has thus far expanded employment as jobs in manufacturing have been lost? The current emphasis on education for employment may appear to be preparation for a race that will soon be over and an emphasis that will serve the needs of the few rather than of the many. Rediscovering a broad view of education as preparation for life, not just preparation for work, may become an urgent priority. Education could make a critical contribution to cohesiveness in future society if those who benefit most and most directly from productivity increases through ICT understand and accept that their interests will be served by a stable society in which benefits are shared.

Finally, this book has emphasised the uncertainty with which individuals, organisations and governments have to contend when making decisions about education. What are the prospects for increasing value for money by reducing that uncertainty? This depends first of all on whether governments and teachers are willing to acknowledge the uncertainty they face. Confidence about 'the right way to organise education' and 'the right way to teach' seems to massively exceed what we currently know. Of course, governments are constrained by the nature of the society they are trying to govern, but they have been culpable of masking dodgy statements with resolute posture. This is the enemy of good education. We do have firm evidence (e.g. Trautwein & Lüdtke, 2007) that students learn better when they regard knowledge as uncertain. It is probably the same for the quality of teaching (Hashweh, 1996). Is it not the same for governments? If our knowledge base about education is rather modest it also makes sense to cooperate in building it up. Claims to be guardians of the 'true knowledge' about education – whether they come from governments, 'special advisers' or teachers, from schools or universities, economists or sociologists – are part of the problem. A good teacher knows how to listen closely, especially when students offer answers they didn't want. The same applies to academics and policy makers. A good education system would foster this kind of culture in society. The future needs it.

Notes

1 It has sometimes been suggested that teaching is a relatively straightforward activity. But teachers require good knowledge of the subject they teach (content knowledge), good knowledge of students' everyday understanding and good knowledge of what will help students to improve their understanding (pedagogic content knowledge), good knowledge of what motivates different children and a strong ability to manage groups of children.

2 George Bernard Shaw who coined the phrase 'he who pays the piper, calls the tune' made this point when he asserted: "the value to me [...] of calling the tune as well as playing it, is so great that it would need much more than a hundred guineas to induce me to forfeit it" (Laurence, 1988, p. 164). This point may have received greater attention in a speech by then Prime Minister James Callaghan (1976), widely regarded in the UK as having initiated a 'great debate' about education.

3 The argument that teaching is relatively unattractive to high achievers was discussed in Chapter 5. O'Leary and Sloane's (2011) analysis of returns to UK graduates shows that the median and upper quartile graduate premia for males with an education degree are relatively low, while those in the lowest quartile earn a graduate premium approximately similar to graduates in other social science disciplines.

4 Data from the Department for Education (2017a). *The School Workforce in England: November 2016*. London, Department for Education. Available at www.gov.uk/government/statistics/school-workforce-in-england-november-2016 (accessed 15 September 2016).

5 Data from the Independent School Council Census. Available at www.isc.co.uk/research/annual-census/ (accessed 29 September 2017).

6 Data from the Australian Bureau of Statistics. Available at www.abs.gov.au/AUSSTATS/abs@.nsf/DetailsPage/4221.02016?OpenDocument (accessed 18 September 2017).

7 Data from the index of average weekly pay in constant prices from the Office of National Statistics. Available at www.ons.gov.uk/employmentandlabourmarket/peopleinwork/earningsandworkinghours/datasets/averageweeklyearningsearn (accessed 15 September 2016).

8 The report (Sellen, 2016) found that US teachers had about the average number of days' CPD (ten), while Australia was below average at six days per year. Interestingly, the list was headed by teachers in Shanghai (40 days). Although government ministers in England have been keen to highlight other aspects of practice they have been rather quiet on this figure, despite recognising that Shanghai teachers also have considerably more time to prepare lessons (see https://schoolsweek.co.uk/schools-minister-admits-shanghai-maths-teachers-only-do-two-lessons-a-day/).

9 On the grounds that rewards to signalling simply redistribute earnings, they do not reflect increases in productive capacity.

10 Even when local politicians and regional political assemblies were prime movers in these foundations.

11 For example, in 2014 Harvard reported that only 21 per cent of its income came from fees from students, while 36 per cent came from income from endowments (see www.harvard.edu/about-harvard/harvard-glance/endowment). In 2016 Cambridge University (UK) reported its assets as valued at approximately £4 billion (www.admin.cam.ac.uk/reporter/2016-17/weekly/6448/section4.shtml#heading2-10).

12 Figures from the statistics portal (www.statista.com/statistics/183995/us-college-enrollment-and-projections-in-public-and-private-institutions/) (accessed 3 November 2017).

13 Stratification is most commonly described in education in terms of the distribution of students among institutions by socio-economic background. Higher education institutions are commonly classified according to the minimum entrance qualifications they accept and this leads to strong stratification by entrance grade and by socio-economic background, since there is a high positive association between the two.

14 Calculated from figures made available by the Higher Education Statistics Agency (on undergraduate enrolments by institution). Institutions were classified into four groups: (1) Oxbridge and Russell Group (including medical training in university hospitals in London); (2) other universities established before 1992; (3) former polytechnics, and (4) institutions granted university status since 1992. Data available at www.hesa.ac.uk/data-and-analysis/publications (accessed 4 November 2017).

15 Such as those offered by national newspapers (e.g. www.thetimes.co.uk/article/good-university-guide-2018-university-of-the-year-2018-h3x7l80vl) or bespoke websites (e.g. www.thecompleteuniversityguide.co.uk/league-tables/rankings?o=Entry+Standards).

16 This quotation from Bowden et al. (2000) is cited in Barrie (2007, p. 440).

17 For information on the ETS Proficiency Profile see www.ets.org/proficiencyprofile/about (accessed 25 November 2017).

18 For information on the Collegiate Learning Assessment see http://cae.org/flagship-assessments-cla-cwra/cla/ (accessed 25 November 2017).

19 For information on the College Assessment of Academic Proficiency see www.act.org/content/act/en/products-and-services/act-collegiate-assessment-of-academic-proficiency.html (accessed 25 November 2017).

20 Although there is some promising work on suitable assessment items (e.g. Hatcher, 2011) and 'Service Learning' (Eyler & Giles, 1999).

21 Alternatively, they may be described (following Foucault) as having been 'captured by the discourse').

22 This does not mean that not-for-profits are immune from problems. See e.g. www.olderiswiser.com/work-career/articles/trouble-in-the-valleys-or-rather-the-universities; www.slate.com/articles/double_x/doublex/2017/09/university_of_rochester_professor_s_alleged_sexual_harassment_of_students.html; www.telegraph.co.uk/education/university education/9360494/Warning-to-universities-in-foreign-student-grades-scandal.html (all accessed 6 November 2017).

23 The core funding 'teaching grant' made up 80 per cent of all teaching-related government grants to universities (HEFCE, 2009). Belfield and colleagues (2017) calculated that the taxpayer subsidy in 2011, the year before the substantial change in funding regime, was 59 per cent of the total expenditure on higher education teaching.

24 For example, DBIS (2016) mentions 'social benefits' once (p. 23) and does not refer to the value of these benefits. This document is only concerned with private benefits: in terms of the graduate premium. The 'Teaching Excellence Framework' introduced for HEIs in England (Department for Education, 2017b, p. 6) declares its purpose as "better meeting the needs of employers, business, industry and the professions". There is no mention of the wider interests of society. A report prepared for HEFCE (Hoareau McGrath et al., 2015) refers to learning gains exclusively in terms of private benefits.

25 Chen and DesJardins (2008) report that the college drop-out rate is almost twice as high for students from low-income households as the drop-out rate for students from high-income households. Their analysis controls for school- and college-level academic attainment.

26 A similar pricing strategy may be observed in UK private schools (Davies, 2011).

27 See e.g. http://admissions.psu.edu/costs-aid/tuition/ or www.baylor.edu/admissions/index.php?id=872111.

28 The College Board data did not show a figure for for-profit universities in 2017/2018, but did not quote a figure of $16,000 for 2016/2017.

29 Variations among countries are, of course, even greater beyond the very restricted comparison of Australia, England and the USA. Indeed, there is great variation within the UK (see Wakeling & Jefferies, 2013).

30 A key argument for this assumption is that students vary in their initial capacity for learning. It takes more resources to enable one student to learn at undergraduate level than it takes to enable another student to learn at undergraduate level.

31 See, for example, in Australia (www.education.gov.au/upholding-quality-quality-indicators-learning-and-teaching) (accessed 14 November 2017) and in England (www.hefce.ac.uk/lt/nss/) (accessed 14 November 2017).

32 See www.gov.uk/government/publications/school-inspection-handbook-from-september-2015 (accessed 14 November 2017).

33 This observation has implications for how we interpret 'productivity increase' in the nation as a whole. It has become commonplace to worry about 'flat-lining productivity'. The rationale for this worry is that improving living standards depends on increasing national productivity per person. But this is not true. We have noted in this book that people believe they are better off if their children are educated in smaller classes. Many people believe they are better off if they spend longer in education. Increases in the total resources devoted to education tend to reduce average 'physical' productivity. Imagine an economy in which there are only two goods: physical productivity in providing Good A (perhaps a manufactured good) can be increased by reducing the labour input. As more of this good is provided, living standards rise. Physical productivity in providing Good B (perhaps education) falls as more resources are devoted to it, but these additional resources also improve the experience of having this good provided to you. Suppose that labour is transferred from production of Good A to production of Good B as technical change allows productivity increase in Good A. Improved productivity in providing Good A will be counterbalanced by deteriorating productivity in providing Good B. This does not mean that living standards have flat-lined. People feel better off by having more of Good A and they also feel better off from the greater resources devoted to Good B because their satisfaction from Good B depends on the resource richness of how it is provided.

34 The majority of privately educated school students in the UK (80 per cent in 1984 and 90 per cent in 2014) were educated in schools affiliated to the Independent Schools Council (ISC). Data published in the ISC annual census show gradual increases in the number of privately educated students and the average size of schools affiliated to the ISC.

35 And stronger claims for the outcomes from ICT mediated learning (see e.g. Allen *et al.*, 2004).

REFERENCES

Abdulkadiroglu, A., Pathak, P. A., Schellenberg, J. & Walters, C. R. (2017). *Do parents value school effectiveness?* NBER Working Paper No. 23912. Cambridge, MA, National Bureau of Economic Research.

Acemoglu, D. & Robinson, J. (2012). *Why nations fail: The origins of power, prosperity, and poverty.* London, Profile Books.

Adnett, N. (2003). Commentary. Reforming teachers' pay: Incentive payments, collegiate ethos and UK policy. *Cambridge Journal of Economics, 27*(1), 145–157.

Adnett, N. (2004). Private-sector provision of schooling: An economic assessment. *Comparative Education, 40*(3), 385–399.

Adnett, N. & Davies, P. (2002). *Markets for schooling: An economic analysis.* London, Routledge.

Adnett, N. & Davies, P. (2003). Schooling reforms in England: From quasi-markets to competition? *Journal of Education Policy, 18*(3), 415–428.

Adnett, N. & Davies, P. (2005). Competition between or within schools? Re-assessing school choice. *Education Economics, 13*(1), 109–121.

Adnett, N., Davies, P. & Bougheas, S. (2002). Market-based reforms of public schooling: Some unpleasant dynamics. *Economics of Education Review, 21*(4), 323–330.

Adonis, A. (2012). *Education, education, education. Reforming England's schools.* London, Biteback Publishing.

Agasisti, T. & Murtinu, S. (2012). 'Perceived' competition and performance in Italian secondary schools: New evidence from OECD-PISA 2006. *British Educational Research Journal, 38*(5), 841–858.

Aghion, P., Caroli, E. & Garcia-Penalosa, C. (1999). Inequality and economic growth: The perspective of the new growth theories. *Journal of Economic Literature, 37*(4), 1615–1660.

Ahonen, S. (2001). Politics of identity through history curriculum: Narratives of the past for social exclusion – or inclusion? *Journal of Curriculum Studies, 33*(2), 179–194.

Ainsworth, H., Hewitt, C. E., Higgins, S., Wiggins, A., Torgerson, D. J. & Torgerson, C. J. (2015). Sources of bias in outcome assessment in randomised controlled trials: A case study. *Educational Research and Evaluation, 21*(1), 3–14.

Ajzen, I. (1991). The Theory of Planned Behavior. *Organizational Behavior and Human Decision Processes, 50*, 179–211.

Akenson, D. H. (2011). *The Irish education experiment: The national system of education in the nineteenth century* (Vol. 1). London, Routledge.

Akerlof, G. A. & Kranton, R. E. (2002). Identity and schooling: Some lessons for the economics of education. *Journal of Economic Literature, 40*(4), 1167–1201.

Akerlof, G. A. & Shiller, R. J. (2010). *Animal spirits: How human psychology drives the economy, and why it matters for global capitalism.* Princeton, NJ, Princeton University Press.

Alavi, M. & Leidner, D. E. (2001). Review: Knowledge management and knowledge management systems: Conceptual foundations and research issues. *MIS Quarterly, 25*(1), 107–136.

Aligica, P. D. & Tarko, V. (2013). Co-production, polycentricity, and value heterogeneity: The Ostroms' public choice institutionalism revisited. *American Political Science Review, 107*(4), 726–741.

Allen, I. E. & Seaman, J. (2007). *Online nation: Five years of growth in online learning.* Newburyport, MA, Sloan Consortium.

Allen, I. E. & Seaman, J. (2011). *Going the distance: Online education in the United States.* Babson Park, MA, Babson Survey Research Group and Quahog Research Group.

Allen, M., Mabry, E., Mattrey, M., Bourhis, J., Titsworth, S. & Burrell, N. (2004). Evaluating the effectiveness of distance learning: A comparison using meta-analysis. *Journal of Communication, 54*(3), 402–420.

Allen, R. (2013). Measuring foundation school effectiveness using English administrative data, survey data and a regression discontinuity design. *Education Economics, 21*(5), 431–446.

Allen, R. & Burgess, S. (2013). Evaluating the provision of school performance information for school choice. *Economics of Education Review, 34*, 175–190.

Allen, R., Burgess, S. & McKenna, L. (2013). The short-run impact of using lotteries for school admissions: Early results from Brighton and Hove's reforms. *Transactions of the Institute of British Geographers, 38*(1), 149–166.

All Party Parliamentary Group on Financial Education for Young People (APPG) (2016). *Financial education in schools two years on – job done?* London, Young Enterprise. Available at www.pfeg.org/sites/default/files/APPG%20on%20Financial%20Education%20for%20Young%20People%20-Final%20Report%20-%20May%202016.pdf.

Altbach, P. G., Reisberg, L. & Rumbley, L. E. (2009). *Trends in global higher education: Tracking an academic revolution.* Report prepared for the 2009 UNESCO World Conference on Higher Education. Paris, UNESCO.

Altonji, J. (1995). The effects of high school curriculum on education and labor market outcomes. *Journal of Human Resources, 30*(3), 409–438.

Amrein, A. L. & Berliner, D. C. (2002). High-stakes testing & student learning. *Education Policy Analysis Archives, 10*(18), 1–72.

Anderson, D. C., Crowell, C. R., Doman, M. & Howard, G. S. (1988). Performance posting, goal setting, and activity-contingent praise as applied to a university hockey team. *Journal of Applied Psychology, 73*(1), 87–95.

Andrew, M. (2010). The changing route to owner occupation: The impact of student debt. *Housing Studies, 25*(1), 39–62.

Andrews, J. (2016). *School performance in multi-academy trusts and local authorities – 2015.* London, Education Policy Institute.

Andrews, R. & Byrne, G. A. (2009). Size, structure & administrative overheads: An empirical analysis of English local authorities. *Urban Studies, 46*(4), 739–759.

Andrews, R. & Mycock, A. (2008). Dilemmas of devolution: The 'politics of Britishness' and citizenship education. *British Politics, 3*(2), 139–155.

Angrist, J. D. & Guryan, J. (2008). Does teacher testing raise teacher quality? Evidence from state certification requirements. *Economics of Education Review, 27*(5), 483–503.

Angrist, J. D. & Lavy, V. (1999). Using Maimonides' rule to estimate the effect of class size on scholastic achievement. *The Quarterly Journal of Economics, 114*(2), 533–575.

Angrist, J. & Lavy, V. (2002). New evidence on classroom computers and pupil learning. *The Economic Journal, 112*(482), 735–765.

Ansell, B. W. (2008). University challenges: Explaining institutional change in higher education. *World Politics, 60*(2), 189–230.

Antoniou, P. & Kyriakides, L. (2011). The impact of a dynamic approach to professional development on teacher instruction and student learning: Results from an experimental study. *School Effectiveness and School Improvement, 22*(3), 291–311.

Apple, M. W. (1982). *Cultural and economic reproduction in education: Essays on class, ideology and the state.* London, Routledge & Kegan Paul.

Apple, M. W. (1993). The politics of official knowledge: Does a national curriculum make sense? *Discourse, 14*(1), 1–16.

Apple, M. W. (2000). *Official knowledge: Democratic education in a conservative age* (2nd edition). New York, Routledge.

Araya, R., Lewis, G., Rojas, G. & Fritsch, R. (2003). Education and income: Which is more important for mental health? *Journal of Epidemiology and Community Health, 57*(7), 501–505.

Arcidiacono, P. (2004). Ability sorting and the returns to college major. *Journal of Econometrics, 121*, 343–375.

Arcidiacono, P. (2005). Affirmative action in higher education: How do admission and financial aid rules affect future earnings? *Econometrica, 73*(5), 1477–1524.

Argimon, I., Gonzalez-Paramo, J. M. & Roldan, J. M. (1997). Evidence of public spending crowding-out from a panel of OECD countries. *Applied Economics, 29*(8), 1001–1010.

Arreman, I. E. & Holm, A. S. (2011). Privatisation of public education? The emergence of independent upper secondary schools in Sweden. *Journal of Education Policy, 26*(2), 225–243.

Arum, R., Gamoran, A. & Shavit, Y. (2007). More inclusion than diversion: Expansion, differentiation, and market structure in higher education. In Y. Shavit, R. Arum & A. Gamoran (Eds), *Stratification in higher education. A comparative study.* Stanford, CA, Stanford University Press (pp. 1–38).

Ashby, J. S. & Schoon, I. (2010). Career success: The role of teenage career aspirations, ambition value and gender in predicting adult social status and earnings. *Journal of Vocational Behavior, 77*(3), 350–360.

Astone, N. M. & McLanahan, S. S. (1991). Family structure, parental practices and high school completion. *American Sociological Review, 56*(3), 309–320.

Atkinson, A., Burgess, S., Croxson, B., Gregg, P., Propper, C., Slater, H. & Wilson, D. (2009). Evaluating the impact of performance-related pay for teachers in England. *Labour Economics, 16*(3), 251–261.

Atkinson, T. (2005). *The Atkinson Review. Final report. Measurement of government output and productivity for the national accounts.* London, Palgrave Macmillan.

Audit Office of New South Wales. (2012). *NSW Auditor General's Report: The impact of raising the school leaving age.* Sydney, Australia, the Audit Office of New South Wales.

Aurini, J. & Davies, S. (2004). The transformation of private tutoring: Education in a franchise form. *The Canadian Journal of Sociology, 29*(3), 419–438.

Australian Government. (2017). *The Higher Education Reform Package.* Canberra, Australian Government.

Autor, D. H., Katz, L. F. & Kearney, M. S. (2008). Trends in US wage inequality: Revising the revisionists. *The Review of Economics and Statistics, 90*(2), 300–323.

Auwarter, A. E. & Aruguete, M. S. (2008). Effects of student gender and socioeconomic status on teacher perceptions. *The Journal of Educational Research, 101*(4), 242–246.

Avery, C. & Turner, S. (2012). Student loans: Do college students borrow too much – or not enough? *The Journal of Economic Perspectives, 26*(1), 165–192.

Bach, S. & Kessler, I. (2011). *The modernisation of the public services and employee relations: Targeted change.* London, Palgrave Macmillan.

Bacolod, M. P. (2007). Do alternative opportunities matter? The role of female labor markets in the decline of teacher quality. *The Review of Economics and Statistics, 89*(4), 737–751.

Bagley, C., Woods, P. A. & Glatter, R. (2001). Rejecting schools: Towards a fuller understanding of the process of parental choice. *School Leadership & Management, 21*(3), 309–325.

Bagwell, L. S. & Bernheim, B. D. (1996). Veblen effects in a theory of conspicuous consumption. *The American Economic Review, 86*(3), 349–373.

Bainbridge, J., Meyers, M. K., Tanaka, S. & Waldfogel, J. (2005). Who gets an early education? Family income and the enrollment of three- to five-year-olds from 1968 to 2000. *Social Science Quarterly, 86*(3), 724–745.

Baker, L., Mackler, K., Sonnenschein, S. & Serpell, R. (2001). Parents' interactions with their first-grade children during storybook reading and relations with subsequent home reading activity and reading achievement. *Journal of School Psychology, 39*(5), 415–438.

Ball, S. J. (1992). *Politics and policy making in education: Explorations in the sociology of policy.* London, Routledge.

Ball, S. J. (2003a). *Class strategies and the education market: The middle classes and social advantage.* London, Routledge.

Ball, S. J. (2003b). The teacher's soul and the terrors of performativity. *Journal of Education Policy, 18*(2), 215–228.

Ball, S. J. (2012a). Performativity, commodification and commitment: An I-spy guide to the neoliberal university. *British Journal of Educational Studies, 60*(1), 17–28.

Ball, S. J. (2012b). *Global education inc: New policy networks and the neo-liberal imaginary.* London, Routledge.

Ball, S. J. & Junemann, C. (2012). *Networks, new governance and education.* Bristol, Policy Press.

Ball, S. J., Bowe, R. & Gewirtz, S. (1995). Circuits of schooling: A sociological exploration of parental choice of school in social class contexts. *The Sociological Review, 43*(1), 52–78.

Ball, S. J., Bowe, R. & Gewirtz, S. (1996). School choice, social class and distinction: The realization of social advantage in education. *Journal of Education Policy, 11*(1), 89–112.

Ball, S. J., Maguire, M. & Braun, A. (2012). *How schools do policy: Policy enactments in secondary schools.* London, Routledge.

Ball, S. J., Davies, J., David, M. & Reay, D. (2002). 'Classification' and 'judgement': Social class and the 'cognitive structures' of choice of higher education. *British Journal of Sociology of Education, 23*(1), 51–72.

Bandura, A., Barbaranelli, C., Caprara, G. V. & Pastorelli, C. (1996). Multifaceted impact of self-efficacy beliefs on academic functioning. *Child Development, 67*(3), 1206–1222.

Bandura, A., Barbaranelli, C., Caprara, G. V., & Pastorelli, C. (2001). Self-efficacy beliefs as shapers of children's aspirations and career trajectories. *Child Development, 72*(1), 187–206.

Banks, J. A. (1993). Multicultural education: Historical development, dimensions, and practice. *Review of Research in Education, 19*, 3–49.

Banks, J., Frawley, D. & McCoy, S. (2015). Achieving inclusion? Effective resourcing of students with special educational needs. *International Journal of Inclusive Education, 19*(9), 926–943.

Banks, M., Bates, I., Bynner, J., Breakwell, G., Emler, N., Jamieson, L. & Roberts, K. (1992). *Careers and identities*. Milton Keynes, Open University Press.

Barich, H. & Kotler, P. (1991). A framework for marketing image management. *Sloan Management Review, 32*(2), 94–100.

Barnes, D. (1976). *From communication to curriculum*. Harmondsworth, Penguin.

Barnett, W. S. (1993). Economic evaluation of home visiting programs. *The Future of Children, 3*(3), 93–112.

Barnett, W. S. & Yarosz, D. J. (2007). Who goes to preschool and why does it matter? *Preschool Policy Matters, 7*. New Brunswick, NJ, National Institute for Early Education Research, Rutgers Graduate School of Education.

Barraclough, S. J. & Smith, A. B. (1996). Do parents choose and value quality child care in New Zealand? *International Journal of Early Years Education, 4*(1), 5–26.

Barrie, S. C. (2007). A conceptual framework for the teaching and learning of generic graduate attributes. *Studies in Higher Education, 32*(4), 439–458.

Barrow, L., Markman, L. & Rouse, C. E. (2009). Technology's edge: The educational benefits of computer-aided instruction. *American Economic Journal: Economic Policy, 1*(1), 52–74.

Bartlett, L., Frederick, M., Gulbrandsen, T. & Murillo, E. (2002). The marketization of education: Public schools for private ends. *Anthropology & Education Quarterly, 33*(1), 5–29.

Bartley, S. J. & Golek, J. H. (2004). Evaluating the cost effectiveness of online and face-to-face instruction. *Journal of Educational Technology & Society, 7*(4), 167–175.

Bartunek, J. M., Greenberg, D. N. & Davidson, B. (1999). Consistent and inconsistent impacts of a teacher-led empowerment initiative in a federation of schools. *The Journal of Applied Behavioral Science, 35*(4), 457–478.

Bassanini, A., Nunziata, L. & Venn, D. (2009). Job protection legislation and productivity growth in OECD countries. *Economic Policy, 24*(58), 349–402.

Bauman, Z. (2001). *Community: Seeking safety in an insecure world*. Cambridge, Polity Press.

Baumert, J., Kunter, M., Blum, W., Brunner, M., Voss, T., Jordan, A. & Tsai, Y.-M. (2010). Teachers' mathematical knowledge, cognitive activation in the classroom, and student progress. *American Educational Research Journal, 27*(1), 133–180.

Baumol, W. J. (2012). *The Cost Disease: Why computers get cheaper and health care doesn't*. New Haven, CT, Yale University Press.

Baumol, W. J. & Blinder, A. S. (2016). *Microeconomics: Principles and policy* (13th edition). Boston, MA, Cengage Learning.

Baumol, W. J., Panzar, J. C. & Willig, R. D. (1982). *Contestable markets and the theory of industry structure*. New York, Harcourt Brace Jovanovich.

Baxter, J. (2013). *Child care participation and maternal employment trends in Australia*. Research Report No. 26. Canberra, Australian Institute of Family Studies, Australian Government.

Baxter, J. & Clarke, J. (2013). Farewell to the tick box inspector? Ofsted and the changing regime of school inspection in England. *Oxford Review of Education, 39*(5), 702–718.

Beal, H. K. O. & Hendry, P. M. (2012). The ironies of school choice: Empowering parents and reconceptualizing public education. *American Journal of Education, 118*(4), 521–550.

Beavis, A. (2004). Why parents choose public or private schools. *Research Developments, 12*(12), 3–4.

Becher, T. & Trowler, P. (2001). *Academic tribes and territories* (2nd edition). Buckingham, SRHE and Open University Press.

Becker, G. (1965). A theory of the allocation of time. *The Economic Journal, 75*(299), 493–517.

Becker, G. (1994). *Human capital: A theoretical and empirical analysis, with special reference to education* (3rd edition). New York, Columbia University Press for the National Bureau of Economic Research.

Becker, G. S. & Tomes, N. (1986). Human capital and the rise and fall of families. *Journal of Labor Economics, 4*(2), S1–39.

Becker, R. & Hecken, A. E. (2009). Higher education or vocational training? An empirical test of the rational action model of educational choices suggested by Breen and Goldthorpe and Esser. *Acta Sociologica, 52*(1), 25–45.

Becker, S. O. & Woessmann, L. (2008). Luther and the girls: Religious denomination and the female education gap in nineteenth-century Prussia. *The Scandinavian Journal of Economics, 110*(4), 777–805.

Bedard, K. & Kuhn, P. (2008). Where class size really matters: Class size and student ratings of instructor effectiveness. *Economics of Education Review, 27*(3), 253–265.

Beecham, J. & Knapp, M. (1999). Inclusive and special education: Issues of cost-effectiveness. In D. Labon (Ed.), *Inclusive Education at Work: Students with Disabilities in Mainstream Schools*. Paris, OECD (pp. 327–370).

Behrman, J. R. & Taubman, P. (1990). The intergenerational correlation between children's adult earnings and their parents' income: Results from the Michigan panel survey of income dynamics. *Review of Income and Wealth, 36*(2), 115–127.

Bekke, A. J. G. M. & Meer, F. M. (Eds). (2000). *Civil service systems in Western Europe*. Cheltenham, Edward Elgar.

Belfield, C. R. & Heywood, J. S. (2008). Performance pay for teachers: Determinants and consequences. *Economics of Education Review, 27*(3), 243–252.

Belfield, C. & Levin, H. M. (2002). The effects of competition between schools on educational outcomes: A review for the United States. *Review of Educational Research, 72*(2), 279–341.

Belfield, C. R. & Sibieta, L. (2016). *Long-run trends in school spending in England, IFS Report R115*. London, Institute for Fiscal Studies.

Belfield, C., Britton, J., Dearden, L. & van der Erve, L. (2017). *Higher education funding in England: Past, present and options for the future*. IFS Briefing Note No. 211. London, Institute for Fiscal Studies.

Belfield, C. R., Nores, M., Barnett, S. & Schweinhart, L. (2006). The High/Scope Perry Preschool Program cost–benefit analysis using data from the age – 40 follow-up. *Journal of Human Resources, 41*(1), 162–190.

Bell, A. D., Rowan-Kenyon, H. T. & Perna, L. W. (2009). College knowledge of 9th and 11th grade students: Variation by school and state context. *The Journal of Higher Education, 80*(6), 663–685.

Bell, C. A. (2009). All choices created equal? The role of choice sets in the selection of schools. *Peabody Journal of Education, 84*(2), 191–208.

Bellei, C. (2009). Does lengthening the school day increase students' academic achievement? Results from a natural experiment in Chile. *Economics of Education Review, 28*(5), 629–640.

Beller, E. & Hout, M. (2006). Intergenerational social mobility: The United States in comparative perspective. *The Future of Children, 16*(2), 19–36.

Belley, P. & Lochner, L. (2007). The changing role of family income and ability in determining educational achievement, *Journal of Human Capital 1*(1), 37–89.

Bénabou, R. & Tirole, J. (2006). Belief in a just world and redistributive politics. *Quarterly Journal of Economics, 121*(2), 699–746.

Ben-Ner, A. (2002). The shifting boundaries of the mixed economy and the future of the non-profit sector, *Annals of Public and Cooperative Economics, 73*(1), 5–40.

Bennett, R., Glennerster, H. & Nevison, D. (1995). Investing in skill: Expected returns to vocational studies. *Education Economics, 3*(2), 99–117.

Benson, C. S. (1961). *The economics of public education.* Boston, MA, Houghton, Mifflin.

Berger, A. N. (2003). The economic effects of technological progress: Evidence from the banking industry. *Journal of Money, Credit, and Banking, 35*(2), 141–176.

Berger, M. C. & Kostal, T. (2002). Financial resources, regulation, and enrollment in US public higher education. *Economics of Education Review, 21*(2), 101–110.

Bergmann, B. R. (2004). A Swedish-style welfare state or basic income: Which should have priority? *Politics & Society, 32*(1), 107–118.

Berkowitz, M. W. & Grych, J. H. (2000). Early character development and education. *Early Education and Development, 11*(1), 55–72.

Berliner, D. C. (2009). MCLB (Much Curriculum Left Behind): A US calamity in the making. *The Educational Forum, 73*(4), 284–296.

Berliner, D. (2011). Rational responses to high stakes testing: The case of curriculum narrowing and the harm that follows. *Cambridge Journal of Education, 41*(3), 287–302.

Bernard, R. M., Borokhovski, E., Schmid, R. F., Tamim, R. M. & Abrami, P. C. (2014). A meta-analysis of blended learning and technology use in higher education: From the general to the applied. *Journal of Computing in Higher Education, 26*(1), 87–122.

Bernard, R. M., Abrami, P. C., Borokhovski, E., Wade, C. A., Tamim, R. M., Surkes, M. A. & Bethel, E. C. (2009). A meta-analysis of three types of interaction treatments in distance education. *Review of Educational Research, 79*(3), 1243–1289.

Bernstein, B. (1982). Codes, modalities and the process of cultural reproduction. In M. W. Apple (Ed.), *Cultural and economic reproduction in education: Essays on class, ideology and the state.* London, Routledge and Kegan Paul (pp. 304–355).

Bertola, G. & Checchi, D. (2013). Who chooses which private education? Theory and international evidence. *Labour, 27*(3), 249–271.

Besley, T. (1988). A simple model for merit good arguments. *Journal of Public Economics, 35*(3), 371–383.

Bettinger, E. P. & Long, B. T. (2010). Does cheaper mean better? The impact of using adjunct instructors on student outcomes. *The Review of Economics and Statistics, 92*(3), 598–613.

Biesta, G. (2007a). Why 'what works' won't work: Evidence-based practice and the democratic deficit in educational research. *Educational Theory, 57*(1), 1–22.

Biesta, G. (2007b). Education and the democratic person: Towards a political conception of democratic education. *The Teachers College Record, 109*(3), 740–769.

Biggs, J. (1996). Enhancing teaching through constructive alignment. *Higher Education, 32*(3), 347–364.

Bills, D. B. (2003). Credentials, signals, and screens: Explaining the relationship between schooling and job assignment. *Review of Educational Research, 73*(4), 441–449.

Birchler, U. & Bütler, M. (2007). *Information economics.* Abingdon, Routledge.

Björklund, A., Lindahl, M. & Plug, E. (2006). The origins of intergenerational associations: Lessons from Swedish adoption data. *The Quarterly Journal of Economics, 121*(3), 999–1028.

Black, S. E. (1999). Do better schools matter? Parental valuation of elementary education. *Quarterly Journal of Economics, 114*(2), 577–599.

Black, S. E. & Lynch, L. M. (2001). How to compete: The impact of workplace practices and information technology on productivity. *Review of Economics and Statistics, 83*(3), 434–445.

Blackbourn, D. & Evans, R. J. (Eds.). (2014). *The German bourgeoisie (Routledge Revivals): Essays on the social history of the German middle class from the late eighteenth to the early twentieth century.* London, Routledge.

Blanchett, W. J. (2006). Disproportionate representation of African American students in special education: Acknowledging the role of white privilege and racism. *Educational Researcher*, *35*(6), 24–28.

Blanden, J. & Gregg, P. (2004). Family income and educational attainment: A review of approaches and evidence for Britain. *Oxford Review of Economic Policy*, *20*(2), 245–263.

Blanden, J. & Machin, S. (2004). Educational inequality and the expansion of UK higher education. *Scottish Journal of Political Economy*, *51*(2), 230–249.

Blanden, J., Katz, I. & Redmond, G. (2012). Family background and child outcomes. In. J. Ermisch, M. Jantti & T. Smeeding (Eds.), *From Parents to Children*. New York, Russell Sage Foundation (pp. 140–163).

Blanden, J., Goodman, A., Gregg, P. & Machin, S. (2004). Changes in intergenerational mobility in Britain. In M. Corak (Ed.), *Generational income mobility in North America and Europe*. Cambridge, Cambridge University Press (pp. 122–146).

Blatchford, P., Bassett, P. & Brown, P. (2011). Examining the effect of class size on classroom engagement and teacher–pupil interaction: Differences in relation to pupil prior attainment and primary vs. secondary schools. *Learning and Instruction*, *21*(6), 715–730.

Blatchford, P., Russell, A. & Webster (2012). *Reassessing the impact of teaching assistants*. London, Routledge.

Blatchford, P., Bassett, P., Goldstein, H. & Martin, C. (2003). Are class size differences related to pupils' educational progress and classroom processes? findings from the institute of education class size study of children aged 5–7 years. *British Educational Research Journal*, *29*(5), 709–730.

Blatchford, P., Goldstein, H., Martin, C. & Browne, W. (2002). A study of class size effects in English school reception year classes. *British Educational Research Journal*, *28*(2), 169–185.

Blatchford, P., Russell, A., Bassett, P., Brown, P. & Martin, C. (2007). The role and effects of teaching assistants in English primary schools (Years 4 to 6) 2000–2003. Results from the Class Size and Pupil–Adult Ratios (CSPAR) KS2 Project. *British Educational Research Journal*, 33(1), 5–26.

Blau, D. M. & Hagy, A. P. (1998). The demand for quality in child care. *Journal of Political Economy*, *106*(1), 104–146.

Blau, F. D. & Kahn, L. M. (2003). Understanding international differences in the gender pay gap. *Journal of Labor Economics*, *21*(1), 106–144.

Bloom, H. & Unterman, R. (2014). Can small high schools of choice improve educational prospects for disadvantaged students? *Journal of Policy Analysis and Management*, *33*(2), 290–319.

Blunkett, D. (2014). *Introducing Citizenship Education was the easy bit. We need to do more to encourage schools to support youth participation*. Blog released on Democratic Audit UK, 23/04/2014. Available at www.democraticaudit.com/2014/06/23/david-blunkett-introducing-citizenship-education-was-the-easy-bit-we-need-to-do-more-to-encourage-schools-to-support-youth-participation/ (accessed 21 July 2017).

Bobbitt, P. (2002). *The Shield of Achilles: War, peace, and the course of history*. New York, Alfred Knopf.

Bodovski, K. (2010). Parental practices and educational achievement: Social class, race, and habitus. *British Journal of Sociology of Education*, *31*(2), 139–156.

Boe, E. E. & Gilford, D. M. (Eds.). (1992). *Teacher supply, demand, and quality: Policy issues, models, and data bases*. Washington, DC, National Academies Press.

Boliver, V. (2011). Expansion, differentiation, and the persistence of social class inequalities in British higher education, *Higher Education*, *61*(3), 229–242.

Boliver, V. & Swift, A. (2011). Do comprehensive schools reduce social mobility? *British Journal of Sociology*, *62*(1), 89–110.

Bolton, P. (2008). *Teachers' pay statistics. Standard Note SN/SG/1877*, London, House of Commons.

Bolton. P. (2012). *Education: Historical statistics. Standard Note SN/SG/4252*. London, House of Commons.

Bolton, P. (2014). *Education spending in the UK. Standard Note SN/SG/1078*. London, House of Commons.

Borman, G. D. & Dowling, N. M. (2008). Teacher attrition and retention: A meta-analytic and narrative review of the research. *Review of Educational Research, 78*(3), 367–409.

Bosetti, L. (2004). Determinants of school choice: Understanding how parents choose elementary schools in Alberta. *Journal of Education Policy, 19*(4), 387–405.

Bowden, J., Hart, G., King, B., Trigwell, K. & Watts, O. (2000). *Generic capabilities of ATN university graduates*. Canberra, Australian Government Department of Education, Training and Youth Affairs.

Brint, S. & Karabel, J. (1989). *The diverted dream: Community colleges and the promise of educational opportunity in America, 1900–1985*. New York, Oxford University Press.

Bronfenbrenner, U. (1979). *The ecology of human development: Experiments in nature and design*. Cambridge, MA: Harvard University Press.

Bong, M., Cho, C., Ahn, H. S. & Kim, H. J. (2012). Comparison of self-beliefs for predicting student motivation and achievement. *The Journal of Educational Research, 105*(5), 336–352.

Borck, R. (2007). Voting, inequality and redistribution. *Journal of Economic Surveys, 21*(1), 90–109.

Borman, K. M., Eitle, T. M., Michael, D., Eitle, D. J., Lee, R., Johnson, L., Cobb-Roberts, D., Dorn, S. & Shircliffe, B. (2004). Accountability in a postdesegregation era: The continuing significance of racial segregation in Florida's schools. *American Educational Research Journal, 41*(3), 605–631.

Boudon, R. (1974). *Education, opportunity and social inequality*. New York, Wiley.

Bourdieu, P. (1973). Cultural reproduction and social reproduction. In R. Brown (Ed.), *Knowledge, Education and Cultural Change*. London, Tavistock (pp. 71–112).

Bourne, C. & Dass, A. (2003). Private and social rates of return to higher education in science and technology in a Caribbean economy. *Education Economics, 11*(1), 1–10.

Bowles, S. & Gintis, H. (1976). *Schooling in capitalist America*. New York, Basic Books.

Bowles, S. & Gintis, H. (2002). Schooling in capitalist America revisited. *Sociology of Education, 75*(1), 1–18.

Bowles, S. & Gintis, H. (2011). *A cooperative species: Human reciprocity and its evolution*. Princeton, NJ, Princeton University Press.

Bowles, T. J. & Bosworth, R. (2002). Scale economies in public education: Evidence from school level data. *Journal of Education Finance, 28*(2), 285–299.

Boyd, D., Grossman, P., Lankford, H., Loeb, S. & Wyckoff, J. (2008). *Who leaves? Teacher attrition and student achievement* (No. w14022). Cambridge, MA, National Bureau of Economic Research.

Bradley, S. & Taylor, J. (1998). The effect of school size on exam performance in secondary schools. *Oxford Bulletin of Economics and Statistics, 60*(3), 291–324.

Bradley, S. & Taylor, J. (2002). The effect of the quasi-market on the efficiency–equity trade-off in the secondary school sector. *Bulletin of Economic Research, 54*(3), 295–314.

Bradley, S., Johnes, G. & Millington, J. (2001). The effect of competition on the efficiency of secondary schools in England. *European Journal of Operational Research, 135*(3), 545–568.

Branigan, A. R., McCallum, K. J. & Freese, J. (2013). Variation in the heritability of educational attainment: An international meta-analysis. *Social Forces, 92*(1), 109–140.

Bratsberg, B., Røed, K., Raaum, O., Naylor, R. & Eriksson, T. (2007). Nonlinearities in intergenerational earnings mobility: Consequences for cross-country comparisons. *The Economic Journal, 117*(519), C72–C92.

Bratti, M., Checchi, D. & De Blasio, G. (2008). Does the expansion of higher education increase the equality of educational opportunities? Evidence from Italy. *Labour, 22*(s1), 53–88.

Bray, M. & Kwok, P. (2003). Demand for private supplementary tutoring: C onceptual considerations, and socio-economic patterns in Hong Kong. *Economics of Education Review, 22*(6), 611–620.

Breen, R. & Goldthorpe, J. H. (1997). Explaining educational differentials towards a formal rational action theory. *Rationality and Society, 9*(3), 275–305.

Breen, R. & Jonsson, J. O. (2005). Inequality of opportunity in comparative perspective: Recent research on educational attainment and social mobility. *Annual Review of Sociology, 31*, 223–243.

Breneman, D. W., Pusser, B. & Turner, S. E. (2006). The competitive provision of for-profit higher education: Mapping the competitive market. In D. W. Breneman, B. Pusser & S. E. Turner (Eds.), *Earnings from learning: The rise of for-profit universities*. Albany, State University of New York Press (pp. 3–22).

Brennan, J. & Naidoo, R. (2008). Higher education and the achievement (and/or prevention) of equity and social justice. *Higher Education, 56*(3), 287–302.

Bright, L. (2008). Does public service motivation really make a difference on the job satisfaction and turnover intentions of public employees? *The American Review of Public Administration, 38*(2), 149–166.

British Chambers of Commerce. (2014). *BCC Workforce Survey 2014: Developing the talents of the next generation*. London, British Chambers of Commerce.

Broadbent, J., Dietrich, M. & Laughlin, R. (1996). The development of principal–agent, contracting and accountability relationships in the public sector: Conceptual and cultural problems. *Critical Perspectives on Accounting, 7*(3), 259–284.

Brockmann, M., Clarke, L., Méhaut, P. & Winch, C. (2008). Competence-based vocational education and training (VET): The cases of England and France in a European perspective. *Vocations and Learning, 1*(3), 227–244.

Brown, D. K. (2001). The social sources of educational credentialism: Status cultures, labor markets, and organizations. *Sociology of Education, 74*, 19–34.

Brown, P., Lauder, H. & Ashton, D. (2011). *The global auction: The broken promises of education, jobs, and incomes*. Oxford, Oxford University Press.

Brown, T., Goodman, J. & Yasukawa, K. (2010). Academic casualization in Australia: Class divisions in the university. *Journal of Industrial Relations, 52*(2), 169–182.

Browne, Lord, J. (2010). *Securing a sustainable future for higher education: An independent review of higher education funding and student finance*. London, HMSO. Available online at www. bis.gov.uk/assets/biscore/corporate/docs/s/10-1208-securing-sustainable-higher-education-browne-report.pdf.

Browning, M. & Heinesen, E. (2007). Class size, teacher hours and educational attainment. *Scandinavian Journal of Economics, 109*(2), 415–438.

Bruinsma, M. & Jansen, E. P. W. A. (2010). Is the motivation to become a teacher related to pre-service teachers' intentions to remain in the profession? *European Journal of Teacher Education, 33*(2), 185–200.

Brunello, G. & Checchio, D. (2007). Does school tracking affect equality of opportunity? New international evidence. *Economic Policy, 22*(52), 782–861.

Brunello, G. & De Paola, M. (2013). *The costs of early school leaving in Europe*. IZA Discussion Paper No. DP 7791. Berlin, IZA.

Bryant, W. K. & Zick, C. D. (1996). An examination of parent–child shared time. *Journal of Marriage and the Family*, 58(1), 227–237.

Buchanan, J. M. (1965). An economic theory of clubs. *Economica*, 32(125), 1–14.

Buchanan, J. & Tullock, G. (1962). *The calculus of consent*. Ann Arbor, University of Michigan Press.

Buchmann, C. & Park, H. (2009). Stratification and the formation of expectations in highly differentiated educational systems. *Research in Social Stratification and Mobility*, 27(4), 245–267.

Buchmann, C., Condron, D. J. & Roscigno, V. J. (2010). Shadow education, American style: Test preparation, the SAT and college enrollment. *Social Forces*, 89(2), 435–461.

Bukodi, E., Erikson, R. & Goldthorpe, J. H. (2014). The effects of social origins and cognitive ability on educational attainment: Evidence from Britain and Sweden. *Acta Sociologica*, 57(4), 293–310.

Burgess, S. & Briggs, A. (2010). School assignment, school choice and social mobility. *Economics of Education Review*, 29(4), 639–649.

Burnard, P. & White, J. (2008). Creativity and performativity: Counterpoints in British and Australian education. *British Educational Research Journal*, 34(5), 667–682.

Busemeyer, M. (2007). Determinants of public education spending in 21 OECD democracies, 1980–2001. *Journal of European Public Policy*, 14(4), 582–610.

Butt, R. & Lowe, K. (2012). Teaching assistants and class teachers: Differing perceptions, role confusion and the benefits of skills-based training. *International Journal of Inclusive Education*, 16(2), 207–219.

Buysse, V., Sparkman, K. L. & Wesley, P. W. (2003). Communities of practice: Connecting what we know with what we do. *Exceptional Children*, 69(3), 263–277.

Byrne, J. (Ed.) (2012). *The occupy handbook*. New York, Back Bay Books.

Caldwell, B. J. (2005). *School-based management* (Vol. 3). Paris, International Institute for Educational Planning.

Caldwell, B. J. (2008). Reconceptualizing the self-managing school. *Educational Management Administration & Leadership*, 36(2), 235–252.

Callaghan, J. (1976). *A rational debate based on the facts*. Speech at Ruskin College, Oxford. Available online at www.educationengland.org.uk/documents/speeches/1976ruskin.html (accessed 1 October 2018).

Callender, C. & Jackson, J. (2005). Does the fear of debt deter students from higher education? *Journal of Social Policy*, 34(4), 509–540.

Callender, C. & Jackson, J. (2008). Does the fear of debt constrain choice of university and subject of study? *Studies in Higher Education*, 33(4), 405–429.

Calvó-Armengol, A., Patacchini, E. & Zenou, Y. (2009). Peer effects and social networks in education. *The Review of Economic Studies*, 76(4), 1239–1267.

Cameron, D. (2014). British values aren't optional, they're vital. That's why I will promote them in EVERY school: As row rages over 'Trojan Horse' takeover of our classrooms, the Prime Minister delivers this uncompromising pledge. *Daily Mail Online*. Published 15 June. Available at www.dailymail.co.uk/debate/article-2658171/DAVID-CAMERON-British-values-arent-optional-theyre-vital-Thats-I-promote-EVERY-school-As-row-rages-Trojan-Horse-takeover-classrooms-Prime-Minister-delivers-uncompromising-pledge.html.

Cameron, S. V. & Taber, C. (2004). Estimation of educational borrowing constraints using returns to schooling. *Journal of Political Economy*, 112(1), 132–182.

Cantoni, D. & Yuchtman, N. (2014). Medieval universities, legal institutions, and the commercial revolution. *The Quarterly Journal of Economics*, 129(2), 823–887.

Cappelen, A. W., Moene, K. O., Sørensen, E. Ø. & Tungodden, B. (2013). Needs versus entitlements – an international fairness experiment. *Journal of the European Economic Association*, *11*(3), 574–598.

Cappelli, P. & Hamori, M. (2005). The new road to the top, research report. *Harvard Business Review, January*, 1–11.

Carneiro, P. & Heckman, J. J. (2002). The evidence on credit constraints in post-secondary schooling. *The Economic Journal*, *112*(482), 705–734.

Carnoy, M., Froumin, I., Loyalka, P. K. & Tilak, J. B. (2014). The concept of public goods, the state, and higher education finance: A view from the BRICs. *Higher Education*, 68(3), 359–378.

Carpenter, D. & Moss, D. A. (Eds.) (2014). *Preventing regulatory capture: Special interest influence and how to limit it*. New York, Cambridge University Press.

Caravita, S. & Halldén, O. (1994). Re-framing the problem of conceptual change. *Learning and Instruction*, *4*(1), 89–111.

Carpenter, H., Papps, I., Bragg, J., Dyson, A., Harris, D., Kerr, K., Todd, L. & Laing, K. (2013). *Evaluation of pupil premium*. Research Report No. RR282. London, Department for Education.

Carr, W. & Hartnett, A. (1996). *Education and the struggle for democracy: The politics of educational ideas*. Buckingham, Open University Press.

Carr, W. & Kemmis, S. (1986). *Becoming critical: Education knowledge and action research*. London, RoutledgeFalmer.

Castells, M. (2010). *The power of identity: The information age: Economy, society, and culture* (Vol. 2) (2nd edition). Chichester, John Wiley & Sons.

Centra, J. A. (2003). Will teachers receive higher student evaluations by giving higher grades and less course work? *Research in Higher Education*, *44*(5), 495–518.

Chakraborty, K., Biswas, B. & Lewis, W. C. (2000). Economies of scale in public education: An econometric analysis. *Contemporary Economic Policy*, *18*(2), 238–247.

Chambers, J. G., Parrish, T. B., Lieberman, J. C. & Wolman, J. M. (1998). *What are we spending on special education in the US? CSEF brief*. Palo Alto, CA, Center for Special Education Finance.

Chan, C. & Bray, M. (2014). Marketized private tutoring as a supplement to regular schooling: Liberal studies and the shadow sector in Hong Kong secondary education. *Journal of Curriculum Studies*, *46*(3), 361–388.

Chandra, V. & Lloyd, M. (2008). The methodological nettle: ICT and student achievement. *British Journal of Educational Technology*, *39*(6), 1087–1098.

Chapman, B. & Lounkaew, K. (2015). Measuring the value of externalities from higher education. *Higher Education*, *70*(5), 767–785.

Chapman, C. (2013). Academy federations, chains, and teaching schools in England: Reflections on leadership, policy, and practice. *Journal of School Choice*, 7(3), 334–352.

Chapman, C. (2015). From one school to many: Reflections on the impact and nature of school federations and chains in England. *Educational Management Administration & Leadership*, *43*(1), 46–60.

Chapman, C. & Muijs, D. (2014). Does school-to-school collaboration promote school improvement? A study of the impact of school federations on student outcomes. *School Effectiveness and School Improvement*, *25*(3), 351–393.

Chapman, C. & Salokangas, M. (2012). Independent state-funded schools: Some reflections on recent developments. *School Leadership & Management*, *32*(5), 473–486.

Chen, R. & DesJardins, S. L. (2008). Exploring the effects of financial aid on the gap in student dropout risks by income level. *Research in Higher Education*, *49*(1), 1–18.

Chen, S. H., Yang, C. C. & Shiau, J. Y. (2006). The application of balanced scorecard in the performance evaluation of higher education. *The TQM magazine, 18*(2), 190–205.

Cheng, H. C., Lehman, J. & Armstrong, P. (1991). Comparison of performance and attitude in traditional and computer conferencing classes. *American Journal of Distance Education, 5*(3), 51–64.

Chetty, R., Friedman, J. N. & Rockoff, J. E. (2014). Measuring the impacts of teachers II: Teacher value-added and student outcomes in adulthood. *The American Economic Review, 104*(9), 2633–2679.

Cheung, A. C. & Slavin, R. E. (2013). The effectiveness of educational technology applications for enhancing mathematics achievement in K-12 classrooms: A meta-analysis. *Educational Research Review, 9*, 88–113.

Chevalier, A. (2007). Education, occupation and career expectations: Determinants of the gender pay gap for UK graduates. *Oxford Bulletin of Economics and Statistics, 69*(6), 819–842.

Chevalier, A. (2011). Subject choice and earnings of UK graduates, *Economics of Education Review, 30*(6), 1187–1201.

Chevalier, A., Harmon, C., O'Sullivan, V. & Walker, I. (2013). The impact of parental income and education on the schooling of their children. *IZA Journal of Labor Economics, 2*(1), 1–22.

Chia, G. & Miller, P. W. (2008). Tertiary performance, field of study and graduate starting salaries. *Australian Economic Review, 41*(1), 15–31.

Chowdry, H. & Sibieta, L. (2011). *Trends in education and schools spending.* IFS Briefing Note BN121. London, Institute for Fiscal Studies.

Chowdry, H., Crawford, C., Dearden, L., Goodman, A. & Vignoles, A. (2013). Widening participation in higher education: Analysis using linked administrative data. *Journal of the Royal Statistical Society: Series A (Statistics in Society), 176*(2), 431–457.

Christensen, C. M. & Eyring, H. J. (2011). *The innovative university: Changing the DNA of higher education from the inside out.* San Francisco, CA, Jossey-Bass.

Christie, H. & Munro, M. (2003). The logic of loans: Students' perceptions of the costs and benefits of the student loan. *British Journal of Sociology of Education, 24*(5), 621–636.

Chubb, J. E. & Moe, T. M. (1990). *Politics, markets and America's schools.* Washington, DC: Brookings Institution.

Ciccone, A. & Peri, G. (2006). Identifying human-capital externalities: Theory with applications. *The Review of Economic Studies, 73*(2), 381–412.

Clark, A. E., Frijters, P. & Shields, M. A. (2008). Relative income, happiness, and utility: An explanation for the Easterlin paradox and other puzzles. *Journal of Economic Literature, 46*(1), 95–144.

Clark, D. (2009). The performance and competitive effects of school autonomy. *Journal of Political Economy, 117*(4), 745–783.

Clark, D. & Linn, M. C. (2003). Designing for knowledge integration: The impact of instructional time. *Journal of the Learning Sciences, 12*(4), 451–493.

Clarke, J. (2004). Dissolving the public realm? The logics and limits of neo-liberalism. *Journal of Social Policy, 33*(1), 27–48.

Clarke, M. (2010). Educational reform in the 1960s: The introduction of comprehensive schools in the Republic of Ireland. *History of Education, 39*(3), 383–399.

Clarke, T. (2013). The advance of the MOOCs (massive open online courses): The impending globalisation of business education? *Education + Training, 55*(4/5), 403–413.

Clotfelter, C. T. (1976). School desegregation, 'tipping' and private school enrollment. *Journal of Human Resources, 11*(1), 28–50.

Clotfelter, C. T., Ladd, H. F. & Vigdor, H. F. (2007). Teacher credentials and student achievement: Longitudinal analysis with student fixed effects. *Economics of Education Review, 26*(6), 673–682.

Coase, R. H. (1937). The nature of the firm. *Economica, 4*(16), 386–405.

Coates, H. (2010). Defining and monitoring academic standards in Australian higher education. *Higher Education Management and Policy, 22*(1), 1–17.

Cobb, P. & McClain, K. (2010). The collective mediation of a high-stakes accountability program: Communities and networks of practice. In A. Sfard, K. Gravemeijer & E. Yackel (Eds.), *A Journey in Mathematics Education Research*. Dordecht, Springer (pp. 207–230).

Coe, R. (1999). *Changes in examination grades over time: Is the same worth less?* Paper presented at the British Educational Research Association Annual Conference, Brighton, September.

Coffield, F., Moseley, D., Hall, E. & Ecclestone, K. (2004). *Learning styles and pedagogy in post 16 learning: A systematic and critical review*. London, The Learning and Skills Research Centre.

Colantone, I. & Stalig, P. (2016). *The Trade Origins of Nationalist Protectionism: Import Competition and Voting Behavior in Western Europe*. Mimeo, Bocconi University, Milan, Italy.

Coldron, J. & Boulton, P. (1991). 'Happiness' as a criterion of parents' choice of school. *Journal of Education Policy, 6*(2), 169–178.

Coleman, J. (1968). The concept of equality of educational opportunity. *Harvard Educational Review, 38*(1), 7–22.

Coleman, J. S. (1988). Social capital in the creation of human capital. *American Journal of Sociology, 94*, S95–S120.

Coleman, J. S. & Hoffer, T. (1987). *Public and private high schools: The impact of communities*. New York, Basic Books.

Coleman, J., Hoffer, T. & Kilgore, S. (1982). *High school achievement: Public, catholic and private schools compared*. New York, Basic Books.

College Board. (2017). *Trends in higher education*. Available at https://trends.collegeboard. org/college-pricing/introduction (accessed 5 November 2017).

Collins, R. (1979). *The Credential Society: An historical sociology of education and stratification*. New York, Academic Press.

Committee on Ways and Means. (1998). *1998 Green Book: Background material and data on programs within the jurisdiction of the House Committee on Ways and Means*. Washington, DC: United States Government Printing Office.

Competition and Markets Authority (CMA). (2015). *An effective regulatory framework for higher education: A policy paper, CMA42*. London, Competition and Markets Authority.

Condron, D. J. & Roscigno, V. J. (2003). Disparities within: Unequal spending and achievement in an urban school district. *Sociology of Education, 76*(1), 18–36.

Confederation of British Industry (CBI). (1989). *Towards a skills revolution. Report of the vocational education and training task force*. London, Confederation of British Industry.

Confederation of British Industry (CBI). (1993). *Routes for success. Careership: A strategy for all 16–19 year-old learning*. London, Confederation of British Industry.

Confederation of British Industry (CBI)/Pearson. (2016). *The right combination. CBI/Pearson Education and Skills Survey 2016*. London, Pearson.

Conlisk, J. (1996). Why bounded rationality? *Journal of Economic Literature, 34*(2), 669–700.

Connelly, R. (1992). The effect of child care costs on married women's labor force participation. *The Review of Economics and Statistics, 74*(1), 83–90.

Connelly, R., Sullivan, A. & Jerrim, J. (2014). *Primary and secondary education and poverty review*. London, Centre for Longitudinal Studies, Institute of Education.

Connor, J. M. (2006). Effectiveness of antitrust sanctions on modern international cartels. *Journal of Industry, Competition and Trade, 6*(3), 195–223.

Conway, J. K. (1974). Perspectives on the history of women's education in the United States. *History of Education Quarterly, 14*(1), 1–12.

Cookson Jr., P. W. & Persell, C. H. (2008). *Preparing for power: America's elite boarding schools.* New York, Basic Books.

Cooper, A., Levin, B. & Campbell, C. (2009). The growing (but still limited) importance of evidence in education policy and practice. *Journal of Educational Change, 10*(2–3), 159–171.

Cooper, H., Robinson, J. C. & Patall, E. A. (2006). Does homework improve academic achievement? A synthesis of research, 1987–2003. *Review of Educational Research, 76*(1), 1–62.

Corak, M. (2013). Income inequality, equality of opportunity, and intergenerational mobility. *The Journal of Economic Perspectives, 27*(3), 79–102.

Corak, M. & Heisz, A. (1999). The intergenerational earnings and income mobility of Canadian men: Evidence from longitudinal income tax data. *Journal of Human Resources, 34*(3), 504–533.

Corcoran, S. & Evans, W. N. (2010). *Income inequality, the median voter, and the support for public education* (No. w16097). Cambridge, MA, National Bureau of Economic Research.

Corcoran, S. P., Evans, W. N. & Schwab, R. M. (2004). Changing labor-market opportunities for women and the quality of teachers, 1957–2000. *American Economic Review, 94*(2), 230–235.

Cousin, G. & Deepwell, F. (2005). Designs for network learning: A communities of practice perspective. *Studies in Higher Education, 30*(1), 57–66.

Cowan, R. & Foray, D. (1997). The economics of codification and the diffusion of knowledge. *Industrial and Corporate Change, 6*(3), 595–622.

Cox, C. B. & Dyson, A. E. (1969). *Fight for education: A black paper.* London, The Critical Quarterly Society.

Cox, D. & Jimenez, E. (1991). The relative effectiveness of private and public schools. *Journal of Development Economics, 34*(1), 99–121.

Craig, D. (2008). *Squandered: How Gordon Brown is wasting over one trillion pounds of our money.* London, Constable & Robinson.

Cremin, H., Thomas, G. & Vincett, K. (2005). Working with teaching assistants: Three models evaluated. *Research Papers in Education, 20*(4), 413–432.

Cremin, L. A. (1961). *The transformation of the school: Progressivism in American education, 1876–1957.* New York, Alfred A. Knopf.

Crewson, P. E. (1997). Public-service motivation: Building empirical evidence of incidence and effect. *Journal of Public Administration Research and Theory, 7*(4), 499–518.

Crisp, B. F., Jensen, N. M., Rosas, G. & Zeitzoff, T. (2010). Vote-seeking incentives and investment environments: The need for credit claiming and the provision of protectionism. *Electoral Studies, 29*(2), 221–226.

Crul, M. & Schneider, J. (2009). Children of Turkish immigrants in Germany and the Netherlands: The impact of differences in vocational and academic tracking systems. *Teachers College Record, 111*(6), 1508–1527.

Cruz, N. F. D. & Marques, R. C. (2012). Delivering local infrastructure through PPPs: Evidence from the school sector. *Journal of Construction Engineering and Management, 138*(12), 1433–1443.

Cuban, L., Kirkpatrick, H. & Peck, C. (2001). High access and low use of technologies in high school classrooms: Explaining an apparent paradox. *American Educational Research Journal, 38*(4), 813–834.

Cummings, C., Dyson, A., Muijs, D., Papps, I., Pearson, D., Raffo, C., Tiplady, L., Todd, L. & Crowther, D. (2007). Evaluation of the full service extended schools initiative: Final report. *DES Research Brief and Report*. London, Department for Education and Skills, Newcastle University.

Cummins, J. (1997). Cultural and linguistic diversity in education: A mainstream issue? *Educational Review, 49*(2), 105–114.

Curren, R. (2013). A neo-Aristotelian account of education, justice, and the human good, *Theory and Research in Education, 11*(3), 231–249.

Currie, J. (2001). Early childhood education programs. *Journal of Economic Perspectives, 15*(2), 213–238.

Dahl, G. B. & Lochner, L. (2012). The impact of family income on child achievement: Evidence from the earned income tax credit. *The American Economic Review, 102*(5), 1927–1956.

Dahlin, B. & Watkins, D. (2000). The role of repetition in the processes of memorising and understanding: A comparison of the views of German and Chinese secondary school students in Hong Kong. *British Journal of Educational Psychology, 70*(1), 65–84.

Dang, H. A. & Rogers, F. H. (2008). The growing phenomenon of private tutoring: Does it deepen human capital, widen inequalities, or waste resources? *The World Bank Research Observer, 23*(2), 161–200.

Darling-Hammond, L. (2000). How teacher education matters. *Journal of Teacher Education, 51*(3), 166–173.

Darling-Hammond, L. (2007). Race, inequality and educational accountability: The irony of 'No Child Left Behind'. *Race Ethnicity and Education, 10*(3), 245–260.

Davey Smith, G., Hart, C. & Hole, D. (1998). Education and occupational social class: Which is the more important indicator of mortality risk? *Journal of Epidemiology and Community Health, 52*(3), 153–160.

Davidson, A., Miskelly, J. & Kelly, A. (2008). *Value for money in schools: Literature and data review*. London, Audit Commission.

Davies, E. & Lea, S. E. (1995). Student attitudes to student debt. *Journal of Economic Psychology, 16*(4), 663–679.

Davies, N., Dickson, M., Davey Smith, G., van den Berg, G. & Windmeijer, F. (in press). The causal effects of education on health, mortality, cognition, well-being, and income in the UK Biobank. *Nature, Human Behavior*.

Davies, P. (2006). Educating citizens for changing economies. *Journal of Curriculum Studies, 38*(1), 15–30.

Davies, P. (2011). Private Schools and public benefit: Fees, fee remissions and subsidies. *Journal of School Choice, 5*(4), 397–413.

Davies, P. (2012). Can governments improve Higher Education through 'informing choice'? *British Journal of Educational Studies, 60*(3), 261–276.

Davies, P. (2015). Towards a framework for financial literacy in the context of democracy. *Journal of Curriculum Studies, 47*(2), 300–316.

Davies, P. & Davies, N. (2014). Paying for quality? Associations between private school fees, performance and use of resources. *British Educational Research Journal, 40*(3), 421–440.

Davies, P. & Hughes, J. (2009). The fractured arms of government and the premature end of lifelong learning. *Journal of Education Policy, 24*(5), 595–610.

Davies, P. & Mangan, J. (2007). Threshold concepts and the integration of understanding in economics. *Studies in Higher Education, 32*(6), 711–726.

Davies, P., Adnett, N. & Mangan, J. (2002). The diversity and dynamics of competition: Evidence from two local schooling markets. *Oxford Review of Education, 28*(1), 91–107.

Davies, P., Davies, N. & Qiu, T. (2017). Information and choice of A-level subjects: A cluster randomized controlled trial with linked administrative data. *British Educational Research Journal, 43*(4), 647–670.

Davies, P., Mangan, J. & Hughes, A. (2009b). Participation, financial support and the marginal student. *Higher Education,* 58(2), 193–204.

Davies, P., Mangan, J. & Telhaj, S. (2005a). 'Bold, reckless and adaptable'? Explaining gender differences in economic thinking and attitudes. *British Educational Research Journal, 31*(1), 29–48.

Davies, P., Qiu, T. & Davies, N. (2014). Cultural and human capital, information and higher education choices, *Journal of Education Policy 29*(6), 804–825.

Davies, P., Slack. K. & Howard, C. (2012). Variation in the length of an undergraduate degree: Participation and outcomes. *Studies in Higher Education, 37*(4), 431–447.

Davies, P., Coates, G., Hammersley-Fletcher, L. & Mangan, J. (2005b). When 'becoming a 50% school' is success enough: A principal–agent analysis of subject leaders' target setting. *School Leadership and Management, 25*(5), 493–511.

Davies, P., Mangan, J., Hughes, A. & Slack, K. (2013). Labour market motivation and undergraduates' choice of degree subject. *British Educational Research Journal, 39*(2), 361–382.

Davies, P., Davies, N., Hutton, D., Adnett, N. & Coe, R. (2009a). Choosing *in* schools: Locating the benefits of specialization. *Oxford Review of Education, 35*(2), 147–167.

Davies, P., Telhaj, S., Adnett, N., Coe, R. & Hutton, D. (2009c). Competition, cream-skimming and department performance within secondary schools. *British Educational Research Journal, 35*(1), 65–81.

Davies, P., Telhaj, S., Hutton, D., Adnett, N. & Coe, R. (2004). *The myth of the bog standard secondary school: A school level analysis of students' choice of optional subjects.* IEPR Working Paper. Stoke-on-Trent, Staffordshire University.

Davies, P., Connolly, M., Nelson, J., Hulme, M., Kirkman, J. & Greenway, C. (2016). 'Letting the right one in': Provider contexts for recruitment to initial teacher education in the United Kingdom. *Teaching and Teacher Education, 60,* 291–302.

Davies, S. & Guppy, N. (1997). Globalization and educational reforms in Anglo-American democracies. *Comparative Education Review, 41*(4), 435–459.

Davis-Kean, P. E. (2005). The influence of parent education and family income on child achievement: The indirect role of parental expectations and the home environment. *Journal of Family Psychology, 19*(2), 294.

Day, C., Elliot, B. & Kington, A. (2005). Reform, standards and teacher identity: Challenges of sustaining commitment. *Teaching and Teacher Education, 21*(5), 563–577.

Deakin, G., James, N., Tickner, M. & Tidswell, J. (2010). *Teachers' workload diary survey 2010 DFE-RR057.* London, Department for Education.

Dearden, L., Machin, S. & Reed, H. (1997). Intergenerational mobility in Britain. *The Economic Journal, 107*(1), 47–66.

Dearden, L., Ryan, C. & Sibieta, L. (2011). What determines private school choice? A comparison between the United Kingdom and Australia. *Australian Economic Review, 44*(3), 308–320.

Dearden, L., Emmerson, C., Frayne, C. & Meghir, C. (2009). Conditional cash transfers and school dropout rates. *Journal of Human Resources, 44*(4), 827–857.

Dearing, Sir R. (1997). *Higher education in the learning society.* London, Her Majesty's Stationary Office.

Dearlove, J. (1998). Fundamental changes in institutional governance structures: The United Kingdom. *Higher Education Policy, 11*(2–3), 111–120.

Deci, E. L., Koestner, R. & Ryan, R. M. (2001). Extrinsic rewards and intrinsic motivation in education: Reconsidered once again. *Review of Educational Research, 71*(1), 1–27.

Dee, T. S. (2004). Are there civic returns to education? *Journal of Public Economics*, *88*(9), 1697–1720.

Dee, T. S. & Jacob, B. (2011). The impact of No Child Left Behind on student achievement. *Journal of Policy Analysis and Management*, *30*(3), 418–446.

Dee, T. S. & Keys, B. J. (2004). Does merit pay reward good teachers? Evidence from a randomized experiment. *Journal of Policy Analysis and Management*, *23*(3), 471–488.

De Graaf, N. D., De Graaf, P. M. & Kraaykamp, G. (2000). Parental cultural capital and educational attainment in the Netherlands: A refinement of the cultural capital perspective. *Sociology of Education*, *73*(2), 92–111.

De Haan, J., Sturm, J. E. & Sikken, B. J. (1996). Government capital formation: Explaining the decline. *Weltwirtschaftliches Archiv*, *132*(1), 55–74.

DeHoog, R. H. (1990). Competition, negotiation, or cooperation: Three models for service contracting. *Administration & Society*, *22*(3), 317–340.

Deissinger, T. (1994). The evolution of the modern vocational training systems in England and Germany: A comparative view. *Compare*, *24*(1), 17–36.

Deissinger, T. & Hellwig, S. (2005). Apprenticeships in Germany: Modernising the dual system. *Education + Training*, *47*(4/5), 312–324.

Deloitte (2015). *The importance of universities to Australia's prosperity. A report prepared for Universities Australia*. London, Deloitte Access Economics Pty.

del Mar Salinas-Jiménez, M., Artés, J. & Salinas-Jiménez, J. (2011). Education as a positional good: A life satisfaction approach. *Social Indicators Research*, *103*(3), 409–426.

Deneulin, S. & Townsend, N. (2007). Public goods, global public goods and the common good. *International Journal of Social Economics*, *34*(1/2), 19–36.

Denis, J. L., Dompierre, G., Langley, A. & Rouleau, L. (2011). Escalating indecision: Between reification and strategic ambiguity. *Organization Science*, *22*(1), 225–244.

De Paola, M. & Scoppa, V. (2011). The effects of class size on the achievement of college students. *The Manchester School*, *79*(6), 1061–1079.

Department for Business, Innovation and Skills (DBIS). (2013). *Privately funded providers of higher education in the UK*. London, Department for Business, Innovation and Skills.

Department for Business, Innovation and Skills (DBIS). (2016). *Success as a knowledge economy: Teaching excellence, social mobility and student choice*. London, Department for Business, Innovation and Skills.

Department for Education. (2010). *Education secretary commits £110m to weakest schools*. Press release 3 November. Available at www.gov.uk/government/news/education-secretary-commits-110m-to-weakest-schools.

Department for Education. (2011). *Training our next generation of outstanding teachers*. London, Department for Education.

Department for Education. (2013a). *The National Curriculum in England: Framework document*, DFE-00177–2013. London, Department for Education.

Department for Education. (2013b). *Review of efficiency in the schools system*, DFE-00091–2013. London, Department for Education.

Department for Education. (2016). *Schools that work for everyone. Government consultation*. London, Department for Education.

Department for Education. (2017a). *Schools, pupils and their characteristics, January 2017*, SFR28/2017. London, Department for Education. Available at www.gov.uk/government/statistics/schools-pupils-and-their-characteristics-january-2017 (accessed 18 September 2017).

Department for Education. (2017b). *Teaching excellence and student outcomes framework specification*. London, Department for Education.

Department for Education and Skills. (2003). *Time for standards – Raising standards and tackling workload: A national agreement*. London, Department for Education and Skills.

Department for Education and Skills. (2007a). *Raising expectations: Staying in education and training post-16* (Cm. 7065). London, The Stationery Office.

Department for Education and Skills. (2007b). *Curriculum Review: Diversity and Citizenship*. London, The Stationery Office.

Department of Education, Employment and Workplace Relations, & Bradley, D. (2008). *Review of Australian higher education: Discussion paper*. Canberra, Department of Education, Employment and Workplace Relations.

Desimone, L. M., Porter, A. C., Garet, M. S., Yoon, K. S. & Birman, B. F. (2002). Effects of professional development on teachers' instruction: Results from a three-year longitudinal study. *Educational Evaluation and Policy Analysis, 24*(2), 81–112.

DesJardins, S. L. & Toutkoushian, R. K. (2005). Are students really rational? The development of rational thought and its application to student choice. In *Higher education: Handbook of theory and research*. Amsterdam, Springer Netherlands (pp. 191–240).

Devereux, P. J. & Hart, R. A. (2010). Forced to be rich? Returns to compulsory schooling in Britain. *The Economic Journal, 120*(549), 1345–1364.

Dewey, J. (1939). *Theory of valuation*. Chicago, IL, University of Chicago Press.

de Wolf, I. F. & Janssens, F. J. G. (2007). Effects and side effects of inspections and accountability in education: An overview of empirical studies. *Oxford Review of Education, 33*(3), 379–396.

Diamond, J. B., Randolph, A. & Spillane, J. P. (2004). Teachers' expectations and sense of responsibility for student learning: The importance of race, class, and organizational habitus. *Anthropology & Education Quarterly, 35*(1), 75–98.

Dickson, M. (2007). *The effect of free pre-school education on children's subsequent academic performance: Empirical evidence from England*. Mimeo, Warwick, University of Warwick.

Dika, S. L. & Singh, K. (2002). Applications of social capital in educational literature: A critical synthesis. *Review of Educational Research, 72*(1), 31–60.

Dill, D. D. (1997). Higher education markets and public policy. *Higher Education Policy, 10*(3–4), 167–185.

DiMaggio, P. (1982). Cultural capital and school success: The impact of status culture participation on the grades of US high school students. *American Sociological Review, 47*(2), 189–201.

DiMartino, C. & Jessen, S. B. (2016). School brand management: The policies, practices, and perceptions of branding and marketing in New York City's public high schools. *Urban Education, 51*(5), 447–475.

DiPasquale, D. & Glaeser, E. L. (1998). The Los Angeles riot and the economics of urban unrest. *Journal of Urban Economics, 43*(1), 52–78.

diSessa, A. A. & Sherin, B. L. (1998). What changes in conceptual change? *International Journal of Science Education, 20*(10), 1155–1191.

Dixit, A. (2002). Incentives and organizations in the public sector: An interpretative review. *Journal of Human Resources, 37*(4), 696–727.

Dobbs, R., Madgavkar, A., Manyika, J., Woetzel, J., Bughin, J., Labaye, E. & Kashyap, P. (2016). *Poorer than their parents? Flat or falling incomes in advanced economies*. London, McKinsey Global Institute. Available at www.mckinsey.com/global-themes/employment-and-growth/poorer-than-their-parents-a-new-perspective-on-income-inequality.

Dollery, B. & Wallis, J. (2003). *The political economy of the voluntary sector*. Cheltenham, Edward Elgar.

Dolton, P. & Marcenaro-Gutierrez, O. D. (2011). If you pay peanuts do you get monkeys? A cross-country analysis of teacher pay and pupil performance. *Economic Policy, 26*(65), 5–55.

Dolton, P. & Vignoles, A. (2002). The return on post-compulsory school mathematics study. *Economica, 69*(273), 113–142.

Donnelly, C. (2004). What price harmony? Teachers' methods of delivering an ethos of tolerance and respect for diversity in an integrated school in Northern Ireland. *Educational Research, 46*(1), 3–16.

Douglass, J. A. & Keeling, R. (2008). *The big curve: Trends in university fees and financing in the EU and US. CSHE Research & Occasional Paper Series 19.08.* Berkeley, CA, Center for Studies in Higher Education, University of Berkeley.

Downes, S. (2010). Learning networks and connective knowledge. In H. H. Yang & S. C.-Y. Yuen (Eds.), *Collective Intelligence and E-learning 2.* New York, Information Science Reference (pp. 1–26).

Downes, T. A. & Zabel, J. E. (2002). The impact of school characteristics on house prices: Chicago 1987–1991. *Journal of Urban Economics, 52*(1), 1–25.

Downey, D. B. (1995). When bigger is not better: Family size, parental resources, and children's educational performance. *American Sociological Review, 60*(5), 746–761.

Dowrick, S. & Gemmell, N. (1991). Industrialisation, catching up and economic growth: A comparative study across the world's capitalist economies. *The Economic Journal, 101*(405), 263–275.

Dreher, A. (2006). The influence of globalization on taxes and social policy: An empirical analysis for OECD countries. *European Journal of Political Economy, 22*(1), 179–201.

Driscoll, A., Jicha, K., Hunt, A. N., Tichavsky, L. & Thompson, G. (2012). Can online classes deliver in-class results? A comparison of student performance and satisfaction in an online versus a face-to-face introductory Sociology course. *Teaching Sociology, 40*(4), 312–331.

Dumais, S. & Ward, A. (2010). Cultural capital and first-generation college success. *Poetics, 38*(3), 245–265.

Duncombe, W. & Yinger, J. (2007). Does school district consolidation cut costs? *Education, 2*(4), 341–375.

Duncombe, W., Miner, J. & Ruggiero, J. (1995). Potential cost savings from school district consolidation: A case study of New York. *Economics of Education Review, 14*(3), 265–284.

Dupriez, V., Dumay, X. & Vause, A. (2008). How do school systems manage pupils' heterogeneity? *Comparative Education Review, 52*(2), 245–273.

Dworkin, R. (1981). What is equality? Part 2: Equality of resources. *Philosophy & Public Affairs, 10*(4), 183–345.

Dwyer, R. E., McCloud, L. & Hodson, R. (2012). Debt and graduation from American universities. *Social Forces, 90*(4), 1133–1155.

Dynarski, S. & Scott-Clayton, J. (2013). Financial aid policy: Lessons from research. *Future of Children, 23*(1), 67–91.

Earley, P. C. (1986). Trust, perceived importance of praise and criticism, and work performance: An examination of feedback in the United States and England. *Journal of Management, 12*(4), 457–473.

Easterlin, R. A. (2005). Feeding the illusion of growth and happiness: A reply to Hagerty and Veenhoven. *Social Indicators Research, 74*(3), 429–443.

Eatwell, R. (2000). The rebirth of the 'extreme right' in Western Europe? *Parliamentary Affairs, 53*(3), 407–425.

Eberts, R., Hollenbeck, K. & Stone, J. (2002). Teacher performance incentives and student outcomes. *Journal of Human Resources, 37*(4), 913–927.

Eccles, J. S. & Harold, R. D. (1993). Parent-school involvement during the early adolescent years. *Teachers College Record, 94*(3), 568–578.

Eckel, C. C., Johnson, C., Montmarquette, C. & Rojas, C. (2007). Debt aversion and the demand for loans for postsecondary education. *Public Finance Review, 35*(2), 233–262.

Economist, The. (2016). Collatoral damage: Britain is unusually open to trade but unusually bad at at mitigating its impact. *The Economist*, 30 July.

Education Scotland. (2016). *Social studies: Assessing progress and achievement*. Edinburgh, Education Scotland. Available at www.educationscotland.gov.uk/Images/SocialStudies Grid_tcm4-832619.pdf.

Edwards, A. (2005). Relational agency: Learning to be a resourceful practitioner. *International Journal of Educational Research, 43*(3), 168–182.

Edwards, D. & Radloff, A. (2013). *Higher education enrolment growth, change and the role of private HEPs*. Melbourbe, Australian Council for Educational Research. Available at www.acpet. edu.au/uploads/files/ACER%20Background%20Paper%20for%20ACPET%20-%20 Growth%20in%20HE%20FINAL%20131115.pdf (accessed 3 November 2017).

Eichhorst, W., Rodríguez-Planas, N., Schmidl, R. & Zimmermann, K. F. (2012). *A roadmap to vocational education and training systems around the world*. IZA Discussion Paper No. 7110. Bonn, IZA.

Eide, E., Goldhaber, D. & Brewer, D. (2004). The teacher labour market and teacher quality. *Oxford Review of Economic Policy, 20*(2), 230–244.

Eika, L., Mogstad, M. & Zafar, B. (2014). *Educational assortative mating and household income inequality*. Federal Reserve Bank of New York Staff Report 682. New York, Federal Reserve Bank of New York.

Eisner, E. W. (2001). What does it mean to say a school is doing well? *Phi Delta Kappan, 82*(5), 367–372.

Eiszler, C. F. (2002). College students' evaluations of teaching and grade inflation. *Research in Higher Education, 43*(4), 483–501.

Elacqua, G., Contreras, D., Salavar, F. & Santos, H. S. (2011). Private school chains in Chile: Do better schools scale up? *Cato Institute Policy Analysis* No. 682. Washington, DC, The Cato Institute.

Elliott, W. & Nam, I. (2013). Is student debt jeopardizing the short-term financial health of US households? *Federal Reserve Bank of St. Louis Review, 95*(September/October), 405–424.

Elmore, G. M. & Huebner, E. S. (2010). Adolescents' satisfaction with school experiences: Relationships with demographics, attachment relationships, and school engagement behavior. *Psychology in the Schools, 47*(6), 525–537.

Elton, Lord. (1989). *Discipline in schools*. London, Department of Education and Science and the Welsh Office.

Emirbayer, M., & Goodwin, J. (1994). Network analysis, culture, and the problem of agency. *American Journal of Sociology, 99*(6), 1411–1454.

Engeström, Y. (2001). Expansive learning at work: Toward an activity theoretical reconceptualization. *Journal of Education and Work, 14*(1), 133–156.

England, J. & Chatterjee, P. (2005). *Financial education: A review of existing provision in the UK Department for Work and Pensions Research Report 275*. London, Department for Work and Pensions.

English, L. M. & Guthrie, J. (2003). Driving privately financed projects in Australia: What makes them tick? *Accounting, Auditing & Accountability Journal, 16*(3), 493–511.

Epple, D. & Romano, R. E. (1996). Ends against the middle: Determining public service provision when there are private alternatives. *Journal of Public Economics, 62*(3), 297–325.

Epple, D., Figlio, D. & Romano, R. (2004). Competition between private and public schools: Testing stratification and pricing predictions. *Journal of Public Economics, 88*(7), 1215–1245.

Epstein, J. L. (2001). *School and family partnerships: Preparing educators and improving schools.* Boulder, CO, Westview Press.

Eren, A. & Tezel, K. V. (2010). Factors influencing teaching choice, professional plans about teaching, and future time perspective: A mediational analysis. *Teaching and Teacher Education, 26*(7), 1416–1428.

Ermisch, J., Jantti, M., Smeeding, T. & Wilson, J. A. (2012). Advantage in comparative perspective. In J. Ermisch, M. Jantti & T. Smeeding (Eds.), *From parents to children: The intergenerational transmission of advantage.* New York, The Russell Sage Foundation (pp. 3–31).

European Council. (2015). *Promoting education for economic growth and employment.* European Council of the European Union. Brussels, European Council. Available at www.consilium.europa.eu/en/policies/education-economic-growth/.

Euzent, P., Martin, T., Moskal, P. & Moskal, P. (2011). Assessing student performance and perceptions in lecture capture vs. face-to-face course delivery. *Journal of Information Technology Education, 10*(1), 295–307.

Evans, B. (1992). *The politics of the training market: From Manpower Services Commission to Training and Enterprise Councils.* Brighton, Psychology Press.

Eyler, J. & Giles Jr., D. E. (1999). *Where's the learning in service-learning? Jossey-Bass Higher and Adult Education Series.* San Francisco, CA, Jossey-Bass.

Faas, D. (2011). The nation, Europe, and migration: A comparison of geography, history, and citizenship education curricula in Greece, Germany, and England. *Journal of Curriculum Studies, 43*(4), 471–492.

Farkas, G., Grobe, R. P., Sheehan, D. & Shuan, Y. (1990). Cultural resources and school success: Gender, ethnicity and poverty groups within an urban school district. *American Sociological Review, 55*(1), 127–142.

Farrell, P., Alborz, A., Howes, A. & Pearson, D. (2010). The impact of teaching assistants on improving pupils' academic achievement in mainstream schools: A review of the literature. *Educational Review, 62*(4), 435–448.

Feinstein, C. (1999). Structural change in the developed countries during the twentieth century. *Oxford Review of Economic Policy, 15*(4), 35–55.

Feinstein, L. & Symons, J. (1999). Attainment in secondary school. *Oxford Economic Papers, 51*(2), 300–321.

Feldman, M. & Desrochers, P. (2003). Research universities and local economic development: Lessons from the history of the Johns Hopkins University. *Industry and Innovation, 10*(1), 5–24.

Fender, V. & Calver, J. (2014). *Human capital estimates 2013.* London, Office for National Statistics.

Fenstermacher, G. D. (1994). The knower and the known: The nature of knowledge in research on teaching. *Review of Research in Education, 20*(1), 3–56.

Ferguson, R. (1998). Teacher perceptions and expectations and the Black–White test score gap. In C. Jencks & M. Philips (Eds.), *The Black–White test score gap.* Washington, DC, Brookings Institution Press (pp. 273–317).

Fernandez, J., Mateo, M. A. & Muniz, J. (1998). Is there a relationship between class size and student ratings of teaching quality? *Educational and Psychological Measurement, 58*(4), 596–604.

Ferrier, G. D. & Porter, P. K. (1991). The productive efficiency of US milk processing co-operatives. *Journal of Agricultural Economics, 42*(2), 161–173.

Fevre, R., Rees, G. & Gorard, S. (1999). Some sociological alternatives to human capital theory and their implications for research on post-compulsory education and training [1]. *Journal of Education and Work, 12*(2), 117–140.

Fiala, P. (2005). Information sharing in supply chains. *Omega, 33*(5), 419–423.

Fierman, W. (2006). Language and education in post-Soviet Kazakhstan: Kazakh-medium instruction in urban schools. *The Russian Review, 65*(1), 98–116.

Figlio, D. N. (1997). Teacher salaries and teacher quality. *Economics Letters, 55*(2), 267–271.

Figlio, D. N., Schapiro, M. O. & Soter, K. B. (2015). Are tenure track professors better teachers? *Review of Economics and Statistics, 97*(4), 715–724.

Fine, B. (2000). Endogenous growth theory: A critical assessment. *Cambridge Journal of Economics, 24*(2), 245–265.

Finn, J. D. & Achilles, C. M. (1999). Tennessee's class size study: Findings, implications, misconceptions. *Educational Evaluation and Policy Analysis, 21*(2), 97–109.

Finn, M. (2015). The politics of education revisited: Anthony Crosland and Michael Gove in historical perspective. *London Review of Education, 13*(2), 98–112.

Firestone, W. A. (2014). Teacher evaluation policy and conflicting theories of motivation. *Educational Researcher, 43*(2), 100–107.

Fitz-Gibbon, C. T. & Stephenson-Forster, N. J. (1999). Is OfSTED helpful? In C. Cullingford (Ed.), *An inspector calls: The effect of OfSTED inspections on school standards, 97–118.* London, Kogan Page (pp. 97–118).

Fives, H. & Gill, M. G. (Eds). (2014). *International handbook of research on teachers' beliefs.* New York, Routledge.

Fletcher, J. D., Hawley, D. E. & Piele, P. K. (1990). Costs, effects, and utility of microcomputer assisted instruction in the classroom. *American Educational Research Journal, 27*(4), 783–806.

Flores, B., Cousin, P. T. & Diaz, E. (1991). Transforming deficit myths about learning, language, and culture. *Language Arts, 68*(5), 369–379.

Forcadell, F. J. & Guadamillas, F. (2002). A case study on the implementation of a knowledge management strategy oriented to innovation. *Knowledge and Process Management, 9*(3), 162–171.

Foreman-Peck, J. & Foreman-Peck, L. (2006). Should schools be smaller? The size–performance relationship for Welsh schools. *Economics of Education Review, 25*(2), 157–171.

Forsyth, H. (2014). *A history of the modern Australian university.* Sydney, NewSouth Publishing.

Francesconi, M. & Nicoletti, C. (2006). Intergenerational mobility and sample selection in short panels. *Journal of Applied Econometrics, 21*(8), 1265–1293.

Francis, B. (2000). *Boys, girls, and achievement: Addressing the classroom issues.* London, Routledge.

Francois, P. (2000). 'Public service motivation' as an argument for government provision. *Journal of Public Economics, 78,* 275–299.

Francois, P. (2003). Not-for-profit provision of public services. *Economic Journal, 113,* C53–C61.

Frank, R. H. (1997). The frame of reference as a public good. *The Economic Journal, 107*(445), 1832–1847.

Freire, P. (2006). *Pedagogy of the oppressed.* 30th anniversary edition. New York, Continuum.

Friedkin, N. E. & Necochea, J. (1988). School system size and performance: A contingency perspective. *Educational Evaluation and Policy Analysis, 10*(3), 237–249.

Friedman, M. (1955). The role of government in education. In R. A. Solow (Ed.), *Economics and the public interest.* New Brunswick, NJ, Rutgers University Press (pp. 123–144).

Friedman, M. (1957). The Permanent Income Hypothesis. In M. Friedman (Ed.), *A theory of the consumption function.* Princeton, NJ, Princeton University Press (pp. 20–37).

Friedman, M. (1962). *Capitalism and freedom.* Chicago, IL, University of Chicago Press.

Fritz, T. (2015). *Public services under attack: TTIP, CETA, and the secretive collusion between business lobbyists and trade negotiators.* Amsterdam, Association Internationale de Techniciens, Experts et Chercheurs (AITEC), Corporate Europe Observatory (CEO), European Federation of Public Services Unions (EPSU), Instytut Globalnej Odpowiedzialności (IGO), Transnational Institute (TNI), Vienna Chamber of Labour (AK Vienna), and War on Want.

Frohlich, N., Oppenheimer, J. A. & Eavey, C. L. (1987). Laboratory results on Rawls's distributive justice. *British Journal of Political Science, 17*(1), 1–21.

Frontier Economics. (2015). *A review of HEFCE capital expenditure.* Bristol, Higher Education Funding Council for England.

Fryer Jr., R. G., Levitt, S. D., List, J. & Sadoff, S. (2012). *Enhancing the efficacy of teacher incentives through loss aversion: A field experiment* (No. w18237). Cambridge, MA, National Bureau of Economic Research.

Fullan, M. (2000). The return of large-scale reform. *Journal of Educational Change, 1*(1), 5–27.

Gailmard, S. & Patty, J. W. (2007). Slackers and zealots: Civil service, policy discretion, and bureaucratic expertise. *American Journal of Political Science, 51*(4), 873–889.

Galor, O. & Moav, O. (2000). Ability-biased technological transition, wage inequality, and economic growth. *Quarterly Journal of Economics, 115*(2), 469–497.

Gamoran, A. (1987). The stratification of high school learning opportunities. *Sociology of Education, 60*(3), 135–155.

Gamoran, A. (1992). The variable effects of high school tracking. *American Sociological Review, 57*(6), 812–828.

Gamoran, A. & Boxer, M. (2005). Religious participation as cultural capital development: Sector differences in Chicago's Jewish schools. *Journal of Catholic Education, 8*(4), 440–462.

Gardner, H. (2011). *Frames of mind: The theory of multiple intelligences.* New York, Basic books.

Garet, M. S., Porter, A. C., Desimone, L., Birman, B. F. & Yoon, K. S. (2001). What makes professional development effective? Results from a national sample of teachers. *American Educational Research Journal, 38*(4), 915–945.

Garrett, G. & Mitchell, D. (2001). Globalization, government spending and taxation in the OECD. *European Journal of Political Research, 39*(2), 145–177.

Gerber, S. B., Finn, J. D., Achilles, C. M. & Boyd-Zaharias, J. (2001). Teacher aides and students' academic achievement. *Educational Evaluation and Policy Analysis, 23*(2), 123–143.

Gerhart, B. & Fang, M. (2014). Pay for (individual) performance: Issues, claims, evidence and the role of sorting effects. *Human Resource Management Review, 24*(1), 41–52.

Gibb, N. (2015). *How autonomy raises standards.* Speech by the Rt. Hon. Nick Gibb MP to the Freedom and Autonomy for Schools National Association (FASNA), 12 November. Available at www.gov.uk/government/speeches/how-autonomy-raises-standards.

Gibb, N. (2016). *The role that freedom and autonomy has played in school improvement.* Speech by the Rt. Hon. Nick Gibb MP to the Freedom and Autonomy for Schools National Association (FASNA), 2 November. Available at www.gov.uk/government/speeches/the-role-freedom-and-autonomy-has-played-in-school-improvement (accessed 16 October 2017).

Gibbons, S. & Machin, S. (2008). Valuing school quality, better transport, and lower crime: Evidence from house prices. *Oxford Review of Economic Policy, 24*(1), 99–119.

Gibbons, S., Machin, S. & Silva, O. (2008). Choice, competition, and pupil achievement. *Journal of the European Economic Association, 6*(4), 912–947.

Gill, B., Hamilton, L. S., Lockwood, J. R., Marsh, J. A. & Zimmer, R. (2005). *Inspiration, perspiration, and time: Operations and achievement in Edison schools.* Santa Monica, CA, Rand Corporation.

Gillborn, D. (2005). Education policy as an act of white supremacy: Whiteness, critical race theory and education reform. *Journal of Education Policy, 20*(4), 485–505.

Gillis, W. & Castrogiovanni, G. J. (2012). The franchising business model: An entrepreneurial growth alternative. *International Entrepreneurship and Management Journal, 8*(1), 75–98.

Goh, S. C. (2002). Managing effective knowledge transfer: An integrative framework and some practice implications. *Journal of Knowledge Management, 6*(1), 23–30.

Gokhberg, L. & Meissner, D. (2013). Innovation: Superpowered invention. *Nature, 501*(7467), 313–314.

Goldin, C. (1999). *A brief history of education in the United States.* NBER Historical Paper No. 119. Cambridge, MA, National Bureau of Economic Research.

Goldin, C. & Katz, L. F. (1997). *Why the United States led in education: Lessons from secondary school expansion, 1910 to 1940.* Cambridge, MA, National Bureau of Economic Research.

Goldin, C. & Katz, L. F. (2007). *The race between education and technology: The evolution of US educational wage differentials, 1890 to 2005. NBER Working Paper No. 12984.* Cambridge, MA, National Bureau of Economic Research.

Goldring, E. B. & Phillips, K. J. (2008). Parent preferences and parent choices: The public–private decision about school choice. *Journal of Education Policy, 23*(3), 209–230.

Goldstein, H. & Spiegelhalter, D. (1996). League tables and their limitations: Statistical issues in comparisons of institutional performance. *Journal of the Royal Statistical Society*, Series A, *159*(3), 385–443.

Goldthorpe, J. H. (2013). Understanding – and misunderstanding – social mobility in Britain: The entry of the economists, the confusion of politicians and the limits of educational policy. *Journal of Social Policy, 42*(3), 431–450.

Goldthorpe, J. H. (2016). *Social class mobility in modern Britain: Changing structure, constant process.* Lecture given to the British Academy, London, 15 March. Available at www. britac.ac.uk/events/2016/Social_class_mobility_in_modern_Britain.cfm.

Golovina, S., Nillson, J. & Wolz, A. (2013). Members' choice of production co-operatives in Russian agriculture. *Post-Communist Economies, 25*(4), 465–491.

Goodhart, C. A. E. (1989). *Money, information and uncertainty*, 2nd edition. Cambridge, MA, MIT Press.

Goodson, I. F. (1993). *School subjects and curriculum change*, 3rd edition. London, Routledge.

Gorard, S., See, B. H. & Davies, P. (2012). *The impact of attitudes and aspirations on educational attainment and participation.* York, Joseph Rowntree Foundation.

Gorard, S., See, B.-H. & Siddiqui, N. (2014). *Switch-on reading: Evaluation report and executive summary.* London, Education Endowment Fund.

Gorard, S., Taylor, C. & Fitz, J. (2002). Does school choice lead to 'spirals of decline'? *Journal of Education Policy, 17*(3), 367–384.

Gore, J. M. & Zeichner, K. M. (1991). Action research and reflective teaching in preservice teacher education: A case study from the United States. *Teaching and Teacher Education, 7*(2), 119–136.

Gottfried, M. A. (2010). Evaluating the relationship between student attendance and achievement in urban elementary and middle schools: An instrumental variables approach. *American Educational Research Journal, 47*(2), 434–465.

Gove, M. (2012). *Michael Gove speech at the BETT Show 2012.* Available at www.pgce.soton. ac.uk/IT/Curriculum/ComputerScience2012/Michael%20Gove%20speech%20at%20 the%20BETT%20Show%202012%20-%20In%20the%20news.pdf.

Gove, M. (2013). *Oral statement by Michael Gove on education reform*. London, Department for Education. Available at www.gov.uk/government/speeches/oral-statement-on-education-reform.

Government Accountability Office (GAO). (2013). *Financial regulatory reform. Financial crisis losses and potential impacts of the Frank-Dodd Act*. Washington, DC, United States Government Accountability Office.

Grace, G. (1989). Education: Commodity or public good? *British Journal of Educational Studies*, *37*(3), 207–221.

Graham, D. & Tytler, D. (1993). *A lesson for us all. The making of the national curriculum*. London, Routledge.

Granovetter, M. (1973). The strength of weak ties. *American Journal of Sociology*, *78*(6), 1360–1380.

Greany, T. (2015). More fragmented, and yet more networked: Analysing the responses of two Local Authorities in England to the Coalition's 'self-improving school-led system' reforms. *London Review of Education*, *13*(2), 125–143.

Green, A. (1990). *Education and state formation. The rise of education systems in England, France and the USA*. London, Macmillan.

Green, C. L., Walker, J. M., Hoover-Dempsey, K. V. & Sandler, H. M. (2007). Parents' motivations for involvement in children's education: An empirical test of a theoretical model of parental involvement. *Journal of Educational Psychology*, *99*(3), 532–544.

Green, F. & Zhu, Y. (2010). Overqualification, job dissatisfaction, and increasing dispersion in the returns to graduate education. *Oxford Economic Papers*, *62*(4), 740–763.

Green, F., McIntosh, S. & Vignoles, A. (2002). The utilization of education and skills: Evidence from Britain. *The Manchester School*, *70*(6), 792–811.

Greenwald, A. G. & Gillmore, G. M. (1997). No pain, no gain? The importance of measuring course workload in student ratings of instruction, *Journal of Educational Psychology*, *89*(4), 743–751.

Gregg, P., Grout, P. A., Ratcliffe, A., Smith, S. & Windmeijer, F. (2011). How important is pro-social behaviour in the delivery of public services? *Journal of Public Economics*, *95*(7), 758–766.

Grice, A. (2016). Theresa May's grammar schools plan based on 'no evidence', warns biggest study of existing schools. *Independent*, 23 September.

Grolnick, W. S. (2009). The role of parents in facilitating autonomous self-regulation for education. *School Field*, *7*(2), 164–173.

Grolnick, W. S. & Ryan, R. M. (1989). Parent styles associated with children's self-regulation and competence in school. *Journal of Educational Psychology*, *81*(2), 143.

Grossman, G. M. & Helpman, E. (1994). Endogenous innovation in the theory of growth, *Journal of Economic Perspectives*, *8*(1), 23–44.

Grossman, J. B., Price, M. L., Fellerath, V., Jucovy, L. Z., Kotloff, L. J., Raley, R. & Walker, K. E. (2002). *Multiple choices after school: Findings from the Extended-service Schools Initiative*. ED468056. Philadelphia, PA, Public/Private Ventures/New York, Manpower Demonstration Research Corporation.

Grubb, W. N. (2009). *The money myth. Schools, resources and equity*. New York, The Russell Sage Foundation.

Gruening, G. (2001). Origin and theoretical basis of New Public Management. *International Public Management Journal*, *4*(1), 1–25.

Gundlach, E., Wössman, L. and Gmelin, J. (2001). The decline of schooling productivity in OECD countries, *The Economic Journal*, *113*(485), C135-C147.

Gurun, A. & Millimet, D. A. (2008). *Does private tutoring pay off?* IZA Discussion Paper No. 3637. Bonn, IZA.

Guskey, T. R. & Yoon, K. S. (2009). What works in professional development? *Phi Delta Kappan, 90*(7), 495–500.

Gutman, L. M. & Feinstein, L. (2008). *Children's well-being in primary school: Pupil and school effects.* Wider Benefits of Learning Research Report No. 25. Centre for Research on the Wider Benefits of Learning, Institute of Education. London, University of London.

Gutman, L. M. & McLoyd, V. C. (2000). Parents' management of their children's education within the home, at school, and in the community: An examination of African-American families living in poverty. *The Urban Review, 32*(1), 1–24.

Hagerty, M. R. & Veenhoven, R. (2003). Wealth and happiness revisited – growing national income does go with greater happiness. *Social Indicators Research, 64*, 1–27.

Hannan, D. F., Raffe, D. & Smyth, E. (1996). Cross-national research on school to work transitions: An analytical framework. *Background paper prepared for the Planning Meeting for the Thematic Review of the Transition from Initial Education to Working Life.* Paris, OECD Publishing (pp. 26–27).

Hanson, G. H. (2001). Scale economies and the geographic concentration of industry. *Journal of Economic Geography, 1*(3), 255–276.

Hanushek, E. A. (2003). The failure of input-based schooling policies. *The Economic Journal, 113*(485), F64–F98.

Hanushek, E. A. & Rivkin, S. G. (2006). Teacher quality. In E. Hanushek and F. Welch (Eds.), *Handbook of the economics of education, 2.* Amsterdam, Elsevier (pp. 1051–1078).

Hanushek, E. A. & Rivkin, S. G. (2007). Pay, working conditions, and teacher quality. *The Future of Children, 17*(1), 69–86.

Hanushek, E. A. & Woessman, L. (2006). Does educational tracking affect performance and inequality? Differences-in-differences evidence across countries. *The Economic Journal, 116*(510), C63–C76.

Hanushek, E. A. & Woessmann, L. (2008). The role of cognitive skills in economic development. *Journal of Economic Literature, 46*(3), 607–668.

Hanushek, E. A., Link, S. & Woessmann, L. (2013). Does school autonomy make sense everywhere? Panel estimates from PISA. *Journal of Development Economics, 104*, 212–232.

Hargreaves, A. (2000). Four ages of professionalism and professional learning. *Teachers and Teaching: Theory and Practice, 6*(2), 151–182.

Hargreaves, A. (2003). *Teaching in the knowledge society: Education in the age of insecurity.* New York, Teachers College Press.

Hargreaves, D. (1999). The knowledge-creating school. *British Journal of Educational Studies, 47*(2), 122–144.

Harland, J., Kinder, K., Lord, P., Stott, A., Schagen, I., Haynes, J., Cusworth, L. & Paola, R. (2000). *Arts education in secondary schools: Effects and effectiveness.* Slough, National Foundation for Educational Research.

Harman, K. & Treadgold, E. (2007). Changing patterns of governance for Australian universities. *Higher Education Research & Development, 26*(1), 13–29.

Harmon, C. & Walker, I. (1995). Estimates of the economic return to schooling for the United Kingdom. *The American Economic Review, 85*(5), 1278–1286.

Harms, P. & Zink, S. (2003). Limits to redistribution in a democracy: A survey. *European Journal of Political Economy, 19*(4), 651–668.

Harris, A. (2004). Distributed leadership and school improvement: Leading or misleading? *Educational Management Administration & Leadership, 32*(1), 11–24.

Hart, O., Shleifer, A. & Vishny, R. (1997). The proper scope of government: Theory and an application to prisons. *Quarterly Journal of Economics, 112*(4), 1126–1261.

Harvard College. (2016). *Mission Statement.* Cambridge, MA, Harvard College. Available at https://college.harvard.edu/about/history (accessed 16 September 2016).

Hashweh, M. Z. (1996). Effects of science teachers' epistemological beliefs in teaching. *Journal of Research in Science Teaching, 33*(1), 47–63.

Haskel, J. & Sanchis, A. (1995). Privatisation and X-inefficiency: A bargaining approach. *The Journal of Industrial Economics, 43*(3), 301–321.

Hastings, J. S., Van Weelden, R. & Weinstein, J. (2007). *Preferences, information, and parental choice behavior in public school choice* (No. w12995). Cambridge, MA, National Bureau of Economic Research.

Hatcher, J. A. (2011). Assessing civic knowledge and engagement. *New Directions for Institutional Research, 2011*(149), 81–92.

Hattie, J. & Timperley, H. (2007). The power of feedback. *Review of Educational Research, 77*(1), 81–112.

Hatton, N. & Smith, D. (1995). Reflection in teacher education: Towards definition and implementation. *Teaching and Teacher Education, 11*(1), 33–49.

Heckman, J. J. (2006). Skill formation and the economics of investing in disadvantaged children. *Science, 312*(5782), 1900–1902.

Heckman, J. J. & Kautz, T. (2012). Hard evidence on soft skills. *Labour Economics, 19*(4), 451–464.

Heckman, J. J. & Masterov, D. V. (2007). The productivity argument for investing in young children. *Applied Economic Perspectives and Policy, 29*(3), 446–493.

Helburn, S. & Howes, C. (1996). Child care cost and quality. *The Future of Children, 6*(2), 62–82.

Heller, D. E. (1997). Student price response in higher education: An update to Leslie and Brinkman. *The Journal of Higher Education, 68*(6), 624–659.

Heller, D. E. (1999). The effects of tuition and state financial aid on public college enrollment. *The Review of Higher Education, 23*(1), 65–89.

Henderson, S. (2016). Welcome from the Headmaster, Eton College. Available at www.etoncollege.com (accessed 18 August 2016).

Heyneman, S. P. (2011). Private tutoring and social cohesion. *Peabody Journal of Education, 86*(2), 183–188.

Higgins, S., Xiao, Z. & Katsipataki, M. (2012). *The impact of digital technology on learning: A summary for the Education Endowment Foundation.* London, The Education Endowment Foundation.

Higgins, S., Katsipataki, M., Kokotsaki, D., Coe, R., Elliott Major, L. & Coleman, R. (2013). *The Sutton Trust-Education Endowment Foundation teaching and learning toolkit: Technical appendices.* London, The Sutton Trust.

Higham, R. (2014). Free schools in the Big Society: The motivations, aims and demography of free school proposers. *Journal of Education Policy, 29*(1), 122–139.

Higher Education Funding Council for England (HEFCE). (2009). *Recurrent Grants for 2009/10. March 2009/08.* Bristol, Higher Education Funding Council for England.

Higher Education Funding Council for England (HEFCE). (2017). *Annual funding allocations for 2017–18.* Bristol, Higher education Funding Council for England. Available at www.hefce.ac.uk/funding/annallocns/1718/lt/ (accessed 10 November 2017).

Hill, N. E. & Tyson, D. F. (2009). Parental involvement in middle school: A meta-analytic assessment of the strategies that promote achievement. *Developmental Psychology, 45*(3), 740–763.

Hill, R., Dunford, J., Parish, N., Rea, S. & Sandals, L. (2012). *The growth of academy chains: Implications for leaders and leadership.* Nottingham, National College of School Leadership.

Hirsch, F. (1977). *Social limits to growth.* London, Routledge.

Hirschman, A. O. (1970). *Exit, voice, and loyalty: Responses to decline in firms, organizations, and states.* Cambridge, MA, Harvard University Press.

260 References

Hoadley, U. & Muller, J. (2010). Codes, pedagogy and knowledge. In M. Apple, S. J. Ball & L. A. Gandin (Eds.), *The Routledge international handbook of the sociology of education*. London, Routledge (pp. 69–78).

Hoareau McGrath, C., Guerin, B., Harte, E., Frearson, M. & Manville, C. (2015). *Learning gain in higher education*. Cambridge, RANDEurope.

Hodgen, J., Pepper, D., Sturman, L. & Ruddock, G. (2010). *Is the UK an outlier? An international comparison of upper secondary mathematics education*. London, Nuffield Foundation.

Hoeckel, K. (2010). *Learning for jobs OECD reviews of vocational education and training: Austria*. Paris, Organisation for Economic Co-operation and Development.

Holzer, H. J. (1986). *Search method use by unemployed youth*. NBER Working Paper No. 1859. Cambridge, MA, National Bureau of Economic Research.

Hoover-Dempsey, K. V. & Sandler, H. M. (1997). Why do parents become involved in their children's education? *Review of Educational Research*, 67(1), 3–42.

Hopkins, D. & Jackson, D. (2002). *Networked learning communities: Capacity building, networking and leadership for learning*. Nottingham, National College for School Leadership.

Hopkins, D., Stringfield, S., Harris, A., Stoll, L. & Mackay, T. (2014). School and system improvement: A narrative state-of-the-art review. *School Effectiveness and School Improvement*, 25(2), 257–281.

Hordósy, R. (2014). Who knows what school leavers and graduates are doing? Comparing information systems within Europe. *Comparative Education*, 50(4), 448–473.

Hornberger, N. H. (1998). Language policy, language education, language rights: Indigenous, immigrant, and international perspectives. *Language in Society*, 27(04), 439–458.

House of Commons Education Committee. (2017). *Recruitment and retention of teachers: Fifth report of session 2016–2017*. London, House of Commons.

Houston, D. J. (2000). Public-service motivation: A multivariate test. *Journal of Public Administration Research and Theory*, 10(4), 713–728.

Hoxby, C. M. (1996). How teachers' unions affect education production. *The Quarterly Journal of Economics*, 111(3), 671–718.

Hoxby, C. M. (2004). Productivity in education: The quintessential upstream industry. *Southern Economic Journal*, 71(2), 209–231.

Hoxby, C. M. & Leigh, A. (2004). Pulled away or pushed out? Explaining the decline of teacher aptitude in the United States. *The American Economic Review*, 94(2), 236–240.

Hoy, W. K., Tarter, C. J. & Hoy, A. W. (2006). Academic optimism of schools: A force for student achievement. *American Educational Research Journal*, 43(3), 425–446.

Hoyle, E. (1974). Professionality, professionalism and control in teaching. *London Education Review*, 3(2), 13–19.

Hoyle, E. (1982). The professionalization of teachers: A paradox. *British Journal of Educational Studies*, 30(2), 161–171.

Huberman, A. M. & Miles, M. B. (1984). *Innovation up close: How school improvement works*. New York, Plenum Press.

Huebner, E. S., Drane, W. & Valois, R. F. (2000). Levels and demographic correlates of adolescent life satisfaction reports. *School Psychology International*, 21(3), 281–292.

Huffington Post. (2014). The US illiteracy rate hasn't changed in 10 years. *Huffington Post*, 12 December.

Hummel-Rossi, B. & Ashdown, J. (2002). The state of cost-benefit and cost-effectiveness analyses in education. *Review of Educational Research*, 72(1), 1–30.

Hurd, S., Mangan, J. & Adnett, N. (2005). Are secondary schools spending enough on books? *British Educational Research Journal*, 31(2), 239–255.

Hussain, I. (2012). *Subjective performance evaluation in the public sector: Evidence from school inspections*. Centre for Economics of Education, CEE DP 215. London, London School of

Economics. Available at http://cee.lse.ac.uk/ceedps/ceedp135.pdf (accessed 26 October 2017).

Hussain, I., McNally, S. and Telhaj, S. (2009). *University quality and graduate wages in the UK.* Centre for Economics of Education, Discussion Paper No. 0099. London, London School of Economics and Political Science.

Iannelli, C., Gamoran, A. & Paterson, L. (2011). Scottish higher education, 1987–2001: Expansion through diversion. *Oxford Review of Education, 37*(6), 717–741.

Ingersoll, R. M. (2001). Teacher turnover and teacher shortages: An organizational analysis. *American Educational Research Journal, 38*(3), 499–534.

Ingersoll, R. M. & May, H. (2012). The magnitude, destinations, and determinants of mathematics and science teacher turnover. *Educational Evaluation and Policy Analysis, 34*(4), 435–464.

Inklaar, R., Mahoney, M. & Timmer, M. (2005). ICT and Europe's productivity performance: Industry level growth account comparisons with the United States. *Review of Income and Wealth, 51*(4), 505–536.

International Labour Office/Organisation for Economic Cooperation and Development (ILO/OECD). (2015). *The Labour Share in G20 countries.* ILO/OECD, Anatalya, Turkey. Available at www.oecd.org/g20/topics/employment-and-social-policy/The-Labour-Share-in-G20-Economies.pdf (accessed 6 September 2017).

Ipsos/MORI. (2010). *Public perceptions of the benefits of higher education. Final report for the Higher Education Funding Council for England.* London, Ipsos/MORI.

Ireson, J. & Rushforth, K. (2011). Private tutoring at transition points in the English education system: Its nature, extent and purpose. *Research Papers in Education, 26*(1), 1–19.

Izzo, C. V., Weissberg, R. P., Kasprow, W. J. & Fendrich, M. (1999). A longitudinal assessment of teacher perceptions of parent involvement in children's education and school performance. *American Journal of Community Psychology, 27*(6), 817–839.

Jackson, A. (2007). *Theatre, education and the making of meanings: Art or instrument?* Manchester, Manchester University Press.

Jacob, B. A. (2002). Where the boys aren't: Non-cognitive skills, returns to school and the gender gap in higher education. *Economics of Education Review, 21*(6), 589–598.

Jacobs, J. A. (1996). Gender inequality and higher education. *Annual Review of Sociology, 22*(1), 153–185.

Jacquemin, A. & Slade, M. E. (1989). Cartels, collusion, and horizontal merger. In R. Schmalensee & R. Willig (Eds.), *Handbook of industrial organization Volume 1.* Amsterdam, North Holland (pp. 415–473).

Jamieson, A., Sabates, R., Woodley, A. & Feinstein, L. (2009). The benefits of higher education study for part-time students. *Studies in Higher Education, 34*(3), 245–262.

Jankowski, N. & Provezis, S. (2014). Neoliberal ideologies, governmentality and the academy: An examination of accountability through assessment and transparency. *Educational Philosophy and Theory, 46*(5), 475–487.

Jäntti, M. & Jenkins, S. M. (2013). *Income mobility. IZA Discussion Paper 7730.* Bonn, Institute for the Study of Labor (IZA). Available at http://ftp.iza.org/dp7730.pdf.

Jencks, C., Smith, M., Acland, H., Bne, M. J., Cohen, D., Gintis, H., Heynes, B. and Michelson, S. (1972). *Inequality: A reassessment of the effects of family and schooling in America.* New York, Basic Books.

Jepson, E. & Forrest, S. (2006). Individual contributory factors in teacher stress: The role of achievement striving and occupational commitment. *British Journal of Educational Psychology, 76*(1), 183–197.

Jerrim, J. & Macmillan, L. (2014). *Income inequality, intergenerational mobility and the Great Gatsby Curve: Is education the key?* Department of Quantitative Social Science, Institute of

Education, University of London, Working Paper No. 14–18. London, Institute of Education.

Jerrim, J., Choi, A. & Rodriguez, R. S. (2014). *Two-sample two-stage least squares (TSTSLS) estimates of earnings mobility: How consistent are they?* Department of Quantitative Social Science Working Paper No. 14–17. London, Institute of Education, University of London.

Jerrim, J., Vignoles, A., Lingam, R. & Friend, A. (2015). The socio-economic gradient in children's reading skills and the role of genetics. *British Educational Research Journal, 41*(1), 6–29.

Jin, S. U. & Moon, S. M. (2006). A study of well-being and school satisfaction among academically talented students attending a science high school in Korea. *Gifted Child Quarterly, 50*(2), 169–184.

Johannesson, I. A., Lindblad, S. & Simola, H. (2002). An inevitable progress? Educational restructuring in Finland, Iceland and Sweden at the turn of the millennium. *Scandinavian Journal of Educational Research, 46*(3), 325–339.

Johnson, D. W., Johnson, R. T. & Stanne, M. B. (2000). *Cooperative learning methods: A meta-analysis.* Available at www.researchgate.net/publication/220040324_Cooperative_Learning_Methods_A_Meta-Analysis.

Johnson, D. W., Maruyama, G., Johnson, R. & Nelson, D. (1981). Effects of cooperative, competitive and individualistic goal structures on achievement: A meta-analysis. *Psychological Bulletin, 89*(1), 47–62.

Johnsson, M. & Lindgren, J. (2010). 'Great location, beautiful surroundings!' Making sense of information materials intended as guidance for school choice. *Scandinavian Journal of Educational Research, 54*(2), 173–187.

Johnston, R. S., McGeown, S. & Watson, J. E. (2012). Long-term effects of synthetic versus analytic phonics teaching on the reading and spelling ability of 10 year old boys and girls. *Reading and Writing, 25*(6), 1365–1384.

Jones, C. I. (1995). Time series tests of endogenous growth models. *The Quarterly Journal of Economics, 110*(2), 495–525.

Jones, G. E. (2000). The debate over the National Curriculum for history in England and Wales, 1989–90: The role of the press. *Curriculum Journal, 11*(3), 299–322.

Jones, R. M. (1992). Beyond identity? The reconstruction of the Welsh. *The Journal of British Studies, 31*(4), 330–357.

Jorgenson, D. W. (2001). Information technology and the US economy. *The American Economic Review, 91*(1), 1–32.

Junemann, C. & Ball, S. J. (2013). ARK and the revolution of state education in England. *Education Inquiry, 4*(3), 423–441.

Jung, I. (2003). Cost-effectiveness of online education. In M. G. Moore & W. G. Anderson (Eds.), *Handbook of distance education.* Mahwah, NJ, Lawrence Erlbaum & Associates (pp. 717–726).

Jussim, L. & Harber, K. D. (2005). Teacher expectations and self-fulfilling prophecies: Knowns and unknowns, resolved and unresolved controversies. *Personality and Social Psychology Review, 9*(2), 131–155.

Kagawa, F. & Selby, D. (Eds.) (2010). *Education and climate change: Living and learning in interesting times.* London, Routledge.

Kahneman, D. & Tversky, A. (1979). Prospect theory: An analysis of decision under risk. *Econometrica: Journal of the Econometric Society, 47*(2), 263–291.

Kakabadse, N. K., Kakabadse, A. P. & Summers, N. (2007). Effectiveness of private finance initiatives (PFI): Study of private financing for the provision of capital assets for schools. *Public Administration and Development, 27*(1), 49–61.

Kalafat, J., Illback, R. J. & Sanders, D. (2007). The relationship between implementation fidelity and educational outcomes in a school-based family support program: Development of a model for evaluating multidimensional full-service programs. *Evaluation and Program Planning, 30*(2), 136–148.

Kamens, D. H. & McNeely, C. L. (2010). Globalization and the growth of international educational testing and national assessment. *Comparative Education Review, 54*(1), 5–25.

Kandiko Howson, C. B. (2017). *Evaluation of HEFCE's learning gain pilot projects: Year 1 report.* London, King's College.

Kane, T. J. & Staiger, D. (2008). *Estimating teacher impacts on student achievement: An experimental evaluation. NBER Working Paper* No. 14607. Cambridge, MA, National Bureau of Economic Research.

Kanji, G. K., Malek, A. & Tambi, B. A. (1999). Total quality management in UK higher education institutions. *Total Quality Management, 10*(1), 129–153.

Karabarbounis, L. & Neiman, B. (2013). The global decline of the labor share. *The Quarterly Journal of Economics, 129*(1), 61–103.

Karseth, B. & Nerland, M. (2007). Building professionalism in a knowledge society: Examining discourses of knowledge in four professional associations. *Journal of Education and Work, 20*(4), 335–355.

Katz, S. & Earl, L. (2010). Learning about networked learning communities. *School Effectiveness and School Improvement, 21*(1), 27–51.

Kaufmann, K. M. M., Messner, M. & Solis, A. (2013). Returns to elite higher education in the marriage market: Evidence from Chile. Available at SSRN: https://ssrn.com/abstract=2313369 or http://dx.doi.org/10.2139/ssrn.2313369.

Kauppinen, T. M. (2008). Schools as mediators of neighbourhood effects on choice between vocational and academic tracks of secondary education in Helsinki. *European Sociological Review, 24*(3), 379–391.

Keane, M. P. & Wolpin, K. I. (2001). The effect of parental transfers and borrowing constraints on educational attainment. *International Economic Review, 42*(4), 1051–1103.

Keeley, B. (2015). *Income inequality: The gap between rich and poor.* OECD Insights. Paris, OECD Publishing.

Keenan, J. & McCabe, B. (2010). Contracting problems? Tales from PFI schools. *Journal of Finance & Management in Public Services, 9*(1), 17–29.

Keep, E. (2005). Reflections on the curious absence of employers, labour market incentives and labour market regulation in English 14–19 policy: First signs of a change in direction? *Journal of Education Policy, 20*(5), 533–553.

Kelly, A. (2012). Sen and the art of educational maintenance: Evidencing a capability, as opposed to effectiveness, approach to schooling. *Cambridge Journal of Education, 42*(3), 283–296.

Kent, T. W. & McNergney, R. F. (1999). *Will technology really change education? From blackboard to web.* Thousand Oaks, CA, Corwin Press.

Kerckhoff, A. C. (1976). The status attainment process: Socialization or allocation? *Social Forces, 55*(2), 368–381.

Kerr, D. (1999). *Citizenship education: An international comparison.* London, Qualifications and Curriculum Authority (pp. 200–227).

Kerr, D., Ireland, E., Lopes, J. & Craig, R. (2004). *Citizenship Education Longitudinal Study: Second Annual Report: First Longitudinal Survey: Making citizenship education real.* Research Report No. RR531. London, Department for Education and Skills.

Kettl, D. F. (2000). The transformation of governance: Globalization, devolution, and the role of government. *Public Administration Review, 60*(6), 488–497.

Keynes, J. M. (1937). The general theory of employment. *The Quarterly Journal of Economics, 51*(2), 209–223.

Kezar, A. & Eckel, P. D. (2004). Meeting today's governance challenges: A synthesis of the literature and examination of a future agenda for scholarship. *The Journal of Higher Education, 75*(4), 371–399.

Kim, J., DesJardins, S. L. & McCall, B. P. (2009). Exploring the effects of student expectations about financial aid on postsecondary choice: A focus on income and racial/ethnic differences. *Research in Higher Education, 50*(8), 741–774.

Kim, M. M. & Ko, J. (2015). The impacts of state control policies on college tuition increase. *Educational Policy, 29*(5), 815–838.

Kim, S. & Lee, J. H. (2006). Changing facets of Korean higher education: Market competition and the role of the state. *Higher Education, 52*(3), 557–587.

Kim, Y-H., Chiu, C.-Y. & Zou, Z. (2010). Know thyself: Misperceptions of actual performance undermine achievement motivation, future performance, and subjective well-being. *Journal of Personality and Social Psychology, 99*(3), 395.

King, P. & Protherough, R. (Eds.). (2006). *The challenge of English in the national curriculum.* London, Routledge.

King Rice, J. (1997). Cost analysis in education: Paradox and possibility. *Educational Evaluation and Policy Analysis, 19*(4), 309–317.

Kirsch, I., & Guthrie, J. T. (1977). The concept and measurement of functional literacy. *Reading Research Quarterly, 13*(4), 485–507.

Kirshstein, R. (2015). Colleges' reliance on part-time faculty: Who wins? Who loses? Available at www.noodle.com/articles/the-rise-of-part-time-faculty-and-its-effect-on-higher-ed131 (accessed 30 January 2018).

Kirzner, I. M. (1997). Entrepreneurial discovery and the competitive market process: An Austrian approach. *Journal of Economic Literature, 35*(1), 60–85.

Kiser, L. L. (1984). Toward an institutional theory of citizen coproduction. *Urban Affairs Review, 19*(4), 485–510.

Kitschelt, H. (1989). The internal politics of parties: The law of curvilinear disparity revisited. *Political Studies, 37*(3), 400–421.

Klandermans, B. & Oegema, D. (1987). Potentials, networks, motivations, and barriers: Steps towards participation in social movements. *American Sociological Review, 52*(4), 519–531.

Klayman, J. (1995). Varieties of confirmation bias. In J. Busemeyer, R. Hastie and D. L. Medin (Eds.), *Decision making from a cognitive perspective.* Academic Press, New York (pp. 365–418).

Kleij, F. M., Feskens, R. C. & Eggen, T. J. (2015). Effects of feedback in a computer-based learning environment on students' learning outcomes: A meta-analysis. *Review of Educational Research, 85*(4), 475–511.

Kleinhenz, E. & Ingvarson, L. (2004). Teacher accountability in Australia: Current policies and practices and their relation to the improvement of teaching and learning. *Research Papers in Education, 19*(1), 31–49.

Kluger, A. N. & DeNisi, A. (1996). The effects of feedback interventions on performance: A historical review, a meta-analysis, and a preliminary feedback intervention theory. *Psychological Bulletin, 119*(2), 254–284.

Koh, A. (2014). The 'magic' of tutorial centres in Hong Kong: An analysis of media marketing and pedagogy in a tutorial centre. *International Review of Education, 60*(6), 803–819.

Kokkelenberg, E. C., Dillon, M. & Christy, S. M. (2008). The effects of class size on student grades at a public university. *Economics of Education Review, 27*(2), 221–233.

Koliba, C. & Gajda, R. (2009). 'Communities of practice' as an analytical construct: Implications for theory and practice. *International Journal of Public Administration, 32*(2), 97–135.

Konow, J. (2003). Which is the fairest one of all? A positive analysis of justice theories. *Journal of Economic Literature, 41*(4), 1188–1239.

Koopman, C. (2005). Art as fulfilment: On the justification of education in the arts. *Journal of Philosophy of Education, 39*(1), 85–97.

Krueger, A. B. (2012). *The rise and consequences of inequality,* Speech to the Center for American Progress on January 12, in his capacity as Chairman of the Council of Economic Advisors. Available at www.whitehouse.gov/sites/default/files/krueger_cap_speech_final_remarks.pdf.

Krugman, P. (1991). Increasing returns and economic geography. *Journal of Political Economy, 99*(3), 483–499.

Kuhn, T. S. (1962). *The structure of scientific revolutions.* Chicago, IL, University of Chicago Press.

Kuziemko, I. (2006). Using shocks to school enrollment to estimate the effect of school size on student achievement. *Economics of Education Review, 25*(1), 63–75.

Kyriacou, C. & Coulthard, M. (2000). Undergraduates views of teaching as a career choice. *Journal of Education for Teaching, 26*(2), 117–126.

Lacireno-Paquet, N., Holyoke, T., Moser, M. & Henig, J. (2002). Creaming versus cropping: Charter schools enrollment practices in response to market incentives. *Educational Evaluation and Policy Analysis, 24*(2), 145–158.

Ladd, G. W. (1990). Having friends, keeping friends, making friends, and being liked by peers in the classroom: Predictors of children's early school adjustment? *Child Development, 61*(4), 1081–1100.

Ladd, H. F. (1999). The Dallas school accountability and incentive program: An evaluation of its impacts on student outcomes. *Economics of Education Review, 18*(1), 1–16.

Ladd, H. F. & Walsh, R. P. (2002). Implementing value-added measures of school effectiveness: Getting the incentives right. *Economics of Education Review, 21*(1), 1–17.

Ladson-Billings, G. & Tate, W. F. (1995). Toward a critical race theory of education. *Teachers College Record, 97*(1), 47–68.

Lam, A. (2000). Tacit knowledge, organizational learning and societal institutions: An integrated framework. *Organization Studies, 21*(3), 487–513.

Lam, C. B., McHale, S. M. & Crouter, A. C. (2012). Parent–child shared time from middle childhood to late adolescence: Developmental course and adjustment correlates. *Child Development, 83*(6), 2089–2103.

Land, R., Meyer, J. H. F., Cousin, G. & Davies, P. (2005). Threshold concepts and troublesome knowledge (3): Implications for course design and evaluation. In C. Rust (Ed.), *Improving student learning: Diversity and inclusivity.* Oxford, Oxford Centre for Staff and Learning Development (pp. 53–64).

Lange, F. & Topel, R. (2006). The social value of education and human capital. In G. Johnes (Ed.), *Handbook of the economics of education.* Cheltenham, Edward Elgar (pp. 459–509).

Langman, L. (2013). Occupy: A new new social movement. *Current Sociology, 61*(4), 510–524.

Lareau, A. (1987). Social class differences in family–school relationships: The importance of cultural capital. *Sociology of Education, 60*(2), 73–85.

Lareau, A. & Horvat, E. M. (1999). Moments of social inclusion and exclusion: Race, class, and cultural capital in family-school relationships. *Sociology of Education, 72*(1), 37–53.

Lauder, H. (1991). Education, democracy and the economy. *British Journal of Sociology of Education, 12*(4), 417–431.

Laurence, D. H. (Ed.). (1988). *Collected letters of George Bernard Shaw, 1926–1950.* London, Max Reinhardt.

Lave, J. & Wenger, E. (1991). *Situated learning: Legitimate peripheral participation*. Cambridge, Cambridge University Press.

Lavy, V. (2007). Using performance-based pay to improve the quality of teachers. *The Future of Children, 17*(1), 87–109.

Lawler 3rd, E. E. & Mohrman, S. A. (1984). Quality circles after the fad. *Harvard Business Review, 63*(1), 65–71.

Lazear, E. P. (2003). Teacher incentives. *Swedish Economic Policy Review, 10*(2), 179–214.

Leckie, G. & Goldstein, H. (2011). A note on 'The limitations of school league tables to inform school choice'. *Journal of the Royal Statistical Society Series A Statistics in Society, 174*(3), 833–836.

Leder, H., Belke, B., Oeberst, A. & Augustin, D. (2004). A model of aesthetic appreciation and aesthetic judgments. *British Journal of Psychology, 95*(4), 489–508.

Lee, J. S. & Bowen, N. K. (2006). Parent involvement, cultural capital, and the achievement gap among elementary school children. *American Educational Research Journal, 43*(2), 193–218.

Lee, V. E. & Ready, D. D. (2009). US high school curriculum: Three phases of contemporary research and reform. *The Future of Children, 19*(1), 135–156.

Lee, V. E. & Smith, J. B. (1997). High school size: Which works best and for whom? *Educational Evaluation and Policy Analysis, 19*(3), 205–227.

Leeds, E. M. & Cope, J. (2015). MOOCs: Branding, enrollment, and multiple measures of success. *Online Journal of Distance Learning Administration, 18*(3).

LeGrand, J. L. (2010). Knights and knaves return: Public service motivation and the delivery of public services. *International Public Management Journal, 13*(1), 56–71.

Leibenstein, H. (1950). Bandwagon, snob, and Veblen effects in the theory of consumers' demand. *The Quarterly Journal of Economics, 64*(2), 183–207.

Leibenstein, H. (1966). Allocative efficiency vs. 'X-efficiency'. *The American Economic Review, 56*(3), 392–415.

Leibenstein, H. (1978). On the basic propositions of x-efficiency theory, *The American Economic Review, 68*(2), 328–332.

Leigh, A. & Ryan, C. (2008). How and why has teacher quality changed in Australia? *Australian Economic Review, 41*(2), 141–159.

Leitch, Lord S. (2006). *Prosperity for all in a global economy – world class skills*. London, HMSO.

Leithwood, K. & Jantzi, D. (2009). A review of empirical evidence about school size effects: A policy perspective. *Review of Educational Research, 79*(1), 464–490.

Leithwood, K. & Menzies, T. (1998). A review of research concerning the implementation of site-based management. *School Effectiveness and School Improvement, 9*(3), 233–285.

Leithwood, K., Jantzi, D., Earl, L., Watson, N., Levin, B. & Fullan, M. (2004). Strategic leadership for large-scale reform: The case of England's national literacy and numeracy strategy. *School Leadership & Management, 24*(1), 57–79.

Lemke, T. (2012). *Foucault, governmentality, and critique*. London, Routledge.

Leschinsky, A. & Mayer, K. U. (Eds.). (1999). *The comprehensive school experiment revisited: Evidence from Western Europe* (2nd edition). Frankfurt, Peter Lang.

Leseman, P. P. & Jong, P. F. (1998). Home literacy: Opportunity, instruction, cooperation and social-emotional quality predicting early reading achievement. *Reading Research Quarterly, 33*(3), 294–318.

LeTendre, G. K., Hofer, B. K. & Shimizu, H. (2003). What is tracking? Cultural expectations in the United States, Germany, and Japan. *American Educational Research Journal, 40*(1), 43–89.

Levačić, R. (2004). Competition and the performance of English secondary schools: Further evidence. *Education Economics, 12*(2), 177–193.

Levačić, R. (2009). Teacher incentives and performance: An application of principal–agent theory. *Oxford Development Studies, 37*(1), 33–46.

Levin, H. M. (1983). *Cost effectiveness: A primer.* Newbury Park, CA, Sage.

Levin, H. (1991). The economics of educational choice. *Economics of Education Review, 10*(20), 137–158.

Levin, H. (2001). Waiting for Godot: Cost-effectiveness analysis in education. *New Directions for Evaluation, 2001*(90), 55–68.

Levin, H. M. & McEwan, P. J. (2001). *Cost-effectiveness analysis: Methods and applications* (2nd edition). London, Sage.

Levine, K. (1982). Functional literacy: Fond illusions and false economies. *Harvard Educational Review, 52*(3), 249–266.

Levine, P. B. & Zimmerman, D. J. (1995). The benefit of additional high school math and science courses for young men and women. *Journal of Business and Economic Statistics, 13*(2), 137–149.

Lewis, P. (2016). Shackle on choice, imagination and creativity: Hayekian foundations. *Cambridge Journal of Economics, 41*(1), 1–24.

Lewis, S. K. & Oppenheimer, V. K. (2000). Educational assortative mating across marriage markets: Nonhispanic whites in the United States. *Demography, 37*(1), 29–40.

Li, Y. & Devine, F. (2011). Is social mobility really declining? Intergenerational class mobility in Britain in the 1990s and the 2000s. *Sociological Research Online, 16*(3), 4.

Lieberman, A. (1995). Practices that support teacher development. *Phi delta kappan, 76*(8), 591.

Lieberman, M. (2000). *The teacher unions: How they sabotage educational reform and why.* San Francisco, CA, Encounter Books.

Lin, N. (2002). *Social capital: A theory of social structure and action.* Cambridge, Cambridge University Press.

Lindley, J. & Machin, S. (2012). The quest for more and more education: Implications for social mobility. *Fiscal Studies, 33*(2), 265–286.

Lindsay, G. (2003). Inclusive education: A critical perspective. *British Journal of Special Education, 30*(1), 3–12.

Lingard, B. (2010). Policy borrowing, policy learning: Testing times in Australian schooling. *Critical Studies in Education, 51*(2), 129–147.

Liu, O. L., Bridgeman, B. & Adler, R. M. (2012). Measuring learning outcomes in higher education: Motivation matters. *Educational Researcher, 41*(9), 352–362.

Long, B. T. (2004). Does the format of a financial aid program matter? The effect of state in-kind tuition subsidies. *The Review of Economics and Statistics, 86*(3), 767–782.

Long, R. F., Huebner, E. S., Wedell, D. H. & Hills, K. J. (2012). Measuring school-related subjective well-being in adolescents. *American Journal of Orthopsychiatry, 82*(1), 50–60.

Lovenheim, M. F. (2011). The effect of liquid housing wealth on college enrollment. *Journal of Labor Economics, 29*(4), 741–771.

Lubienski, C. (2003). Innovation in education markets: Theory and evidence on the impact of competition and choice in charter schools. *American Educational Research Journal, 40*(2), 395–443.

Lubienski, C. (2007). Marketing schools consumer goods and competitive incentives for consumer information. *Education and Urban Society, 40*(1), 118–141.

Luginbuhl, R., Webbink, D. & de Wolf, I. (2012). Do inspections improve primary school performance? *Educational Evaluation and Policy Analysis, 34*(1), 221–237.

Lupton, R. & Thomson, S. (2015). Socio-economic inequalities in English schooling under the Coalition Government 2010–15. *London Review of Education, 13*(2), 4–20.

Lux, T. (1995). Herd behaviour, bubbles and crashes. *The Economic Journal*, *105*(431), 881–896.

Luyten, H. (2014). Quantitative summary of research findings. In H. Luyten (Ed.), *School size effects revisited*. Dordecht, Springer (pp. 177–218).

Lynch, K. (2006). Neo-liberalism and marketisation: The implications for higher education. *European Educational Research Journal*, *5*(1), 1–17.

Lyubomirsky, S., King, L. & Diener, E. (2005). The benefits of frequent positive affect: Does happiness lead to success? *Psychological Bulletin*, *131*(6), 803–855.

Maaz, K., Trautwein, U., Lüdtke, O. & Baumert, J. (2008). Educational transitions and differential learning environments: How explicit between-school tracking contributes to social inequality in educational outcomes. *Child Development Perspectives*, *2*(2), 99–106.

MacDonagh, O. (1958). IV. The nineteenth-century revolution in government: A reappraisal. *The Historical Journal*, *1*(1), 52–67.

Macdonald, J. (2004). *Calling a halt to mindless change: A plea for commonsense management*. Washington, DC, Beard Books.

MacDonald, K. & Parke, R. D. (1984). Bridging the gap: Parent–child play interaction and peer interactive competence. *Child Development*, *55*(4), 1265–1277.

Machin, S. & McNally, S. (2008). The literacy hour. *Journal of Public Economics*, *92*(5), 1441–1462.

Machin, S. & Van Reenen, J. (1998). Technology and changes in skill structure: Evidence from seven OECD countries. *The Quarterly Journal of Economics*, *113*(4), 1215–1244.

Machin, S. & Vernoit, J. (2011). *Changing school autonomy: Academy schools and their introduction to England's education*. CEE DP 123. London, Centre for the Economics of Education (NJ1).

Machin, S. & Vignoles, A. (2006). *Education policy in the UK*. Centre for Economics of Education Discussion Paper No. CEE DP 57. London, London School of Economics.

Machin, S. & Wadhwani, S. (1991). The effects of unions on organisational change and employment. *The Economic Journal*, *101*(407), 835–854.

MacLeod, S., Bernardinelli, D., Skipp, A. & Higgins, S. (2015). *Supporting the attainment of disadvantaged pupils: Articulating success and good practice*. Research Brief, November. London, Department for Education.

MacLeod, W. B. & Urquiola, M. (2009). *Anti-lemons: School reputation and educational quality*. Working Paper No. 15112. Cambridge, MA, National Bureau of Economic Research.

Mahony, P., Menter, I. & Hextall, I. (2004). The emotional impact of performance-related pay on teachers in England. *British Educational Research Journal*, *30*(3), 435–456.

Mahony, P. & Hextall, I. (2013). 'Building schools for the future': 'Transformation' for social justice or expensive blunder? *British Educational Research Journal*, *39*(5), 853–871.

Malloy, L. C. (2015). Loss aversion, education, and intergenerational mobility. *Education Economics*, *23*(3), 318–337.

Mangan, J., Davies, P. & Adnett, N. (2001). Movers and stayers: The determinants of post-16 educational choice. *Research in Post-Compulsory Education*, *6*(1), 31–50.

Mangan, J., Hughes, A. & Slack, K. (2010a). Student finance, information and decision making. *Higher Education*, *60*(5), 459–472.

Mangan, J., Hughes, A., Davies, P. & Slack, K. (2010b). Fair access: Explaining the association between social class and students' choice of university. *Studies in Higher Education*, *35*(3), 335–350.

Mansell, W. (2012). *Should Pearson, a giant multinational, be influencing our education policy?* Guardian. 16 July. Available at www.theguardian.com/education/2012/jul/16/pearson-multinational-influence-education-policy.

Manski, C. F. (2000). *Economic analysis of social interactions*. Working Paper No. 7580, Cambridge, MA, National Bureau of Economic Research.

Marburger, D. R. (2006). Does mandatory attendance improve student performance? *The Journal of Economic Education*, *37*(2), 148–155.

Marchetti, C. (1980). Society as a learning system: Discovery, invention, and innovation cycles revisited. *Technological Forecasting and Social Change*, *18*(4), 267–282.

Marginson, S. (2006). Dynamics of national and global competition in higher education. *Higher Education*, *52*(1), 1–39.

Marsh, A. J. (1995). The effect on school budgets of different non-statemented special educational needs indicators within a common funding formula. *British Educational Research Journal*, *21*(1), 99–105.

Marsh, H. W., Seaton, M., Trautwein, U., Lüdtke, O., Hau, K. T., O'Mara, A. J. & Craven, R. G. (2008b). The big-fish–little-pond-effect stands up to critical scrutiny: Implications for theory, methodology, and future research. *Educational Psychology Review*, *20*(3), 319–350.

Marsh, J., Hamilton, L. & Gill, B. (2008a). Assistance and accountability in externally managed schools: The case of Edison Schools, Inc. *Peabody Journal of Education*, *83*(3), 423–458.

Marston, G. & Watts, R. (2003). Tampering with the evidence: A critical appraisal of evidence-based policy-making. *The Drawing Board: An Australian Review of Public Affairs*, *3*(3), 143–163.

Marton, F. (2014). *Necessary conditions of learning*. London, Routledge.

Maslowski, R., Scheerens, J. & Luyten, H. (2007). The effect of school autonomy and school internal decentralization on students' reading literacy. *School Effectiveness and School Improvement*, *18*(3), 303–334.

Matsumoto, A., Merlone, U. & Szidarovszky, F. (2012). Some notes on applying the Herfindahl–Hirschman Index. *Applied Economics Letters*, *19*(2), 181–184.

Matthews, P. & Berwick, G. (2013). Teaching schools: First among equals. *Nottingham, National College for Teaching and Leadership*.

Matthews, P., Holmes, J. R., Vickers, P. & Corporaal, B. (1998). Aspects of the reliability and validity of school inspection judgements of teaching. *Educational Research and Evaluation*, *4*(2), 167–188.

Matthews, R. C. O. (1991). The economics of professional ethics: Should the professions be more like businesses? *The Economic Journal*, *101*(407), 737–750.

Maudos, J. & de Guevara, J. F. (2007). The cost of market power in banking: Social welfare loss vs. cost inefficiency. *Journal of Banking & Finance*, *31*(7), 2103–2125.

Maxwell, J. A. (2004). Causal explanation, qualitative research, and scientific inquiry in education. *Educational Researcher*, *33*(2), 3–11.

May, T. (2016). Full text of Theresa May's speech on grammar schools. *The New Statesman*, 9 September.

McCauley, D. P. & Kuhnert, K. W. (1992). A theoretical review and empirical investigation of employee trust in management. *Public Administration Quarterly*, *16*(2), 265–284.

McClellan, B. E. (1999). *Moral education in America: Schools and the shaping of character from colonial times to the present*. Williston, VT, Teachers College Press.

McCune, V. & Entwistle, N. (2011). Cultivating the disposition to understand in 21st century university education. *Learning and Individual Differences*, *21*(3), 303–310.

McDonnell, L. M. (2005). No Child Left Behind and the federal role in education: Evolution or revolution? *Peabody Journal of Education*, *80*(2), 19–38.

McGregor, D. (1964). *The human side of enterprise*. New York, McGraw-Hill.

McKnight, A., Naylor, R. and Smith, J. (2002). *Sheer class? The extent and sources of variation in the UK graduate earnings premium*. LSE STICERD Research Paper No. CASE 054. London, London School of Economics.

McMahon, W. W. (2009). *Higher learning, greater good: The private and social returns of higher education*. Baltimore, MD, The Johns Hopkins University Press.

McNeal, R. B. (1999). Parental involvement as social capital: Differential effectiveness on science achievement, truancy, and dropping out. *Social Forces, 78*(1), 117–144.

McNeil, L. M. (2002). Private asset or public good: Education and democracy at the crossroads. *American Educational Research Journal, 39*(2), 243.

McPherson, M. S. & Schapiro, M. O. (1999). *The student aid game: Meeting need and rewarding talent in American higher education*. Princeton, NJ, Princeton University Press.

Meek, V. L. (1990). The rise and fall of the binary policy of higher education in Australia. *Journal of Education Policy, 5*(3), 282–292.

Melhuish, E. C., Phan, M. B., Sylva, K., Sammons, P., Siraj-Blatchford, I. & Taggart, B. (2008). Effects of the home learning environment and preschool center experience upon literacy and numeracy development in early primary school. *Journal of Social Issues, 64*(1), 95–114.

Meltzer, A. H. & Richard, S. F. (1981). A rational theory of the size of government. *Journal of Political Economy, 89*(5), 914–927.

Meltzer, A. H. & Richard, S. F. (1983). Tests of a rational theory of the size of government. *Public Choice, 41*(3), 403–418.

Meyer, J. H. F., Parsons, P. & Dunne, T. T. (1990). Individual study orchestrations and their association with learning outcome. *Higher Education, 20*(1), 67–89.

Miller, L. & Olson, J. (1994). Putting the computer in its place: A study of teaching with technology. *Journal of Curriculum Studies, 26*(2), 121–141.

Milligan, K., Moretti, E. & Oreopoulos, P. (2004). Does education improve citizenship? Evidence from the United States and the United Kingdom. *Journal of Public Economics, 88*(9), 1667–1695.

Mincer, J. (1991). *Education and unemployment*. NBER Working Paper No. 3838. Cambridge, MA, National Bureau of Economic Research.

Mintrom, M. (1997). Policy entrepreneurs and the diffusion of innovation. *American Journal of Political Science, 41*(3), 738–770.

Mintrom, M. & Vergari, S. (1998). Policy networks and innovation diffusion: The case of state education reforms. *The Journal of Politics, 60*(1), 126–148.

Mintzberg, H. (1979). *The structuring of organizations*. Englewood Cliffs, NJ, Prentice Hall.

Mintzberg, H. & Waters, J. A. (1985). Of strategies, deliberate and emergent. *Strategic Management Journal, 6*(3), 257–272.

Mitra, S. & Chaya, A. K. (1996). Analyzing cost-effectiveness of organizations: The impact of information technology spending. *Journal of Management Information Systems, 13*(2), 29–57.

Moore, J., Sanders, J. & Higham, L. (2013). *Literature review of research into widening participation to higher education. Report to HEFCE and OFFA. AimHigher Research & Consultancy Network*. Bristol, Higher Education Funding Council for England.

Moore, T. (2004). The critical thinking debate: How general are general thinking skills? *Higher Education Research & Development, 23*(1), 3–18.

Moran, A., Kilpatrick, R., Abbott, L., Dallat, J. & McClune, B. (2001). Training to teach: Motivating factors and implications for recruitment. *Evaluation & Research in Education, 15*(1), 17–32.

Moretti, E. (2004). Estimating the social return to higher education: Evidence from longitudinal and repeated cross-sectional data. *Journal of Econometrics, 121*(1–2), 175–212.

Morris, E. W. (2005). From 'middle class' to 'trailer trash:' Teachers' perceptions of White students in a predominately minority school. *Sociology of Education, 78*(2), 99–121.

Morris, R. (2014). The admissions criteria of secondary Free Schools. *Oxford Review of Education, 40*(3), 389–409.

Morris, R. & Perry, T. (2017). Reframing the English grammar schools debate. *Educational Review, 69*(1), 1–24.

Moser, S. C. A. & Moser, S. C. (1999). *Improving literacy and numeracy: A fresh start.* London, DfEE Publications.

Mouw, T. (2006). Estimating the causal effect of social capital: A review of recent research. *Annual Review of Sociology, 32*, 79–102.

Muijs, D. (2015). Improving schools through collaboration: A mixed methods study of school-to-school partnerships in the primary sector. *Oxford Review of Education, 41*(5), 563–586.

Muijs, D. & Lindsay, G. (2008). Where are we at? An empirical study of levels and methods of evaluating continuing professional development. *British Educational Research Journal, 34*(2), 195–211.

Muijs, D. & Reynolds, D. (2003). The effectiveness of the use of learning support assistants in improving the mathematics achievement of low achieving pupils in primary school. *Educational Research, 45*(3), 219–230.

Muijs, D., West, M. & Ainscow, M. (2010). Why network? Theoretical perspectives on networking. *School Effectiveness and School Improvement, 21*(1), 5–26.

Murnane, R. J., Singer, J., Willett, D., John, B. & Kemple, J. J. (1991). *Who will teach? Policies that matter.* Cambridge, MA, Harvard University Press.

Musgrave, R. A. (1957). A multiple theory of budget determination, *Finanzarchiv*, N.F., *17*, 333–343.

Muzaka, V. (2009). The niche of graduate teaching assistants (GTAs): Perceptions and reflections. *Teaching in Higher Education, 14*(1), 1–12.

Myers, D. G. (2003). Close relationships and quality of life. In D. Kahneman, E. Diener & I. Schwartz (Eds.), *Well-being: Foundations of hedonic psychology.* New York, Russell Sage Foundation (pp. 374–391).

National Audit Office (NAO). (2009). *The Building Schools for the Future Programme. Renewing the secondary school estate.* London, Stationery Office.

National Audit Office (NAO). (2017). *Retaining and developing the school workforce, HC 307.* London, the National Audit Office.

National College for Teaching and Learning. (2014). *Governance in multi-academy trusts.* Nottingham, NCTL.

National Curriculum Task Group on Assessment and Testing. (1987). *Report of the Task Group on Assessment and Testing.* London, Department of Education and Science and the Welsh Office.

National Research Council. (2002). *Scientific research in education.* Washington, DC, National Academy Press.

National Union of Students (NUS). (2013). *Postgraduates who teach.* London, National Union of Students.

Naval, C., Print, M. & Veldhuis, R. (2002). Education for democratic citizenship in the New Europe: Context and reform. *European Journal of Education, 37*(2), 107–128.

Neal, D. (1997). The effect of Catholic secondary schooling on educational attainment. *Journal of Labour Economics, 15*(1), 98–123.

Nelson, F. (2014). The Blob gobbled up Michael Gove – now it's coming for David Cameron. *Daily Telegraph*, 12 December. Available at www.telegraph.co.uk/education/11288932/The-Blob-gobbled-up-Michael-Gove-now-its-coming-for-David-Cameron.html.

Nelson, R. R. & Phelps, E. S. (1966). Investment in humans, technological diffusion, and economic growth. *The American Economic Review, 56*(1/2), 69–75.

Newcastle Commission. (1861). The Royal Commission on the State of Popular Education in England, Parliamentary Papers. In G. M. Young & W. D. Hancock (Eds.). *English historical documents, XII(1), 1833–1874.* New York, Oxford University Press, pp. 891–897.

Newman, M., Garrett, Z., Elbourne, D., Bradley, S., Noden, P., Taylor, J. & West, A. (2006). Does secondary school size make a difference? A systematic review. *Educational Research Review, 1*(1), 41–60.

Newman-Ford, L., Fitzgibbon, K., Lloyd, S. & Thomas, S. (2008). A large-scale investigation into the relationship between attendance and attainment: A study using an innovative, electronic attendance monitoring system. *Studies in Higher Education, 33*(6), 699–717.

Newmann, F. M., Rutter, R. A. & Smith, M. S. (1989). Organizational factors that affect school sense of efficacy, community, and expectations. *Sociology of Education, 62*(4), 221–238.

Nickell, S. & Nicolitsas, D. (1997). Wages, restrictive practices and productivity. *Labour Economics, 4*(3), 201–221.

Nickell, S. & Quintini, G. (2002). The consequences of the decline in public sector pay in Britain: A little bit of evidence. *The Economic Journal, 112*(477), 107–118.

Nielsen, F. & Roos, J. M. (2015). Genetics of educational attainment and the persistence of privilege at the turn of the 21st century. *Social Forces, 94*(2), 535–561.

Nilsson, J. (2001). Organisational principles for co-operative firms. *Scandinavian Journal of Management, 17*(3), 329–356.

Noailly, J., Webbink, D. & Jacobs, B. (2011). Should the government stimulate enrolment in science and engineering studies? *Applied Economics Letters, 18*(4), 371–375.

Noble, J. & Davies, P. (2009). Cultural capital as an explanation of variation in participation in Higher Education. *British Journal of Sociology of Education, 30*(5), 591–605.

Noddings, N. (2003). *Happiness and education.* Cambridge, Cambridge University Press.

Nonaka, I. (1994). A dynamic theory of organizational knowledge creation. *Organization Science, 5*(1), 14–37.

Norris, P. (1995). May's law of curvilinear disparity revisited: Leaders, officers, members and voters in British political parties. *Party Politics, 1*(1), 29–47.

Nunnery, J. A. & Ross, S. M. (2007). The effects of the School Renaissance program on student achievement in reading and mathematics. *Research in the Schools, 14*(1), 40–59.

Nutley, S., Davies, H. & Walter, I. (2002). Evidence based policy and practice: Cross sector lessons from the UK. *Working Paper No. 9.* St Andrews, ESRC UK Centre for Evidence Based Policy and Practice.

Nye, B., Konstantopoulos, S. & Hedges, L. V. (2004). How large are teacher effects? *Educational Evaluation and Policy Analysis, 26*(3), 237–257.

Oates, T. (2011). Could do better: Using international comparisons to refine the National Curriculum in England. *Curriculum Journal, 22*(2), 121–150.

Odden, A. & Busch, C. (1998). *Financing schools for high performance: Strategies for improving the use of educational resources.* San Francisco, CA, Jossey-Bass.

OECD. (1997). *Technology incubators: Nurturing small firms.* OCDE/GD(97)202. Paris, OECD Publishing.

OECD. (2007). *Human capital: How what you know shapes your life.* OECD Insights. Paris, OECD Publishing.

OECD. (2009). *Learning for jobs: England and Wales.* Paris, OECD Publishing.

OECD. (2010). *The high cost of low educational performance: The long-run impact of improving PISA outcomes.* Paris, OECD Publishing.

OECD. (2011). *Teachers matter: Attracting, developing and retaining effective teachers.* Paris, OECD Publishing.

OECD. (2014a). *Education at a glance 2014 OECD indicators*. Paris, OECD Publishing.

OECD. (2014b). *Society at a glance 2014 OECD social indicators*. Paris, OECD Publishing.

OECD. (2014c). *Does homework perpetuate inequalities in education?* PISA in Focus 46. Paris, OECD Publishing. Available at www.oecd-ilibrary.org/docserver/download/5jxrhqhtx 2xt-en.pdf?expires=1492862684&id=id&accname=guest&checksum=8D43F1B3125D 90EC1B8ABDDD3E7B37C9 (accessed 23 April 2017).

OECD. (2015). *How's life? 2015. Measuring well-being*. Paris, OECD Publishing. Available at www.oecd.org/statistics/how-s-life-23089679.htm (accessed 19 October 2017).

OECD. (2017). *Education at a glance 2017 OECD indicators*. Paris, OECD Publishing.

OECD/CERI. (2001). *Learning to change: ICT in schools*. Paris, OECD Publishing.

Office for Fair Access (OFFA). (2017). *Analysis, data and progress reports*. Bristol, Office for Fair Access. Available at www.offa.org.uk/publications/analysis-data-and-progress-reports/ (accessed 6 November 2017).

Office for National Statistics (ONS). (2014). *Measuring national well-being: Exploring the well-being of children in the UK*, 2014. London, Office for National Statistics. Available at www. ons.gov.uk/ons/rel/wellbeing/measuring-national-well-being/exploring-the-well-being-of-children-in-the-uk-2014/rpt-measuring-national-wellbeing-children-uk-2014.html (accessed 11 November 2015).

Office for National Statistics (ONS). (2015). *Summary of public sector finances November 2015*. London, ONS. Available at www.ons.gov.uk.

Office for National Statistics (ONS). (2016). *Percentile points from 1 to 99 for total income before and after tax*. London, Office for National Statistics. Available at www.gov.uk/government/ statistics/percentile-points-from-1-to-99-for-total-income-before-and-after-tax.

Office for National Statistics (ONS). (2017). *Housing affordability in England and Wales: 1997 to 2016*. London, Office for National Statistics. Available at www.ons.gov.uk/people populationandcommunity/housing/bulletins/housingaffordabilityinenglandandwales/19 97to2016 (accessed 17 October 2017).

Office for Standards in Education (Ofsted). (2005). *Remodelling the School Workforce*, HMI 2596. London, Ofsted.

Office for Standards in Education (Ofsted). (2014). *The report of Her Majesty's Chief Inspector of Education, Children's Services and Skills 2013/14. Schools*. Manchester, Ofsted.

Office for Standards in Education (Ofsted). (2015). *The report of Her Majesty's Chief Inspector of Education, Children's Services and Skills 2014/15. Schools*. London, Ofsted.

Ohmae, K. (1995). *The end of the nation state: The rise of regional economies*. New York, Free Press Paperbacks.

Okagaki, L. & Frensch, P. A. (1998). Parenting and children's school achievement: A multiethnic perspective. *American Educational Research Journal*, *35*(1), 123–144.

Okbay, A., Beauchamp, J. P., Fontana, M. A., Lee, J. J., Pers, T. H., Rietveld, C. A. & Oskarsson, S. (2016). Genome-wide association study identifies 74 loci associated with educational attainment. *Nature*, *533*(7604), 539–542.

O'Leary, N. C. & Sloane, P. J. (2011). The wage premium for university education in Great Britain during a decade of change: Wage premium for university education. *The Manchester School*, *79*(4), 740–764.

Oliner, S. D. & Sichel, D. E. (2000). *The resurgence of growth in the late 1990s: Is information technology the story?* FEDS Working Paper No. 2000–20. Available at SSRN: http://ssrn. com/abstract=233139 or http://dx.doi.org/10.2139/ssrn.233139.

Olsen, L. (1994). *The unfinished journey: Restructuring schools in a diverse society. A California Tomorrow Research and Policy Report from the Education for a Diverse Society Project*. ED 371 431. San Francisco, CA, California Tomorrow.

Olson, J. (1981). Teacher influence in the classroom: A context for understanding curriculum translation. *Instructional Science, 10*(3), 259–275.

Olssen, M. & Peters, M. A. (2005). Neoliberalism, higher education and the knowledge economy: From the free market to knowledge capitalism. *Journal of Education Policy, 20*(3), 313–345.

Oosterbeek, H. & van den Broek, A. (2009). An empirical analysis of borrowing behaviour of higher education students in the Netherlands. *Economics of Education Review, 28*(2), 170–177.

Orcutt, G. H. (1970). Data, research, and government. *The American Economic Review, 60*(2), 132–137.

Oreopoulos, P. (2006). Estimating average and local average treatment effects of education when compulsory schooling laws really matter. *The American Economic Review, 96*(1), 152–175.

Oreopoulos, P. & Salvanes, K. G. (2011). Priceless: The nonpecuniary benefits of schooling. *The Journal of Economic Perspectives, 25*(1), 159–184.

Orr, D. (2011). Illiteracy in London's schools is a scandal. *The Guardian*, 2 June.

Ost, B. (2014). How do teachers improve? The relative importance of specific and general human capital. *American Economic Journal: Applied Economics, 6*(2), 127–151.

Osterman, K. F. (2000). Students' need for belonging in the school community. *Review of Educational Research, 70*(3), 323–367.

Ostrom, E. (1996). Crossing the great divide: Coproduction, synergy, and development. *World Development, 24*(6), 1073–1087.

Ostrom, E. (2010). Beyond markets and states: Polycentric governance of complex economic systems. *The American Economic Review, 100*(3), 641–672.

Oswald, A. J. & Wu, S. (2010). Objective confirmation of subjective measures of human well-being: Evidence from the USA. *Science, 327*(5965), 576–579.

Ouseley, Sir H. (2001*). Community pride not prejudice: Making diversity work in Bradford.* Bradford, Bradford Vision.

Ouston, J., Fidler, B. & Earley, P. (1997). What do schools do after OFSTED school inspections – or before? *School Leadership & Management, 17*(1), 95–104.

Ozga, J. (2009). Governing education through data in England: From regulation to self-evaluation. *Journal of Education Policy, 24*(2), 149–162.

Page, L., Garboua, L. L. & Montmarquette, C. (2007). Aspiration levels and educational choices: An experimental study. *Economics of Education Review, 26*(6), 747–757.

Pang, M. F. & Marton, F. (2003). Beyond 'lesson study': Comparing two ways of facilitating the grasp of some economic concepts. *Instructional Science, 31*(3), 237–257.

Papay, J. P. & Johnson, S. M. (2012). Is PAR a good investment? Understanding the costs and benefits of teacher peer assistance and review programs. *Educational Policy, 26*(5), 696–729.

Parcel, T. L. & Dufur, M. J. (2001). Capital at home and at school: Effects on student achievement. *Social Forces, 79*(3), 881–911.

Parish, B. & Bryant, B. (2015). *Research on funding for young people with special educational needs.* London, Department for Education.

Parks, R. B., Baker, P. C., Kiser, C., Oakerson, L, Ostrom, E., Ostrom, V., Percy, S. L., Vandivort, M. B., Whitaker, G. P. & Wilson, R. (1981). Consumers as coproducers of public services: some economic and institutional considerations. *Policy Studies Journal, 9*(7), 1001–1011.

Parry, G. (2009). Higher education, further education and the English experiment. *Higher Education Quarterly, 63*(4), 322–342.

Parry, G. & Thompson, A. (2002). *Closer by degrees: The past, present and duture of higher education in further education colleges.* London, Learning and Skills Development.

Paulsen, M. B. & St John, E. P. (2002). Social class and college costs: Examining the financial nexus between college choice and persistence. *The Journal of Higher Education, 73*(2), 189–236.

Payne, J. (2008). Sector skills councils and employer engagement – delivering the 'employer-led' skills agenda in England. *Journal of Education and Work, 21*(2), 93–113.

Payne, J. (2010). Scoring opportunity or hospital pass? The changing role of local authorities in 14–19 education and training in England. *Journal of Education Policy, 25*(4), 519–545.

Payton, J. W., Wardlaw, D. M., Graczyk, P. A., Bloodworth, M. R., Tompsett, C. J. & Weissberg, R. P. (2000). Social and emotional learning: A framework for promoting mental health and reducing risk behavior in children and youth. *Journal of School Health, 70*(5), 179–185.

Pearce, S., Power, S. & Taylor, C. M. (2017). Private tutoring in Wales: Patterns of private investment and public provision. *Research Papers in Education* (i-first).

Peel, M. (2015). *The new meritocracy. A history of UK independent schools 1979*–2015. London, Elliott & Thompson.

Perez, P. A. & McDonough, P. M. (2008). Understanding Latina and Latino college choice: A social capital and chain migration analysis. *Journal of Hispanic Higher Education, 7*(3), 249–265.

Peri, G. (2005). Determinants of knowledge flows and their effect on innovation. *Review of Economics and Statistics, 87*(2), 308–322.

Perna, L. W. & Titus, M. A. (2005). The relationship between parental involvement as social capital and college enrollment: An examination of racial/ethnic group differences. *The Journal of Higher Education, 76*(5), 485–518.

Perou, R., Bitsko, R. H., Blumberg, S. J., Pastor, P., Ghandour, R. M., Gfroerer, J. C. & Parks, S. E. (2013). Mental health surveillance among children – United States, 2005–2011. *MMWR Surveillance Summaries, 62*(Suppl 2), 1–35.

Perri, S. (2002). Can policy making be evidence based? *MCC Building Knowledge for Integrated Care, 10*(1), 3–9.

Perry, T. (2017). Inter-method reliability of school effectiveness measures: A comparison of value-added and regression discontinuity estimates. *School Effectiveness and School Improvement, 28*(1), 22–38.

Perry, T., Davies, P. & Qiu, T. (2017). Great grade expectations? The role of pupil expectations in target setting. *International Journal of Educational Research*, published online 6th December 2017, doi.org/10.1016/j.ijer.2017.10.010.

Perryman, J. (2006). Panoptic performativity and school inspection regimes: Disciplinary mechanisms and life under special measures. *Journal of Education Policy, 21*(2), 147–161.

Peters, H. E. (1992). Patterns of intergenerational mobility in income and earnings. *Review of Economics and Statistics, 74*(3), 456–466.

Peters, M. A. (2002). Foucault and governmentality: Understanding the neoliberal paradigm of education policy. *School Field, 12*(5/6), 59–80.

Peters, S. J. (2003). *Inclusive education: Achieving education for all by including those with disabilities and special needs.* Mimeo. Prepared for the World Bank Disability Group. Available at http://documents.worldbank.org/curated/en/614161468325299263/pdf/266900WP0 English0Inclusive0Education.pdf (accessed 18 October 2017).

Petras, J. (2008). Global ruling class: billionaires and how they 'make it'. *Journal of Contemporary Asia, 38*(2), 319–329.

Phillips, D. & Ochs, K. (2003). Processes of policy borrowing in education: Some explanatory and analytical devices. *Comparative Education*, *39*(4), 451–461.

Pick, D. (2006). The re-framing of Australian higher education. *Higher Education Quarterly*, *60*(3), 229–241.

Pierson, P. (1998). Irresistible forces, immovable objects: Post-industrial welfare states confront permanent austerity. *Journal of European Public Policy*, *5*(4), 539–560.

Pigou, A. (1920). *The economics of welfare*. London, Macmillan.

Piketty, T. (2014). *Capital in the 21st century*. Cambridge, MA, Harvard University Press.

Piketty, T. & Zucman, G. (2014). Capital is back: Wealth–income ratios in rich countries 1700–2010. *The Quarterly Journal of Economics*, *129*(3), 1255–1310.

Pillinger, C. & Wood, C. (2014). Pilot study evaluating the impact of dialogic reading and shared reading at transition to primary school: Early literacy skills and parental attitudes. *Literacy*, *48*(3), 155–163.

Pimlott-Wilson, H. (2011). The role of familial habitus in shaping children's views of their future employment. *Children's Geographies*, *9*(1), 111–118.

Pinto, L. (2013). When politics trump evidence: Financial literacy education narratives following the global financial crisis. *Journal of Education Policy*, *28*(1), 95–120.

Popham, W. J. (2001). Teaching to the test? *Educational Leadership*, *58*(6), 16–21.

Popkewitz, T. S. (1985). Ideology and social formation in teacher education. *Teaching and Teacher Education*, *1*(2), 91–107.

Poterba, J. M. (1997). Demographic structure and the political economy of public education. *Journal of Policy Analysis and Management*, *16*(1), 48–66.

Powell, T. C. (1995). Total quality management as competitive advantage: A review and empirical study. *Strategic Management Journal*, *16*(1), 15–37.

Powell, W. (2003). Neither market nor hierarchy. In M. J. Handel (Ed.), *The sociology of organizations: Classic, contemporary, and critical readings*. Thousand Oaks, CA, Sage, pp. 315–330.

Power, S., Edwards, T., Whitty, G. & Wigfall, V. (2003). *Education and the middle class*. Buckingham, Open University Press.

Pratt, J. (1997). *The Polytechnic Experiment: 1965–1992*. Buckingham, Society for Research into Higher Education & the Open University Press.

Presley, A., Damron-Martinez, D. & Zhang, L. (2010). A study of business student choice to study abroad: A test of the theory of planned behavior. *Journal of Teaching in International Business*, *21*(4), 227–247.

Pressley, M., Wharton-McDonald, R., Allington, R., Block, C. C., Morrow, L., Tracey, D., Baker, K., Brooks, G., Cronin, J., Nelson, E. & Woo, D. (2001). A study of effective first-grade literacy instruction. *Scientific Studies of Reading*, *5*(1), 35–58.

Preston, C., Goldring, E., Berends, M. & Cannata, M. (2012). School innovation in district context: Comparing traditional public schools and charter schools. *Economics of Education Review*, *31*(2), 318–330.

Price, C. (1999). The Education Secretary. In D. Leonard (Ed.), *Crosland and New Labour*. London, Macmillan, pp. 57–66.

Price, I. F., Matzdorf, F., Smith, L. & Agahi, H. (2003). The impact of facilities on student choice of university. *Facilities*, *21*(10), 212–222.

Prieur, A. & Savage, M. (2011). Updating cultural capital theory: A discussion based on studies in Denmark and in Britain. *Poetics*, *39*(6), 566–580.

Psacharopoulos, G. & Patrinos, H. (2004). Returns to investment: A further update. *Education Economics*, *12*(2), 111–134.

Pugh, G., Davies, P. & Adnett, N. (2006). Should we have faith in not-for-profit providers of schooling? *Journal of Education Policy, 21*(1), 19–33.

Punch, K. F. & Tuetteman, E. (1996). Reducing teacher stress: The effects of support in the work environment. *Research in Education, 56*(1), 63–73.

Putnam, R. D. (2001). *Bowling alone: The collapse and revival of American community.* New York, Simon & Schuster.

Quartz, K. H. & TEP Research Group. (2003). 'Too angry to leave': Supporting new teachers' commitment to transform urban schools. *Journal of Teacher Education, 54*(2), 99–111.

Quintas, P., Wield, D. & Massey, D. (1992). Academic–industry links and innovation: Questioning the science park model. *Technovation, 12*(3), 161–175.

Radnor, Z. J. & Barnes, D. (2007). Historical analysis of performance measurement and management in operations management. *International Journal of Productivity and Performance Management, 56*(5/6), 384–396.

Raffe, D. (2003). Pathways linking education and work: A review of concepts, research, and policy debates. *Journal of Youth Studies, 6*(1), 3–19.

Raftery, A. E. & Hout, M. (1993). Maximally maintained inequality: Expansion, reform, and opportunity in Irish education, 1921–75. *Sociology of Education, 66*(1), 41–62.

Randle, K. & Brady, N. (1997). Further education and the new managerialism. *Journal of Further and Higher Education, 21*(2), 229–239.

Rao, H., Morrill, C. & Zald, M. N. (2000). Power plays: How social movements and collective action create new organizational forms. *Research in Organizational Behavior, 22,* 237–281.

Rauh, J. (2011). Online education as a toll good: An examination of the South Carolina virtual school program. *Computers & Education, 57*(2), 1583–1594.

Ravallion, M. (2005). A poverty-inequality trade off? *The Journal of Economic Inequality, 3*(2), 169–181.

Rawls, J. (2009). *A theory of justice.* Cambridge, MA, Harvard University Press.

Reardon, J., Hasty, R. & Coe, B. (1997). The effect of information technology on productivity in retailing. *Journal of Retailing, 72*(4), 445–461.

Reay, D. (1998). 'Always knowing' and 'never being sure': Familial and institutional habituses and higher education choice. *Journal of Education Policy, 13*(4), 519–529.

Reay, D. (2004). 'It's all becoming a habitus': Beyond the habitual use of habitus in educational research. *British Journal of Sociology of Education, 25*(4), 431–444.

Reay, D. (2015). Habitus and the psychosocial: Bourdieu with feelings. *Cambridge Journal of Education, 45*(1), 9–23.

Reback, R. (2005). House prices and the provision of local public services: Capitalization under school choice programs. *Journal of Urban Economics, 57*(2), 275–301.

Reeves, E. (2008). The practice of contracting in public–private partnerships: Transaction costs and relational contracting in the Irish schools sector. *Public Administration, 86*(4), 969–986.

Reeves, J. & Drew, V. (2012). Relays and relations: Tracking a policy initiative for improving teacher professionalism. *Journal of Education Policy, 27*(6), 711–730.

Reimann, N. (2004). First-year teaching-learning environments in economics. *International Review of Economics Education, 3*(1), 9–38.

Renfrew, K., Baird, H., Green, H., Davies, P., Hughes, A., Mangan, J. and Slack, K. (2010). *Understanding the information needs of users of public information about higher education,* Bristol, Higher Education Funding Council for England.

Restakis, J. (2010). *Humanizing the economy: Co-operatives in the age of capital.* Gabriola Island, Canada, New Society Publishers.

Reynolds, D., Treharne, D. & Tripp, H. (2003). ICT – the hopes and reality. *British Journal of Educational Technology, 34*(2), 151–167.

Rhoades, S. A. (1993). The herfindahl-hirschman index. *Federal Reserve Bulletin, 79*(3), 188.

Rice, P. G. (1987). The demand for post-compulsory education in the UK and the effects of educational maintenance allowances. *Economica*, 54(216), 465–475.

Rietveld, C. A., Medland, S. E., Derringer, J., Yang, J., Esko, T., Martin, N. W. & Albrecht, E. (2013). GWAS of 126,559 individuals identifies genetic variants associated with educational attainment. *Science, 340*(6139), 1467–1471.

Riew, J. (1986). Scale economies, capacity utilization, and school costs: A comparative analysis of secondary and elementary schools. *Journal of Education Finance, 11*(4), 433–446.

Riley-Smith, B. (2016). *Theresa May to end ban on new grammar schools. The Daily Telegraph*, 6 August.

Rist, R. (1970). Student social class and teacher expectations: The self-fulfilling prophecy in ghetto education. *Harvard Educational Review, 40*(3), 411–451.

Robbins, L. (1963). The Robbins Report on Higher Education. *Report of UK Government Committee on Higher Education*. London, Her Majesty's Stationary Office.

Robertson, S. L. (2005). Re-imagining and rescripting the future of education: Global knowledge economy discourses and the challenge to education systems. *Comparative Education, 41*(2), 151–170.

Robinson, D., Hammersley-Fletcher, L., Davies, P. & Vigurs, K. (2006). *A comparative study of the leadership, governance and management (LGM) issues of three FE/HE partnerships*. Report to HEFCE. Huddersfield, University of Huddersfield.

Roemer, J. E. (2009). *Equality of opportunity*. Cambridge, MA, Harvard University Press.

Rogers, E. M. (2003). *Diffusion of innovations, fifth edition*. New York, Free Press.

Roksa, J. & Potter, D. (2011). Parenting and academic achievement intergenerational transmission of educational advantage. *Sociology of Education, 84*(4), 299–321.

Romer, P. M. (1986). Increasing returns and long-run growth, *Journal of Political Economy, 94*(5), 1002–1037.

Ronfeldt, M., Loeb, S. & Wyckoff, J. (2013). How teacher turnover harms student achievement. *American Educational Research Journal, 50*(1), 4–36.

Rose, H. & Betts, J. R. (2004). The of high school courses on earnings. *Review of Economics and Statistics, 86*(2), 497–513.

Rosenberg, N. (1965). Adam Smith on the division of labour: Two views or one? *Economica, 32*(126), 127–139.

Rothstein, J. M. (2006). Good principals or good peers? Parental valuation of school characteristics, Tiebout equilibrium, and the incentive effects of competition among jurisdictions. The effect. *American Economic Review, 96*(4), 1333–1350.

Rothstein, J. (2010). Teacher quality in educational production: Tracking, decay, and student achievement. *The Quarterly Journal of Economics, 125*(1), 175–214.

Rothstein, J. & Rouse, C. E. (2011). Constrained after college: Student loans and early-career occupational choices. *Journal of Public Economics, 95*(1), 149–163.

Rowe, K. J. (2000). Assessment, league tables and school effectiveness: Consider the issues and get real. *The Journal of Educational Enquiry, 1*(1), 73–98.

Rubie-Davies, C. M. (2007). Classroom interactions: Exploring the practices of high- and low-expectation teachers. *British Journal of Educational Psychology, 77*(2), 289–306.

Rubie-Davies, C. M., Flint, A. & McDonald, L. G. (2012). Teacher beliefs, teacher characteristics, and school contextual factors: What are the relationships? *British Journal of Educational Psychology, 82*(2), 270–288.

Rubinfeld, D. L. & Shapiro, P. (1989). Micro-estimation of the demand for schooling: Evidence from Michigan and Massachusetts. *Regional Science and Urban Economics, 19*(3), 381–398.

Rubinstein, D. & Simon, B. (1969). *The evolution of the comprehensive school: 1926–1972.* London, Routledge and Kegan Paul.

Ruggiero, J., Duncombe, W. & Miner, J. (1995). On the measurement and causes of technical inefficiency in local public services: With an application to public education. *Journal of Public Administration Research and Theory, 5*(4), 403–428.

Rumble, G. (2003). Modeling the costs and economics of distance education. In M. G. Moore & W. G. Anderson (Eds.), *Handbook of distance education.* Mahwah, NJ, Lawrence Erlbaum & Associates, pp. 703–716.

Runkle, D. E. (1991). Liquidity constraints and the permanent-income hypothesis: Evidence from panel data. *Journal of Monetary Economics, 27*(1), 73–98.

Ryan, R. (2009). Making VET in Schools work: A review of policy and practice in the implementation of vocational education and training in Australian schools. *The Journal of Educational Enquiry, 3*(1), 1–16.

Ryan, R. M. & Deci, E. L. (2000). Self-determination theory and the facilitation of intrinsic motivation, social development and well-being. *American Psychologist, 55*(1), 68–78.

Rymarz, R. & Graham, J. (2006). Australian core Catholic youth, Catholic schools and religious education. *British Journal of Religious Education, 28*(1), 79–89.

Sacerdote, B. (2011). Peer effects in education: How might they work, how big are they and how much do we know thus far? In E. Hanushek, S. J. Machin & L. Woessman (Eds.), *Handbook of the economics of education, Volume 3.* Amsterdam, North Holland, pp. 249–277.

Sallis, E. (2014). *Total quality management in education, 3rd edition.* London, Routledge.

Saltman, K. J. (2005). *The Edison Schools: Corporate schooling and the assault on public education.* New York, Routledge.

Samdal, O., Wold, B. & Bronis, M. (1999). Relationship between students' perceptions of school environment, their satisfaction with school and perceived academic achievement: An international study. *School Effectiveness and School Improvement, 10*(3), 296–320.

Samuelson, Paul A. (1954). The pure theory of public expenditure. *Review of Economics and Statistics, 36*(4), 387–389.

Sanderson, I. (2002). Evaluation, policy learning and evidence-based policy making. *Public Administration, 80*(1), 1–22.

Sanderson, I. (2003). Is it 'what works' that matters? Evaluation and evidence-based policy-making. *Research Papers in Education, 18*(4), 331–345.

Sanderson, I. (2009). Intelligent policy making for a complex world: pragmatism, evidence and learning. *Political Studies, 57*(4), 699–719.

Sappington, D. E. (1991). Incentives in principal–agent relationships. *The Journal of Economic Perspectives, 5*(2), 45–66.

Saracho, O. N. & Spodek, B. (2010). Parents and children engaging in storybook reading. *Early Child Development and Care, 180*(10), 1379–1389.

Scheerens, J. (1990). School effectiveness research and the development of process indicators of school functioning. *School Effectiveness and School Improvement, 1*(1), 61–80.

Schmidt, W. H. (2009). *Exploring the relationship between content coverage and achievement: Unpacking the meaning of tracking in eighth grade mathematics.* East Lansing, Michigan State University Education Policy Center.

Schmidt, W. H. & McKnight, C. C. (2012). *Inequality for all: The challenge of unequal opportunity in American schools.* New York, Teachers College.

Schmidt, W. H., Burroughs, N. A., Zoido, P. & Houang, R. T. (2015). The role of schooling in perpetuating educational inequality: An international perspective. *Educational Researcher, 44*(7), 371–386.

Schneider, M., Marschall, M., Roch, C. & Teske, P. (1999). Heuristics, low information rationality, and choosing public goods. Broken windows as shortcuts to information about school performance. *Urban Affairs Review, 34*(5), 729–741.

Schön, D. A. (1987). *Educating the reflective practitioner: Toward a new design for teaching and learning in the professions*. San Francisco, CA, Jossey-Bass.

Schultz, T. W. (1961). Investment in human capital. *The American Economic Review, 51*(1), 1–17.

Schülz, W., Fraillon, J., Ainley, J., Losito, B. & Kerr, D. (2008). *International civic and citizenship education study: Assessment framework*. Amsterdam, NL, International Association for the Evaluation of Educational Achievement.

Schütz, G., Ursprung, H. W. & Wößmann, L. (2008). Education policy and equality of opportunity. *Kyklos, 61*(2), 279–308.

Schwartz, A. E., Stiefel, L. & Wiswall, M. (2013). Do small schools improve performance in large, urban districts? Causal evidence from New York City. *Journal of Urban Economics, 77*, 27–40.

Schwartz, H. M. (1994). Public choice theory and public choices bureaucrats and state reorganization in Australia, Denmark, New Zealand, and Sweden in the 1980s. *Administration & Society, 26*(1), 48–77.

Schweers Cook, K. (2005). Networks, norms, and trust: The social psychology of social capital. 2004 Cooley Mead Award Address. *Social Psychology Quarterly, 68*(1), 4–14.

Scott, D. (2013). *Education, epistemology and critical realism*. London, Routledge.

Scott, J. C. (2006). The mission of the university: Medieval to postmodern transformations. *The Journal of Higher Education, 77*(1), 1–39.

Seels, B., Fullerton, K., Berry, L. & Horn, L. J. (2004). Research on learning from television. In D. H. Jonassen (Ed.), *Handbook of research on educational communications and technology, 2*. Mahwah, NJ, Lawrence Erlbaum Associates, pp. 249–334.

Sellen, P. (2016). *Teacher workload and professional development in England's secondary schools: Insights from TALIS*. London, Education Policy Institute.

Sen, A. (2017). *Collective choice and social welfare, 3rd edition*. London, Penguin.

Shackle, G. L. S. (1974). *Keynesian Kaleidics*. Edinburgh, Edinburgh University Press.

Shah, M. & Sid Nair, C. (2013). Private for-profit higher education in Australia: Widening access, participation and opportunities for public–private collaboration. *Higher Education Research & Development, 32*(5), 820–832.

Shann, M. H. (1998). Professional commitment and satisfaction among teachers in urban middle schools. *The Journal of Educational Research, 92*(2), 67–73.

Sharples, M. & Pea, R. (2014). Mobile learning. In K. Sawyer (Ed.), *The Cambridge handbook of the learning sciences, 2nd edition*. New York, Cambridge University Press, pp. 501–521.

Shattock, M. L. (2004). The Lambert Code: Can we define best practice? *Higher Education Quarterly, 58*(4), 229–242.

Shattock, M. (2013). University governance, leadership and management in a decade of diversification and uncertainty. *Higher Education Quarterly, 67*(3), 217–233.

Shavit, Y., Arum, R. & Gamoran, A. (2007). (Eds). *Stratification in higher education. A comparative study*. Stanford, CA, Stanford University Press.

Sheldon, S. B. (2007). Improving student attendance with school, family, and community partnerships. *The Journal of Educational Research, 100*(5), 267–275.

Sherer, P. D., Shea, T. P., & Kristensen, E. (2003). Online communities of practice: A catalyst for faculty development. *Innovative Higher Education, 27*(3), 183–194.

Shircliffe, B. J. (2002). Desegregation and the historically Black high school. *Urban Review, 34*(2), 135–158.

Shulman, L. (1987). Knowledge and teaching: Foundations of the new reform. *Harvard Educational Review, 57*(1), 1–22.

Siegelbaum, L. H. (1990). *Stakhanovism and the Politics of Productivity in the USSR, 1935–1941.* Cambridge, Cambridge University Press.

Silverberg, G., Dosi, G. & Orsenigo, L. (1988). Innovation, diversity and diffusion: A self-organisation model. *The Economic Journal, 98*(393), 1032–1054.

Simon, H. A. (1955). A behavioural model of rational choice. *The Quarterly Journal of Economics, 69*(1), 99–118.

Siraj-Blatchford, I., Clarke, K. & Needham, M. (Eds.). (2007). *The team around the child: Multi-agency working in the early years.* Stoke-on-Trent, Trentham Books.

Skinner, E. A., Wellborn, J. G. & Connell, J. P. (1990). What it takes to do well in school and whether I've got it: A process model of perceived control and children's engagement and achievement in school. *Journal of Educational Psychology, 82*(1), 22–32.

Slack, K., Mangan, J., Hughes, A. & Davies, P. (2014). 'Hot', 'cold' and 'warm' information and higher education decision-making. *British Journal of Sociology of Education, 35*(2), 204–223.

Slater, H., Davies, N. M. & Burgess, S. (2012). Do teachers matter? Measuring the variation in teacher effectiveness in England. *Oxford Bulletin of Economics and Statistics, 74*(5), 629–645.

Slaughter, S. & Rhodes, G. (2004). *Academic capitalism and the new economy.* Baltimore, MD, The Johns Hopkins University Press.

Slavin, R. E. (1990). Research on cooperative learning: Consensus and controversy. *Educational Leadership, 47*(4), 52–54.

Smith, A. (1937). *The Wealth of Nations.* New York, The Modern Library.

Smith, G. (2000). Research and inspection: HMI and OfSTED, 1981–1996 – A commentary. *Oxford Review of Education, 26*(3–4), 333–352.

Smyth, J. (Ed.). (1993). *A socially critical view of the self-managing school.* London, The Falmer Press.

Solon, G. (1999). Intergenerational mobility in the labor market. In O. C. Ashenfelter & D. Card (Eds.), *Handbook of labor economics 3(A).* Amsterdam, Elsevier, pp. 1761–1800.

Soysal, Y. N. & Strang, D. (1989). Construction of the first mass education systems in nineteenth-century Europe. *Sociology of Education, 62*(4), 277–288.

Spence, M. A. (1974). *Market signaling: Information transfer in hiring and related screening procedure.* Cambridge, MA, Harvard University Press.

SPICe (Scottish Parliament Information Centre for Education. (2017). *Education and Skills Committee Teacher Workforce Planning 10th May 2017.* Edinburgh, SPICe. Available at www.parliament.scot/S5_Education/Inquiries/20170505ES.workforce_planning_SPICe_paper.pdf (accessed 18 September 2017).

Spielhofer, T., Walker, M., Gagg, K., Schagen, S. & O'Donnell, S. (2007). *Raising the participation age in education and training to 18: Review of existing evidence of the benefits and challenges.* DCSF Research Report No. DCSF RR012. London, Department for Children, Schools and Families.

Spillane, J. P. (2005). Distributed leadership. *The Educational Forum, 69*(2), 143–150.

Stanca, L. (2006). The effects of attendance on academic performance: Panel data evidence for introductory microeconomics. *Journal of Economic Education, 37*(3), 251–266.

Stankov, L. & Lee, J. (2014). Quest for the best non-cognitive predictor of academic achievement. *Educational Psychology, 34*(1), 1–8.

Steedman, H. (2010). *The state of apprenticeship in 2010: International comparisons – Australia, Austria, England, France, Germany, Ireland, Sweden, Switzerland: a report for the Apprenticeship Ambassadors Network.* London, Apprentice Ambassadors Network.

Steelman, L. C., Powell, B. & Carini, R. (2000). Do teacher unions hinder educational performance? Lessons learned from State SAT and ACT scores. *Harvard Educational Review, 70*(4), 437–467.

Steinberg, L., Lamborn, S. D., Dornbusch, S. M. & Darling, N. (1992). Impact of parenting practices on adolescent achievement: Authoritative parenting, school involvement, and encouragement to succeed. *Child Development, 63*(5), 1266–1281.

Stevens, M. (2001). Should firms be required to pay for vocational training? *The Economic Journal, 111*(473), 485–505.

Stevenson, D. L. & Baker, D. P. (1992). Shadow education and allocation in formal schooling: Transition to university in Japan. *American Journal of Sociology, 97*(6), 1639–1657.

Stevenson, H. (2007). Restructuring teachers' work and trade union responses in England: Bargaining for change? *American Educational Research Journal, 44*(2), 224–251.

Stiglitz, J. (1975). The theory of screening education and the distribution of income. *American Economic Review, 65*(3), 283–300.

Stiglitz, J. (1999). Knowledge as a global public good. In I. Kaul, I. Grunberg & M. A. Stern (Eds.), *Global public goods: International co-operation in the 21st century*. New York, Oxford University Press, pp. 308–325.

Stiglitz, J. (2013). *The price of inequality*. London, Penguin Books.

St John, E. P. & Asker, E. H. (2003). *Refinancing the college dream: Access, equal opportunity, and justice for taxpayers*. New York, The Johns Hopkins University Press.

St John, E. P., Paulsen, M. B. & Carter, D. F. (2005). Diversity, college costs, and postsecondary opportunity: An examination of the financial nexus between college choice and persistence for African Americans and Whites. *The Journal of Higher Education, 76*(5), 545–569.

Stoll, L., Bolam, R., McMahon, A., Wallace, M. & Thomas, S. (2006). Professional learning communities: A review of the literature. *Journal of Educational Change, 7*(4), 221–258.

Stoll, L. & Louis, K. S. (Eds.). (2007). *Professional learning communities: Divergence, depth and dilemmas*. Maidenhead, McGraw-Hill/Open University Press.

Strand, S. (2010). Do some schools narrow the gap? Differential school effectiveness by ethnicity, gender, poverty and prior achievement. *School Effectiveness and School Improvement, 21*(3), 289–314.

Strawczynski, M. & Zeira, J. (2003). What determines education expenditure in Israel? *Israel Economic Review, 1*(1), 11–33.

Sturt, M. (1967). *The education of the people*. Abingdon, Routledge.

Sullivan, A. (2001). Cultural capital and educational attainment. *Sociology, 35*(4), 893–912.

Sundberg, D. & Wahlström, N. (2012). Standards-based curricula in a denationalised conception of education: The case of Sweden. *European Educational Research Journal, 11*(3), 342–356.

Sung, J. (2010). Vocational education and training and employer engagement: An industry-led sectoral system in the Netherlands. *International Journal of training and Development, 14*(1), 16–31.

Sutton Trust. (2014). *Extra-curricular inequality. Research Brief*. London, The Sutton Trust.

Svanum, S. & Bigatti, S. (2006). Grade expectations: Informed or uninformed optimism, or both? *Teaching of Psychology, 33*(1), 14–18.

Swain, J. & Hammond, C. (2011). The motivations and outcomes of studying for part-time mature students in higher education. *International Journal of Lifelong Education, 30*(5), 591–612.

Swann, M., McIntyre, D., Pell, T., Hargreaves, L. & Cunningham, M. (2010). Teachers' conceptions of teacher professionalism in England in 2003 and 2006. *British Educational Research Journal, 36*(4), 549–571.

Talbert, J. E. & McLaughlin, M. W. (1994). Teacher professionalism in local school contexts. *American Journal of Education, 102*(2), 123–153.

Tan, C. (2008). Creating 'good citizens' and maintaining religious harmony in Singapore. *British Journal of Religious Education, 30*(2), 133–142.

Tan, C. (2012). The culture of education policy making: Curriculum reform in Shanghai. *Critical Studies in Education, 53*(2), 153–167.

Tansel, A. & Bircan, F. (2006). Demand for education in Turkey: A tobit analysis of private tutoring expenditures. *Economics of Education Review, 25*(3), 303–313.

Taylor, C. & Gorard, S. (2001). The role of residence in school segregation: Placing the impact of parental choice in perspective. *Environment and Planning A, 33*(10), 1829–1852.

Taylor, J. S., Brites, Ferreira, J., de Lourdes Machado, M. & Santiago, R. (Eds.). (2008). *Non-university higher education in Europe.* Dordecht, Springer.

Telhaj, S., Adnett, N., Davies, P., Hutton, D. & Coe, R. (2009). Increasing within school competition: A case for department-level performance indicators? *Research Papers in Education, 24*(1), 45–55.

Temple, J. (1999). The new growth evidence. *Journal of Economic Literature, 37*(1), 112–156.

Tharp, R. & Gallimore, R. (1988). *Rousing minds to life: Teaching, learning and schooling in social context.* New York, Cambridge University Press.

Thomas, G. (2013). A review of thinking and research about inclusive education policy, with suggestions for a new kind of inclusive thinking. *British Educational Research Journal, 39*(3), 473–490.

Thomas, H., Butt, G., Fielding, A., Foster, J., Gunter, H., Lance, A., Rayner, S., Rutherford, D., Potts, L., Powers, S., Selwood, I. & Szwed, C. (2004). *The evaluation of the Transforming the School Workforce Pathfinder Project, Research Report 541.* London, HMSO.

Thompson, G. (2003). *Between hierarchies and markets: The logic and limits of network forms of organization.* Oxford, Oxford University Press.

Thompson, P. & Alvesson, M. (2005). Bureaucracy at work: Misunderstandings and mixed blessings. In P. du Gay (Ed.), *The values of bureaucracy.* New York, Oxford University Press, pp. 89–114.

Thomson, M. M., Turner, J. E. & Nietfeld, J. L. (2012). A typological approach to investigate the teaching career decision: Motivations and beliefs about teaching of prospective teacher candidates. *Teaching and Teacher Education, 28*(3), 324–335.

Thoonen, E. E., Sleegers, P. J., Oort, F. J., Peetsma, T. T. & Geijsel, F. P. (2011). How to improve teaching practices: The role of teacher motivation, organizational factors, and leadership practices. *Educational Administration Quarterly, 47*(3), 496–536.

Thorelli, H. B. (1986). Networks: Between markets and hierarchies. *Strategic Management Journal, 7*(1), 37–51.

Thrupp, M. (1995). The school mix effect: The history of an enduring problem in educational research, policy and practice. *British Journal of Sociology of Education, 16*(2), 183–203.

Tiebout, C. M. (1956). A pure theory of local expenditures. *Journal of Political Economy, 46*(5), 416–424.

Tierney, W. G. (1988). Organizational culture in higher education: Defining the essentials. *The Journal of Higher Education, 59*(1), 2–21.

Timmermans, S. & Epstein, S. (2010). A world of standards but not a standard world: Toward a sociology of standards and standardization. *Annual Review of Sociology, 36,* 69–89.

Todd, P. E. & Wolpin, K. I. (2003). On the specification and estimation of the production function for cognitive achievement. *The Economic Journal, 113*(485), F3–F33.

Tollefson, T. A. (2009). Community college governance, funding, and accountability: A century of issues and trends. *Community College Journal of Research and Practice*, *33*(3–4), 386–402.

Tomaskovic-Devey, D. (1993). The gender and race composition of jobs and the male/female, white/black pay gaps. *Social Forces*, *72*(1), 45–76.

Tomlinson, H. (2000). Proposals for performance related pay for teachers in English schools. *School Leadership & Management*, *20*(3), 281–298.

Tonnies, F. (1957). *Community and society*. East Lancing, Michigan State University Press.

Torio, C. M., Encinosa, W., Berdahl, T., McCormick, M. C. & Simpson, L. A. (2015). Annual report on health care for children and youth in the United States: National estimates of cost, utilization and expenditures for children with mental health conditions. *Academic Pediatrics*, *15*(1), 19–35.

Torres, C. A. (2002). Globalization, education, and citizenship: Solidarity versus markets? *American Educational Research Journal*, *39*(2), 363–378.

Tramonte, L. & Willms, J. D. (2010). Cultural capital and its effect on educational outcomes. *Economics of Education Review*, *29*(2), 200–213.

Trautwein, U. & Lüdtke, O. (2007). Epistemological beliefs, school achievement and college major: A large-scale longitudinal study on the impact of certainty beliefs. *Contemporary Educational Psychology*, *32*(3), 348–346.

Treweek, S. & Zwarenstein, M. (2009). Making trials matter: Pragmatic and explanatory trials and the problem of applicability. *Trials*, *10*(1), 1–9.

Tullock, G., Brady, G. L. & Seldon, A. (2002). *Government failure: A primer in public choice*. Washington, DC, Cato Institute.

Turner, S. E. (2004). Going to college and finishing college: Explaining different educational outcomes. In C. M. Hoxby (Ed.), *College choices: The economics of where to go, when to go and how to pay for it*. Chicago, IL, University of Chicago Press, pp. 13–62.

UCU (University and College Union). (2010). *Student:teacher ratios in higher and further education*. London, UCU. Available at www.ucu.org.uk/article/4624/Studentteacher-ratios-in-higher-and-further-education.

UKCES (United Kingdom Commission for Employment and Skills). (2014). *The labour market story: Skills for the future*. Wath-upon-Dearne, UKCES.

Universities UK. (2015a). *University funding explained*. London, Universities UK.

Universities UK. (2015b). *Patterns and trends in UK higher education 2015*. London, Universities UK.

Urquiola, M. (2005). Does school choice lead to sorting? Evidence from Tiebout variation. *The American Economic Review*, *95*(4), 1310–1326.

US Department of Education. (2001). *Subpart 13 – Excellence in economic education* (Sections 5531–5537 of the No Child Left Behind Act). Available at www.ed.gov/print/policy/elsec/leg/esea02/pg78.html (accessed 10 October 2016).

US Department of Education. (2010). *The condition of education 2010*. Washington, DC, US Department of Education.

US Department of the Treasury, Office of Financial Education. (2006). *Taking ownership of the future: The national strategy for financial literacy*. Available at www.treas.gov (accessed 7 November, 2016).

Usher, D. (1997). Education as a deterrent to crime. *Canadian Journal of Economics*, *30*(2), 367–384.

Vandenberghe, V. (2002). Evaluating the magnitude and the stakes of peer effects analysing science and math achievement across OECD. *Applied Economics*, *34*(10), 1283–1290.

Vandenberghe, V. (2006). Achievement effectiveness and equity: The role of tracking, grade repetition and inter-school segregation. *Applied Economics Letters*, *13*(11), 685–693.

Vandenbroeck, M., De Visscher, S., Van Nuffel, K. & Ferla, J. (2008). Mothers' search for infant child care: The dynamic relationship between availability and desirability in a continental European welfare state. *Early Childhood Research Quarterly, 23*(2), 245–258.

Vandenbussche, J., Aghion, P. & Meghir. C. (2006). Growth, distance to frontier and composition of human capital. *Journal of Economic Growth, 11*(2), 97–127.

van de Werfhorst, H. G. (2011). Skills, positional good or social closure? The role of education across structural–institutional labour market settings. *Journal of Education and Work, 24*(5), 521–548.

van de Werfhorst, H. G. & Mijs, J. J. (2010). Achievement inequality and the institutional structure of educational systems: A comparative perspective. *Annual Review of Sociology, 36*, 407–428.

van Gelder, S. (Ed.). (2011). *This changes everything: Occupy Wall Street and the 99% movement.* San Francisco, CA, Berrett-Koehler.

van Kempen, R. & Özüekren, A. S. (1998). Ethnic segregation in cities: New forms and explanations in a dynamic world. *Urban Studies, 35*(10), 1631–1656.

van Rossum, E. J. & Schenk, S. M. (1984). The relationship between learning conception, study strategy and learning. *British Journal of Educational Psychology, 54*(1), 73–83.

van Slyke, D. M. (2006). Agents or stewards: Using theory to understand the government–nonprofit social service contracting relationship. *Journal of Public Administration Research and Theory, 17*(2), 157–187.

van Treeck, T. (2014). Did inequality cause the US financial crisis? *Journal of Economic Surveys, 28*(3), 421–448.

Vecchio, G. M., Gerbino, M., Pastorelli, C., Del Bove, G. & Caprara, G. V. (2007). Multifaceted self-efficacy beliefs as predictors of life satisfaction in late adolescence. *Personality and Individual Differences, 43*(7), 1807–1818.

Vella, F. (1999). Do Catholic schools make a difference? Evidence from Australia. *Journal of Human Resources, 34*(1), 208–224.

Ver Eecke, W. (2003). Adam Smith and Musgrave's concept of merit good. *The Journal of Socio-economics, 31*(6), 701–720.

Verger, A., Bonal, X. & Zancajo, A. (2016). What are the role and impact of public–private partnerships in education? A realist evaluation of the Chilean education quasi-market. *Comparative Education Review, 60*(2), 223–248.

Verkuyten, M. & Thijs, J. (2002). School satisfaction of elementary school children: The role of performance, peer relations, ethnicity and gender. *Social Indicators Research, 59*(2), 203–228.

Vescio, V., Ross, D. & Adams, A. (2008). A review of research on the impact of professional learning communities on teaching practice and student learning. *Teaching and Teacher Education, 24*(1), 80–91.

Vidovich, L. & Currie, J. (2011). Governance and trust in higher education. *Studies in Higher Education, 36*(1), 43–56.

Vining, A. R. & Weimer, D. L. (1990). Government supply and government production failure: A framework based on contestability. *Journal of Public Policy, 10*(1), 1–22.

Voitchovsky, S. (2009). Inequality, growth & sectoral change. In E. Nolan, W. Salverda & T. M. Smeeding (Eds.), *The Oxford handbook of economic inequality.* Oxford, Oxford University Press, pp. 549–574.

von Krogh, G., Ichijo, K. & Nonaka, I. (2000). *Enabling knowledge creation: How to unlock the mystery of tacit knowledge and release the power of innovation.* Oxford, Oxford University Press.

Vosniadou, S. (2013). Conceptual change in learning and instruction: The framework theory approach. In S. Vosniadou (Ed.), *International handbook of research in conceptual change, 2nd edition.* London, Routledge, pp. 11–30.

Vosniadou, S. & Brewer, W. F. (1992). Mental models of the earth: A study of conceptual change in childhood. *Cognitive Psychology, 24*(4), 535–585.

Vossensteyn, J. J. H. (2005). *Perceptions of student price-responsiveness; A behavioural economics exploration of the relationships between socio-economic status, perceptions of financial incentives and student choice.* Enschede, CHEPS/UT.

Waddell, G. R. (2012). Adolescent drug use and the deterrent effect of school-imposed penalties. *Economics of Education Review, 31*(6), 961–969.

Wæraas, A. & Solbakk, M. N. (2009). Defining the essence of a university: Lessons from higher education branding. *Higher Education, 57*(4), 449.

Waite, E., Evans, K. & Kersh, N. (2014). The challenge of establishing sustainable workplace 'Skills for Life' provision in the UK: Organisational 'strategies' and individual 'tactics'. *Journal of Education and Work, 27*(2), 199–219.

Waite, L. J., Leibowitz, A. & Witsberger, C. (1991). What parents pay for: Child care characteristics, quality, and costs. *Journal of Social Issues, 47*(2), 33–48.

Wakeling, P. & Jefferies, K. (2013). The effect of tuition fees on student mobility: The UK and Ireland as a natural experiment. *British Educational Research Journal, 39*(3), 491–513.

Waldo, S. (2007). Efficiency in Swedish public education: competition and voter monitoring. *Education Economics, 15*(2), 231–251.

Walford, G. (1988). The privatisation of British higher education. *European Journal of Education, 23*(1/2), 47–64.

Walford, G. (2002). Classification and framing of the curriculum in evangelical Christian and Muslim schools in England and the Netherlands. *Educational Studies, 28*(4), 403–419.

Walford, G. (2006). *Private education: Tradition and diversity.* London, Continuum.

Walker, D. G. & Jan, S. (2005). How do we determine whether community health workers are cost-effective? Some core methodological issues. *Journal of Community Health, 30*(3), 221–229.

Walker, I. & Zhu, Y. (2008). The college wage premium and the expansion of higher education in the UK. *The Scandinavian Journal of Economics, 110*(4), 695–709.

Walker, I. & Zhu, Y. (2011). Differences by degree: Evidence of the net financial rates of return to undergraduate study for England and Wales. *Economics of Education Review, 30*(6), 1177–1186.

Walshok, M. L. (1995). *Knowledge without boundaries: What America's research universities can do for the economy, the workplace, and the community.* The Jossey-Bass Higher and Adult Education Series. San Francisco, CA, Jossey-Bass.

Wang, M., Shen, R., Novak, D. & Pan, X. (2009). The impact of mobile learning on students' learning behaviours and performance: Report from a large blended classroom. *British Journal of Educational Technology, 40*(4), 673–695.

Warhurst, C., Nickson, D., Commander, J. & Gilbert, K. (2014). 'Role stretch': Assessing the blurring of teaching and non-teaching in the classroom assistant role in Scotland. *British Educational Research Journal, 40*(1), 170–186.

Waslander, S., Pater, C. & Van Der Weide, M. (2010). *Markets in education: An analytical review of empirical research on market mechanisms in education.* OECD Education Working Papers No. 52, EDU/WKP(2010)15. Paris, OECD Publishing.

Watson, D. & Bowden, R. (1999). Why did they do it? The Conservatives and mass higher education, 1979–97. *Journal of Education Policy, 14*(3), 243–256.

Watson, G. & Crossley, M. (2001). Beyond the rational: The strategic management process, cultural change and post-incorporation further education. *Educational Management & Administration, 29*(1), 113–125.

Watson, T. (2009). Inequality and the measurement of residential segregation by income in American neighborhoods. *Review of Income and Wealth, 55*(3), 820–844.

Watt, H. M. & Richardson, P. W. (2007). Motivational factors influencing teaching as a career choice: Development and validation of the FIT-Choice Scale. *The Journal of Experimental Education, 75*(3), 167–202.

Watt, H. M. & Richardson, P. W. (2008). Motivations, perceptions, and aspirations concerning teaching as a career for different types of beginning teachers. *Learning and Instruction, 18*(5), 408–428.

Wechsler, H., Devereaux, R. S., Davis, M. & Collins, J. (2000). Using the school environment to promote physical activity and healthy eating. *Preventive Medicine, 31*(2), S121–S137.

Weis, L. (1990). *Working class without work: High school students in a de-industrializing economy.* New York, Routledge.

Weiss, A. (1995). Human capital vs. signalling explanations of wages. *The Journal of Economic Perspectives, 9*(4), 133–154.

Welch, A. R. (1998). The cult of efficiency in education: Comparative reflections on the reality and the rhetoric. *Comparative Education, 34*(2), 157–175.

Wells, A. S., Slayton, J. & Scott, J. (2002). Defining democracy in the neoliberal age: Charter school reform and educational consumption. *American Educational Research Journal, 39*(2), 337–361.

Wells, J., Barlow, J. & Stewart-Brown, S. (2003). A systematic review of universal approaches to mental health promotion in schools. *Health Education, 103*(4), 197–220.

Wenger, E. (1998). *Communities of practice: Learning, meaning, and identity.* Cambridge, Cambridge University Press.

Wenger, E., McDermott, R. A. & Snyder, W. (2002). *Cultivating communities of practice: A guide to managing knowledge.* Cambridge, MA, Harvard Business Press.

West, A., Hind, A. & Pennell, H. (2004). School admissions and 'selection' in comprehensive schools: Policy and practice. *Oxford Review of Education, 30*(3), 347–369.

West, E. G. & McKee, M. (1983). De Gustibus Est Disputandum: The phenomenon of 'merit wants' revisited. *American Economic Review, 73*(5), 1110–1121.

White House. (2015). *Knowledge and skills for the jobs of the future.* White House briefing. Washington, DC, The White House. Available at www.whitehouse.gov/issues/education/reform.

Whitty, G. (1998). New Labour, education and disadvantage. *Education and Social Justice, 1*(1), 2–8.

Whitty, G. & Edwards, T. (1998). School choice policies in England and the United States: An exploration of their origins and significance. *Comparative Education, 34*(2), 211–227.

Wiborg, S. (2004). Education and social integration: A comparative study of the comprehensive school system in Scandinavia. *London Review of Education, 2*(2), 83–93.

Wigfield, A. & Eccles, J. S. (2000). Expectancy–value theory of achievement motivation. *Contemporary Educational Psychology, 25*(1), 68–81.

Wiggins, A. & Tymms, P. (2002). Dysfunctional effects of league tables: A comparison between English and Scottish primary schools. *Public Money Management, 22*(1), 43–48.

Wilcox, P., Winn, S. & Fyvie-Gauld, M. (2005). 'It was nothing to do with the university, it was just the people': the role of social support in the first-year experience of higher education. *Studies in Higher Education, 30*(6), 707–722.

Wilkinson, G. (2007). Civic professionalism: Teacher education and professional ideals and values in a commercialised education world. *Journal of Education for Teaching, 33*(3), 379–395.

Williams, L. (2015). What is TTIP? And six reasons why the answer should scare you. *The Independent*, 12 October.

Willis, P. E. (1977). *Learning to labor: How working class kids get working class jobs.* New York, Columbia University Press.

Willms, J. D. (2010). School composition and contextual effects on student outcomes. *Teachers College Record, 112*(4), 1008–1037.

Wilson, D. & Piebalga, A. (2008). Performance measures, ranking and parental choice: An analysis of the English School League Tables. *International Public Management Journal, 11*(3), 344–366.

Wilson, J. Q. (1989). *Bureaucracy. What government agencies do and why they do it.* New York, Basic Books.

Winch, P. (2008). *The idea of a social science and its relation to philosophy, 3rd edition.* London, Routledge.

Winters, J. V. (2014). STEM graduates, human capital externalities, and wages in the US. *Regional Science and Urban Economics, 48*, 190–198.

Wisman, J. D. (2013). Wage stagnation, rising inequality and the financial crisis of 2008. *Cambridge Journal of Economics, 37*(4), 921–945.

Witte, J. F. & Thorn, C. A. (1996). Who chooses? Voucher and interdistrict choice programs in Milwaukee. *American Journal of Education, 104*(3), 186–217.

Wohlstetter, P. & Chau, D. (2004). Does autonomy matter? Implementing research-based practices in charter and other public schools. In K. Bulkley & P. Wohlstetter (Eds.), *Taking account of charter schools: What's happened and what's next.* New York, Teachers College Press, pp. 53–71.

Wohlstetter, P., Datnow, A. & Park, V. (2008). Creating a system for data-driven decision-making: Applying the principal–agent framework. *School Effectiveness and School Improvement, 19*(3), 239–259.

Wohlstetter, P., Smith, J. & Malloy, C. L. (2005). Strategic alliances in action: Toward a theory of evolution. *Policy Studies Journal, 33*(3), 419–442.

Wolf, A. (2010). *More than we bargained for: The social and economic costs of national pay bargaining.* London, CentreForum.

Wolf, A. (2011). *Review of vocational education: The Wolf report.* London, Department for Education.

Wolf, A., Aspin, L., Waite, E. & Ananiadou, K. (2010). The rise and fall of workplace basic skills programmes: Lessons for policy and practice. *Oxford Review of Education, 36*(4), 385–405.

Wolf, M. (2001). Will the nation-state survive globalization? *Foreign Affairs, 80*(1), 178–190.

Wood, K. (2000). The experience of learning to teach: Changing student teachers' ways of understanding teaching. *Journal of Curriculum Studies, 32*(1), 75–93.

Wood, L, Egger, M., Gluud, L. L., Schulz, K. F., Juni, P., Altman, G. G., Gluud, C., Martin, R. M., Wood, A. J. G. & Sterne, J. A. C. (2008). Empirical evidence of bias in treatment effect estimates in controlled trials with different interventions and outcomes: Meta-epidemiological study. *British Medical Journal, 336*(7644), 601–605.

Woolner, P., Hall, E., Higgins, S., McCaughey, C. & Wall, K. (2007). A sound foundation? What we know about the impact of environments on learning and the implications for Building Schools for the Future. *Oxford Review of Education, 33*(1), 47–70.

Wyse, D. (2003). The National Literacy Strategy: A critical review of empirical evidence. *British Educational Research Journal, 29*(6), 903–916.

Wyse, D. & Styles, M. (2007). Synthetic phonics and the teaching of reading: The debate surrounding England's 'Rose Report'. *Literacy, 41*(1), 35–42.

Yaacob, N. A., Osman, M. M. & Bachok, S. (2014). Factors influencing parents' decision in choosing private schools. *Procedia-Social and Behavioral Sciences, 153*, 242–253.

Yang, P. Q. & Kayaardi, N. (2004). Who chooses non-public schools for their children? *Educational Studies, 30*(3), 231–249.

Young, H. P. (1996). The economics of convention. *Journal of Economic Perspectives, 10*(2), 105–122.

Yuan, K., Le, V. N., McCaffrey, D. F., Marsh, J. A., Hamilton, L. S., Stecher, B. M. & Springer, M. G. (2013). Incentive pay programs do not affect teacher motivation or reported practices: Results from three randomized studies. *Educational Evaluation and Policy Analysis, 35*(1), 3–22.

Yuen, T. & Byram, M. (2007). National identity, patriotism and studying politics in schools: A case study in Hong Kong. *Compare: A Journal of Comparative and International Education, 37*(1), 23–36.

Zemsky, R., Shapiro, D., Iannozzi, M., Cappelli, P. & Bailey, T. (1998). *Transition from initial education to working life in the United States of America. A report to the Organisation for Economic Co-operation and Development (OECD) as part of a comparative study of transitions from initial education to working life in 14 member countries.* NCPI Project Paper No. 1. Washington, DC, Office of Educational Research and Improvement.

Zheng, S., Rosson, M. B., Shih, P. C. & Carroll, J. M. (2015). Understanding student motivation, behaviors and perceptions in MOOCs. In *Proceedings of the 18th ACM Conference on Computer Supported Cooperative Work & Social Computing.* New York, ACM, pp. 1882–1895.

Zimmer, R. & Buddin, R. (2007). Getting inside the black box: Examining how the operation of charter schools affects performance. *Peabody Journal of Education, 82*(2–3), 231–273.

Zimmer, R. W. & Toma, E. F. (2000). Peer effects in private and public schools across countries. *Journal of Policy Analysis and Management, 19*(1), 75–92.

INDEX

Page numbers in **bold** denote tables, those in *italics* denote figures.

"Bigfoot, Who Are You"

"A Bigfoot Discovery Book for Kids"

Frank Hendersen

Table of Contents

Chapter 1: We've All Heard of Bigfoot

Bigfoot tales date back beyond recorded history and span the globe. Tales of seven-foot-tall hairy men haunting the woods, occasionally terrifying campers, lumberjacks, hikers, and others may be found all across the United States from the tip of Washington state to the bottom of the swamps of Florida.

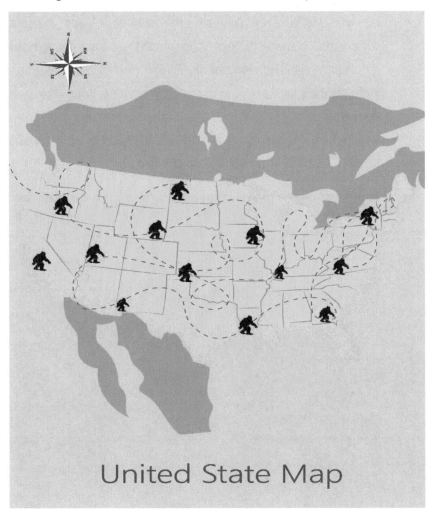

United State Map

Bigfoot stories have become part of regional folklore as they have become part of oral tradition, or, storytelling.

★ Bigfoot's presence in Oregon dates back to 1904 when residents in the Sixes River area of the Coast Range reported seeing a hairy "wild man."

★ Miners on top Mount St. Helens claimed to have been assaulted by enormous "apes" in 1924. Local Native Americans then shared their knowledge about tsiatko hirsute "wild Indians" of the woods. Most Native American tribes across the country have long-held legends about the woodsman. These beings are known as feral tribes or "stick Indians" by others. Many Native Americans believe that Sasquatch is no different from any other animal seen in the woods. They occur with birds, bears, and fish in their culture.

2

★ Lumberjacks and woodworkers east and west of the Cascade Mountains began reporting seeing animals and discovering their massive tracks along logging routes after 1958, boosting popular awareness of Bigfoot. Since then they have been seen crossing highways at night, marching stealthily over woodland and mountain terrain, and digging for and devouring ground squirrels in rock heaps, according to witnesses.

Chapter 2: What Was That?

Bigfoot could be a Gigantopithecus.

No, that's not an insult!

We don't know much about Gigantopithecus except that it was bigger than a gorilla and had human-like teeth. We don't even know when it went extinct. Sounds like a bigfoot, right? It gets a little more complicated when we admit that we aren't sure that Gigantopithecus are completely extinct...

If bigfoot isn't a Gigantopithecus, it could be another kind of ape.

The orangutan, the closest living cousin of Gigantopithecus, matches several of the traits that eyewitnesses say bigfoot has. Orangutans have long, reddish-brown hair, are extremely clever, and show a strong interest in human behavior, just like bigfoot. Although they are not extremely talkative, they will occasionally produce loud, wailing sounds to warn other orangutans about their presence. Again, just like bigfoot...

So, bigfoot could also be a type of orangutan!

The reason that bigfoot researchers believe this could be possible is because orangutans live a little differently than other species of ape in nature; they live on their own, or solitarily, compared to other apes and monkeys who live in groups and families like we do.

No matter what the explanation may be, all of them explain why it is so rare to see a bigfoot and why no skeletons have been found yet.

As human cities have expanded into their habitat, it makes sense for an intelligent animal that wants to be alone to push further back, deep into the deep forests or up into the mountains to escape, and if it was smart enough, it might maybe hide from humans for hundreds of years. After all, the chances of a fast-food restaurant or shopping mall being built high in the caves of a mountain or the depths of a forest reserve are pretty small!

Aliens?

Maybe Bigfoot is a UFO pilot who has landed on Earth to do research. On the flip side, what if bigfoot and his friends are "guinea pigs" to test our Earth's health?

As an example, on December 9, 1974, at 10:30 p.m., dairy farmer William Bosak of Frederic, Wisconsin, was driving home after a co-op meeting when he almost collided with a globular UFO on the road in front of him, its bottom half obscured in fog.

A six-foot-tall ape-like creature with reddish-brown fur covering its body except for its face, which was hairless, and unique pointed ears stood inside the clear dome on the top of the spacecraft. It seemed like it was controlling a control panel.

Just as William drove by, the spacecraft lifted from the ground and disappeared into the sky.

Notice here that the description of the creature - six foot tall and covered in reddish-brown hair –it matches with most accounts from interactions with bigfoot!

A Government Experiment?

The United States Army isn't unfamiliar with the idea of changing the human genetic code to engineer supersoldiers. A paper written in 2020, *CCDC CBC-TR-1599, Cyborg Soldier 2050: Human/Machine Fusion and the Implications for the Future of the DOD,* written by army doctors explores the not-too-far-in-the-future idea of genetically modified soldiers taking to the battlefield. Think; bigfoot is muscular, able to hide, tall, and supremely strong – remove the bigfoot aspect, and you've got traits any army general would want.

A Fake!

Less fun, some think that bigfoot could be a big fake!

Casts of enormous footprints are one of the most common pieces of sasquatch evidence. Those who doubt that bigfoot exists argue that this evidence is easy to whip up at home, and doesn't prove much – all it takes is some plaster from the hardware store and a fake foot, and the sounds that bigfeet are said to make could easily be created on a computer with basic software.

Chapter 3: Not the Only One

Bigfoot is a tale that has no bounds. There are over 50 distinct versions of Bigfoot across the world, with just as many of the same features; a hard-to-capture, hairy, upright-walking, humanlike creature.

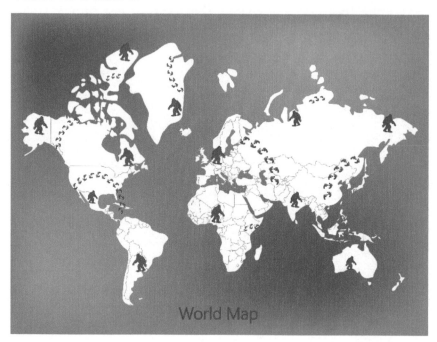

World Map

The Yeti

The Yeti, the Abominable Snowman, is a strange monster who is claimed to live in Asia's high mountains. It is known to leave traces in the snow and to live below the Himalayan snow line, meaning it doesn't live in the mountain, but close to the base. Much of this area hasn't been explored even to this day, leaving the Yeti free to roam the place.

The Yeti is described as strong, with mostly white hair that may also come in shades of dark grey or reddish-brown, and a weight range of 200 to 400 pounds. (between 91 and 181 kilos) It stands around 6 feet (1.8 meters) tall, which is small in comparison to Bigfoot in North America, and can come in a few different muscular shapes.

The Skunk Ape

Skunk Apes are thought to be descended from orangutans who escaped from traveling circuses that frequented Florida in the 1950s, researchers believe.

Skunk Apes have shaggy reddish to dark brown hair, are around seven feet tall, and weigh between 400 and 500 pounds on average. Then there's the odor, which has been described as a disgusting combination of wet dog, skunk, and rotting eggs.

The Sarasota Sheriff's Department received an anonymous letter, and two pictures from a woman on December 29, 2000, claiming to show what her husband claimed was an escaped orangutan eating fruit from their back porch.

The photographs were shot when she walked outdoors to investigate a series of deep hooting noises on the third night – the first two, the creature had come up and eaten fruit off of her porch. The creature disappeared into the bushes after clicking two shots, each with a dazzling flash. Its "terrible scent" lingered long after it left. She left their dog leashed in the backyard, and it never came back.

Orang Pendek and Orang Mawas

The Orang Pendek, Indonesian meaning "Short Person," is the name for the creature claimed to live in distant, mountainous jungles on the island of Sumatra, according to Indonesian legends. Forest tribes, local people, Dutch colonists, scientists, and visitors are said to have witnessed and documented the animal for at least 100 years.

Witnesses agree that the animal is bipedal, it walks on two legs, and is a ground-dwelling monkey with short fur that stands between 30 and 60 inches tall.

The Orang Mawas, also known as the Orang Dalam, is a Malaysian folklore creature said to live in the jungles of Johor, Malaysia. It's around 10 feet tall, bipedal, and coated with black fur, and it's been seen eating fish and invading orchards. The monster, which the local Orang Asli people name "hantu jarang gigi," or "Snaggle-toothed Ghost," has been seen several times.

Seeing how they are similar?

While Orang Pendek and other similar species have long been thought to live in the jungles of Sumatra, Indonesia, and Southeast Asia, reported sightings have been concentrated in the Kerinci Regency in central Sumatra, particularly within the boundaries of Kerinci Seblat National Park (Taman Nasional Kerinci Seblat or TNKS).

The park is located 2 degrees south of the equator, inside of the Bukit Barisan mountain range, and has some of the world's most isolated primary rainforest. Perfect, right?

The Orang Rimba of Bukit Duabelas talk about a monster called "Hantu Pendek," which closely looks like the Orang Pendek. Hantu Pendek, whose name translates to "short ghost," is regarded to be a supernatural being or demon rather than an animal.

D'Sonoqu

The D'Sonoqu (or Dzunukwa) mythology may be found all across the world, from Canada and the Pacific Northwest to the jungles of South America. While Bigfoot is sometimes shown as gigantic, the D'Sonoqu might be a whole separate species. They combine the characteristics of monkeys, apes, and humans.

Francois de Loys, a Swiss geologist, someone who studies the Earth's rocks and formations, returned from the Venezuelan jungle with a spectacular picture in the 1920s. A five-foot-tall ape, propped up on a carton – an ape that nobody else had seen before, with a strange, long, crested face almost like it was wearing a mask.

Professor Georges Montandon, one of France's most prominent zoologists at the time, confirmed the photograph and named the new species Ameranthropoides Loysi after de Loys. However, the story was widely called a fake and was quickly forgotten.

Legends of apelike animals in South America back up de Loys' discoveries. The creatures are said to be roughly five feet tall, bipedal (they walk on two feet, like humans), and noted for their unusual communication style, which involves loud whistling. D'Sonoqu masks, or tribal masks, are the ape's two most distinguishing features; a strong circular eye ridge, where a human's eyebrow would be, and a puckered mouth that represents the whistling sound they make.

Yowie

The Yowie is thought to be Australia's Bigfoot, with many ape-like characteristics, causing some to think that they could be a previously unknown species of big ape or prehistoric humans. The Yowie is one of the more dangerous Bigfoot species, with reports of it ripping the heads off of kangaroos and dogs. It has also been observed attacking humans.

According to Aboriginal stories, the Yowie stands 5 to 9 feet tall, has a big crimson mouth, and talon-like claws. It's also worth mentioning that the Yowie has two huge fang-like canines that set it apart from other Bigfoot species. Its fur is normally dark or reddish in color. Watch out for those teeth!

Yeren

The Yeren, also known as the Yiren, Yeh Ren, Chinese Wildman, or Man-Monkey, is China's Bigfoot. The Yeren is a strange ape that lives in China's mountains, with it being seen usually in the distant Hubei region, where few people other than locals go.

It has reddish-brown hair and a big jaw like the Yowie. It stands six to eight feet tall (in some extreme cases, up to 12 feet tall), and is normally friendly but shy near humans.

Over 400 people have reported seeing the Yeren, according to newspapers in China. The Chinese government has combed the country in pursuit of the Yeren – that's right, the government there has been looking for it!

There have been several footprints and hair traces discovered. The creature, like the Yeti or Sasquatch, has never been proven by science and remains a legend and a subject of cryptozoology, the study of unknown creatures. It is reported to be less strong and stocky than its other relatives, despite how big it is.

This doesn't mean they can't cause chaos, though! A news story from 1980 detailed the account of a lady who claimed to have been kidnapped by one and had a child with it. When the offspring passed away, a study of his bones revealed that he had traits of both man and ape!

Bukit Timah Monkey Man

The Bukit Timah Monkey Man is a monkey that, according to stories, has been living in the Bukit Timah region of Singapore, safely hiding in the jungles from anyone who could hurt him.

The Monkey Man is claimed to have a greyish coat of fur and a height of about 6-9 feet, and its upright-walking motion is supposed to mimic that of a person closely.

Chapter 4: Common Features

Most eyewitness accounts report bigfeet that are colored anywhere from black to brown, reddish-brown, and red. These coats, their fur, are usually long and shaggy like a carpet. They also claim that Bigfoot's face is a little flat, with wide cheekbones, a square jaw, and a mouth that juts out of their chin a little. Some people have claimed that the being has eyes that glow red in the dark, like a deer or cat in either yellow or red.

Bigfoot families will live in tiny family groups of two to four; however, sometimes single males can be spotted. Typically families of bigfeet will follow herds of deer through the year.

Nesting Behaviors

Experts agree that bigfeet have evolved to avoid people, and are loyal to their homes as long as they aren't being bothered by humans.

They sleep in largely temporary handmade huts padded with whatever plants they can find. Ferns, moss, bear grass, soft evergreen or rhododendron branches, and leaves make up the padding like a mattress.

The nest is usually abandoned once it has been discovered, and there is evidence that bigfeet families even keep pets like abducted puppies and kittens.

Movement

When most bigfoot are seen walking, it is easy to notice their smooth, long, and fluent stride with wide arm swings like they are skiing or riding a motorcycle. This is because they have a "compliant gait" which means they don't lock their knees when they walk, like humans do. If you're really interested, search for the Patterson Tape on YouTube. This famous tape, taken in the sixties, gives a good view of a bigfoot moving. While the tape is still debated today as to if it is real or fake, the famous ape expert Jane Goodall, who is considered one of the highest experts on apes, has looked at the tape and said it is likely real...

Running

Sightings of running bigfeet make up for around 10% of all sightings. Their top speed, when running, has been compared to the speed of a horse. That makes them pretty fast! They're even able to catch up to vehicles driving at up to 40 miles per hour and run uphill at the same rate.

Swimming

They appear to be strong swimmers, as seen by lucky witnesses who have seen them swimming to and from the uninhabitable tiny islands off the coast of British Columbia – in fact, they're able to kick and perform well in the water, which is shocking for their size.

Throwing Objects When Confronted

Their upper-body power is famous, being able to lift basketball-sized rocks and throw them to scare off intruders with ease, lifting the edges of mobile homes, cars, or trailers, lifting and throwing full 50-gallon drums that can weigh hundreds of pounds, and spirally twisting the trunks of small trees, possibly as territorial or markers.

Scaring Instead of Fighting

Of course, we can't brush over the most obvious and important fact here; bigfoot families are most likely responding in the way that any animal would; they are protecting their young. This behavior matches many others in the animal kingdom, including the closest connection, primates, that are also known to use rocks, sticks, and pebbles as weapons in protecting their young.

Communication

Bigfoot moves in quiet for the most part. Long-distance communication appears to be accomplished by hitting boulders or thick branches against other rocks or dead trees in a patterned, repeating knocking sound, almost like making music if they aren't using grunts, growls, and screams.

They appear to rely on vocalizations, sounds made with their mouths like grunts or screams, more than diurnal primates because they are a nocturnal species. Starting with whistling, they may generate a wide range of noises, including moans, howls, hoots, grunts, extremely deep growls, roars ("like a lion from the bottom of a 50-gallon drum"), and frightening screams that rise from a low roar over many seconds. Rarely, they make melodic and imitative noises or complicated vocalizations that resemble a basic language, called "samurai chatter."

Specific Calls

The "Ohio" Call

The forests of southern Ohio are the state's thickest and least inhabited territory. It's also home to the eerie 'Ohio Howl,' an unexplained animal sound.

The combination of a howl and moan was first recorded in the Ohio River highlands north of Wellsville near the West Virginia border in the mid-1990s.

The howl transforms into a siren-like shriek. Similar screams have been reported in Kentucky and the Ohio River basin, as well as in the Georgia and north Florida woodlands and the Pacific Northwest.

You can make this sound as well! Start out with a deep, scary moan and quickly change it into a shriek!

Wood Knocks

Bigfeet are thought to communicate by beating sticks against trees, according to several bigfoot experts. Bigfeet frequently mimic human-made wood knocks to warn us to their presence. In essence, wood knocking is both a method of communication, and as a warning sign to announce "this is my territory, please stay clear!"

Wood knocks, according to researchers, are utilized in a variety of ways to send different meanings depending on the setting. Single loud wood knocks, accompanied by a loud whoop or other sound, could be interpreted as a "are you there?"

The wood knock element of a knock/vocal combination could be used for two purposes: punctuation ("!") and confirmation (".") just like we use in speech and writing.

When in close proximity and/or when danger is present, softer wood knocks appear to be employed to keep track of each other, then there's the intimidation type of wood knock, which field researchers have noticed on a few instances.

While many people assume that wood knocking is made by slamming trees or sticks together, some researchers suggest that Bigfoot could just be clapping or using his hands to make the sound. This strategy is used by many researchers to identify bigfeet and establish their presence. Some researchers have noted the use of wood knocks in response to non-wood knock sounds, such as the closing of car doors or the moving of equipment, indicating that it is likely that primarily wood knocks are used for announcing presence and occupation of marked territory. Some bigfoot experts have also noticed the use of wood knocks to count out the number of encroachers in territory as if the information was being communicated to others over long distances – for instance, two knocks would indicate that two bigfoot seekers have entered a territory.

Whoops

Whoops are the usual bigfoot sound, and they sound like just what their name suggests. The best whoops start low and quickly increase in tone and volume before ending suddenly. Try it out!

In primates, howling and whooping are also used with territorial defense and mate guarding. Their enlarged basihyal or hyoid bone, which allows them to emit powerful vocalizations, is responsible for these noises. A loud, deep guttural yell or howl is the main vocal sound. While we can't do it perfectly, since we don't have the hyoid bone, we can get pretty close!

There are a few types of whoop sounds that have been heard by many researchers and firsthand witnesses:

"The Scream"

This piecing, high-pitched scream is often compared to a woman's shriek of horror. It's classic – and you'll know it when you hear it, as this shriek often starts the human fight or flight response in motion. It makes you want to run away when you hear it!

"The Grunt"

These are frequently used as warnings against those getting too close, but have also been observed in conversational use between bigfeet. Bigfoot grunts are deeper and louder than people can make, because of their larger lungs.

"The Bark"

These vocalizations are grunts, but forced out quickly, rather than slowly as in a grunt. If you've ever tried to mimic the sound of a big dog barking, you will reach a similar effect to the sound bigfeet have been recorded making.

Samurai Chatter

Al Berry, a skeptical reporter researching the Bigfoot, and his friend Ron Moorehead recorded the Samurai Chatter recordings in the Sierra Nevada foothills of California in 1971.

They were pitching their tent somewhere between Lake Tahoe and Yosemite National Park for the night. They were awakened one night by some rather odd cries. Of course, he organized and produced the recordings, which are widely accessible online.

The name comes from Japanese kabuki performances, in which exaggerated sounds are used to express action and emotion onstage. It is believed by most bigfoot researchers that so-called "Samurai Chatter" serves as an early language, meaning it is a language that exists but is not fully developed yet. Think of it as "caveman speak."

Howls and Human Alarms

Howls, in bigfoot language, are likely very similar to their use in the primate world. Primates use howls to call out to each other as a sort of homing call or location device. Bigfeet likely also use these calls to locate each other or share information, such as the location of food, a hurt member of their family unit, or to alert other members to danger.

It isn't uncommon for firsthand witnesses of bigfoot to recall or even record high-pitched calls directly before a sighting or associated event such as a rock being thrown. The high-pitched call or scream likely relates to the primate world where the call is used as a multitool – to ward off humans, and also to warn other bigfeet in the area that humans are near.

Chapter 5: When Can I See One?

Most animals either have a period of little activity sometime in the year or "hibernate" like bears do, in which they find shelter and lie low for a time to rest and wait out the cold months. The question is, then, do bigfeet hibernate?

Currently, there are no known primates, which Bigfoot would be considered, that enter into what we know as hibernation. In areas that are cold enough to make hibernation necessary, it is likely that the bigfoot population would migrate to a warmer climate to stay, or find a way to keep out of the weather until it starts to warm up again.

Knowing this, we can make a few educated guesses.

Fall is a good time to stock up on food and look for comfortable places to stay throughout the winter. It is natural that bigfeet would be busy settling in and storing away food for the winter, so it is likely you can see one during the fall months.

During the winter, bigfeet will probably be nestled in waiting out the winter, making it unlikely to see one during the colder months.

Spring is also a strong contender for the busiest time for bigfoot populations. Why? With the growth of new vegetation and breeding seasons of most prey animals falling under this period, food will be plentiful, and there's no better time, as food stored for the winter period is likely beginning to grow dry at this point. It will be high-time for getting out of their hides and burrows to find food. On top of these points, spring likely falls within breeding time for bigfoot populations; young will be born at this stage of the season.

What Else is Out There?

Bigfoot sightings are frequently paired with other strange phenomena. Could they be connected? While firsthand bigfoot accounts paired with paranormal sightings may or may not be correlated, it is important to have an understanding ahead of time to respond appropriately, should you come across one of these situations.

Orbs

Many people believe that unusual balls of light seen on still pictures or videos are spirits exiting in our world.

Orbs come in different colors, beyond clear, which is the most common type. Investigators over time have narrowed down what these colors could mean.

White

White or silver orbs are thought to be kind or helpful spirits, but they might also signal that a soul or energy is stranded or trapped where they don't belong.

Red

Warm red or orange orbs are said to be warm and protecting spirits. They might also represent the spirit of a guardian or a caregiver, someone who was always on the lookout, like a mother, teacher, or nurse.

Black

Brown or dark-colored orbs have a reputation for being nasty or angry spirits, although they might simply be sad spirits or warning the person seeing them that the place they are is loaded with negative energy.

Green

Green is usually connected with nature, and in the case of orbs, it often represents oneness with the Earth and the heart - the connection between the body, soul, and the Earth. It can also refer to souls who have never lived on Earth.

Blue

Blue orbs often are calming or healing energy or spirit. It might also mean the truth, especially if you're looking for answers or attempting to communicate with a specific ghost from the afterlife.

Why An Orb May be Something Else

The fact is that some orbs are caused by dust, insects, mold spores, or pollen – the things that are always in the air, we just never notice them.

Bugs

Because insects have a larger density than dust – they're thicker and heavier, these orbs are brighter on camera. These will be very easy to spot!

Rain

Because raindrops contain the majority of their mass at the bottom owing to gravity, the light from the flash enters the raindrop along the path of least resistance, which is straight out the top. This is why they'll look like they're flying up toward the sky.

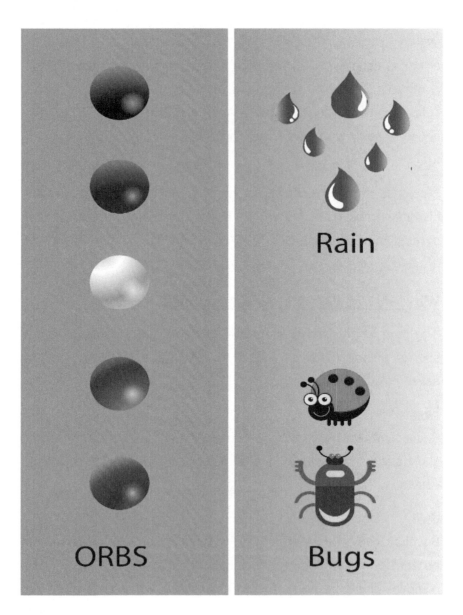

ORBS

Rain

Bugs

Snow

You've probably heard that no two snowflakes are precisely the same, right? It's true! Orbs that are truthfully snow will look unalike because of the water content in each flake, which will always be different.

Dust

The truth is that you can capture a ball of dust in any color of the rainbow. Think about it. How many distinct colors are there in today's fabrics? You can easily catch any color of the rainbow from any shirt or blanket!

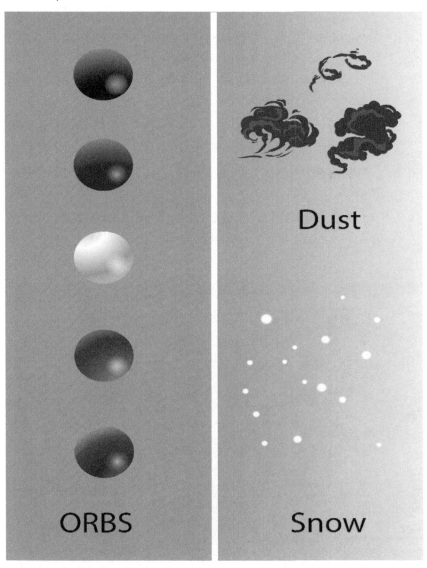

ORBS

Dust

Snow

Chapter 6: I'm Seeing Bigfoot! What Do I Do?

Ok, you're seeing or have seen bigfoot. What next? You have to act fast!

1. The most important thing to remember is to KEEP CALM! Remember that you may be experiencing a once-in-a-lifetime experience and will want to record every detail. Be ready to move out of the way, if the creature moves toward you.

2. Not everything you see is a bigfoot. First, rule out all other options. After that, you can start trying to figure things out. Are there animals in your area that could match the description? Could this be a prank?

3. Record everything if you can. If not, draw pictures of what you saw and the surroundings around it.

4. Record the details as soon as you can on paper or video. Make sure you give "reference points" as you talk. "I'm around 10 feet from the large oak tree, and the ship is 30 feet past that, near the car." If you don't have the chance to make these notes, make them as soon as possible afterward.

5. If anyone else saw, have them write down or record their observations. Investigators want to know what you saw, so don't talk about it with them! (At least until after your observations have been taken down).

6. Check for broken branches and limbs in the path of where the bigfoot walked to see if there is any collectible hair that has been left behind; remember, the bigfoot is covered in it, they probably left some behind! Use gloves if you can, and bag the hair samples. Make sure to label the bag with the time, date, and location of the sample.

7. Report the incident to a research group right away so that it may be investigated. There are a number of similar organizations operating all around the world that can help.

If you come up on a bigfoot footprint, or what's called a track, you'll probably want to take a cast of it!

To take a cast of footprints, you don't need much!

- ★ Craft plaster (Plaster of Paris is a really common brand, but there are plenty out there. Your guardian likely already has some around the house!)

- ★ Water

- ★ A container and paddle or spoon-like device for mixing the water and plaster.

<u>Once you have your materials, you can get to work!</u>

1. Mix the water and plaster in the plastic cup, 1 part water to 2 parts plaster. It should have the same feel as pancake batter. Fill the track (the footprint) with enough plaster to fill it up. Within 10 minutes of being mixed, it will begin to harden. You can scrape any extra off the top to get a flat cast of the print.

2. Allow it to sit for 30 minutes to 1 hour. If it's in a safe area, you can leave it overnight, but if it's not, you can dig around and underneath it to get it out once it's hardened. It's still fragile, so don't try to pull it out of the ground, because you could break it like a clay plate.

3. Using a brush, remove the dirt from the cast. You can wipe it down with a moist towel after it has dried for another day or so to remove any lasting dirt.

Why Do Some People See Bigfoot Multiple Times?

Don't worry – it isn't likely that they have some special ability like "the sixth sense" where people see ghosts.

To understand why some "hunters" have multiple encounters, we need to understand "the Observable Effect." The behavior of African mountain gorillas is used to support the observable effect argument. It is assumed that Gigantopithecus in North America would live similarly.

* Surviving Gigantopithecus would form family groups, similar to African mountain gorillas.
* Like African mountain gorillas, Gigantopithecus would stay in the same places for years.
* Gigantopithecus, like African mountain gorillas, would be strictly herbivores.
* African flora and trees are similar to those found in North America.
* Mountain gorillas feed in tropical African woods when Gigantopithecus would browse in North American coniferous forests that are similar.

If the number of surviving Gigantopithecus (bigfoots) in North America is anywhere between 2000 and 6000, with a breeding population of around 300, there are many more deer and elk sharing the same ecosystem.

Really, the deer and elk would cover up any signs of bigfeet being around!

Did You See A UFO Too?

Do you believe you've seen a UFO? More than 70,000 reports of UFO sightings are received by UFO research organizations around the world each year.

Here are some pointers to assist you in figuring out what that strange light in the sky is.

1. Many people have seen something in the sky that they couldn't explain at first, but be patient, thought may often help you both identify that mystery light and improve your stargazing skills.

2. Strangely enough, take a look at heatmaps available online of bigfoot sightings through arcgis, then compare the heatmap to the one available through the UFO research organization MUFON; you'll start to see that the same

locations on the map are highlighted for both UFOs and Bigfoot. Are the two related?

3. It seems like it could be true, especially considering witness stories – in fact, many bigfoot witnesses have come forward explaining that they had a UFO encounter during or shortly after a bigfoot sighting.

What Could That Have Been?

Okay, now, you've seen a bigfoot and now think you're seeing a UFO! Don't run for your camera just yet; make sure it's a UFO you're seeing first!

Frisbees

The toy, which is shaped like a flying saucer, is usually connected with fake UFO sightings because they're easy to get and easy to use.

The Moon

A woman reported a "bright stationary object" floating in the air for half an hour to South Wales Police in 2007. The police investigators quickly found out that the call was about the moon.

Planes

During the Cold War, many top-secret, high-flying spy planes were mistaken for UFOs. UFO spotters in the 1950s and 1960s were horrified and thrilled by the strange aircraft witnessed skimming across the clouds.

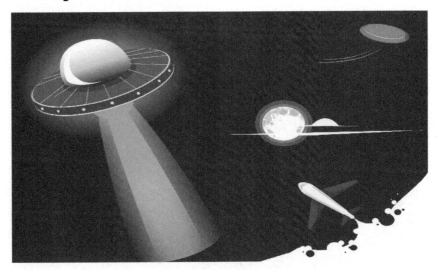

Paper Lanterns

Many UFO reports of orange lights in the sky can be attributed to paper lanterns used at Chinese New Year.

Stars and Planets

The British UFO Research Association calculated that more than a third of all UFO encounters were just the result of seeing stars and planets more clearly than usual. Venus is a frequent one, as it is highly visible during certain points of the year.

Blimps and Balloons

Could it just be a balloon or a drone? While seeing a blimp or a balloon isn't common, they still sometimes can be spotted in the sky; especially around sports games.

Rockets

Many Los Angeles residents rushed to social media after the SpaceX Falcon 9 launched in December, believing the object floating through the sky surrounded by a white trail of smoke was an alien spaceship.

If You See a UFO During a Bigfoot Sighting

Ok, the chances of it being a fake have been eliminated; now it's time to file a report.

To assist more experienced viewers in identifying the object, contact your local astronomy club and have the following information handy:

★ The date and time of the event.

★ How long did you spend looking at this object? How long did it take to complete its journey?

★ How bright was it in comparison to the brightest stars? Did the brightness change?

★ When you first saw this object, where were you?

After you've collected this information, make sure to try and get a clear photograph or video of the object if there is enough time remaining after the shock of seeing it has worn off.

* The same tips and techniques of taking photos and video under normal conditions apply. Try and get a good angle and good lighting!

* Hold the camera steady – be sure to control your breathing and not yell or talk, to keep from shaking the camera.

* Remember; UFO sightings are over as quickly as they start. Use your time getting the best footage you can, rather than focusing on how long you can record.

Refer to the steps earlier in this chapter for sighting bigfoot and creating a report. Run through the both of these lists, making sure that you've made a report that is as complete as possible.

Chapter 7: Tracking Bigfoot Yourself

Tracking bigfoot means examining a variety of landscape features, including footprints, trails, bedding, feeding signs, scat, scrapes, hair, bone, chews, feathers, and kill sites. All of these provide information about the creatures in our environment, allowing us to become more aware of and comprehend bigfoot's existence.

Use Online Heatmaps

Of course, one of the best places to go searching for bigfoot is where someone already reported seeing one!

Utilize this list of resources to find more information on bigfoot, of course, but also to find bigfoot sighting heatmaps:

1. BFRO – Bigfoot Field Researchers Organization
2. ARCGIS
3. GISLounge
4. Kaggle
5. Google Maps

What better place to start than where people have already seen one?

Spotting Bigfoot Tracks

You'll know them when you see them! They range in size from 4"-5", making it clear when you've found a baby bigfoot's footprint or an adult bigfoot's footprint.

The average length of the 702 prints (collected over nearly 50 years) is 15.6 inches, with a range of 4 to 27 inches and a mean length across of 0.45 times the length.

As a side note, be aware of handprints as well!

Compared to a human hand, you'll definitely be able to tell that a bigfoot has been around! The fingers on a bigfoot's hand are much larger, and the fingers are much shorter.

Try looking at the palm of your hand – feel along the space where your thumb muscle is – a bigfoot will not have this feature on their hand! The palm will also be much wider.

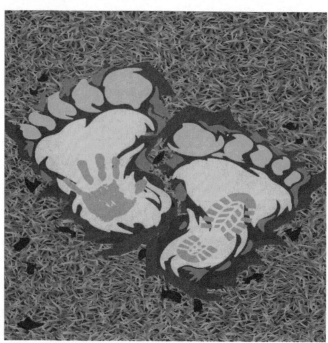

Tunnels and Barrows

In fact, some bigfoot experts lay their stake on that bigfoot lives exclusively underground because this could be an excellent way to avoid detection since, in the wild, the chances of deep-penetrating scanning technology being used is fairly low – bigfoot, as a species, could easily go about their lives with little interruption or chance of coming across human habitation, deep beneath the ground in dug-out tunnel systems, like moles.

Nests, Lays, and Beds

Many bigfoot investigators have come across signs that bigfoot families bed down in temporary lean-to style structures consisting of logs or downed trees put together in a shelter formation or, in areas where they can, bed down in nest formations within caves and cave systems – either way, the ultimate goal is to be hidden away; as you can expect, with a bigfoot!

Les Stroud in the television show Survivorman Bigfoot found a few of these and asked the obvious question, "-if these are out in the middle of nowhere and go unreported, they rule out hoaxes. Why are they here?"

Urine and feces

Animal feces is known as scat, and it can reveal a lot about the animal that deposited it. Scat is used by many mammals, animals that breathe air and have live babies, particularly carnivores, to express specific information to their neighbors. This could include details about the animal's age, gender, health, and disposition.

In the case of finding bigfoot feces, we do have a reference point; a piece is currently part of a traveling experience, Expedition: Bigfoot! The same is a whopping thirty-six inches long, to be expected for bigfoot's size, and is dark brown in color, also to be expected, judging from the cryptid's omnivorous diet. Knowing this, when tracking a bigfoot, a feces sample would be expected to be as similarly large, dark-colored, and is likely to contain embedded elements such as undigestible leaves, fruit seeds or husks, and small animal bones.

Several hoax fecal samples have come up over the years, leading to the question "where does the bigfoot poop go?"

The answer is actually quite simple.

1. Just as bigfoot buries their dead like other animals such as elephants, proving that this behavior is possible, they also bury their feces. For this idea, look no further than pet housecats and their wild relatives – they cover their feces in an attempt to hide their scent from predators.

2. Living in such wild and remote areas, any feces created has the chance to sink into the ground before it is found.

Signs on Vegetation or Parts Left Behind

With tracking bigfoot we're in luck here, something that big will knock leaves and branches off of trees – this includes pulled-up trees, broken branches, moved rocks, or significant dents in tall-growing grasses.

We have to remember that bigfoot is a huge creature; it's bound to leave at least some evidence behind, no matter how good it is at avoiding humans – this can include fingernails, toenails, hair and skin samples left behind as it moves through the limbs, branches, and leaves of the forest.

Bones

Bones are another intriguing sign to uncover while tracking animals. Skulls are the most useful bones to uncover, as they may often be used to identify an animal down to species level. Skulls may reveal a lot about an animal, such as what its dominant senses are, what it consumes, how it finds food, its approximate age, and much more. Of course, bigfoot bones are incredibly rare, and most often are hoaxes when hunters claim to find them, but they're an important idea to keep in mind, as, since bigfoot exists, there of course have to be bones out there somewhere.

Killsites

Carnivorous creatures such as birds of prey, weasels, wild cats, wild dogs, bears, and other predators leave behind their leftovers. Kill sites, even if they are gross, may teach you a lot about animal tracking, including the lives of both the predator and its prey.

As bigfoot has been confirmed to be an omnivore, potential sites where a deer or other large prey was consumed could be a great hint toward if a bigfoot population is in or has been in an area, depending on how fresh the features of the area are, like the blood being present still, or bones having not turned to dust yet.

Tools to Utilize

Alright, you know how to track bigfoot; what about some extra tools to accomplish the job? There have to be some out there, right?

Bigfoot Call Apps

Of course, plenty of research has been done on bigfoot calls and the noises they can make. Multiple cell phone applications have shown up, some free, that utilize recorded bigfoot calls, some fake and some taken from real recordings, to help bigfoot searchers on their hunts.

Range Finders

Range finders are typically used by hunters; they are designed to assist hunters in determining the exact distance to their target – they are often used for ranged observation and marking spots frequented by bigfoot populations within the bigfoot investigation community.

Trail Cameras

Trail cameras are battery-powered camera or video devices that work like home security cameras, are triggered by movement, or in some cases, noise. They can have their files digitally downloaded or physically downloaded by flash drive or storage SD card.

Bigfoot Calls app

 Range Finders

Trail Cameras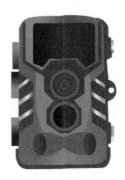

Thermal Cameras

Like trail cameras, thermal cameras take video or pictures after being triggered by the presence of body heat generated by a living being.

Audio Recording Devices

Similar to outdoor cameras, outdoor audio recording devices are triggered at a significant decibel level (loud sounds,) allowing the user to pull the sounds later off the device.

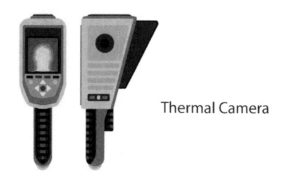

Thermal Camera

Audio recording device

Why Hasn't Bigfoot Been Spotted on These Devices?

Bigfoot has been spotted on a few trail cameras here and there, with some of the reports being revealed as hoaxes or plain fakes later on. Outside of these times, the lack of trail cam footage is often used as ammunition by skeptics looking for reasons why bigfoot does not exist.

The reason, can be linked back to human scents, called pheromones, the smells we leave behind at locations after a visit. These pheromones can last for a few hours up to days, and deliver subtle chemical signals to wildlife that we have been present in an area recently – these pheromones would alert a bigfoot family, in an essence, to "stay away, humans are present!"

Chapter 8: The Bigfoot World

Just like the existence of bigfoot, the answer is probably right under your nose!

Learning More About Bigfoot

1. Search google for bigfoot keywords.
2. Follow bigfoot organizations listed here on social media.
3. Set a Google Alert for bigfoot keywords to stay abreast of new links.
4. Check out Wikipedia for extended links. While you always must be careful on open source websites like Wikipedia, they can be a valuable branching tree of information from many websites.
5. Watch bigfoot shows.
6. Of course, check out your local bookstore or library! Libraries can be great resources for finding (and reading for free!) older books on bigfoot and other cryptids.

And of course, most obviously, go out on your own bigfoot hunts! Practice makes perfect!

Associations and Events

Bigfoot Field Researchers Association

https://www.bfro.net/

The BFRO, which was founded in 1995, is today the oldest and largest organization of its kind, consisting of a virtual community of scientists, journalists, and specialists from many fields. The BFRO's researchers are working on a variety of studies, including field and laboratory investigations, to understand the bigfoot phenomena better. The BFRO is widely regarded as the most reputable and respected investigative network active in the research of this issue, according to its members' education and experience, as well as the quality of their efforts.

The Gulf Coast Bigfoot Research Organization

http://gcbro.com/

Bobby Hamilton (Texas) created the Gulf Coast Bigfoot Research Organization in February 1997. Jim Lansdale (Louisiana) joined as a Co-Founder a few months later, and the two of them worked together to build the G.C.B.R.O. into what it is today. It's still one of the most popular bigfoot search organizations in the country.

Smoky Mountain Bigfoot Conference

https://gatherupevents.com/smoky-mountain-bigfoot-conference/

The organizer of this event runs multiple bigfoot events, including another conference in Florida. They are considered a viable gathering ground for minds within the bigfoot circle.

The Ohio Bigfoot Conference

https://ohiobigfootconference.org

The Ohio Bigfoot Conference was founded in 2012 by Marc DeWerth and the Ohio Bigfoot Organization, along with several other groups and friends. Since then, the conference has evolved to become the world's largest Bigfoot gathering, attracting thousands of individuals each year. Top-rated speakers from throughout the Bigfoot community will share their experiences and knowledge on the subject of Sasquatch at the event. The conference provides something for everyone, including media stars, academics, local and national investigators, and other significant persons. Many free events are scheduled over the weekend, including the world's largest vendor fair of Bigfoot products, an advanced hike, the Bigfoot Festival, and a family hike. It's a fantastic weekend full of entertaining and educational activities for the entire family to enjoy. In fact, the latest iteration of the event was sold out.